Where I Was Born and Raised

Books by David L. Cohn

GOD SHAKES CREATION

PICKING AMERICA'S POCKETS

THE GOOD OLD DAYS

NEW ORLEANS: AND ITS LIVING PRESENT

LOVE IN AMERICA

COMBUSTION ON WHEELS

THIS IS THE STORY

WHERE I WAS BORN AND RAISED

Where I Was Born and Raised

DAVID L. COHN

Preface by
JAMES W. SILVER

UNIVERSITY OF NOTRE DAME PRESS
NOTRE DAME – LONDON

First Paperback Edition 1967
Copyright © 1967 by University of Notre Dame Press

This Edition by special arrangement with
Mrs. David L. Cohn

Grateful acknowledgment is made to
Tomorrow magazine for permission
to reprint two selections in this book
and to *The Atlantic Monthly* for permission to reprint one selection.

Part I of this book was published
in 1935 under the title, *God Shakes
Creation.*

Library of Congress Catalog Card No. 67-22152
Manufactured in the United States of America

To the memory of my father and mother
who sleep in the soil of the Delta

Preface

No NEGRO living in Mississippi in the first half of the twentieth century had any reason to hope that he could break free of the caste system. Segregation, the form of white supremacy which had replaced slavery, had been thoroughly institutionalized by the state constitution of 1890 and the white primary. Every person, Negro and Caucasian, had drilled into him from early childhood the inflexible role he must play concerning race, as well as the inexorable penalty he would pay for attempting to crack the barriers of law and custom.

In one of his most poignant scenes, in the section called "The Fire and the Hearth" of *Go Down, Moses*, William Faulkner describes the disruption of the intimacy of two seven-year-old boys who had previously played and hunted, eaten and slept together. The white lad entered into his heritage, accepting "the old curse of his fathers, the old haughty ancestral pride based not on any value but on an accident of geography, stemmed not from courage and honor but from wrong and shame. . . ."

Today in Mississippi, as indeed in the rest of the United States, the promises of the Declaration of Independence and of the Emancipation Proclamation are slowly becoming reality for the colored minority. But a great many of the tens of thousands caught up in the civil rights crusade of the past decade have expressed shock and amazement at the recalcitrance of Mississippi in refusing to accept at once the national mandate for change in her social order. For these people an understanding of Faulkner or Richard Wright and/or a reading of the nonfiction of another native Mississippian, David L. Cohn of Greenville, might have made the dimensions and intensity of the country's most absolute degree of segregation more comprehensible.

In 1935 Cohn published *God Shakes Creation,* a personal memoir which attempted to explain the meaning of the Mississippi Delta to which he had returned after an absence of two decades. In 1948 he brought his story up to date with *Where I was Born and Raised,* now republished in paperback.

As Faulkner linked short stories into novels, Cohn expanded essays into books. During his quarter of a century of writing he firmly established himself as Editor Edward Weeks' "cabinet member for the South," publishing more than sixty articles in the *Atlantic Monthly.* Beyond these he wrote ten books, including *The Good Old Days, Picking America's Pockets, The Life and Times of King Cotton, The Fabulous Democrats,* and *Love in America.* A professional speaker himself (as well as a magnificent storyteller), David Cohn may have set a record of sorts in the middle months of 1952 by writing political essays (speeches mainly) for William J. Fulbright, Sam Rayburn, Estes Kefauver, Averell Harriman, Stuart Symington, and Adlai Stevenson. He was an inveterate, usually an amusingly indignant, "letter to the editor" writer, quite often to the *Washington Post* and the *New York Times.* Trained in the law and highly successful in business, Cohn wrote as journalist, folklorist, economist, historian, political scientist, sociologist, and philosopher.

Mr. Cohn started the second chapter of *God Shakes Creation* with that imperishable sentence: "The Mississippi Delta begins in the lobby of the Peabody Hotel in Memphis and ends on Catfish Row in Vicksburg." One reviewer thought that Mississippians found Cohn's sane and authentic description of themselves "as familiar as the black earth and cotton rows." Perhaps so, but it should be remembered today that in the middle of the Depression thirties, native whites were more likely to look upon any critic of the racial and economic (sharecropper) system as a meddlesome troublemaker. Twenty years later the author would have been excoriated. In any case, the fact remains that the problem children of the nation after World War II, the underprivileged Negroes of the Southern and Northern ghettoes and the poorer whites of the rural South who resisted racial changes so bitterly, can best be comprehended in the light of their blighted environment between the two world wars in such areas as the Mississippi Delta. Herein lies a chief source of Negro and white frustration *everywhere* today.

Among the 293,000 Negroes and 98,000 whites in the Delta were found taboos "as rigid as may be found in a Melanesian village." Slaves liberated into poverty and dubious freedom were still largely exploited economically, degraded spiritually, neglected educationally, and encouraged in moral profligacy. A Negro must not raise his hand against a white man regardless of the latter's brutality, injustice, or lust. Cohn examines sympathetically the black man's religion, crime, sexuality, disease, and ability as "an actor who never steps out of character." In 1935 there was no reason to quarrel with his dicta that the Negro was politically "as dead as the Indian" and that racial problems were "without hope of solution in the present and without direction in the future." Yet the community, he was certain, could not avoid the "ultimate penalty for its neglect of the Negro." Surely this was a hopeless situation made tolerable only by the mellowing effects of the strong bonds of affection between individual whites and Negroes playing their roles as masters and servants.

By 1948 air-conditioning, crop diversity, cattle, industrial jobs, medical clinics, and increased wealth had come to the Delta without really influencing the status of the Negro or challenging segregation. Mechanization was leading to that efficiency in agricultural production of the 1960's when one man could do the work ten had done before the Depression. Hence the beginning of the mass exodus of rural unskilled Negroes (prompted also by increasing dissatisfaction with their lot) into the towns and cities of the South and the North. In Mississippi, though, Negroes were hardly ever allowed to work in factories and mills and were exploited by "monstrously exorbitant" rents in city slums whose scanty municipal services and outrageous police brutalities led inevitably to misery, disease, adult crime, juvenile delinquency, and even lowered efficiency. *Noblesse oblige* had pretty much evaporated, and Negro leadership and responsibility were puny things at best.

Though Cohn believed the Negro could make considerable gains (as some did) within the bounds of segregation, he saw the race problem as insoluble. Miscegenation was ebbing and Negro migration was diluting the blackness of the Delta, but grossly inadequate educational and medical facilities as well as lack of economic opportunity doomed the Negro to cultural as well as economic inferiority. Cohn warned that those who contemplated breaking the barriers of segregation "run risks of incalculable gravity." He had little doubt that any serious movement in the direction of social equality would find the country "nearing civil war."

At the end of World War II, then, David Lewis Cohn, a native Mississippian of high intelligence, great personal charm, and complete integrity, a lawyer and business man with impeccable collegiate antecedents (Virginia and Yale), a citizen of the world with a reputation for urbane writing, looked with compassion and wisdom on the racial situation in the Delta. Like Faulkner he saw no easy or immediate solution for black-white problems nor any prospect of social equality. Since Cohn's death in 1960 revolutionary changes have taken place in Mississippi and the ultimate future is clear. But the next decade will be as filled as the last with great soul-searching, tribulation, and anguish on the part of all Mississippians and indeed all citizens of the deep South. For a profound comprehension of the basic society whence America's racial problems originated there is no better source than Cohn's *Where I was Born and Raised*. It can now be placed on the paperback shelf along with *Caste and Class in a Southern Town, Deep South,* and perhaps *Mississippi: The Closed Society.*

James W. Silver
University of Notre Dame

March 15, 1967.

Foreword

THIS BOOK was first begun, nearly fifteen years ago, as an exercise in the rediscovery of the land where I was born. During a period of two decades I had not returned to my native Mississippi Delta except for brief visits. Upon my return I stood half alien, in a familiar-unfamiliar land. My childhood came back to me in blinding surges. I felt again the kindness that I had known and the hospitality of the country. I knew once more the courtesy that manifests itself not only outwardly in form but inwardly in the willingness of men to do you a favor without hope or thought of reward. I observed the lack of emphasis on the possession of money and the absence of passion for its acquisition; a leisurely manner of living today without morbid occupation for the morrow; the provincialism of a people geographically remote from the great centers of the United States but free from the acrid arrogance of city provincials; cotton and unending talk of cotton; the great river; and Negroes, Negroes everywhere.

I began to discover that this apparently simple society was highly complex. It was marked by strange paradoxes and hopelessly irreconcilable contradictions. It possessed elaborate behavior codes written, unwritten, and unwritable. It was clear that these codes were evolved because of the presence of the Negro in great numbers. He is a problem to the white man. And the white man, however unconscious he may be of it, is a problem to the Negro. It was obvious that both would be different if each lived in an all-white or an all-Negro society.

I scarcely knew my own Delta country except in the misty memories of youth. I wanted now to see it with eyes of maturity, and come to understand it. I knew that it was still a land of huge plantations, feudalistic in many ways, cotton-intoxicated, Negro-obsessed, fearing the wrath of God and the Mississippi River. Here are more Negroes in proportion to whites than elsewhere in the United States. Here members of two races are born, live, and die, each within his own separate group. They seem to be as remote from one another as Aldebaran is from Ittabena. But they are not. The Negro profoundly affects the white man, and the white man profoundly affects the Negro. They largely go their own ways but neither functions freely in a world of his own.

The attempt of these races to live side by side in harmony has been productive of amazing disharmonies and clashing contradictions in the social structure of the Delta, and in the beings of those who compose it. Whites and Negroes know intuitively how to conduct themselves in the presence of each other and under almost any circumstance, however novel. The races muddle along in peace, adjusting their often irreconcilable differences as best they can. Yet at intervals a feeling of helplessness and hopelessness sweeps the thinking members of each group as they survey the difficulties of the situation, without hope of solution in the present and with little direction for the future.

What follows in these pages is an attempt to set down some of the salient features of this society, based upon long months of observation and contact in the Delta.

I talked with all kinds of white men about Negroes, and with all kinds of Negroes about white men. It is part of the legend of the Negro that he will not talk frankly and truthfully with a white man about the relationships of Negroes and whites, nor tell the truth about his own people. Unless I have been greatly deceived, the legend is legend and nothing more. I found that once Negroes had accepted me as a serious student of their problems, they spoke eagerly, frankly, and I believe honestly, about their difficulties. My informants in both groups ranged from landowners to day hands, from preachers to prostitutes, from college graduates to the illiterate.

So far as possible, I have avoided the use of statistics, preferring to study the people of the Delta as human beings of blood and brains and bone, living their lives in the light that is given them, loving, hating, acquiring, losing, dying, and being born again in their children. A man is not a sterile statistic. He is rational and irrational, just and unjust, glorious and inglorious, seeing and blind. It is impossible, I believe, to understand a complex society, or a simple society, except in flesh-and-blood terms of those who compose it.

Does the war stir your heart with agony because millions of men lost their lives in it? Or does it sink deeply into your being because your neighbor's son went off to war in the glory of his youth and came back a broken body in a coffin? That is why I deal so largely here with red blood and marrowy bone and so little with pale percentages.

This, then, is a picture of the land where I was born and of the people among whom I grew up; of the country which I left as a youth and to which I returned as a man. It is, I know in my heart, a blurred and incomplete picture. I have painted it out of such affection and understanding as has been given me, but even the great painter rarely penetrates to the secret soul of his sitter, and it is there that the ultimate truth resides.

Many persons gave me liberally of their time and counsel in aiding me to write this book. I acknowledge with thanks help given me by Mrs. Balfour Miller, Mrs. George Marshall, and Judge Charles Patterson, of Natchez; Mr. Will Dockery and Mr. Joe Rice Dockery, of Dockery, Mississippi; Mrs. Selden Humphreys, of Memphis; Mr. O. G. Tann, Superintendent, Mississippi State Penitentiary, Parchman, Mississippi; Mr. Oscar Carr, Clarksdale, Mississippi; Mr. and Mrs. Charles P. Williams, Greenville, Mississippi; and Miss Hortense Powdermaker, Yale Institute of Human Relations, Yale University.

Three persons toiled over this volume more than I did. They are Roark and Mary Rose Bradford, of New Orleans, and the late William Alexander Percy, of Greenville, Mississippi. They struggled with the manuscript, gave me freely of their funds of information, and retained a sense of humor when I lost mine. More than that, they provided for long intervals those things without which even the most zealous student cannot proceed —

bed and board and warming fire. For all these I give them my thanks.

This book at best would be but a pale tract without the aid of hundreds of Delta Negroes. With such articulateness as they could summon, with unending patience, and with complete frankness, they bared to me their sorrows, their aspirations, their way of life. I am deeply grateful to them.

I owe an especial debt of gratitude to the Reverend Kid Scott, because it was from him that I derived the title for the first section of this book. Attending services one day at his church, I heard him say:

> *Gawd sends us His rain in de summer time so de cotton and corn will grow. De fall brings de cool of the evening. Snow draps from His shoulders in winter tell de mountain tops is covered and snow veils de face of de valley. De seeds dey sleeps in de ground and de birds dey stops dey singing. Den Gawd shakes creation in de spring.*

So it was that my book came to be called *God Shakes Creation.*

Since the first section of this book was published in 1935, under the title *God Shakes Creation,* many changes have occurred in the life of the Mississippi Delta as elsewhere. Whether for that small spot upon the American earth, or a Pacific atoll, there is not in our times, "any hiding place down there." We had scarcely emerged from a shattering economic depression following upon the First World War, before we were plunged into man's most catastrophic war. The foundations of our faith are severely shaken. We no longer devoutly believe, as we once did, in the inevitability of progress. Our compass is aberrant; our course erratic. We are more than a little fearful that we shall not make our landfall.

The changes and fears of the world are reflected, as they must be, in the lives of the people of the Delta. Yet they, subject to the stresses that affect all men, are affected by special stresses. These arise from two factors. The one is that the Delta is largely a cotton economy in a period when cotton, under attack from many sides, is a wobbly economic underpinning for the area. The other is that the Delta is a classical land of Negro settlement at a time when the attitudes of Negroes and whites toward one another are in a state of violent transition. The Negro question, as it exists in the United States, is without counterpart elsewhere. And the same question, as it exists in the Delta, is almost without counterpart in the United States.

Since the question is of paramount importance in our national life and the Delta is an area where it finds extreme expression, I have noted in the second section significant changes that have occurred in its economy and in Negro-white relations during more than a decade. It is not less important to point out those things that have not changed, for the unchanging — perhaps unchangeable — affords as much insight into men's minds as the changing.

The second section of this book is a report on the Delta as of 1947. The first section is a report as of 1935. It remains as it was originally written. The reader may therefore compare the society studied during the period covered and draw his own conclusions.

I make no claim to complete objectivity in this report. If I did so, I should hold myself superior in this respect to the Lord God Jehovah and the Twelve on Parnassus who, upon many a fateful occasion in the lives of mortals, found it impossible to constrict themselves with the bounds of that divine indifference which is an attribute of godhead. I have simply, within the frailties of human limitations, and deeply conscious of the gravity of the matters discussed, indicated what seems to me to be true. If the reporter is not the voice of mankind, he is the servant of truth so far as it may be revealed to him. His duty, therefore, is clear, while he cannot, for the life of him, deviate from his path whether it lead to the dark wood or the sunny clearing.

D. L. C.

December, 1947.

Contents

PART ONE
1935

PART TWO
1947

Part One
1935

CHAPTER 1

Jesus Comes to the Americas

CORTEZ marched into Mexico and Pizarro into Peru with the sword in one hand, the Cross in the other, and sacks to carry loot slung over their shoulders. The heathen were invited to come to God and give up their gold. Those who came and gave were merely robbed; those who did neither were robbed and slain. The unregenerate dead were buried naked without benefit of prayer. The living meek were stripped to their skins and taught to pray. Te Deums were declared with dividends. Paternosters were recited with profits.

Aztec and Inca perished that Spain might become greater and her cathedrals more golden. The stench of rotting bodies in the clear air of high Mexico and mountainous Peru became by transubstantiation the sweet-smelling incense of Toledo and Seville. Ancient cultures vanished amid the agony of millions, and the gathered gold of the heathen paid for masses for the repose of the souls of those who had brought about their destruction. In the name of Christ and for His sake, Amen.

The Spanish conquistadors inaugurated the great age of the exporting of hypocrisy and the importing of loot. The one cost nothing to manufacture; the other cost little to acquire save the lives and happiness of the heathen. Europe was rich in the possession of the one true faith. It was poor in gold, and cancerous with greed. The West Indies and South America worshiped false gods, were rich and were naïve. Spain would be generous about it. She would make a swap with the heathen, giving them

3

prayers for pearls, and hope of heaven for silver and gold. It is far better to store up treasure in heaven than on earth. Nor was that all. She would confer upon the benighted people of these backward countries what the white races call the blessings of civilization. These ranged from syphilis to tight-fitting shoes.

In Cuba the clean seas piled upon the clean sands. The sun rose upon the fruits and upon the flowers. Fish swam glittering among the coral and deer stood sun-dappled in the shade. Multicolored birds sang and screamed in the lush foliage. An eternal benediction of happiness seemed to rest upon the land, while the people sat idly beneath their trees, sharing their simple goods in common, plucking their food with little effort from bush and sea, making love and quietly dying. In Haiti, too, there were peace and contentment and leisure. In all the islands of the Caribbean men walked their ancient ways and there was gladness.

Then the Spaniards came. If there was gold, they seized it. If there was no gold, the people were made to dig for it. But they were an ungrateful race who shirked their tasks and evaded the blessings that were about to be conferred upon them by the simple expedient of quickly dying. Soon the man power of the islands was almost gone. But sugar cane had been discovered, the mines perhaps held gold, and the seas pearls. Beyond the horizon there was helpless Africa with its teeming millions of stalwart men inured to the tropical sun.

For more than three hundred years white Europe and America ravaged black Africa for slaves. The principal nations engaged in the slave trade were the great nations of the earth. They were proud, strong, enlightened, and Christian. They were the fierce and powerful who, strangely enough, worshiped the meek and gentle Jesus.

For long years, stinking slave ships of the English, the French, the Dutch, the Spanish, the Portuguese, the Danish, and the Americans stood off the coasts of Africa. There were an inexhaustible supply of blacks and insatiable demand. The wombs of black mothers were fertile. The unworked mines and the untilled lands of the whites were endless. The cost of human raw material was low in Africa. The selling prices of the same material abroad were high. Profits mounted. Huge country houses were erected in England; the foundations of great fortunes were laid in Massachusetts.

So long as business was good and dividends were high, there were eloquent defenders of slavery among the nations of the West who proved to their own satisfaction that the white men had come just in time to rescue millions of Negroes from the bitter domestic slavery of Africa, and transfer them to the beneficent slavery of the Americas. They made it clear that slavery was God's device to bring the dark heathen soul of the Negro into the light of the true religion; to pluck him from the sterile life of the jungle and transplant him into the better and more abundant life of the West. Jungle Negroes made war upon one another; tribe raided tribe. In well-policed Brazil they would be safe. On the broad acres of Virginia plantations they would be far beyond the alarms of war. Trade-slaving was indeed a humanitarian movement upon the greatest scale that the world has ever known. The fact that profit flowed in its train was entirely incidental. If it had any significance at all, it proved conclusively that the Lord rewards those who do His work on earth, as well as in heaven.

Years later, when the traffic began, for natural reasons, to decline and dividends to fall, slavery was seen to be cruel, inhuman, and barbarous. It was denounced in the English Parliament, and New England, enriched by the trade, found it foul and loathsome. What had been God's work was now the devil's device. Good had become evil, and righteousness was wickedness.

Queen Elizabeth was among the earliest to profit by the operations of the Spanish in the Indies and in South America. The Spaniards excelled at slave-driving and the English excelled on the sea. The wise and efficient course to pursue, therefore, was to let the Spanish accumulate gold conveniently and compactly in ships and send English seamen to rob them of it. The English, masters of euphemism, called their pirates privateers, and for years their activities swelled the English treasury and provided funds for wars upon the Continent and expansion abroad. The

Spanish, the industrious honey-bees that they were, roamed widely over the world, gathering the gold of the weak, and when they had assembled it in the combs of their great clumsy galleons, their masters, the English, came and robbed them of it. There is a balance among nations as there is in nature.

Foremost among the pirates was Sir John Hawkins, who eventually turned from robbing the robber Spanish, to the more honest trade of slaving. The great queen herself was his partner. Among the ships of his second expedition to Africa was the *Jesus of Lübeck*, lent to him by Elizabeth in payment for her shares. Success attended his efforts, for he was a good man and pious, as may be clearly seen from his sailing orders to the captains who accompanied him: "Serve God daily — love one another — preserve your victuals — beware of fire — and keepe good companie."

A hundred years later English royalty still shared in the profits of slaving, and lent the trade the prestige and encouragement of their names. In 1662, with the Duke of York as its titular head, there was formed in London the Company of Royal Adventurers for Carrying on a Trade to Africa. The adventurers themselves were not royal. They stayed in England. There was no adventure save the perils of the sea. The trade was not trade save in the sense of bartering goods for slaves. The real purpose of the company was to supply three thousand blacks annually to the English plantations in the New World, and its brave and splendid sounding title effectively hid its real purpose. So vigorously did the English embark upon the slave trade that by 1790 the Spanish had been almost forced out of it, and the flag of England floated in the warm breezes of West Africa above fourteen forts where blacks were gathered in cages to await shipment overseas.

Negro slaves of Africa, like the people of the West Indies, were enormously inconsiderate of their white masters and ungrateful for their attempts to remove them from a way of life which the whites regarded as degraded and barbarous. They committed suicide, maimed themselves, died at the forts and on the ships. Captain Thomas, who commanded the ship *Hannibal*, of London, in a voyage to Africa for slaves in 1693, comments in his journal upon the unfairness of his human cargo:

We spent in our passage from St. Thomas to Barbadoes two months eleven days, in which time there happened such mortality among my poor men and negroes, that of the first we buried 14, and of the last 320, which was a great detriment to our voyage, the Royal African Company losing ten pounds on every slave that died, and the owners of the ship ten pounds ten shillings, being the freight agreed upon to be paid . . . for every negro delivered alive to the African Company's agents at Barbadoes; whereby the loss in all amounted to near 6500 pounds sterling. . . . No gold-finders can endure so much noisome slavery as they do who carry negroes; for these have some respite and satisfaction but we endure twice the misery; and yet by their mortality our voyages are ruined, and we pine and fret ourselves to death, to think that we should undergo so much misery and take so much pains to so little purpose.

Slave-trading was a three-way traffic with a three-way profit. Ships were built and fitted to carry slaves. Their out-cargoes, if they were English, were Manchester and Yorkshire goods which were bartered in Africa for blacks. These were then taken to the West Indies and sold for spices, rum, and other commodities, which in turn were sold in England. The result was that the companies engaged in the trade made three profits on each voyage, and, given the cupidity of human beings, the helplessness of Africa, and the insatiable demands of a rapidly expanding world for labor, it was inevitable that the trade should mount to huge proportions.

The white peoples did not, themselves, raid the villages and take slaves. They incited petty native chieftains to capture men and women wherever possible and sell them into slavery. They fomented tribal wars and disputes. The losers became slaves. They held out visions of wealth and European luxuries to powerful native kings who systematically organized raiding expeditions and swept over huge stretches of territory, burning, killing, pillaging, and capturing. The weak, the infirm, and the aged were ruthlessly killed. The able-bodied men, women, and children were marched hundreds of miles to the coasts in chains. Those who faltered were clubbed to death or left to starve; frequently one-half or two-thirds of a caravan of slaves perished on its way to the sea. Here they were gathered into compounds to await the coming of the traders, and while they waited some died and others killed themselves. When they were put out for sale, the men and women, stark naked, were examined for defects by the ship's surgeon. Those who were rejected as unfit were killed by their black owners or patched up to be offered again for sale. Those who were accepted were branded on the breast with a hot iron bearing the mark of the company or the individual trader who had bought them.

Domestic slavery had always existed on a relatively small scale in Africa. The boom period came with the whites. Human beings died by the millions because greed hungered for their black helpless bodies. Millions of other human beings died in slavery for sake of the dollars.

From remote vistas of time, down long corridors of space, swells the overtone of melancholy that lingers today in the singing of Negroes. Alexander Falconbridge, who was a member of a slave ship's company, reported in 1788, that "the poor wretches are frequently compelled to sing, but when they do so, their songs are generally melancholy lamentations of their exile from their native country."

Incredible brutalities and hardships were suffered by the slaves on the long passages to the Indies and the Americas. Falconbridge writes that "on board some ships the common sailors are allowed to have intercourse with such of the black women whose consent they can procure. The officers are permitted to indulge their passions among them at pleasure and sometimes are guilty of such brutal excesses as disgrace human nature."

The trade of slaving was inseparable from disease, death, and brutality. The lowest scum and degenerates of the water-fronts of many nations manned the vessels engaged in this trade. They were restrained in their brutalities and excesses by no laws or dictates of humanity. The only restraint upon them was imposed by the profit motive of bringing as many of their slaves alive to market as possible.

The voyage from Europe to America to the west coast of Africa was a long one. Once there, it sometimes took weeks to collect a cargo, and weeks again to take the slaves to the markets of the Americas and the Indies. The ships could not make more than one or two round trips a year, and it was therefore imperative that they should be packed as tightly as possible with slaves. The Negroes, both men and women, were stripped to the skin to prevent infections arising from their filthy loin-cloths. They were stowed in close-packed layers in the holds. There was little room to lie down, and little to stand erect. There were almost no sanitary conveniences, and they were without fresh air save on clear days when they were taken out on deck and exercised. During storms they were battened down and remained in their filth, in the stinking air and darkness, with little food and little water, until the skies cleared. Sometimes a slave ship took fire at sea, and then it was abandoned to burn while the crew took to the boats, and the shackled slaves died between crackling columns of flame and the wide expanse of the unseeing ocean.

Frightful diseases broke out among the Negroes while they were being transported. Small-pox ravaged their ranks, and when the small pink pimples which herald it appeared on the face of a slave, he was immediately thrown overboard to drown. The more merciful captains first killed the slave before throwing his body into the sea. Ophthalmia afflicted them and whole cargoes of slaves became blind and were destroyed. Sometimes the crews caught the disease and there are chronicles of the slaving era which depict blind crew, blind passengers, and blind ship drifting helplessly upon the ocean. Dysentery wreaked havoc among the blacks, and following sharks made short work of their corpses. Revolts broke out among the slaves and were put down with savage fury; occasionally they were successful and horrible punishments were wreaked upon the whites. But the traffic continued while millions died in the bush and at sea, and other millions were transferred to the finer amenities of white civilization scattered from the sugar estates of Jamaica to the mines of Brazil.

The Americans entered the lucrative slave traffic early by way of the ship *Desire*, built at Marblehead, Massachusetts, in 1636. The stern New Englanders, passionate for God, gave the trade a novel turn. The *Desire,* on her first trading voyage to the West Indies in 1637, took with her as part of her cargo two women and fifteen men of the Pequot tribe of Indians who had been captured in a fight. They were sold into slavery. Yankee capacity for trading was soon to astonish the world and make New England rich.

Newport, Rhode Island, was a well-known slaving port during the eighteenth century. The slave-ship owners of Newport worked not only for profit, but also for God, for when their ships came into the harbor well laden with slaves who had escaped the manifold perils of the long voyage, they gave thanks to God that another cargo of the pagan had been brought to a Christian country, where they might enjoy the blessings of the religion of love and peace.

For more than a century, impelled by that most luscious of all combinations — religion and dividends — the ships of New England journeyed around the world with outward cargoes of hardware and rum and inward cargoes of slaves. Later, the New Englanders were to fight to destroy an economy based upon the labor of slaves profitably imported by them. And they fought to liberate the slaves, as they had worked to bring them to America — in the name of humanity.

In 1819 the President of the United States was empowered by Congress to employ the navy for the suppression of the slave trade. In 1843 — seventeen years before the beginning of the Civil War — Horatio Bridge, of the United States Navy, was an officer on a naval vessel off the west coast of Africa. In his *Journal of an African Cruiser* he reports:

> More vessels come to the coast of Africa from Salem than from any other port in the United States; although New York, Boston, and Providence, all have their regular traders. . . . All the vessels bring New England rum, leaf tobacco, powder, guns, large brass pans, and cotton cloth. . . . The bills of Pedro Blanco, the notorious slave-trader at Gallinas, on an eminent Spanish house in New York, and another in London, are taken as readily as cash. Some of the large English houses give orders to their captains not to traffic with men reputed to be slave-dealers; but if a purchaser comes with money in his hand, it requires a tenderer

conscience and sterner integrity than are usually met with on the coast of Africa, to resist the temptation. The merchant at home, possibly, is supposed to know nothing of all this. It is quite an interesting moral question, however, how far either Old or New England can be pronounced free from the guilt and odium of the slave trade, while, with so little indirectness, they both share in its profits and contribute essential aid to its prosecution.

The trade went on despite prohibitions, peachments, and naval vessels. The last cargo of slaves came to the United States in 1860. Profits, like the breath of life, are not lightly surrendered.

On the plantations of the Delta today, and in its little towns, walk Negroes whose ancestors were plucked from the Gold Coast and the Tooth Coast; from Gorée and Gambia; from Dahomey and Old Calabar. At night there is silence upon the Mississippi; at night the rivers of Africa are still. The winds eternally blowing stir the leafy cottonwoods of the Yazoo and play in the palms of Accra; waves pile upon the coast of Coromandel and waves beat against the mud embankments of the Sunflower; fires burn in the jungle dusk and blue wood-smoke ascends from cabins in the cotton. Melancholy pulses in the voices of Negroes singing along Delta creeks; drums talk from hill to hill in Africa. For the blowing winds and the beating waves and the sounding voices and the throbbing drums are one with the sea and the air and the stars; so, too, are tears and lamentations and pain and wrong.

Four centuries ago the first Negroes came to America, and for a hundred years they have lived in the Delta. Their forefathers are dead; dead, too, are those who brought them and those who decreed their bringing. The slave stockades of Whydah are vanished and the slave markets of the Place Congo in New Orleans are no more. The conquered and the slain are perished. The weak are lost in the sea. Long ago they moldered in the warm earth and dissolved in the blood-wet bellies of sharks.

The living whites and the living blacks go on together under the immense and immutable dome of heaven, they know not to what end.

CHAPTER 2

The Delta Land

THE MISSISSIPPI DELTA begins in the lobby of the Peabody Hotel in Memphis and ends on Catfish Row in Vicksburg. The Peabody is the Paris Ritz, the Cairo Shepheard's, the London Savoy of this section. If you stand near its fountain in the middle of the lobby, where ducks waddle and turtles drowse, ultimately you will see everybody who is anybody in the Delta and many who are on the make.

Memphis is the metropolis of the Delta. It is its financial, social, and cultural capital. Many of its citizens grew wealthy by lending money at exorbitant rates of interest to Delta planters. When a gentleman of the old school needed a loan he did not quibble about the cost, especially if there had been a disastrous stud-poker game the night before. Other Memphians founded their dynasties in lumber. They leaped from cypress to Cézanne in one generation. Some of them brought fortunes to Memphis from Arkansas. They had lived on land which "wasn't fitten fur a houn'dawg." But oil spouted underneath their feet. On the whole, however, Memphis draws its sustenance from its immense surrounding territory, and the Delta is one of its richest tributary provinces.

Culturally, Memphis is to the Delta what Paris is to Toulouse. One day I wandered into a bookshop there. I asked for a book by William Faulkner. The clerk, a fragilely lovely woman of the old régime, flew into a rage. "That man!" she said. "He ought to be run out of the country, writing about the South the way he does." I retreated rapidly to my second line of defense. "Have you anything by Thomas Wolfe? Isn't he one of your famous Southern writers?" "Well, he might be, but we don't approve of him, either." Finding that both my authors were on the Index, and that I had been mistaken for an upstart Yankee, I browsed among the shelves for a while, quietly licking my wounds. Then I asked delicately whether books were not at least a minor passion of the people of Memphis. "No, people don't read many books here. Do you live in town?" I regretted profoundly that I did not. "Then," she said, in a sudden burst of confidence, "I'll tell you the truth. We don't have any real culture in Memphis. We have culturine. You know, like oleo-margarine. Looks like butter but isn't."

That may or may not be true. There are many cultures in the world composed of many things ranging from sauces to symphonies. I do know that Memphis has beaten biscuit, rambler roses, and luscious lawns. To Delta citizens in search of light it glows with the beauty of the honey-colored pile of the Erechtheum seen at sunrise from a high Athenian hill. Here they all come in good time to see the occasional flesh-and-blood actors who appear upon its stage, to hear the rare symphony orchestra that straggles down from the north like a lone lost wild duck, and to dance to the music of some radio band advertising the virtues of a genteel purgative.

Here, too, come the business men of the Delta to make loans, sell cotton, buy merchandise, and attend conventions. For a day or two the lobby of the Peabody is filled with ice-cream men and their ice-cream wives. They suddenly melt into nothingness and are succeeded by ant-exterminators bent upon destroying the termite, which, like the politician, is blind but destructive. Then the undertakers appear. They discuss embalming by day. By night they dance delicate dances macabre with their necrophilic ladies under the scared and disapproving eyes of the Negro waiters. Finally they vanish into the outer darkness from which they came, giving way to hay-and-feed men who year long have cherished harlequins in their hearts now to be released in this place of bright carnival. Month after month come the conventions. The banners of business adorn the railings of the mezzanine, songs and resounding speeches come like the roar of the distant sea to lesser citizens as they sit at lunch or dinner in the hotel dining-rooms, and town competes with town for the honor of entertaining the carbonated-beverages men next year. During these periods the panoplied life of the sixteeth century guilds is created anew. The lobby glows briefly with the glory of the vanished Cloth Hall of Ypres.

The Delta, however, loves life as well as art and profits, and in Memphis the stern business man shows the world his other soul-side. Here he meets his inamorata, come up from his home town to sit for a little while together under a mango tree and lose the noisy sentient world. Here he goes in search of frail women, human, all too human, who live in houses with shades perpetually drawn, or he stumbles perhaps with a sudden gasp of delight upon some peripatetic beauty strolling sloe-eyed and lost in the soft darkness of the hotel mezzanine. Sin, a hydra-headed monster at home, becomes in Memphis a white dove cooing in the shade of tall cathedral columns.

Women of the Delta pass transiently through the lobby of the Peabody as they go to buy clothes or to get a permanent wave. A trip of two hundred miles is but a pilgrim's tribute to loveliness. Or sometimes they track culture to its lair in the recesses of a metropolitan woman's club where the nineteenth century in Europe is taken up intact at three o'clock and set down in fragments among the tea things at four.

Here the young men and young women of the Delta stop between trains en route to schools and colleges. Everybody in the area is whole-heartedly for what is vaguely called "education," but the reasons for it are always a little dim. For a while they fill the lobby with their laughter, and suddenly, like migratory birds, are gone, to come again at Christmas and in June.

All in all, at one time or another, everybody passes this way, and here one begins to glimpse the civilization of the Delta and to bruise his perceptions on the jagged points of its paradoxes.

Catfish Row, far to the south in Vicksburg, is a typical gathering-place of Negroes. Here are no marble fountains, no orchestras playing at dinner, no movement of bell-boys in bright uniforms. Tumble-down shacks lean crazily over the Mississippi River far below. Inside them are dice games and "Georgia skin"; the music of guitars, the aroma of love, and the soul-satisfying scent of catfish frying to luscious golden-brown in sizzling skillets. In Vicksburg Negroes eat catfish as catfish at fifteen cents a plate. In the cities white folks eat it as filet of sole at a dollar a portion. Negroes are realists and purists. They are satisfied with the catfish as God made it without benefit of the expensive euphemisms of a white *maître d'hôtel*.

Racially the white of the Delta are largely Anglo-Saxon. Religiously they are Protestant. The Episcopalians are smallest in numbers and largest in membership of old families. Baptists are myriad. They assail the ear of heaven with stentorian voice on Sundays. There are a few Catholics. They walk alien ways lighted by tall candles and perfumed with incense redolent of Rome, intent upon their own purposes, seeking salvation with Latin incantations. But they are lost in the Protestant mass.

This is a church-going and whisky-drinking society. That which is due to the church and to the bootlegger is offered up with such smooth harmony that the life of the body and the life of the spirit go happily in mystic marriage. Mississippi is legally dry, but the liquors of Louisiana are brought across the river, and potent brews are distilled in the swamps. The Delta has indeed the distinction of having created its own *vin de pays,* the corn whisky of one of its towns being famous for hundreds of miles around.

The churches of the Delta are not content merely to assure the salvation of their own members. The woes of the world impinge upon them and they mourn for the lost of Africa and of China. Bazaars, dinners, and "socials" are held continually for the purpose of raising money for foreign missions. Occasionally the bread cast upon the waters returns tenfold when a missionary comes from overseas to report how the sweating heathen of Africa have been taught, in the midst of a thousand false gods worshiped in a thousand false ways, to render homage to the one true God in the one true way which is the

sole possession of his sect. Then there ensues a great feasting
and communion of souls mystically joined in the common task of
bringing light into the darkness of hearts which God for some
strange reason failed to illuminate with the brilliance of Godhead. Amid music and song eyes are lifted on high in gratitude.
If they are blurred by a myopia which reveals the plight of
Bechuanaland blacks ten thousand miles away, and obscures the
fate of poor whites near by as they descend from degradation to
degradation, who shall question the wisdom of God's plan and
the works of his appointed ministers on earth?

The civilization of the Delta is on the surface simple and
almost naïve. Actually it is filled with complexities, with clashing contradictions and irreconcilable disharmonies. In its tolerance it shelters without hindrance every sect and creed within
its borders. In its fanaticism it has descended to the hatreds and
bigotries of the Ku Klux Klan. Devoting large sums to secondary
education, it scarcely considers that literacy has profounder
meanings than the ability to read and write. College-going, its
students largely miss the point. They rarely return with a passion
for truth, with an intellectual curiosity aroused and a desire to
pursue beauty and wisdom for their own sakes.

Culture is distrusted. One who bears it or seeks it is regarded
as being unfitted for the stern struggle of life. If a man should
collect Byzantine textiles or Persian ceramics, his business ability
would be discounted and serious doubts thrown upon his sexual
virility. It is suspect to read good poetry and catastrophic to
one's reputation as a normally functioning male to write it. Red-
blooded men simply do not do that kind of thing. Fine distinctions are, however, drawn and exceptions made. A man may
with impunity collect firearms, stamps, daggers, and stuffed
birds. These are protoplasmic. He may like bird dogs, but not
Persian cats. Coffee, but not tea. Whisky, but not wine. The
Delta, in the midst of a Western civilization, cherishes taboos as
rigid and as all-inclusive as may be found in a Melanesian
village.

The field of intellectual culture is a matriarchy ordered and
pre-empted by women. This is done with the cheerful consent

of the men, who feel that the manifestations of culture are things with which their wives may harmlessly amuse themselves in the long afternoons. And they do.

It is no feat at all for a study club to toss off the Periclean age of Greece in an hour and send its members away in plenty of time to get the dinner going before their husbands come home. The jump from Aristotle to trailing arbutus is easily made because there is a magnificent indifference to relevancy and continuity. Subject matter is not of much importance provided that it be non-controversial and delicately ladylike. Shelley is a favorite. Little essays on religious leaders are always welcome. Marie Antoinette, gentle, fragile, beautiful, and queenly, dies a merciful death just before the ice-cream and cake are served. Napoleon, torn without benefit of anaesthetic from the encyclopaedia, collides with the tea and comes out second best. The veil is torn from the mysteries of ancient Egypt by a member just returned from a cruise, while the audience sinks into a mood sweetly-sad as another plays *Humoresque* on the violin. Sometimes poets read original poems. Virgin brides entangled in disappointment and false rhyme die in the white moonlight. Gallant youths stammer of undying love in metaphors hopelessly mixed. Mockingbirds sing among the poison ivy. For poetry, too, is of the company of the seven arts and every member must have her fling.

The pursuit of knowledge is not, however, the sole diversion of the Delta. The people are kind, gregarious, and genuinely hospitable. Isolated from theaters and night clubs, few in number in the towns and fewer in the country, they visit and are visited by innumerable friends and relatives throughout the year. The length of visits is usually vague in the minds of both host and guest. Hospitality is not chilled by the blight of a parsimonious invitation for a weekend, and if the visit of days lengthens into months the host is usually pleased. A gracious elderly woman of the old régime told me, without sense of the unusual, that "Mary Bruce came to stay for six weeks and remained eight years." So hospitable indeed are these people that if you are at all presentable and have any charm — fortunately for civilization charm remains here the passport to all homes and all hearts — you will be passed on from family to family in the Delta for as long as you like. When you leave one town in the Delta to go to another, your host insists upon telephoning his Aunt Clara to meet you. You stay then at her house. She in turn passes you on to her Uncle Fred who lives on Swan Lake plantation, and thus you may go on for years moving from one house to another, paying for your keep in the bright coin of chatter and conversation.

Summerlong, when the crops are growing, the youngsters are at home from school, and there is little business to be done, the roads are alive with automobiles, and the nights are merry with the music of dance orchestras. Everybody within a radius of fifty or a hundred miles knows when a dance is to be held, and neither heat, perspiration, nor rutted roads keep them away. Often these gatherings are held in the courthouse. Then one may see girls in bouffant frocks of organdie powdering their noses in the jury-box or nursing their weary feet on the judge's rostrum, while a sweat-bedrenched Negro orchestra hurls jagged bits of jazz into the heavy heated air.

At rare intervals a large steamboat built solely for dancing comes up the river from New Orleans. The old-fashioned "floating palace" or showboat has vanished. The drama has given way to the dance. The huge boat glows with light, and its orchestra, through amplifiers, hurls its music out upon the river, against the banks of the levee, high up to the unblinking swarming stars of summer. Its searchlights play upon the streaming crowds as they ascend the hill of the levee and march over the gangplank to fairyland within. On the crown of the levee stand or sit hundreds of Negroes, their ears wooed by the music, their eyes enchanted by the myriad lights, their souls weary in the presence of this other-world beauty suddenly come within their view but beyond their grasp. Crowds stream down to the river's edge, and when all those who are going have finally been assembled after repeated hootings of the whistle to warn the lagging, the boat shoves off downstream.

The dance floor is thick-clotted with people moving to the

music of a Negro orchestra whose members are resplendent in uniforms which are a doorman's dream of heaven. There are loud laughter, shouts of recognition, tilting of bottles, and hurried introductions. The dancing is energetic. In it is a bit of Saint Vitus and the movements of standing upon a hot stove. Dark splotches soon appear upon the white linen suits of the men. On the faces of the women the make-up runs in tiny rivulets. The rich voice of a Negro baritone floats above the heads of the dancers. He recalls the sadly voluptuous fortunes of that

"St. Lopis woman with the diamond ring,
St. Louis woman with that man tied to her apron string."

The close-packed mass of humanity pillows itself upon the soft bosom of a waltz. It becomes excited by the hot staring eyes of jazz. It oscillates a bit wonderingly to the alien rhythm of the rumba. The night slips by.

Outside on the top deck there is darkness. Restless breezes of the river come coolly blowing. There is no sound save the far-away murmur of the music, the muted voices of lovers, and the drip, drip, drip of water on the paddlewheel. The boat is suspended between river and sky. Its fingers of light search the nether banks both sides. Green willows of Arkansas suddenly appear out of the black night. Shantyboats of fishermen pop up shining white out of the dark waters. The lanterns of the aroused occupants glow like insect's eyes for a moment and vanish. It is nearing midnight and the boat slowly turns to begin its homeward voyage.

When the passengers disembark the moon has risen. The land lies drowned beneath a flood of silver. Cows lie sleeping on the levee, resting heavily upon their folded feet. Mules move about, cropping grass, looking like questing creatures out of a dream. Negroes gaze at the incredible blaze of the steamboat's lights, and watch the white folks as they get into their automobiles and go away. Over the levee's rim the town lies sleeping and the roads that lead to plantation homes far away shine in the white moonlight. The air is alive for a little while with the coughing of motors and the shouts of good-bye. Then there is stillness. The lights of the boat go out. Only the beams of its searchlight are alive now as they search the shores. Its paddle-wheel makes silver circles as it slowly turns and goes downstream to bring beauty and enchantment to another river town. Far off there is the baying of a dog. A mockingbird essays a fugitive note or two from the top of a tree. Silence then. The Delta sleeps the hot night through.

If the Delta is radical about its jazz, it is conservative about its social and legalistic points of view. In rapidly changing America it remains a society almost feudal. It fears change. It does not welcome political innovations. Its whole system of codes and criteria of conduct are set up to preserve the *status quo* based upon the plantation tradition, the one-party political order, and white domination of a numerically black majority.

The voters are almost entirely Democrats. The few Republicans straying lost and alone seem prehistoric creatures miraculously surviving into modern life. They are so rare indeed as seldom to be seen in the flesh, and rich rewards are open to the showman who captures a few of these strange animals and exhibits them here in a cage for a fee. This is the land of the Democratic party, come hell and high water.

The non-Anglo-Saxon portion of the population is composed of Sicilians, Chinese, Syrians, Greeks, and Jews. The first generation of Sicilian men in the Delta wore gold earrings and celebrated the feast of Saint Joseph with colored candles and tiny cakes intricately wrought. The second generation wear dandruff like an aura on their tight-fitting suits and cheer the home team from the bleachers. The Chinese, celebrated for their thrift and industry, have lost the one and retained the other. They are victims to the American passion for the automobile. They have Negro mistresses who support black lovers out of their largesse. The Syrians traffic in little grocery stores not for ivory, apes, and peacocks, but for tinned milk and snuff. They lend neither their culture nor their color to the Delta. The Greeks, far from the wine-dark sea, conduct fruit stands and concoct greasy messes in smelly restaurants faintly reminiscent of the crowded anterooms of free venereal clinics. The Jews, by legend both intellectual and shrewd, seem in this soft climate to have lost both these qualities. They are distinguished neither by learning nor by riches. The national frenzy for uniformity is at work here as elsewhere in the United States.

The Negroes, who constitute a vast numerical majority of the population, are of every kind and intermixture. The white man's blindness to differentiations among them was long ago summed up in one of his songs: "All coons look alike to me." They exhibit, as a matter of fact, an astounding diversity. They are, to begin with, descendants of hundreds of tribes torn from every part of Africa. Many of them were markedly different from others in color, physique, language, culture, and occupation. Some lived by hunting, others by agriculture, by keeping herds, by warring on their neighbors. They dwelt on coastal plains, in the hot interior, in the foothills of mountains, in every kind of climate and against every kind of background. They had many cultures. Some were rude barbarians. Others created those sculptures of wood and bronze which have enormously influenced the world of modern art.

A curious case based upon this diversity of Negro peoples came to light some years ago in a criminal trial in the Delta. A Negro woman stabbed a Negro man. Her reason was that he had called her a "Nigger." "I'm no nigger," she said. "My grandma told me not to let nobody call me no nigger. I'm a Molly Glasser and an ink-spitter." Upon examination it developed that she was descended from the tribe of Malagasi. They were a strong and superior people who themselves had owned slaves. They were betel-chewers and expectorated black. Unfortunately, the law does not recognize distinctions of this kind. The descendant of the Malagasi went to jail.

Some of the slaves brought to America had been kings, chiefs, and warriors. They were men of spirit, proud and dignified. Others had been slaves in Africa. They were craven and obsequious. To the white trader they were all "black ivory," ethnologically indistinguishable. And the white planter, if they were strong and obedient, had no deeper curiosity about them.

After three hundred years in America the blood of these

diverse peoples has been improved or debauched — it depend upon one's point of view — with the blood of nearly all the whites who inhabit this continent, and with many of the Indian and Asiatics. Negro women have borne children to men who were members of the first families of the land and to the lowes white degenerates. They have been mothers to impossible hy brids and nurtured inconceivable mixtures of blood. These hybrids have in turn bred and interbred with other full-blooded and hybrid Negroes, so that the strains are hopelessly confused and mixed.

In the Delta one finds Negroes with the clearly defined fea tures of the best Anglo-Saxons. There is a song about it:

> I had a baby and its eyes are blue,
> It can't be mine, Cap'n; it must be you.

Others have the slant eyes of the Chinese, or the nose of the Jew. The bed of the Negro woman has been a leveling-ground of democracy. A doctrine upon which all could agree. Delta Negroes are of every shade. There are at least three gradations of brown — dark brown, deep brown, and reddish brown. They are black, pale black, and profoundly deep black. Some have the golden-yellow of the banana. Others are smoothly chocolate. A man passes you, the color of ripe olive. Another is copper. In a church choir a man of bronze stands next to a girl the color of cream. The eye searching for color is enchanted observing the delicate variations of shade in a Negro crowd. Because, however, of the isolation of the Delta and the overwhelming majority of the Negro population, thousands of Delta blacks are still full-blooded.

All of these people, white, black, and yellow, live in the ten counties which make up the Mississippi Delta. It stretches from a point just south of Memphis to a point just north of Vicksburg. It is one hundred and fifty miles long and fifty miles wide. The Mississippi washes its entire western side, and the Yazoo much of its eastern.

Here live 293,000 Negroes and 98,000 whites.

The Negro completely dominates the Delta in numbers. This

s the one fact indispensable to an understanding of this society. Dut of it flow the contradictions, complexities, and paradoxes which characterize its social and economic systems. It is the cause of distortions and stresses in the beings of the whites. It orings about inevitable repercussions in the blacks. It is largely he reason for the restrictions and disabilities placed upon Negroes. It is the source of difficulties which perplex the governing whites. The men who control the Delta never forget for a moment that the Negro is the majority. It colors their actions and stands in the forefront of their thoughts.

Mississippi is the only state in the union having a preponderance of Negroes in its population. At the census of 1930 there were slightly more than one million Negroes among the two million people of the state. Negroes made up 50.2 per cent of the whole. But in the Delta more than 70 per cent of the population is black.

Unless you have lived here, the density of Negroes in the population seems incredible. A comparison of this section with other parts of the country brings out the disparity in high relief. Figures are taken from the census of 1930 and are in round numbers.

In New England, for instance, there are 8,000,000 people. Only 90,000 are Negroes. The Delta has less than 400,000 people. And nearly 300,000 are Negroes.

The state of Maine has 795,000 whites and 1000 Negroes. The Delta county of Issaqueena has 1000 whites and 4600 Negroes.

Many Delta plantations have more Negroes than are to be found in the entire state of Vermont with its 565 blacks.

Massachusetts has over 4,000,000 whites and 52,000 Negroes. That is precisely the number to be found in the one Delta county of Bolivar.

The Middle Atlantic States have a total population of 25,-000,000. They have 265 times as many whites as are in the Delta. But only 3 times as many Negroes.

There are more Negroes in Sharkey County than in all of Minnesota. But Minnesota has 700 times more whites than this county.

North Dakota's whole Negro population of 377 would no[t] make an impressive "turn-out" for the funeral of a Delta Negr[o] preacher. South Dakota's 646 Negroes are just about the numbe[r] to be found working in many Delta lumber-mills.

The combined states of Montana, Idaho, Wyoming, Colorad[o] New Mexico, Arizona, Utah, and Nevada have fewer Negroe[s] than live in Coahoma County in the Delta.

More than 7,000,000 people live in the Pacific States. But th[e] two counties combined of Bolivar and Leflore in the Delta hav[e] as many Negroes.

If the population of the Delta is considered with referenc[e] only to its own components, the dominance of the Negro remain[s] strikingly apparent.

In Coahoma County there are 3000 Negroes for every 100[0] whites. In Humphreys County there are 5000 Negroes for every 1000 whites. And in Tunica County there are 7000 Negroes fo[r] every 1000 whites. These ratios apply to every county in th[e] Delta. At his fewest, as in Humphreys County, the Negro constitutes 68 per cent of the population. At his most numerous as in Tunica County, he makes up 85 per cent of the whole.

It is obvious that there can be no Negro problem where there are no Negroes. Nor where there are few Negroes, as in Vermont. Nor where there are many Negroes lost in an overwhelmingly white population, as in New York. But there is a Negr[o] problem where a few whites live among vastly dominant masses of Negroes. That is the situation in the Delta.

The Negro's identification with the life of the Delta is fundamental and complete. He came here as a slave with the earliest settlers. He has remained to live and multiply as a freedman. This land is first and last his handiwork. It was he who brought order out of a primeval wilderness, felling the trees, digging the ditches, and draining the swamps. He erected the homes which shelter him and the white man. He built the schools, the courts, the jails, the factories and warehouses. He was a roustabout on the river boats which connected the Delta with the outside world, and toiled up the steep banks of the landings bearing incredible loads on shining black shoulders singing:

"O Lawd, O Lawdie.
All right, boys.
De man done called us
An' let us go.

"O Lawdie, de Cap'n
Done called us
But us didn't send for you.
We sent for a bar'l er pork
An' looked up de road
An' seen you come pokin'.
O Lawdie, O Lawd,
O Lawdie, let us go."

The Negro was builder, too, of the railroads which were forever to extinguish the glory of steamboating on the Mississippi and the gorgeous dynasty of the river captains. Later he built the concrete roads which in turn were to cripple the railroads. The vast ramparts of the levees upon whose existence the life of the Delta depends sprang from the sweat and brawn of the Negro. Wherever one looks in this land, whatever one sees that is the work of man, was erected by the toiling, straining bodies of blacks.

The white men with whom the Negro came to the Delta as slave were unique among pioneers. Here were no lean Yankees marching with rifle, family, and meager possessions across the illimitable plains. No refugees from the Germany of forty-eight. No Irish of the famine years, empty-handed and eager, searching for a new home in a new world. These men were the embodiment of a seeming contradiction — pioneers with means. They were sons of wealthy and moderately wealthy planters of Virginia, Kentucky, South Carolina, and Tennessee. They had a definite gentle culture and the deep-rooted sense of responsibility common to their kind. Used to wealth and possessing it, they were men of property moving with their families, their slaves and manifold possessions, like princely patriarchs of the Old Testament.

The land to which they came was land of the loins of the river. It had sprung from the body of the Mississippi in a gestation eons long. Untold centuries ago it began to deposit here the rich detritus of mountains and plains borne on its bosom as it flowed from the north to the south to sea. Accretion by slow accretion, without foundation of rock or shale, it laid down this land. Here are no hills, no rocks, no thin earth barely hiding the stones beneath, but pure soil endlessly deep, dark and sweet, dripping fatness.

And when, after tens of thousands of years, the land had been built, the forests came. There were oaks and cypresses, sweet gum and leafy cottonwood, persimmon and pecan, walnut, and maple. Cane grew to great heights to make an impenetrable jungle. Vines and creepers laced and interlaced in intricate tangle. Here was an animal's paradise of bear, deer, opossum, raccoon, rabbit, squirrel, panther, and mink. Birds native and migratory filled the silent woods with the loud music of the singing. In the autumn, dawn rose on the wings of myriads of wild ducks. Darkness fell with their swift-descending flight to the bosoms of lakes and ponds. Snakes swarmed on the land and in the water; mosquitoes ascended from the steaming swamps in clouds; bullfrogs disturbed the austerity of the night with their obscene croakings; turtles elongated their reptilian heads on logs rotting in green-scummed creeks.

Century after century the land lay as in a dream. The rich earth became ever richer with the decay of leaf mold and vegetation; the passionate embrace of deep-rooted trees and close-clinging vines made it secure against washing and erosion in torrential rains. The Spaniard came and Hernando de Soto was buried in the Delta's river, but the land did not stir in its sleep. More than a century later, when Cornwallis surrendered at Yorktown, it was still primeval wilderness. It sent no soldiers to the War of 1812 because there were no men to send. It was not until 1825, scarcely more than thirty years before the Civil War, that the first settlers came. The civilization of the Delta is little more than one hundred years old.

At this time many planters in the more northerly states of the South began to find that their farming operations were becoming unprofitable. Their lands under an unwise system of cultivation were losing their fertility. Some of them suspected that slavery was eating into their profits. These doubts, however, were not to be resolved for forty years and were then to be expressed not in rows of black figures on white paper, but in rows of white grave-markers on the dark earth.

Rumors of the fertility of the soil of the Delta, then called "the swamps," began to drift back to Kentucky, Tennessee, Virginia, and South Carolina. Planters made inquiries about this virgin land inhabited by only a few Indians, fugitives from justice, and wild animals. Then they purchased huge tracts and came with armies of slaves to clear the ground and open plantations along the rivers and on the creeks. Roads, too, after a fashion, were constructed. If they were mule-belly deep in mud in the winter and storm-swept with dust in the summer, it did not greatly matter, for there were the rivers, the Mississippi, the Yazoo, and the Sunflower, to serve as arteries of transportation. And here on the banks of the rivers, in the bends of the streams, on ridges or high ground safe from the floods, the pioneer planters of the Delta built their homes.

This was a régime of the wealthy well-born planter; an economy of the huge plantation worked by large numbers of slaves. In it there was no room and no welcome for the small non-slave-holding farmer who with his family's labor might till a few acres. This was a society of gentlemen, overseers, and slaves. If now the gentlemen have almost vanished, if the sons and grandsons of overseers rule where they once reigned, and the slaves liberated into a dubious freedom, it still remains true that neither then nor now has the Delta ever welcomed the so-called "poor white." He took to the sterile hills of Mississippi. There he raised large crops of children and meager crops of cotton. He worshiped a fierce God, hated aristocrats and Negroes, dwelt in poverty and darkness, and awaited the day when he might descend upon these fat lands. Now two terms out of three his Governor rules the state, his Senator sits in the seats of the mighty, and he himself is coming down from his hills.

The tradition and fact of the Delta's dependence upon Negro labor began in the earliest days of the settling of the country. The men worked in the fields and performed the manifold tasks that make up the daily round of the plantation. The women cooked, washed, sewed, baked, and nursed in the planter's home. Younger boys served in the stables, waited at table, and were companions in hunting and fishing to their master's young sons. When the Civil War came they rode off with them as body servants. Hundreds of others, suddenly liberated from slavery and without hope of tangible reward, remained behind to help and protect the planter's defenseless womenfolk and children. The bonds of slavery were sundered. The stronger ties of affection held these alien peoples together.

In the beginning the labor of every man and every tool was needed for clearing the land, and while this task was being done time ran swiftly toward the conflagration of the Civil War. It is for this reason, perhaps, that one does not find in the Delta, ruined or intact, homes that remotely resemble in beauty or magnificence the mansions that stood along the James and the Potomac or high above the Mississippi at Natchez. Men contented themselves in the present with comfortable, if modest, homes. They dreamed dreams which were never to be realized of the day when they might erect replicas of the great houses they had known and recreate the gracious culture they had abandoned.

The pioneers of the Delta, faced with a host of difficulties and intent upon founding a civilization in a wilderness, did not know that this land sheltered one of the most stubborn and dangerous diseases known to man. It lurked in the swamps and lowlands of their new home. Its symptoms were still identical with those described by Hippocrates more than two thousand years ago. Its effects were as deadly here as they had been in Greece and Rome and India where it had decimated armies and depopulated cities. That disease was malaria.

In the spring and summer and often until late in the autumn nearly every man, woman, and child in the community was ill with malaria. They burned with fever. They froze with chills. Their teeth chattered and their temples flamed. In the intervals between the attacks which came every third or fourth day they were listless and exhausted; too dull to think and too tired to work. Traveler after traveler noted the physical debility of the people. The more charitable ascribed it to unknown causes. The less charitable said that they were lazy. But the disease went on and its cause was unknown. Each year the bodies of the victims were drained of vitality and their minds of vigor. Each year many died and found premature graves where they had hoped to find happy homes.

There is no way to estimate accurately the social and economic damage caused by malaria in the Delta. Its destruction in terms of human pain and suffering is immeasurable, but it was undoubtedly a factor of grave importance in impeding the progress of this section. Men are not active in the white shadows of anaemia. They do not create in exhaustion. They cannot function in fever. Life, to be fruitful, must be more than a rhythm swinging from chill to chill.

Malaria came year after year at almost mathematically regular intervals. The community knew when it would come, how long it would stay, and what it would do. They saw it so often that they became accustomed to it despite its pain and suffering. But when the deadly yellow fever came among them they were stricken with terror. It did not come at regular intervals. Its victims did not linger. They quickly died horrible deaths, or in rare cases recovered. The cause of the disease and its treatment were equally unknown. The people were helpless before this deadly scourge.

When the stricken began to vomit black and cough up their life's blood in thick clots, when their chests turned yellow and their enfeebled bodies were storm-swept with dreadful retchings, the living could do nothing to assuage the agony of the dying save to pray at their bedsides and await the coming of merciful death. Safety, they knew, lay in flight to the north. Many would not go, others could not go, and still others would not leave their friends and relatives behind. Through the long, hot, melancholy summer in 1878 hundreds sickened and died of yellow fever, while the living, worn with pain and grief, nursed the sick and buried the dead. Volunteer nurses, one after one, contracted the illness and died. Others stepped promptly forward to take their places. There seemed to be no way to arrest the busy, inexorable hand of death, until, as the Greenville *Times* reported in November of that year:

> A big white frost last Monday morning was a glorious sight for our people to see. To those within the infected districts it was a token of rescue and rest; to those who were shut off from their homes it was an assurance that their exile would soon be over, and the sad homecoming was near at hand. With what agony of heart the white robes of the blessed frost was watched and prayed for, none can know save those who passed the fearful hours within the death-haunted districts, and friends and relatives who watched and waited for the dark clouds to pass away.

The white frost of the autumn of 1878 marked the passing of yellow fever for that year, but not its final end. It came again and again to claim its victims in the summer and retreat before the frost in the autumn, and when it did not come the threat of its coming chilled the hearts of the people every year. It inflicted untold suffering and grief, kept prospective settlers and investors away from the Delta, and wrought enormous damage to the entire economic and social structure.

The Delta was founded and wrought in pain. By legend it is a land of *dolce far niente* where the sun shines, Negroes work, white men loaf on the verandas of white-porticoed mansions, and money mysteriously rolls in. As a matter of fact the pioneers who founded this land fought against enemies as grim as those confronted by the men who opened the west. The Delta has struggled for its existence against a dark company. It has wrestled with malaria, yellow fever, the Civil War, Reconstruction, and the floods of the river. A handful of white men without enormous wealth or political power, without gold or oil under their feet to bring them sudden affluence, and against great odds, converted wilderness and tangled swamps into a fat land. It is a measure of their effort that today, one hundred years after the first settlers came, one of the most powerful enemies of the Delta is yet unconquered, although the resources of the federal government have now been thrown into the scales against it. That is the Mississippi River.

The landscape of the Delta subject to the attacks of the river is both beautiful and ugly. In the spring and summer the fields are touched with the never failing beauty of green growing things. Under the wide sky and immense horizon of this flat land cotton marches in endless ranks of green save where it is joined by tall troops of corn to which peavines cling, piling richness upon richness and color upon color. The humble okra at capricious intervals thrusts its fuzzy fruit into the warm air. Watermelons lie like fat helpless drunkards, their dark bellies turned upward to the sun. Pumpkins lie pale yellow upon the earth attached to the slender umbilical cords of their vines. Sorghum stands in thick tropical jungles. Great stretches of alfalfa carpet the earth lushly with deep green. Soy beans pile their vines thick-clustered upon the warm land. Clover matches the blue of its flowers with the blue of the azure sky. From hour to hour as the sun burns with a greater or a lesser whiteness the landscape changes color. The tin roofs of Negro cabins become burnished silver. The gray coat of a mule far away in the fields becomes suddenly black. A passing cloud shades a field to darkness so that it seems in the shimmering light surrounding it a bit of dark driftwood afloat on a tossing sea of bright green. From sunrise to sunset in the spring and summer the white light of the Delta creates miracles of shadow and shade under the vast arch of the heavens.

As the brief spring glides imperceptibly into the hot days of summer, the crops grow with furious rapidity, forced upward by the rich earth, the warm rains, and the long hours of sunlight. Weeds grow with equal rapidity, and as they come up the fields become alive with the chatter and laughter of Negroes wielding hoes. The contest between man and nature for the rich prize of the annual crops is never ending. In this warm climate, this teeming soil, the earth throbs to give birth to myriad forms of plant life, little caring whether they are friend or foe to excrescent man clinging to its surface by the sweat of his brow.

In June the fields are starred with the beauty of millions of cotton blossoms cream-white, soft-red, shell-pink. They vanish after a brief day in the sun and give way to bolls; hard tight little globes of green containing the embryo of cotton. For three months they grow until suddenly in August the cotton begins to burst through its confining walls. Bits of white here and there fleck the sea of green. As the days pass the whiteness spreads rapidly and more rapidly until it undulates in waves and rolls in billows, drowning the land beneath its softness. Now the Negroes come to gather the harvest. With long sacks of coarse canvas slung over their shoulders and trailing the ground they pick the cotton. In time only the stalks remain to become brown and withered with the frosts of autumn and rattle forlornly in the winds of winter until they are plowed under in the spring. The flat fields stretch away mile after mile in a brown monotony unbroken by the surge or lift of hills. Stumps of trees that were hidden by the thick-clustering leaves of the cotton now splotch the fields. Beauty has flown from the Delta. It will come again in the spring.

The roads become, in cotton-picking time, a thronged Appian Way leading to the gins. Their rusty tin roofs shine now in the eyes of Negroes with as great a glory as the dome of Saint Peter's ever shone for home-haunted Romans returning from exile. The fields are filled with cottonpickers, and as fast as wagons and trucks can be filled they move to the gins in an almost unending procession around the hands of the clock. Here the cotton vanishes, at one end into the maw of a suction pipe, and emerges, stripped of its valuable seed, at the other as the jute-wrapped bale of commerce. Long lines of wagons and trucks wait their turn. Negroes lie sound asleep aloft on the high-piled cotton under the shining sun or the starry sky. Ginned bales rumble down inclines and are stacked by black brawny arms for shipment. The gins make a fearful clatter in the quiet air of the countryside. For nine months of the year they are silent. For three months they run. They seem now to crowd into this too-brief season of activity the repressed forces of strength that must lie dormant for most of the year. Plumes of steam wave in the autumn breezes. Columns of black smoke stain the immaculate blue of the sky. Cotton seed rattles loudly in tin pipes as it is blown under pressure into the seedhouses.

At night sudden blasts of flame assault the darkness as the fire doors of boilers are opened and shut. The gin is the annual journey's end for Negro share-croppers and white farmers.

This is the glad time of the year for Negroes. The long road down which they have toiled for months now opens upon enchanting vistas of cash money and uninterrupted leisure. For weal or woe the crop has been made and gathered. They will soon taste its first fruits in the form of "seed money" — the cropper's share of the cotton seed. Later there will be a final settlement of accounts for the year's work.

The cropper sees but little cash during the cultivating and growing season. Now that he has money in hand he goes on a spending spree. The little country grocery stores which summerlong have had in stock only the most utilitarian foods such as beans, fat meat, flour, lard, and coffee, now flaunt on their shelves the unaccustomed luxuries of dried figs and raisins, apples and oranges, lemons and grapes, and tinned California fruit. The dry-goods stores, which have sold only work clothes and cheap cotton dresses, now display wondrous suits for men dyed strange shades and richly adorned with multicolored buttons. "Sunday" shoes, too, are now to be worn every day. Rayon socks and rayon neckties are bright with shine, dripping color. Caps will be worn, jauntily backwards, and there are shotgun shells for rabbit-hunting.

For the women there are dresses of fairy-like splendor woven of the mist ingeniously mixed with satin, billowing with ruffles, bouffant with lace, smart with pink and blue marabou, and all for less than five dollars. Admirable dresses for walking in the rain across muddy fields to visit neighbors; superbly smart when worn with long white kid gloves to stand long hours in hot dusty streets, waiting for the circus parade. Underwear, too — Negroes in their conservatism still wear it — of maize and purple rayon embroidered with magenta roses. Shiny panties are only seventy-five cents, and that is merely the garnered sweat of ten hours' work with a hoe in the hot sun magically crystallized into silver. Love flourishes, beauty burns, and "us sho gwine have us a good time while us can." So with the buying of this and that, with the garnering of trinkets and bright trash, the stores are crowded and the money is spent. The paean-obituary of a year of hard work is then written by the financial agencies reporting that "business in the Delta section of Mississippi is 5 per cent ahead of last year."

Delta white folks complain bitterly that the Negro with a few dollars in his pocket will not work until the money is gone. Fortunately for the white folks, these periods of spasmodic prosperity do not last long. The Negro and his money are soon parted. It is as difficult for him to hold money as it would be to cling life-long to the face of a precipice by his fingers. In his opinion thriftiness is utterly silly — a characteristic of "mean mens." Tomorrow does not press, a crown of thorns upon his brow. And when the last extremity has been reached there may be always found somehow a white man to assume the burden of his meager keep.

> 'Taint no use fer to work so hard,
> I got a gal in de white folks' yard;
> She gives me biscuits and she gives me lard.
> Ef it wa'n't fer de bulldog I'd go in de yard,
> Skeered he bite me, we shall be free,
> Skeered he bite me, we shall be free,
> 'Cause de good Lawd done set us free.

This is true of the majority of Delta Negroes. There is a tiny minority who are far-sighted, thrifty, parsimonious, and even miserly. By virtue of their thrift they rise to economic independence and places of importance in their communities. But they are lost in the thriftless mass.

Whether the Negro acquired his thriftlessness from the white man or he acquired it from the Negro is a moot question. It is certain in the Delta that both are guilty of it. When money is plentiful the planter and townsman commit the same crimes against economy that the Negro does, differing from him only in kind. In prosperous years they recklessly buy expensive automobiles. They travel up and down the country to visit friends or merely to move about. They buy whatever they see and want at the moment with the fatal inability to resist that marks the swiftly-upward open-mouthed flight of a trout to the lure of a fly. One bale of cotton buys a case of whisky. Two pay for the "fixings" for the party at which its is drunk. Five bales buy a trip to Chicago, and ten to New York. It is not hard to spend a cotton crop if one works devotedly at the task. Soon the money vanishes. Usually it leaves no traces of beauty or grace garnered; no utility gained; no memories of things done and places seen to shine in arid after-years like unquenchable stars.

White folks complain, too, that the Negro won't work unless he is driven. This is true of many Negroes, but not of all. In the Delta there are Negroes who are hard-working and industrious. They prosper without supervision and point the way to their less energetic fellows. The attitude of the average Negro toward work, however, is tempered by several considerations. He feels, for one thing, that "he ain't goin' ter have nuthin' nohow," arising either from a fear that he will be exploited or a knowledge of his own inability to save or both. His wants are simple and easily satisfied. A little labor suffices. He does not burn with the white man's passion for acquisition. He does not seek power. Money is a form of power, but the Delta Negro could not wield it if he had it. He cannot, therefore, see why he should continue to work when he is in possession of enough money to provide for his simple wants in the immediate present.

He feels deeply that work is an unmitigated evil. It is a form of dark penance which he must suffer if he would win through to the bright pleasures of women, train-riding, gambling, and picnics. De Lawd put man on earth to enjoy hisself, and when this life has done gone He's gwine take us all to a better lan' where don't nobody work and Jesus sets on a golden throne, a little white chile-angel on one side an' a little black chile-angel on de yother. Only white folks and fools work for the sake of working. They have no time to enjoy the pleasures of this life nor to anticipate joyfully the glories of the eternally happy life to come.

The Delta Negro has a high capacity for the artless employment of leisure. Time does not hang heavy on his hands when he is free of labor. The wellsprings of his being have not been poisoned at their source by the white man's virus of let us then be up and doing. On Sundays he does not have the haunted, unhappy appearance common to many whites who shift from foot to foot in drug stores through a day unbearably long, or, impelled by some demon of discontent, drive aimlessly in wide circles through city streets or over country roads. The Negro's soul does not harbor the boredom which so often drills with the insensate ruthlessness of a dentist's instruments into the white man's soul, driving him to strange excesses of escape or to obliterating narcotics of violence. He does not feel strongly the white man's need for the complicated paraphernalia of organized entertainment. Out of his sheer gusto for living, his warm and earthly animalism, he creates his own amusements. He makes his own songs and sings them, enjoys the company of his fellows, the thrills and solace of religion, and the never-ending pleasures of conversation.

The Delta Negro likes to talk. His images are illumined by vivid imagination. His speech drips color. It is filled with a sense of wonder and biblical simplicity; often with an extraordinary quality of epigram and precision. He is a maker and teller of stories. A creator and singer of songs. A speculator on the origins of the universe. The birth of man and his destiny; the sweetness of Jesus; the humanness of God; the mysteries of the Scriptures; and the vagaries of the white folks — are stock themes of conversation among Delta Negroes. They sit for hours on end in their cabins, at the gins, and in country stores, talking in groups without cease. If one leaves, another, entering, throws himself headlong into the conversation, although he has not the slightest idea of the subject under discussion. The Delta Negro — and this he probably learned from his preacher — is a master of the *non sequitur*. He throws sentences recklessly about as he throws dice, uncertain where they are going to land or what they are going to reveal, but praying for the best.

On a Saturday morning two reverend elders of the Bright Morning Star Baptist Church sit on smooth-worn benches in front of the Crescent Café (for colored only), to remain until they go home hours later at nightfall. They talk for a long time about Jesus. Their discussion ends with a review of the day when He walked upon the waters — an alluring theme in this land of floods — and they turn then to Nebuchadnezzar, who strongly appeals to the imagination of the rural Delta Negro.

"Does you 'member dat day," says one of the elders, "we'en de zebers chased ole Nebuchadnezzar clean back in dat cave where de Lawd had wrote on de wall in letters of fire, 'Mene, Mene, Tikel, Tikel'?"

"Sho I 'members dat," replies the other elder. With bewildering irrelevancy and devastating assurance he reminds his friend that "hit's jes' lak I tole you. Dey wa'n't no people at de beginnin' of de worl'. Dey wa'n't nuthin' but apes an' monkeys an' A-rabs. Right fum dat po' start de Lawd He made everything — hawgs, chickens, dawgs, contrary wimmens, Shetlan' ponies, white folks, niggers, and Chinermens."

His companion gravely agrees that this is true according to the Bible. In turn they wonder "w'en us gwine git a sho-nuf price for us cotton." They assert that "Gawd sho will strike you dead if you 'fends His commanderments," and reiterate that their plantation manager "don't know nuthin' 'bout makin' no cotton nohow." They praise their preacher because "dat's a squallin' nigger if dere ever wuz one in dis country." From time to time their conversation is interrupted to greet effusively, and as though they had come from a far country, members of their community whom they had just left that morning, would see again that night, with whom their whole lives had been spent.

A white planter passing stops to ask the elders, "Have y'all seen any of my niggers?" The language of slavery still carries over into freedom, although its implications are softened now by paternalism. "Naw, suh, Mister Ed, I ain't see a one of 'em," replies an elder. His is the language of caution and secretiveness in the presence of the white man. It is a survival, too, of slavery and still flourishes in the Delta. "Well, I got room for two or three of 'em in my car and I thought I'd take 'em on out home with me to save 'em walking." "I b'leeve I knows whar dem niggers at," says the other elder, who had been silent. "Dey's at the Chinermen's gittin' theyself somethin' t'eat." The need for caution has vanished. The information is freely given and the planter goes off to the "Chinermen's" in search of "his niggers."

Sometimes Negroes illuminate with a single sentence the differing points of view which motivate the white man of the North and the white man of the South in his conduct and attitude toward Negroes. A man migrated from a small Delta town to Boston. He was dissatisfied there and returned home. "Dey calls a nigger 'mister' up dere," he said, "but it ain't a white man will give you two bits to put somethin' in yo' stomach when you's hongry. And de niggers dey is jes' as bad. Dey won't do nuthin' to he'p nobody if dey down."

In the Delta no white man will call a Negro mister. But thousands of white men will cheerfully give almost any Negro two bits "to put somethin' in yo' stomach." He will indeed give small sums to the Negro more quickly than he will to a fellow white man. But he will never under any circumstances "mister" a Negro. This democratic title is reserved exclusively for white men, as "Mrs." and "Miss" are for white women only. Any Negro seeking to be called by these titles by whites is deemed guilty of a serious breach of the prevailing customs. And conversely, a white man using them in addressing Negroes would fall under the grave suspicion of the community.

The code of the Delta white man is in many respects less severe toward the Negro than whites. He is not held up to the same standards of conduct. The people are enormously indulgent of his faults and petty vices. Negro servants, for instance, go on year after year committing the same crimes of inattention, negligence, and extravagance with their employer's goods and money. Only the repetition of the grossest misconduct brings about their discharge. They are severely reprimanded and forgiven in the same breath. These reprimands are governed usually by well-understood conventions on both sides. They have the rigid stylization of a Japanese Noh play. Each acts his part as though he were on a stage, knowing full well that the speeches of castigation on the one side and the appearance of humble submission on the other have no contact with reality. The white employer storms and shouts. He makes dire threats of dismissal. He will not tolerate that kind of conduct again. The

Negro looks sad and contrite. He fervently promises to mend his ways. His head is bowed to the storm. He "yassuhs" everything his employer says. Yet the white man knows even as he flings the lightnings of his wrath that he will forgive his servant. And the servant knows that he will be forgiven.

Not long ago I was the guest of an old family in Vicksburg. We sat talking one afternoon and drinking sherry. My hostess, usually a talkative and abstemious woman, drank steadily and silently. Finally she left the room. "My wife rarely drinks anything," her husband said, "but she has been sitting here trying to get tight so that she could get up enough nerve to fire the cook. She's been trying to do it for eight years. When the time comes she just can't see it through."

In a little while my hostess returned, sadly triumphant. She had told Louisa that she must leave. She would give her a month's pay and another month in which to find a job, but when the time came she reckoned she just couldn't bear to see her go. Louisa was so fond of the children and they of her. She was such a good cook. She did take care of the house when they went to New York. What did it matter, after all, if she took too much food out of the house, and occasionally went off, without warning, for a week at a time with that good-for-nothing Negro from across the river?

It had taken her eight years and half a bottle of sherry to summon strength to fire the cook. Now that it had been done she spent the afternoon miserably searching for reasons to keep her. When I left the issue remained undecided. I feel, however, that Louisa will continue to cook for the Hennings for a long time to come, that her large family will always flourish on the Henning groceries, and that Louisa herself will leave the household without warning when love calls, to go off for a week at a time with that good-for-nothing Negro from across the river.

The unwritten and unwritable codes which govern the conduct of white men toward the Negro in the Delta function in strange ways. There are men here who would lynch a Negro without the slightest hesitation or compunction. And equally without the slightest hesitation they would risk their lives to save Negroes as they did in the great flood of 1927.

There was a famous physician in the Delta. He was a handsome figure of a man, gentle, kind, and soft-spoken. He might always be depended upon for aid at the lynching of a Negro guilty of a sexual attack upon a white woman or a brutal homicide upon a white man. Yet the Negroes knew him and loved him as one to whom they might always unfailingly turn in time of illness.

During his life he spent hundreds of nights in forlorn Negro cabins, waiting often until the dawn for the arrival of a child. His car stood frequently in muddy streets outside the homes of Negroes. His office was daily crowded with blacks to whom he gave aid and comfort. If they could pay, they paid. If they could not pay they received the same treatment. And if they had no money for medicine, he bought it for them. Illness alone was the passport to his skill, and it mattered not whether those who carried it were poor and black. Hundreds of Negroes in the Delta mourned his passing and venerate his memory as their true friend.

There are white men in the Delta who exploit Negroes ruthlessly. There are others who treat them with every consideration of fairness and justice. There are whites who cherish a venomous hatred of Negroes. There are Negroes who bitterly hate whites. And there are thousands of whites and Negroes between whom there exist long-sustained relations of good will, confidence, and affection.

If the Negro in the Delta is isolated by ignorance and distance from the intellectual currents of the outside world, the white man is isolated by lack of curiosity. Year after year the Delta functions in almost complete detachment in the land of the radio. All kinds of "isms" come and go beyond its borders, but it hears little of them or, hearing, little heeds. The roaring sounds of revolution in a changing world dwindle in this far distance to tiny whispers. Change shatters itself upon the breast of this society as Pacific breakers upon a South Sea reef.

The Delta does not go far afield in its reading. It has an instinctive Anglo-Saxon dislike for ideas. It reads the local newspapers which report what everybody already knows, and the

newspapers of Memphis which have a distinctly sectional tinge.
Among books it prefers non-controversial best sellers. For
critiques of the whole America it goes to the syndicated col-
umnists. Disturbing ideas crawl like flies around the screen of
the Delta. They rarely penetrate. It is only when the price of
cotton is affected that the Delta takes cognizance of the outside
world.

Cotton is more than a crop in the Delta. It is a form of mysti-
cism. It is a religion and a way of life. Cotton is omnipresent
here as a god is omnipresent. It is omnipotent as a god is omnipotent, giving life and taking life away. Here the industrial revolution is an academic adumbration dimly heard, an alien device
scarcely comprehended. In an age of machines, the patient mule
lost in prehistoric thought, followed by a plodding Negro down
a turnrow, remains the machine age of the Delta.

Year after year the Delta struggles to maintain itself upon an
economy resting squarely on cotton. And cotton is produced by
Negroes, who bring in their train a whole set of difficult and
delicate problems. They are largely bound to the land as share-
croppers on large plantations, and out of this system, essentially
unchanged since the Civil War, flows another set of problems
which no man has been able to solve. The result is that the
Delta is affected not only by the general economic conditions
prevailing in the world, but also by those peculiar to its economy.

Spiritually the white man here constantly struggles with his
desire to be just to a people who are helpless beneath white
domination, and the all too human temptation to exploit them.
He is tortured by his indecision whether to attempt to raise their
educational and cultural level, or to leave them where they are.
Racially he is determined that the white race shall be kept free
of Negro blood. But he makes no serious objection if white
blood is poured into the veins of Negroes. Individually he must
accede to the prevailing codes governing racial relations, whether
he agrees with them or no, and traditionally he moves within
the shadows of *noblesse oblige* cast by the founders of his society.

The Negro, for his part, must work out his destiny within a
framework created and ordained for him by the white man. He

must be all things to all people, an actor who never steps out of character. He must adapt himself with the fluidity of water to all the varied personalities of the white community with whom he comes in contact. He must be prepared to play clown or tragedian at a moment's notice. He must accept, silently and unhesitatingly, the conditions of living laid down by the dominant race. He must not forget that he dwells in a white man's country. Within these limits, and subject to these exceptions, he may pursue to the best of his ability the way of life that he prefers.

This, briefly, is the Mississippi Delta. Under these conditions, against this background, and in this environment nearly one hundred thousand white and three hundred thousand Negroes live and have their being. It is a strange and detached fragment thrown off by the whirling comet that is America.

CHAPTER 3

The Mississippi River

THE PEOPLE of the Delta fear God and the Mississippi River. On Sunday mornings the air of the little towns vibrates with the ringing of church bells as the faithful of many sects and both races gather for worship. And in the springtime when the waters of the river are high against the levees, the faithful go, after services, to look at the yellow flood and ponder the possibilities of disaster. Its roaring can be heard in the Sabbath stillness of the streets, and steamboats on the swollen stream pass high above the level of the earth like monstrous birds in slow flight. It is then that the devout turn to God with prayers of supplication against the devouring Mississippi. It is to Him that thanks are given when at long last it flows safely on to the sea. And it is in His bosom that they nestle for comfort when they are engulfed by its waters.

For God and the river are immortal and immemorial. Like life the river gave birth to this land; like death it comes to reclaim what it has given. Then the hand of man is impotent and refuge is in God alone.

The Mississippi has never been conquered. Secretive and unpredictable, it betrays its plans to no man. Seers cannot cast its future in a horoscope of stars, nor can engineers foretell its movements upon charts. A law unto itself, it abides by no fixed laws. This river does not rise and fall with the mathematical accuracy of the Nile, so that those who live upon its banks may know when the floods will come and when they will recede.

One year it may overwhelm the land, and for many succeeding years flow peacefully onward. It continues on no certain course. It is forever changing and altering its channel.

Sleepless and untiring, the waters of the river nibble ceaselessly at its banks until they cave and are lost. Bit by bit, slowly and surely, they are undermined, bringing with them trees, gardens, homes, factories, and sometimes whole towns. Changeable and uncertain, it makes navigation dangerous. Mudflats appear one day where water had flowed deeply the day before. Sandbars are thrown up to block the accustomed channels for boats. The Mississippi is subject to no sure restraint. More than two hundred years ago the first levee was built at New Orleans for protection from the river. Only eight years ago the largest city of the South was saved from the threat of destruction by dynamiting the levees above the town at enormous expense. The accumulated engineering knowledge of two centuries was of no avail. The American genius that built the Panama Canal, tunneled the rivers, and pierced the heavens with skyscrapers, has faltered and frequently failed in the presence of the Mississippi.

The waters of thirty-one states of the union reach the sea through the Mississippi. Its drainage basin extends from the Alleghenies to the Rockies, from the St. Lawrence to the Gulf of Mexico. Its extremities are in western New York, western Montana, southern Louisiana, and western Canada.

Into the Mississippi empty great rivers and thousands of lakes and lesser streams. The snows of the Yellowstone, the hail of Iowa, the ice of the Dakotas, and the torrential rains of the South find their way eventually into its bosom. It is the final repository of the storms and blizzards and melting snows of a gigantic empire.

When the accumulated waters of more than a million square miles of plains and hills and mountains have been gathered together, the Mississippi hurls them against the levees of the Delta. Past the towns and fields of this section flow the Wabash, the White, and the Wisconsin; the Cimarron, the Cumberland, and the Cheyenne; the Kansas, the Kanawha, and the Des Moines; the Powder, the Platte, and the Tennessee; the Ohio, the

Osage, and the Black; the Arkansas, the Yellowstone, and the Missouri. A river-sea composed of the gathered streams of America rushes with stupendous force through the Delta.

For protection against the floods there are the levees — massive, man-piled ramparts of dirt. Behind them are the people, the land, and the accumulated wealth of the whole area. For fifty years the Delta fought the river alone and unaided. The federal government was aloof and far away. All the people were Democrats. They would vote the Democratic ticket in any event. Their administrations did nothing, therefore, for them. The Republicans naturally were not interested. All of their party within the Delta could be gathered into the rest-room of a railroad station without crowding. So far as federal aid for the levees was concerned, both parties were in agreement that there should be none. The drowning of a few Democrats was of no more political or humanitarian interest than the drowning of a thousand Chinese on the Yangtse.

In its battle to keep floods from its door the Delta built its levees higher and broader and stronger. The river in turn massed its strength in greater concentration and hurled it with titanic force against them. Then the bases of the levees were broadened again, and their tops made higher. The river returned to the attack with greater power. In this battle there was no ultimate victory. Triumph rested first with one side and then with the other. The Delta could never rest upon its laurels. The threat of destruction always remained.

This section never knows when a flood will come. It lives precariously from year to year. In order for the river to burst the levees a great many malefic circumstances must simultaneously appear and act in combination. The choked and swollen streams and rivers of half of America must pour their waters into the Mississippi at one time so that it cannot carry them off quickly enough to the sea, and the mounting pressure of millions of tons of water crashes through the levees. When these factors appear and act in unison the might of money, the skill of engineers, the labor of thousands of men, and the prayers of the people are as if they had never been.

Finally in 1927 the river swept the levees away as though they had been of straw and caused the greatest peacetime disaster in the history of the United States. The Delta suffered grievously. The number of human beings drowned will never be accurately known. Cattle and stock were lost by the thousands. Myriads of wild animals perished. Towns became deserts. Plantations became inland lakes. Property losses ran into the millions. Misery and suffering reached prodigious heights.

The little town of Greenville with its population of fifteen thousand people is the largest town of the Delta. It has beauty and a quiet dignity. Summer long it lies drowsing, protected from the hot sun by its innumerable trees. In the autumn and winter its streets throb with unwonted activity as the cotton crop comes in. In the spring flowers bloom upon its breast.

Here there is no great wealth and no great poverty. The wide dome of its sky is unstained by the greasy smoke of factories. The vast acres of cotton plantations surround it and creep up to its very threshold; from these the town draws its life. Here the remnants of an older and more gracious culture still survive. Kindliness and neighborliness flourish in its soil. Whites and Negroes dwell in peace and amity. There yet remain the instinctive impulse to help others and the informed graciousness that knows how to help without hurting. There are compassion for human frailty and pity for human suffering. Men are still men here, not atoms of a state. The brawling world is over the horizon's rim. Its alarms and revolutions do not reach it. And at the end there is the cemetery where the slender limbs of weeping-willow trees descend in cascades of leafy green, and the many-throated voices of birds make music above the graves of Catholic, Protestant, and Jew.

Greenville's houses are lost among its trees. On the borders and edges of its streets grow huge oaks with wide-spreading boughs in which squirrels play. Tall magnolias bear leaves of rich leathery green, and flowers cream-white, heady with perfume. Cotton drifts summer long like driven snow from leafy cottonwoods. Children prowl the autumn through beneath pecan trees in search of nuts. One comes suddenly upon long vistas of cloudy fire of the locust. Wild phlox blows blue through the open gates of gardens.

Yearlong, birds live in the town and thrice repay with the music of their song and chatter the debt of their protection. Red-breasted robins play on its lawns. Jaybirds scream in high indignation in its trees. Hummingbirds hover on wings beating with miraculous swiftness above its flowers. In the autumn blackbirds glisten purplish black in the sun, and nightlong in the summer when the leaves of the trees bend beneath the molten silver of the moonlight mockingbirds sing in a delirium of abandon.

The town lies in a great curve of the river, within the encompassing arms of its broad grass-grown levees. It seems in its peace and quietude always to have lived happily and serenely, but it has fought for its right to live against the might of the river.

The Mississippi has made war on Greenville forthrightly with great booming walls of water, and secretively with furtive underminings of its banks. The town that Mark Twain saw in 1870 has almost vanished. Suckings and lashings of the river's currents caused the land to cave in and slide into the stream, bringing with it the structures on its surface. Where the stream now flows once stood streets and buildings. Year after year the river has encroached on the town, and the levees have moved nearer and nearer to its heart.

Prospective investors have been frightened away from the Delta. There is no safe six per cent upon the slopes of Vesuvius, and every investment here is made doubly hazardous. The river has broken the hearts of people upon its banks, ruined the reputations of engineers who sought to control it, and spread dark shadows of jeopardy upon the land. Yet as the vine is still cultivated upon Vesuvius, cotton is planted within sight and sound of the Mississippi.

In the autumn of 1926 rain fell heavily and long upon wide areas of American mountains and plains. Soot-stained snow drifted deep in Pennsylvania. Cloudbursts tortured Kansas. Tennessee mountaineers huddled in their cabins while wild waters beat down upon their roofs. Sleet pelted the farmhands of Iowa as they fed their hogs. The wheat of Manitoba lay deep beneath a blanket of white. Shepherds could not reach their flocks in Colorado. Oceans and seas of water accumulated in rivers and lakes of which the Delta knows not even the names; snow piled upon mountains which it has never seen and never dreams of seeing; all to come gurgling, rushing, tumbling, roaring into the Mississippi.

Day after day, week after week, the river rose before the levees of the Delta. The currents ran swifter. The walls of yellow grew higher. The stream spoke with stentorian voice. Finally the waters stood at the tops of the levees and men on passing steamboats looked down upon the houses of Greenville. Between it and the obliterating destruction of fifty roaring Niagaras stood a wall of water-soaked earth and the weary, mud-stained bodies of toiling men. When little streams began to trickle over the levees they were dammed with puny sacks of earth; a gesture of bootless bravery as futile as the attempt of children to hold back an avalanche with the bird's strength of their fragile hands. Thousands of men, black and white, toiled day and night. The songs of labor-inured convicts from the state prison mingled with the curses of accountants as they wielded unaccustomed shovels with blistered hands. Guards with rifles kept constant watch lest men from Arkansas across the river should dynamite the levees in order to relieve the pressure on their side. And in Arkansas rifles were raised against the Mississippians. In the town, every man, woman, and child knew that if the levees broke in its midst their lives would be snuffed out in a demoniac sea. Fear lay upon their hearts at going to bed. Thanks arose upon their lips at awakening.

In the early morning of April 21, 1927, after weeks of heartbreaking struggle, the screaming of sirens in Greenville announced that the levees had broken. The entire population, dazed and wildly excited, rushed into the streets. Wild rumors of disaster flew from tongue to tongue. Automobiles dashed through the streets on a thousand errands. Families were hastily gathered. Children whimpered or laughed in high excitement.

The schools did not open. There was utter confusion. For a little while death and disaster seemed imminent.

Then it was ascertained that the levees had broken twenty miles to the north. There fifteen hundred men had labored all night in a cold hard rain at the peril of their lives while they piled sacks against the ever-rising wind-driven might of the river. When this became known in Greenville the citizens rushed wildly to place their goods and possessions on hastily constructed scaffolds and on the second floors of homes and buildings. Provisions were assembled and the town prepared for a siege. Trains leaving the town that morning were trapped and remained engulfed until the waters receded. It would be seventy days before another departed or entered. Within a week the inundation extended over an area thirty miles wide and one hundred miles long. The water stood from four to fifteen feet in depth.

The flood moved swiftly. Hundreds of persons in the country, white and black, were marooned in treetops and on the roofs of houses. Those who did not heed the warnings to flee were lost. Within a few hours after the break the quiet air of the countryside was loud with the sound of rushing waters, the screams of the drowning, and the cries of terror-stricken animals. Motorboats, skiffs, rafts, and anything that would float were sent to the rescue. They were so few in number, however, the area of the flood so vast, the movement of the waters so swift, and some of the spots so inaccessible, that they could not succor all. Many persons dropped like stones into the stream from the tops of trees and the roofs of houses.

Two days after the break the Greenville *Democrat-Times* reported that "efforts are being made to build a board walk from the river to the Y. & M. V. depot from the wharf on Main Street. The current is swift and dangerous crossing the streets. Several boats capsized and were carried away at street intersections. . . . The fire department has had a few fires, but none so far but could be handled. If a big one should break out they would be powerless to stop it. . . . Ernest Clark, a white man, reported that his wife, mother, and children were swept away in the current and drowned while he was helpless to save them." The newspaper itself was produced by printers who stood knee-deep in water while they set the type by hand.

Thousands of refugees with some of their stock and a few possessions swarmed into the town, and in this land where there are no hills and the earth had become a sea, sanctuary was upon the levee. A great camp of ten thousand Negroes and thousands of head of stock was established. The lowing of frightened cattle, the whinnying of mules, the shouts and laughter of Negroes, and the mournful wail of their songs mingled with the roaring of the waters. Children searched for their parents and parents for their children. A fat black woman sat reading the Bible upon a coop of chickens, her abundant buttocks liquidly flowing over the wire netting. A boy chased a squealing pig through the oozing mud. A reverend elder, well fed and cheerful, beamed a gold-toothed smile upon a group of distracted admiring sisters, and bade them put their trust in the Lawd. Three young bucks dressed in Sunday clothes snatched from the flood sat upon a battered dresser and sang:

> "A nigger'll be a nigger, don't care what you do;
> Tie a bow of ribbon round the top of his shoe;
> Button his pants up around his th'oat,
> Put him on a collar, don't need no coat.
> He's spo'tin', we shall be free,
> He's spo'tin', we shall be free,
> 'Cause de good Lawd done set us free."

Suddenly there is a fight. Two tiny little Negro boys are slugging each other with impotent fists. Patches of black skin show beneath their tattered shirts. Their trousers hang perilously by strings. Mankind seemed to be getting the better of Sugar until an older Negro separated them. "Shame on y'all," he said. "What is you boys quarlin' 'bout?" Sugar, who is the smaller, replies: "Mankin' say I ain't big enough to eat nuthin' 'cep' sugar teat. I'm gwine bus' him in de mouf." Mankind rolls his eyes solemnly before replying: "Yassuh, dat's what I tole him. But I didn't mean no harm." "Well, you boys quit yo' fightin'. Don't, I'm gwine tell yo' mammies to split you wide open."

The combatants move slowly and sorrowfully away, a little distance between them. Suddenly they join hands and run swiftly together. From far up the river the wind has brought them the shrill sound of a woman's voice. "You Mankind! You Sugar! You chilluns come and git yo' supper."

Thousands of refugee Negroes were sent to Red Cross camps in Memphis and Vicksburg. The others encamped upon the levee at Greenville. Most of the white women and children left the community. The men remained and sheltered themselves as best they could in buildings and homes. Looting began in the town and voluntary military rule was enacted. Curfew tolled at eight o'clock and lights were out at ten. Then darkness lay upon the largest town of the Delta, and silence save for the gurgling of swift running currents in the streets and the coughing of motorboats bent upon missions of mercy. The moon rose upon a watery desolation of half-drowned houses and the submerged acres of plantations. A sea stretched for a hundred miles upon whose bosoms floated the bodies of men and women, their houses and their possessions.

In war or peace, in danger or stress, whatever may come to the Delta, the Negro looms as an all-important factor. In flood-time, when great strains were thrown upon the community, incidents both amusing and tragic revealed the inseparable gulf between the races and the difficulties of bridging it even momentarily in times of common danger and suffering.

The rigid separation of the races continued without the slightest change. Five days after the coming of the flood the local newspaper of Greenville reported that "John Hardin, colored, told the *Democrat-Times* today that he will give away free to both white and colored free vegetable dinners from his café on South Walnut Street. The front entrance is for white people and the rear of the café will be used for serving colored people."

Negroes displayed heroism in rescuing whites from the flood. White people at great risk to their lives snatched hundreds of Negroes from watery graves. On the night when the waters first swirled into Greenville making boating perilous, a Negro woman gave birth to a child in a hardware store surrounded by rushing torrents of water. Others bore children in almost inaccessible spots of the county. White physicians made their way in every case to the women. Between individual members of both races there existed relations of mutual helpfulness. But finally a rift came. Two peoples already in the shadow of a tragedy were about to face another.

The principal duty of the white men of Greenville during the flood was to care for the thousands of Negroes encamped upon the levee. With the aid of the Red Cross they erected miles of tents in which the Negroes were installed. Food, medicines, medical services, and blankets were provided for them. Kitchens were set up and supervised by the whites. A tented hospital was organized and manned by volunteer white physicians. The whites made every provision for the health and comfort of the marooned Negroes.

There was little work for the Negroes to do. Their principal task was to unload boats containing food largely for their use, and to aid in feeding the stock much of which belonged to them. They were well fed and content in their novel environment with its combination of free food, little work, and much loafing. So long as they were in dire danger they were tractable. When the crisis had begun to pass they rebelled. Out of this situation arose a profoundly disturbing incident which reveals how fragile are the foundations upon which rest the relations of the races in this Negro-teeming land.

The chairman for flood relief for Greenville and its county was one of its citizens, William Alexander Percy. He is a member of an old Southern family with a long record of distinguished public service. He served with the Commission for Belgian Relief before America entered the First World War. He earned the Croix de Guerre for bravery in the Argonne as a captain of infantry after America entered the war. He is a lawyer, poet, and landowner. Deeply conscious by inheritance of the traditions of *noblesse oblige*, he is sensitive to the plight of the underdog and zealous for his welfare. High-minded and idealistic, fearless and just, he is infinitely patient with Negroes and sympathetic with their difficulties. A man of fragile physical strength and indomitable will, he worked himself to the point of exhaustion during the flood and largely for the welfare of Negroes. His reward was to be bitterly assailed by the Northern Negro press. One newspaper, for instance, exhausted its repertoire of invective in denouncing his actions. It charged, among other things, that while the Negroes at Greenville did all the work, the whites played golf. (The course was then under four feet of water.) It concluded, finally, that not until the South rid itself of its Percys could the Negro expect justice.

These incendiary denunciations were read by Delta Negroes, and in combination with local causes almost brought about a clash between the races.

As the waters receded Negroes in the levee camps clamored for permission to return to their homes. Permission was denied. It was impossible to feed them save in one central place. The town could not be policed and would be at the mercy of marauders. The standing waters had made homes insanitary and dangerous to health until they had been cleaned and disinfected. Negroes, none the less, slipped out of the camp in large numbers to spend the day loafing in town, leaving fewer men to unload the boats laden with supplies. And those who remained exhibited a greater and greater reluctance to work, although the food which they unloaded was largely for their own use. No compensation was paid for this work because it was a regulation of the Red Cross that where it provided food the beneficiaries must disembark it from the boats without pay. Nor was any compensation paid or sought by the white volunteers — save some of the boatmen — who labored largely in behalf of the Negroes for two months. It finally became necessary, although there were thousands of unemployed Negroes within the area, to commandeer by force the labor necessary to unload the boats. In the process a Negro was unfortunately shot and killed by a white policeman.

Bitter resentment immediately arose in the breasts of many Negroes against Percy. He was warned by Negroes that some of them had threatened to kill him at sight and were going armed for that purpose. Courage, however, is one of his cardinal characteristics. He immediately called a meeting of Negro leaders to convene with him in a Negro church. Alone, save for the company of a friend and both unarmed, he went to the church.

At the minute appointed for the meeting no one was present. After a while, one by one, Negroes slowly drifted into the church and finally filled it to overflowing. They were silent, sullen, and hostile. Percy knew that they were armed to a man. Finally the preacher arrived and asked the audience to join with him in a hymn. They sang, not with the usual Negro joy and gusto, but with bitterness and hatred. Percy was then introduced by the preacher without the usual eulogy or compliment, as the chairman of the flood relief committee.

He immediately said what he felt to be true: that the slaying of the Negro by the policeman had been wrong and unjustified; that not he but his audience had caused his death. No white man save the boatmen who had come from afar had received pay for his work during the flood. Why should the Negroes? Had they not been installed in such comfort as could be had under the circumstances? Had they not been provided with food, shelter, medicines, and medical services without cost? Had not every white man and white woman in the community labored unceasingly for their benefit? And what, after all, had they been called upon to do? Merely to work two or three hours a day unloading food for their own mouths.

What had they actually done? When the land was a sea and fear clutched at their throats and they had nowhere to turn, they did this bit of work. Now that the waters were falling they slipped off to town and evaded their obligations. Unless the already overburdened whites now unloaded the boats there would be no food even for the Negroes. The final result was that since the Red Cross would not pay for work of this kind, since food was vital and there were no funds for work, it became necessary to commandeer labor. In so doing a Negro wrongly came to his death.

Under the circumstances his real murderers were the shirkers within the Negro community. He concluded finally with a plea for volunteers on the morrow, and a dozen Negroes, joining with him, asked the volunteers to stand. Not a man arose.

Thereafter the Red Cross was compelled to revise its regulations. It paid Negroes to unload boats bringing them food for their own use.

The implications of this incident were profoundly distressing to many white men and women in the Delta who are sincerely interested in the welfare of the Negro, and who seek to awaken in him a sense of moral responsibility toward his own if not the white community. A common danger had enveloped both whites and blacks. The whites responded. The Negroes did not. They had lost an opportunity to demonstrate by action that they are worthy of wider opportunities. The whites then are driven to the conclusion that the average Negro in the Delta will discharge even the most rudimentary social obligations only under compulsion; that he will take as much as he can and give as little as he can. And so long as he continues in these ways there can be neither whole-hearted sympathy nor effective co-operation between the races.

For seventy days the waters remained upon the lands and in the towns. Business was suspended and farming was impossible. The flooded area was cut off from the world and maintained communication with it only by boats. Relief agencies and the federal government poured millions of dollars into the Delta for aid and reconstruction. Slowly the waters receded, the land began to appear, and for the first time in two months thousands of houses could be entered without boat or boots.

The people of the Delta were scattered, their possessions left in their homes were water-soaked and destroyed. Plaster walls had crumbled; furniture had fallen apart; clothes had rotted; utensils had rusted; sometimes the foundations of houses had been undermined. Slime and mud lay thick in homes; dead mules lay rotting upon door-sills; millions of crayfish crawled in thick masses upon the ground.

The planter found that his Negro share-croppers were scattered all over the country; his stock was drowned or lost; his implements floated away or ruined; his cabins wrecked or injured; his home and possessions seriously damaged.

The communities, too, faced large outlays. It was necessary

to restore roads, bridges, and public buildings. They had exhausted their funds in fighting the flood and could not tax a suddenly stricken people. The Delta faced the aftermath of another Appomattox. Its people returned to their homes to undertake the heavy responsibilities of rehabilitation.

Now the land and its homes have again been restored, Commerce is transacted in the towns of the Delta and cotton grows in the wide fields. The levees have been built higher and stronger and the river flows to the sea. But when the snow drifts deep on the Continental Divide and ice piles up in the Yellowstone and the creeks of Oklahoma flow choked to the Cimarron, the Delta looks to its defenses and wonders when a watery Armageddon will be its fate. Then they remember what S. S. Prentiss, a fellow Mississippian, said long ago: "When God made the world, He had a large amount of surplus water which he turned loose and told to go where it pleased; it has been going where it pleased ever since and that is the Mississippi River."

CHAPTER 4

Sex Without Shackles

W HEREVER men have lived in the world sexual relations have existed between conqueror and conquered, invader and invaded, master and slave. It was thus that Holofernes lost his head, that Napoleon dallied with his Polish mistress on his catastrophic Russian campaign, and white men of the South took Negro women as concubines during slavery and after freedom.

The records of these relationships are written for all to read in the physiognomies of thousands of Negroes, and in the probated wills of white men leaving their property to their dark mistresses and mulatto children. In the slave-markets there was a constant demand for especially attractive women. Spirited bidding ensued for them at the auctions where the prices rose as high as twenty-five hundred dollars — the modern equivalent of seventy-five hundred dollars — for a rarely desirable bed companion. And in New Orleans aristocratic young men deserted their aristocratic young women at stately balls to rush to the quadroon balls where women with magnolia-petal skins and sinuous bodies danced to barbaric music.

The Delta, in the deep South, was no exception to the general rule. Here, too, white men resorted more or less openly to Negro prostitutes or mistresses. Their progeny are everywhere. These relationships are known to nearly every Negro in the community and to many of the white people, but they seldom come to the knowledge of the families of the men involved. Sometimes, however, they are discovered, occasionally under tragic circumstances, and then the children bear, as best they can, the sins of their fathers visited upon their innocent heads, while the half-breed Negroes suffer in silence or groan in their impotent wrath.

It is not uncommon for a white man to install his Negro mistress in a home which he has provided, live with her, maintain her economically, and in every way assume toward her and their children the relationship and duties of husband and father. They dwell in peace or devotion more or less openly until they are separated by death, and no pressure of family, public opinion, or church is strong enough to make him break the ties that bind him to his mistress. And sometimes there comes to light the manner in which a Negro woman demonstrates the depths of her affection for a white man.

Many years ago a young man came to a Delta town without friends, money, or position, to begin his career in the cotton business. He found a small job at a low salary, took a room in a boarding-house, and went to work. Driven by ambition, he worked long hours, and when at leisure studied the books available on the cotton trade. He was a stranger to the nightly poker games in the lonely little town, to the cheering whisky bottle, and the gentle pleasures of buggy-riding on Sundays with some young lady of the neighborhood. He lead a monastic, almost ascetic existence. His world revolved around his work. But even a budding genius of business has his human side, and in keeping with the custom of the country he took as mistress a young Negro girl.

He remained three years in the little town. When he left it to move to Memphis he knew more about the cotton business than men who had spent their lives at it. It was plain that in the larger arena he would make a brilliant success. He took with him some money which he had saved, his accumulated knowledge of business, an overweening ambition, and his mistress.

In Memphis he moved rapidly from success to success. The larger part of his time was given to work; the rest was devoted to the Negro girl whom he had brought from the country. As he grew in business stature and in wealth he began to receive invitations to dine at the best homes, to dance at the best dances, to join the best clubs. Mothers of marriageable daughters discerned virtues in him which were not patent to less penetrating eyes. Within two years he had married and rid himself of the impedimenta of his Negro mistress. She promptly and quite obligingly disappeared from the community and was heard of no more for years.

The young cotton merchant advanced from youth to middle age, from moderate wealth to great wealth, from obscurity to influence, and in his private life, from happiness to happiness. He built a great house, bought some bad pictures, entertained lavishly, and traveled widely with his family. He made the refreshing discovery that money confers omniscience, so that he gave interviews to the press on religion, politics, immortality, prison reform, and the Boy Scouts. On the fifteenth birthday of his eldest daughter he gave large sums to charity. On the twenty-fifth anniversary of his happy marriage he endowed a hospital.

Six months later his wife fled to New York with a trombone-player. Eighteen months afterward, through a convulsion in the cotton market, he was stripped of every cent in his possession. He was now growing old and faced with a desolate end because he neither had nor could borrow money with which to recoup his fortunes.

The great house was abandoned and the lavish offices closed. The cotton merchant moved into a one-room office in a cheap building. There he sat one day in his despair, when he became conscious of the presence of a person standing at his desk. He looked up to see a Negro woman. "You don't know me, do you, Mister Ed?" She smiled in vast good humor, enormously amused by the situation. "No, I'm afraid I don't," he said, wearily. "You sure you ain't never seen me before, nowhere?" "No, I've never seen you before. What can I do for you?" She burst into peal after peal of laughter. "That is the beatinest thing I ever heard tell of," she said. "Well, I must 'a' changed. You used to know me kinder well. I ain't nobody else but Lilly Clutcher. I was mighty sorry to hear about your troubles an jes' thought I'd come in to see you whilst I was passing by."

Here stood his mistress of nearly thirty years before who had never lost track of him during all this time, maintaining a kind of surveillance easy for Negroes, through his successive servants. When he married she went to Saint Louis, where she had at first been a prostitute. Then she became the owner of a house of prostitution frequented by wealthy white men, and with the passage of time had herself become wealthy. The one love of her life, the one passion which she had sustained, had been for the young white man to whom she had been mistress long years before in the little country town. She had watched his rise and fall and knew every detail of his life. Now she came again to see him in his agony and poverty. She gave him a check for a large sum with which to make a new start. A little later he died.

Not all relationships between white men and Negro women have the dark beauty or the tragic-happy ending that came to this couple. Usually they are casual and transitory contacts between man and woman which leave no marked impress on either. These contacts are so widespread, however, that they have become crystallized in crude jokes and epigrams which are part of white folk-lore sharply pointing the attitude of the white community in its acceptance of them as being well within the current morality.

Occasionally a white man goes completely native, living openly with a Negro woman in a Negro section of a town, associating only with Negroes, withdrawing himself entirely from the world of whites, in the manner of men living with Polynesian women in remote atolls of the South Seas.

In a small town in the southern part of the Delta there was such an instance. A white man there of good family completely forsook his own people and his own world to live with a Negro woman. He came in contact with whites only in the daytime as he went about his work. Three daughters came of this union. They were quite pretty, with straight soft hair, skins of *café au lait,* softly Oriental eyes, sharply defined features of face, and voluptuous bodies. Long before they reached adolescence he had planned to move them away from the town, knowing from intimate association with Negroes that sexual relations began among them at a tender age, and if his daughters did not fall prey to disease-infested Negroes they would be promptly seduced by worthless white men in search of luscious light-colored Negro virgins. Out of these fears and his ambition for them to marry white men or cultured Negroes, he moved with his family to Chicago. There he lives in an alien world of Negroes, an exile for life from his own family and his own ways, for love of a Negro woman.

For the casual dilettante of sex there are in some Delta towns and in Memphis houses of prostitution whose inmates are Negro women and all of whose patrons are white men. White men come in through the front door at any hour of the evening. Negro men enter by the back door at four o'clock in the morning when the whites have gone. White men pay and black men spend the money they have paid. They sleep with the same women, but do not sit together in the same parlor. Thus the properties and conventions of racial separation are satisfied and everybody is made happy in his own way.

Sometimes the woman who presides over one of these houses becomes famous for hundreds of miles around, and connoisseurs travel long distances to visit them. None was ever more famous some years ago than Lulu White, whose "Mahogany Hall" in New Orleans was favorably known throughout a vast stretch of territory. Once a year Miss White issued a brochure to which she herself contributed an introduction in the first person, and a biographical note about herself written with becoming modesty in the third person. There were also photographs of her "boarders" and brief notes on their personalities.

In an introductory passage Miss White says:

> In presenting this souvenir to my multitude of friends, it is my earnest desire to, in the first place, avoid any and all egotism, and, secondly, to impress them with the fact that the cause of my success must certainly be attributed to their hearty and generous support of my exertions in making their visits to my establishment a moment of pleasure. While deeming it necessary to give the history of my boarders from their birth, which would, no doubt, prove reading of the highest grade, I trust that what I have mentioned will not be misconstrued, and will be read in

the same light as it was written, and in mentioning the fact that all are born and bred Louisiana girls, I trust that my exertions in that direction will be as appreciated as yours has been to me.

It is unfortunate for the student and historian of manners that Miss White in her morbid modesty does not tell us more about herself and the great house over which she so graciously presided. In a too-brief biological note we catch tantalizing glimpses of her as a sublimated Madame de Staël conducting a salon for the gifted men of music, letters, and conversation, who sought her out in the old quarter of New Orleans.

According to this note we find that

> this famous West Indian octoroon first saw the light of day thirty-one years ago. Arriving in this country at a tender age, and having been fortunately gifted with a good education, it did not take long for her to find out what the other sex were in search of.
>
> In describing Miss Lulu, as she is most familiarly called, it would not be amiss to say that, besides possessing an elegant form, she has beautiful black hair and blue eyes which have justly gained for her the title of the "Queen of the Demi-Monde."
>
> Her establishment, which is situated in the central part of the city, is unquestionably the most elaborately furnished house in the city of New Orleans, and, without a doubt, one of the most elegant places in this or in any other country.
>
> She has made a feature of boarding none but the fairest of girls — those gifted with nature's greatest charms, and would, under no circumstances, have any but that class in her house.
>
> As an entertainer Miss Lulu stands foremost, having made a lifelong study of music and literature. She is well read and one that can interest anybody and make a visit to her place a continued round of pleasure.
>
> And when adding that she would be pleased to see her old friends and make new ones, what more could be added?

Much could have been added, Miss Lulu, had you given as frequent thought to posterity as to your "life-long study of music and literature." How we should like to know more about the "good education" with which you were "fortunately gifted"; that education which enabled you to peer with such unclouded vision into the vagrant souls of men and "find out what the other

sex were in search of." If only you had catalogued the books
in your house, or left us, at least, a list of those that appeared
most often on the night table by your bed. Did you cry yourself
to sleep over the fate of Paolo and Francesca? Or did you close
the book out of sheer pain and "in its leaves we read no more
that day"? Did you smile at the delicious naïvetés of the Courts
of Love of old Provence? Surely you collected pages' road songs
of the thirteenth century, and wept when the children went to
the crusades and came home no more to England and to France?

We strain our eyes, Miss Lulu, to see you through the mists
of time. Your portrait is a little blurred, although you have left
to a world hungry for beauty a tiny picture of yourself drawn
with Oriental economy and delicacy of line. We see you again
with "your elegant form, beautiful black hair, and blue eyes,"
amid a circle of enraptured men at your feet, in a house which is
"without doubt one of the most elegant places in this or any
other country." The Spanish War has just ended and men long
absent from the soft amenities of civilization have rushed to
your side from the boats that brought them up from Cuba. They
know that "Miss Lulu is well read and one that can interest
anybody and make a visit to her place a continued round of
pleasure."

Here poetry dwells and harpsichords tinkle in the dusk while
your boarders, "gifted with nature's greatest charms," wander
pensive and lost in halos of mist like figures in a Watteau. Or,
sometimes, the brawling world being too painful to bear, they
turn the yellowing pages of old manuscripts gold-illuminated, to
read how the young Dauphin of France lay dying in a wide-
canopied bed beneath a silken coverlet given him by the Chinese
ambassador to the Court, while the ladies-in-waiting to the
Queen murmur Latin prayers on their little round knees, and
tears drop into the laced sleeves of unashamed slender courtiers.

The clumsy groping fingers of the camera could not catch the
fleeting tenuous beauty of Miss Lulu's boarders, but she has de-
picted them for all time in imperishable prose. We see again Miss
Corine Meyers, who "can sing a song and rob the canary of his
sweet voice. She can perform on any musical instrument and

become a bosom friend in a short while." Surely the gods smiled on Miss Corine when they dowered her at once with the gift of intimacy and the gift of music. Miss Clara Miller was a shy, friendly, fragile creature of great spiritual strength and beauty: "demure, everybody's friend, and can sit up all night if necessary. Why? Because that is her disposition and who don't want to meet such a young lady?"

Miss Clara Morris smiles for us, a rose between her teeth. She describes a parabola of light illuminating the black darkness of no-time in Miss Lulu's portrait of her. "Pretty Miss Clara Morris is how this young lady's friends speak of her. Accomplished, beautiful, and charming. Born and bred right here in this city and a girl which any city should be proud of." New Orleans, dreaming by your river, remember as you toss fitfully in the hot nights that that beauty which once came to you shall never be lost. And finally, there was Miss Alda Halendar, who had a heart of gold and a tremendous talent for friendship. In her presence the leopards of lust lay still; the lions of desire switched their tails playfully upon the floor. Miss Alda was "everybody's friend; one that is liked for her sterling worth. Why is this thus? Because of her amiable disposition. She has been in the large European cities and learned how to entertain."

Miss Lulu, stars swarm above the Greek headlands on nights of summer and the lights of little boats en route to the craggy islands shine dimly in the darkness of the sounding sea. For a little while they seem to stand still in the immensity of great waters. Then they vanish and there is only time and space and nothingness. Yet shepherds keeping lonely vigil high above Corinth note their passing and are less lonely; peasant lovers clasping hands on wooded Olympus see them swim out of the dark ocean and feel for a moment a deeper wonder and a closer drawing together under the sky. So, too, you came briefly, with your boarders the color of cream and of old ivory, bringing with you the illusion of warm love and mirth and gaiety. Your company is scattered and dead; winds rattle the shutters of your abandoned house; mice play on its floors. But old men remember you and, remembering, conjure up again their lost youth and rapturous hours in your presence.

When the octoroon girls who made up Miss Lulu's establishment left their respective communities to join her, it was no more a matter of general concern to the Negro group at large than similar departures are to the white group at large. But Negro men frequently resent deeply as individuals the fact of sexual relations between some particular Negro girl and a white man. They become deeply embittered because there is no tribunal or law or public opinion to which they can resort. Unless they acquiesce their only resort for satisfaction is to violence.

Sometimes a white man, by virtue of larger means or his authority as a member of the dominant race, literally takes a woman away from a Negro man to become his concubine. And sometimes the Negro in his rage and frustration ambushes the white man, kills him, and is in turn killed. Occasionally tragedy is wrought in quite a different way. In one of the towns of the Delta there is living a Negro man of intelligence and sensitivity who does not want to live. He had one young daughter upon whom he lavished great affection and care, rearing her to womanhood as carefully and as gently as he could, hoping that she would eventually marry some worthy member of her race. (There are among Negroes of this section so-called "respectable families," who not only conform to the usual conventions, but are quite puritanical in their outlook.) Shortly after her adolescence she was seduced by a young white man of the community in which she lived. When it became apparent to her that she was with child, she told her father. She blamed no one but herself. He upbraided neither her nor her seducer. Quietly he took poison and tried to die. The poison failed. Now he is a wreck of a man and is drinking himself to death.

Given the conditions under which whites and blacks have for so many years lived together in the Delta, it seems inevitable that sexual relationships should have existed between white men and Negro women. The white man seeking sexual contacts felt that he was in no way impairing the morals of the Negro community when it was clearly apparent to him that these morals according to his standard or any standard, simply did not exist. The women were on the whole willing and even eager to assume a sexual relationship with him, and they were quite venial in their attitude. The white man could give them finery, money, protection, and prestige. There were not, therefore, from his point of view, any reasons for forbearing, and, human nature being what it is, he did not forbear. The white man of the Delta was merely writing his chapter in the long record of the white race throughout the world wherever it has come in contact with colored peoples of a simpler culture or weaker fiber.

It is none the less clear that the history of miscegenation in the Delta is interwoven with dark threads of blood and grief and pain. It is in startling contrast with the principles of the white man's religion which he shares with the Negro. It marks a strange contradiction in his already contradictory relationship with this race. The white man presses certain disabilities and restrictions upon the Negro. The full-blooded Delta Negro, provided the restrictions are not too onerous and he is given a chance to lead his own way of life, brushes them lightly aside and goes gaily on. Half-breeds and quarter-breeds feel the disabilities more sharply and are restive under them. Yet white men have not hesitated to pour their blood into the veins of Negroes and increase the number of those who suffer because of that blood.

The great and inflexible taboo of sexual relationships in the Delta is that there shall not be, under any circumstances whatsoever, a sexual relationship between a white woman and a Negro. The inescapable punishment, when discovery is made, is death. It does not matter that the woman gave consent. Some years ago a white woman gave birth to a Negro child in a Delta hospital. Within a few hours her brother had come in from the country and tried to kill her, and the Negro had been quietly lynched. He had offended an inflexible taboo of which he had full knowledge and of whose penalty for offending he was aware.

Rape is a crime shockingly abhorrent to men all over the world. The white man of the Delta, living among masses of Negroes overwhelmingly superior in numbers and well armed, fears them only in one respect. He does not fear bodily harm to himself, nor an armed uprising *en masse*. There has never been such an uprising in the history of the Delta. He does, however, fear sexual attacks upon his women.

You cannot rationalize a fear of this kind out of a man, nor make it seem ridiculous in his eyes with structures of smooth syllogisms. He is not comforted by the fact that crimes of this kind are of infrequent occurrence, nor calmed by the thought that the chances of a rape committed upon his womenfolk are perhaps one in a million. His wife and daughters are not to him mere figures in tables of averages. They are flesh and blood whom he loves and cherishes, and he cannot ever be brought to see that the ravished body of one dear to him represents merely the haphazard workings of chance which the averages assert will not occur again in a million times.

The planter or overseer away on distant acres from his isolated home, the townsman absent from his house on some lonely street of the outskirts of a town, simply does not feel secure unless his womenfolk are protected in some manner in his absence. (Often the protector may be a Negro.) These people live among great masses of Negroes. They know that rapes and attempted rapes have occurred. Why may they not occur again? And why may not the victims the next time be in their own families?

Out of this fear, out of this horror at the sexual approach of a Negro man to a white woman, out of this vague and gnawing dread, grow lynchings and excesses against Negroes. The Delta was recently the scene of such an attack upon a white woman. The events which followed the commission of the crime, and the capture and trial of the criminal, show clearly the conflicts within the various strata of the white community, and the distortions and stresses which small groups of whites suffer in the presence of masses of Negroes.

The little town of Cleveland, Mississippi, is one of the two county seats of Bolivar County. Its population of about three thousand persons is almost evenly divided between whites and blacks, although within the county itself there are twenty-five hundred Negroes for every one thousand whites, and in some sections there are as many as fifty Negroes to one white person. There are, indeed, as many Negroes in Bolivar County as in all of Massachusetts, although that state has a population of over four millions and the county has only about eighty thousand. Of these fifty-two thousand are Negroes and eighteen thousand are whites.

These Negroes when gathered in groups are seen to be largely full-blooded blacks, although here, as elsewhere, there is a marked leaven of mulattoes. They are, on the whole, poor, darkly ignorant, prey to magic and hoodoo doctors, unpredictable in conduct and temperament, and to the white man, however sympathetic or sensitive, essentially unknowable. They are black, with squat noses and thick lips, shambling arms and low foreheads, kinky of hair and frequently with a yellowish tinge in the whites of their eyes. They still stand close to the parent stock of Africa from which they sprang.

In the latter days of December, 1934, a family of whites composed of father, mother, and young son, were living in a little house on the outskirts of Cleveland. They were simple and obscure people, honest and industrious, awaiting now the joyful coming of Christmas within a few days, and a new baby in the spring. On an evening in December the father returned from work and took his modest meal alone. His wife, in an advanced state of pregnancy, lay in bed. His meal finished, he went in to talk to her. Their little son was asleep. Then darkness.

In the morning, when the neighbors came, they found man and woman dead, the boy's head battered, though he was still living. The man lay face downward stretched across the bed, a bullet hole in the back of his head and his eye torn out where the bullet emerged. The woman's body was dismembered. Her brains, beaten out of her head, splattered a pillow-case. Scattered about the room were portions of her intestines, uterus, and vagina. Her abdomen yawned an empty hole. Great slabs of flesh had been sliced from her legs and thighs. Blood stained the floors, the walls, and bedclothing.

Horror and dread filled the little town. The ghoulish, unfathomably savage character of the crime gripped men's minds with a fearful fascination. Women were afraid to go into the streets, and when they did were then irresistibly drawn to drive past the little house where a man and a woman had been found lying battered in their gore. Young children, fascinated by this incredible terror in their midst, could think of nothing else. A bond of sympathy for the victims and hatred for the criminal enveloped the entire community. People in small towns live in close communion, although they may not know one another. Up and down the length of the Delta and across its breadth crept a shudder of fear and horror. In Cleveland itself one question lay like lead on the throats of every man and woman. Who would be the next victim? Christmas came sorrowfully to the town.

Shortly after the victims had been buried, obscene letters were received by white women in Cleveland, and similar letters by white women in Indianapois, Indiana, postmarked at Cleveland, Mississippi. Federal post-office inspectors then came into the case. They learned that a local Negro, sharing a letter-box with two other Negroes, subscribed to an Indianapolis newspaper. One day the newspaper lay in the box and officers waited in the post-office. One of the men who shared the box came and took his mail. Then the other came and, finding nothing for himself, departed. In the afternoon a third Negro came, took the newspaper, and was arrested.

It was quickly learned from the prisoner that he had been born in Bolivar County and had left it eighteen years before to live in Indiana and Michigan. He had but recently returned to the Delta and was working as a farmhand on his mother's little piece of land about a mile from Cleveland. Convinced that they had their man, the officers placed him in an automobile and lodged him safely in jail at Jackson, 150 miles away, before anyone in Cleveland realized that a suspect had been caught.

After a few days the prisoner made a complete confession before forty or more officials and newspaper men. He confessed committing not only the crime in Cleveland, but also that he had served a prison term in Michigan for robbing graves, and had successfully committed the same crime in Indiana without detection. He had lived in Indianapolis and obtained from the newspapers of that city the names of prominent white women to whom he had addressed obscene letters from Cleveland.

Immediately a loud outcry arose in Cleveland for the return and trial of the criminal. Threats of lynching were heard on many sides, particularly from the poor whites living in Bolivar and adjoining counties as far as fifty miles away. It became increasingly evident that the prisoner would be lynched unless strong armed forces were present at his trial. The militia may not be sent in such a case unless it is requested of the governor by the sheriff of the county. He was not a candidate for re-election, but the district attorney who must prosecute the criminal had announced his intention to seek the office again. His chances of election would be seriously impaired if he joined with the sheriff in requesting troops. Many voters were would-be lynchers. The district attorney none the less joined with the sheriff in asking that the militia be sent to the trial. The faculty and students of Delta State Teachers' College situated in Cleveland requested the sheriff to ask for troops. Churches, clubs, and influential citizens added their voices.

Governor Conner commanded the adjutant-general of the Mississippi National Guard to order out enough men and equipment to take the prisoner from Jackson to Cleveland, protect him during the trial, and in the event of his conviction, return him to Jackson for safe-keeping, pending his appeal or execution.

Nearly six hundred militiamen converged upon Jackson from all parts of the state, care being taken to pick men from counties remote from the scene of the crime. Guardsmen from Bolivar County participated in the mobilization only to the extent of acting as kitchen police. They took no part in guarding the prisoner. An hour before the special train carrying the prisoner and troops was to depart from Jackson, pedestrians and automobiles in the vicinity of the jail were kept moving, and the car containing the prisoner moved to the railway station between marching columns of bayonets in the hands of troops instructed by their commander to "shoot to kill."

The prisoner, heavily manacled, was placed for the night-long ride in a baggage car surrounded by picked officers and men. As the train moved across the state he aired his opinions to them at great length; quoted from his favorite philosophers,

William James and Arthur Schopenhauer; discussed his theories of fatalism; couched his thoughts in excellent concise English and evinced little interest in his possible fate.

While the train was en route to Cleveland, the courthouse where the trial was to be held had been converted by other guardsmen into a fortress. It was surrounded completely by an intricate barbed-wire entanglement. The streets immediately adjacent to it were closed and barred to traffic. Machine-gun nests built of sand-bags were erected in the grounds, and other machine-guns were mounted in the windows and on the roofs to sweep every approach. Morning found troops with rifles and tear-gas guns thick on the lawn of the courthouse, swarming on the steps outside and the stairs inside, guarding every passage leading to and from the courtroom and the courtroom itself. The jail where the prisoner was to be held bristled with rifles and bayonets, and the passage along which he must pass to the courthouse was lined both sides with heavily armed men. Here were force and determination enough to overawe the strongest mob.

At four o'clock in the morning, when Cleveland was asleep, the prisoner arrived and was safely conveyed to the brightly lighted militia-guarded jail. A few hours later crowds began to descend on the town from all over the Delta, some to be admitted with passes to the courthouse, others to stand enviously behind the barbed-wire entanglements, or to talk in little groups on street corners near the scene of the trial.

In the crowd were many Negroes. They talked, laughed, and watched with keen interest and proud eyes the goings and comings of the guardsmen. They speculated on the destructiveness of their guns. "Nigger, ef I had me a swamp-injin like dat I could sho raise me a ruckus," said a tall, gangling black boy, dancing with excitement. "Go 'head, man," replied his companion, pointing to a gas gun in the hands of a trooper, "I'd druther have me one er dem Gatlin' guns. They shoots clean th'oo er oak tree and keeps a-goin'." "Lawd have mussy, what you reckon us gwine do settin' up here in de mouf er dem smoke-poles if dem white folks starts shootin'?" shrilly inquired a stripling yellow girl who had suddenly abandoned the washtub to come to this scene of carnival. "Dey ain't studdin 'bout shootin' nobody," boomed the voice of a man next to her. "De President told 'em not to lessen folks got too bad."

The mere presence of Negroes at such a time was extraordinary. Negroes usually remain indoors in the Delta when trials of this kind are in progress, for fear that the crowd may overpower the officers, lynch the prisoner, and inflict injuries upon them. Now however, completely reassured by the presence of troops, they were *en fête,* and the more business-like among them did a thriving business selling soft drinks to the soldiers and to the onlookers.

The Negroes were sure that the government at Washington had sent troops to protect them as well as the prisoner. They know that it was Lincoln who "sot 'em free," that he once lived in Washington and that ever since his day the white folks there have been on the alert to help the Negro in times of stress. It would have been difficult to make many of them believe that the guardsmen had been sent to Cleveland at the request of the officials of the local county. They could never have understood that they were present not primarily to protect anyone, but to uphold the processes of law and order of which the present prisoner was merely the transient object. The Negroes' belief that the President of the United States had sent troops to Bolivar County for their benefit was an unfortunate conclusion for them to reach, given the conditions under which the two races live in the Delta. It might lead them to think that the federal government was ready to spread its sheltering wings to protect them in all their doings; they would then step out of the place to which white domination had assigned them and inevitably produce a series of racial conflicts. It is part of the hopeless tragedy of these utterly diverse peoples living in close juxtaposition, that the white man's effort to do the right thing is as likely to cause trouble as his actual doing the wrong thing.

The majority of the crowd was composed of poor whites, or, as they are called in the Delta, "rednecks" or "peckerwoods." There is no love lost between them and the Negro. They stand on the same economic level and are in direct competition as croppers and laborers. Despite the fact that they are as ignorant and as poor as Negroes and are looked down upon by landed or propertied whites, they feel themselves, as white men, to be immensely superior to the Negro. Their superiority is expressed by hating and humiliating him as much as they can. The Negro in turn hates the redneck and expresses his scorn of the whole tribe with the contemptuous phrase, "Dey ain't nuthin' but po' white trash."

The poor whites stood in groups outside the barbed wire, looking out of pale-blue eyes glittering with hatred at the troops who had cheated them of their prey. They wore faded blue overalls covered sometimes by an old overcoat, and rubber boots caked with wet mud. Stubbles of beard were on their faces, blond heads bore dust-stained hats, their hands were gnarled and dirty, their broken nails were rims of black at the extremities of their fingers. Fanatically and narrowly religious, poor and superstition-ridden, hating Negroes and whites of a better class, they boiled with anger and impotence as they stood frustrated by the force of steel before them.

I spoke with many of them about the trial. They spat in disgust. Their sheriff had betrayed them by asking for the militia when they could so handily have lynched "the nigger." "He couldn't git elected to dog-ketcher in this county no mo'." I pondered that statement. This, after all, is a democracy. The vote of an idiot is as potent as that of a savant. They were outraged by the expense of bringing the troops. A toothless old man, tin of snuff in hand, interrupted his "dipping" to tell me, "I bet it cost nigh onto twenty thousand dollar to pertect that black son of a bitch, and if they'd 'a' turned him over to us we'd 'a' made hash out of him in no time and it wouldn't 'a' cost nuthin' but a piece of rope."

Another said that "what it cost to pertect this danged nigger who ain't nuthin' but a half-human varmint would 'a' screened ever' share-cropper's house in Bolivar County." A man wearing an old army overcoat informed me that "I spent two years in the World's War a-fightin' them Germans what never done anything as bad as this nigger done sawin' up people. A white man ain't a-goin' to be able to live in this country if we let niggers start gittin' biggity. I wish they'd lemme have him. I'd cut out his black balls and th'ow 'em to the hawgs." He meant it. Near by stood three men debating. "If a fellow knowed whether they got orders to shoot or not," said one, "then he'd know what to do." "They got them orders, all right," said another. "I seen it in the paper." "Well, that might be," said the first speaker, "but they ain't a-goin' to shoot into this crowd where they's women and children. That ain't constitutional and it's ag'in' the guverment."

They were certain that the display of force would convince the Negroes that the government of the United States would protect them whatever they might do, and thus make them "uppity." One of them pointed to the machinegun nests and rifles and said to me, "That's what's a-ruinin' 'em and makin' fools out of the niggers. Niggers air a-braggin' on ever' plantation in this county that the guverment's a-pertectin' 'em and we gonna haf to kill a lot of the black bastards to knock some sense into their kinky heads."

Daylong they stood outside the courthouse, airing their grievances to one another, shifting from foot to foot, walking wearily about, talking to the guardsmen, trying to snatch news of the progress of the trial. It was not until night fell and the trial was ended that they left the scene. They went home mollified by the verdict of the jury, but discontented because they had not been permitted to torture the prisoner slowly to death and hack his body to pieces.

In the jail the prisoner, James Coyner, sits unconcernedly through the morning, and eats his lunch quietly at noon. He is six feet four inches tall and of gigantic strength. He is dressed in a blue overall coat, a blue workshirt open at the throat, rough work trousers and heavy black shoes. His hands and feet are huge. He has soft brown eyes, sharply defined features, and his gentle countenance appears at times almost benign. He looks a shepherd of men, one in whom complete trust could be reposed; a mild giant who would use his great strength but to shelter and protect. As he sits with folded hands and bowed head he is a gargantuan ginger-bread man conjured up by the vision of a child fairy-tale haunted.

He is asked if he has any regret for committing the crime. "No," he says, slowly, "no more than if I had spilled a glass of milk. What's done is done. What's bothering me right now is that this jailhouse is cold."

Shortly after one o'clock in the afternoon the prisoner was led into the courtroom between double rows of militiamen. Every seat on the ground floor was taken by spectators. The balcony was jammed with guardsmen. They stood, too, at the doors and entrances, in the aisles, and occupied the entire row of seats directly behind the prisoner. It would have been suicidal to attempt to harm him.

The prisoner did not want a lawyer to defend him. He merely wanted to plead guilty and have done with it. The court, none the less, ordered that every member of the local bar submit his name for the defense and one of the most capable was chosen by lot to represent the defendant. Then a jury was impaneled and sat to hear the case of the State of Mississippi *v.* James Coyner.

The trial proceeded according to the niceties of the law in a courtroom completely orderly and silent save for the wheezings and coughings of the crowd. One by one the state's witnesses testified. A post-office inspector outlined the circumstances under which the prisoner was arrested. A watchmaker identified the watch of the dead man later found in the prisoner's possession, and a Negro identified the victim's pocketknife. The brother of the dead man gave his testimony, and a timid, frightened little woman, an *attaché* of the Circuit Court clerk's office, presented records bearing on the location of the farm where the prisoner lived with his mother. The confession was introduced and those portions of it admitting crimes committed elsewhere were deleted. Finally the sheriff took the stand and opened a yellow box. From it he took some objects which made the crowd gasp with horror. Here were slabs of the woman's flesh and squares of her skin tanned as leather is tanned, found where the prisoner had secreted them in his corn-crib.

James Coyner, the only Negro in a crowd of twelve hundred whites, sat unconcerned, bored or half asleep. He asked once to go to the toilet, and was led out and brought back by a squad of soldiers. That apparently was his only contact with the world around him. His intelligent and rather sensitive face remained buried most of the time in his huge hands as he walked dreamways remote from this courthouse in Bolivar County where he had been born and was so soon to die.

In the courtroom a strange game was being played according to archaic rules laid down long ago in England, still expressed in stilted English and Anglicized Latin. The judge, a middle-aged graying mammal, sat upon a platform peering out of his skullcase with bespectacled eyes at other mammals, the lawyers. They stood upright, in contradistinction to the generality of the animal kingdom, clothed in the wool of sheep and the fiber of cotton. Their eyes looked out of bony sockets at the twelve skullcases and twenty-four eyes which sat in the jury-box; at the twelve hundred skullcases in the audience, some of which, by their thick-piled hair, one knew to be the heads of women. The judge leaned over. The lawyers whispered to him. He seemed to be quietly admonishing children. The heads separated and seated themselves on opposite sides of a long table.

Someone had died. Someone had indeed been brought to his death. Whence had come the bringer of death? Eyes sought him out in the courtroom. Fingers sliding along the leaves of lawbooks groped for him. Why had that man living in his little house awaiting Christmas and his new baby been chosen to die without even the garlands of a sacrificial bull about him? Where is he now? Where has he gone? What is death?

Do you know, omniscient Judge, sitting high above the heads of men in your wide-backed chair? Do you know, Mr. District Attorney, who seem so familiar with death that you talk about it constantly? Surely you can tell us, Mr. Attorney for the Defense, for it is plain that if you defend one against something you must know the face and nature of the thing against which you interpose your learning and your strength? Or it may be that you will enlighten us, Young Guardsman, standing there with your bayoneted rifle? You are young. The down of youth is on your cheeks. Your mother is worried that you are in peril far from her side. Long ago it was written: Out of the mouths of babes shall come wisdom. But you won't tell us. You lean silent on your long rifle, gazing into the yard below where your fellows are making the flames of bonfires leap ever higher with fresh-piled fagots.

James Coyner, a ginger-colored giant, sits at the table, half asleep, his immense strength in repose, his huge hands folded upon his knees. Then perhaps it is he who is to die, he of the more than thousand persons in the room? He about whose brown throat a hempen rope will be drawn and stretched tighter and tighter by the weight of his dangling body until his windpipe sputters and rattles, his dry lips fleck with bubbly foam, and his vertebrae, ingeniously made, are twisted and broken.

Yet at this very moment the beating of his heart floods the veins of his body to overflowing, touches to color the tiny capillaries of his toes, pours with sanguinary stream over the soft pinkish tissues of his brain. This body began to die when it was born, and all these years it has been dying to the unremitting music of his heart. The judge there on the bench, James Coyner, has a heart, too, and although he is white and free and you are black and imprisoned, it races in his separate body toward the grave even as your heart, and beats the separate tattoo which is his dirge. You are shackled and he is as free as a bird of the air, but he does not race more quickly than you nor cover the ground with firmer stride or longer step. Soon, James Coyner, you will draw away from him and his pale white figure will recede into the mist. In a little while, a day, a week, a month, some subtle chemistry will be made to work in your body so that you will be catapulted into the intersteller spaces and arrive at your dark destiny years ahead of him who now sits high and triumphant above you in his wide-backed chair.

The long afternoon wears wearily on. Outside in the gathering shadows guardsmen begin to spread the dishes for their evening meal on long wooden tables. Inside, the law goes through its measured rhythm with, "I object, Your Honor," and,

"Objection overruled," and "Objection sustained." In a world irreverent of form the law goes its ceremonious stylized way. There is no recess for dinner. Seven o'clock stands on the face of the clock. Is it, I wonder, really seven o'clock? It is so puzzling. How is one to know? Men measure time with superb impudence, but it is of their nature to thrust arrogantly at forces that brought about their being and will inexorably encompass their end. Yet even the magnificent egoists are confused, for if it is indeed seven o'clock here in the Mississippi courtroom where James Coyner is on trial for his life, I know that at this moment Parisians are leaving the Opéra Comique at midnight, having just heard *Manon*; Polynesians on Mangareva are awakening to the tropical dawn; and the ship's bells of a British tramp in the Tasman Sea are tapping out the noon of tomorrow.

At fifteen minutes before eight the state rests. The prisoner does not take the stand. The jury is addressed by the lawyers. They receive the instructions of the court and march out. Twelve gods in rumpled suits force their way through the crowd to the jury-room. The crowd is hushed. James Coyner sleeps. On the stroke of eight the jury returns. Deity, multi-headed, sits on twelve chairs. "We, the jury, find the defendant guilty as charged."

The crowd remains silent. There is no demonstration. Egyptian Thebes is vanished, but men still keep Books of the Dead. Now another little entry is to be made in the crowded leaves. The judge says, "James Coyner, stand up." James stands six feet four and the color of ginger. "Have you anything to say?" "No, sir." The judge resumes. "You have heard the verdict of the jury. You have been represented by able counsel and have had a fair trial. I now sentence you to be hanged by the neck until you are dead on Tuesday, March the fifth, between the hours specified by law. And may God Almighty in His infinite wisdom have mercy upon your soul."

The prisoner is returned to the jail. The crowd dissolves. The courtroom is deserted. A mouse comes to nuzzle its soft gray nose among the peanut-scented papers on the floor. In the railroad yards a black locomotive coughs stertorously and backs down upon a string of cars. James Coyner will soon be on his way to Jackson, sitting manacled nightlong between rows of rifles, until he shall be brought again to Cleveland and his body buried in the rich earth of the Delta from which he sprang.

The sexual relations of Delta Negroes, particularly on the plantations where the majority of them live, are marked by a simplicity and naturalness which the white man cannot ever acquire nor fully understand. He is a creature of conventions and inhibitions. He must consider public opinion and the force of the law. Marriage, the child, and the family are still the basic units of the society in which he moves. His religion casts shadows on Eros. If it be that he is natively as sexually vigorous as the Negro, his vigor is lessened by the worries of one kind or another that constantly assail him; it is debilitated by forebodings and dark fears; it is weakened by inherited cautions of restraint, by circumlocutions of address and conflicts within his mind.

The Negro, on the other hand, is sexually completely free and untrammeled. "W'en I wants me a woman, I gits me a woman." To him the expressions and manifestations of sex are as simple and as natural as the manifestations of nature in the wind and the sun and the rain, in the cycles of the seasons and the rounds of the growing crops. Sexual desire is an imperative need, raw and crude and strong. It is to be satisfied when and wherever it arises. It is not embroidered with the roses and raptures of romantic love. It does not proceed tortuously through devious détours of flirtation, but flies straight to its mark with the blind compulsion and devouring intensity of a speeding bullet.

Many plantation Negroes think of sexual relationships as a "po' man's delight." "Cap'n," a big black field hand told me as he shook with laughter, "niggers is as good as white folks in two places — in de bed and in de graveyard." These Negroes, remote from the moving-picture theaters of the towns, illiterate and ignorant so that they can only spell out the Bible and the mail-order catalogues, with abundant leisure which they turn to no use, regard sex as a Heaven-sent form of amusement.

Upon the structure of the Negro's own sexual freedom another

freedom is superimposed. He is in his sexual and domestic relations beyond the pale of the white man's law and the white man's
opinion. One of my friends one day asked her gardener how
many times he had been married. He scratched his head in distress, trying to remember all the ladies whom he had espoused.
Finally he replied. "Ole Miss, I jes doesn't recollect." An hour
later he brought her a pad of paper and a pencil. "Does you
write down dey names, us can figger hit out." There were
Lagirtha, Pocahontas, Chlorine, Exceptional, Ruby Pearl, Arcele,
Cora Maud, Ruth Rebecca, Waterene, and his present wife,
Honey Bunch. He had married the first of the ladies to whom
he gave his name. He had "'vorced" the others by the simple
process of leaving them or being left.

The white community, so potent in so many activities of
Negroes, does not in the slightest degree concern itself with their
domestic or sexual relations save in the exceedingly rare cases
of incest which come to light, and occasional complaints of rape
which are received with the greatest skepticism. Authentic cases
of rape occur among Negroes and rapists are sent to the state
penitentiary. Often, however, Negroes knowing the gravity with
which white folks regard this crime, use the charge of rape as a
means of revenge.

A justice of the peace in a Delta town told me of such a case
which had come before him. He cross-examined the alleged
victim. "How much underwear did you have on?" he asked.
"I was wearin' a pair drawers an' a pair teddies," she said. "Did
this man here tear your underwear?" "Naw, suh, he didn't tear
it. He was fixin' to tear it, so I pulled 'em down."

The judge exploded in his wrath. "Get out of here!" he yelled.
"Lilie Mae," he said to the accuser, "if I ever catch you trying to
mess up a man again, I'm going to put you in jail and keep you
there until the devilment gets out of your mean hide if it takes
twenty years." "Yassuh," she said. The defendant, a 'spectable
married man, glared at her and stepped haughtily out into the
sunshine of freedom.

The laws governing marriage and divorce are rarely if ever
enforced against Negroes. They are free to marry or not to

marry, as they see fit, although they may live in what appears to be a state of marriage. They may commit adultery, bigamy, polyandry, or polygamy, or devise any combination of relationships, however fantastic, which their fancies may create or their needs demand. There is utterly no external compulsion of law or of white opinion to confine their sexual and domestic relations within an ordered framework.

In his religion and in his sex the Negro is on his own. It is true that he took his religion from the whites, but he has adapted it to his own uses, and he is little influenced by the white churches. Nor do they in turn attempt to press their views and motivations upon him. The life of the body and the life of the spirit are his to do with as he pleases. They are beyond the reach of the white man's pervasive influence.

Within his own community and among his own people the Negro finds himself in complete sexual freedom. Life is a long moral holiday. It is obvious that you cannot incur the wrath of group opinion for doing that which the group itself almost without exception is doing. You cannot lose caste for committing a crime which is being universally committed. You cannot offend conventions which do not exist nor contravene standards which have never been set up. The average Delta Negro has almost no criteria of conduct by which sexual and domestic relations may be judged. The few shadowy codes which exist concern themselves almost entirely with the care in infancy of bastard children.

Sexual relations among Delta Negroes begin at a tender age — puberty comes early in this warm climate — and last as long as strength lasts. A girl at the age of twenty is sexually an experienced woman of the world. A boy of the same age is a mosquito-bitten Casanova of the swamps. The crowded conditions of their cabins make them *au courant* to the manifestations of sex when they are children. The absence of restrictions upon them flowing from their elders gives them freedom and tacit approval when they grow older. Complete sexual license within the community keeps them life long within the frame of the current morality. Both boys and girls live more or less in sexual promiscuity until they take up an arrangement which bears some of the aspects of permanency. They then confine their activities not solely to each other, but merely to a few persons in the neighborhood. That is being "respectable." Sexual fidelity, a manifestation of romantic love, is a conception almost entirely unknown and utterly without value physical or spiritual.

Legal marriage and legal divorce are, of course, largely disregarded. It costs money to hire a preacher and get a license. It is just too much trouble to take. If a man and a woman want to live together, they do it. They have children, remain together as long as they please, leave each other when whim dictates, and repeat the same pattern with another man or another woman. If a man and two women want to live together — a not uncommon arrangement — they set up housekeeping in common and that is all there is to it. And similarly, if a woman can engage and hold the attentions of two men, all three dwell together under the same roof for as long as they desire to continue the relationship. Whatever they may do and however they may do it, they do not offend the mores of the community.

In recent years many Delta Negroes have begun to contract legal marriages for unexpectedly strange reasons. Some of the men have found that if they have a "cotehouse license to live with a lady," and in the course of living with her kill another Negro who has been tampering with her affections, the white folks in their inexplicable ways are not likely to regard such a crime seriously. One Negro on a plantation boasted to me that he was not only married, but had a "cotehouse license." "I had me a commissary license onct, and a levee camp license onct. Now I done got me de pyore-D license from the Circus Cote clerk in Greenville. Ef I catches me a nigger kickin' in my stall, I'm sure gwine crack down on him now." Holy matrimony has become a thing not made in heaven, but rather a home-made product of the plantation as a form of insurance against some uncontemplated but not improbable homicide.

Negro women, too, have latterly begun to insist upon legal marriage so that they may be undisputed claimants of the funds of life insurance policies of which they are beneficiaries. Sometimes a man lives with a woman without marriage, naming "my wife" in the policy as beneficiary. He may leave her, legally marry another woman, and die. A contest over the funds then ensues between the women, each claiming that she is the wife. Or the man may marry a woman and, without legal divorce, marry or live with another. This relation again gives rise to a contest between the two women. The courts of Mississippi have been filled with cases involving disputed insurance moneys arising from these confused relationships. But sacred matrimony is slowly coming in to its own through the roundabout way of life insurance policies. If there were enough of them, the Negroes of the Delta might eventually succumb to the ways of white folks.

On the plantations there is a constant shifting about of women among the men, as well as the constant carrying on of sporadic sexual relationships with dwellers on adjoining plantations. It is a not uncommon thing for a Negro to work from sunup to sundown in the hot fields, then walk ten miles up the road to see a woman, spend most of the night with her, and arrive on his own plantation just in time to catch his mules for the plow and begin a long day's work. In the summer the roads are alive with Negroes at all hours of the night from the coming of darkness to dawn, as they go to and fro on missions of love to distant cabins.

During the season of almost uninterrupted leisure, which runs from the gathering of the crop in October until the planting and plowing in early spring, a man may seek a woman to live with him during these months who has a reputation for sexual ardor. It does not matter that she is a poor cook, an indifferent housekeeper, and an incompetent if not useless field worker — qualities which frequently dictate the Negro's choice when he is contemplating a union of some permanency. During the long period of leisure which stretches before him he prefers *décor* and warmth to utility. When however, the time comes to get the cotton out of the grass and hoe-hands are badly needed to pull the crop through, he quite unceremoniously kicks his fragile light of love out of the house and installs a strong, muscular woman who knows how to work daylong under the hot sun.

There is at least one definite strongly rooted sexual convention among the Delta Negroes. It is that if a man is living with a woman he may quite freely have sexual relations with other women with the more or less tacit knowledge and consent of his wife or mistress, and the same freedom is permitted the woman. However, neither may carry on these extra-marital relations under the nose of each other nor flaunt them in each other's faces. They sum up this convention in these words: "If you does it in a nice kinder way — don't disturb nobody's peace — keeps peace at home and peace where it's at — and wipes yo' mouf [that is, the relationship must be secret], dat's all right and won't no trouble come."

Delta Negroes neither know nor recognize such a status as the illegitimacy of children. If a child is the result of a casual sexual contact with a passer-by in a haystack or a henhouse, no stigma is cast upon it at birth or thereafter. The prospective mother may sometimes leave the neighborhood to bear the child. Upon her return with it she will invariably reply to questions concerning its paternity that, "Its papa he dead"; or, "Its papa he runned off." There is a tacit and dignified acceptance of this explanation, although every person in the community knows that it is untrue. A child is a child, for all that, whether it was born within or without the bonds of wedlock. It is a creature to be loved at birth and later on will be useful in the fields.

The mother of an illegitimate child loses neither caste nor the opportunity of marriage. Plantation Negro men feel, indeed, that there is something vaguely amiss with a girl who has not had sexual relations with a number of men, or has not borne a child or two before she has gone to live with some one man. They much prefer a woman of this kind to the rare virgin or non-promiscuous woman.

Negroes undoubtedly love children. It is for this reason, perhaps, that Negro women in the South are prized as nurses and often achieve lifelong attachments with the children they nurse. The child, too, has a definite economic value in the rural family as a farmhand. For these reasons and because no stigma attaches to an unmarried mother or to illegitimate children, a man has no hesitation in marrying or taking to live with him a woman who has had children by unnamed and unknown men. If she does not find a man and is unable to care for them, dozens of Negro families will eagerly adopt them into their households. Despite the fact that there are nearly three hundred thousand Negroes in the Delta, there is no orphan problem.

The use of contraceptives among Delta Negroes is almost unknown, although in the towns there is some knowledge of contraceptual devices. In the country women occasionally use for this purpose a tea brewed from the roots of the cotton plant at a certain stage of its growth. On a plantation I saw a young Negro woman pull up two young cotton plants. The Negro overseer yelled at her across the fields. "I sees you, gal," he shouted. "Gwine be big doin's tonight. Dat ole big-headed nigger mus' be done come back fum town." The girl giggled. "How come you sees so much, Mr. Galley?" she said. "Dat's what de boss-man keeps me for," he replied. She went giggling down the dusty road, the green plants clutched to her bosom.

The majority of Negroes here see no need for contraceptives. Children are a definite economic asset. It is unwise, therefore, to limit the size of families. If too many arrive, the Negro household is extraordinarily flexible. If there isn't room in the beds there is always room on pallets laid on the floor or by the chimney-corner. The Negro may with complete assurance invite more people to dinner than there are places at the table. Nor have contraceptives any value in preventing the birth of children whose coming would cast a social stigma upon the unmarried mother.

In quite the same way sexual prophylaxis as a preventive of venereal diseases is frequently unknown, and when known is almost completely disregarded. Those who know of the existence of prophylactics — and the knowledge is fairly general in the towns — feel that they are either too expensive to use or too troublesome to apply. The incidence of syphillis and gonnorrhea in the Delta is incredibly high. In the opinion of physicians, health officers, prison officials, plantation managers, and others who come in contact with masses of Negroes, nearly

80 per cent of the Negroes in the whole area suffer from venereal diseases.

It is inevitable under the circumstances that this condition should arise. These illnesses are regarded as having the transiency and triviality of common head colds. They are worthy of thought only to the extent that they interrupt normal sexual activities. The person infected is interested not primarily in curing the disease, but merely in arresting its symptoms so that he may resume his sexual life. It is common knowledge that when a white man offers to send a Negro at his own expense to a reputable physician for the treatment of syphilis, the Negro usually will not go. In the first place, he regards the illness as of no great importance to his health or happiness. In the second place, it is too much trouble to go for frequent and perhaps prolonged treatments. The regimen of the cure is too severe, and pending its duration he is sternly forbidden to drink or indulge in sexual relations. He goes, therefore, to some white or Negro quack who quickly arrests the symptoms and discharges the patient as cured. Or he applies some patent nostrum purchased at a drug store and skips merrily on his way, a victim and a carrier for life of a dread disease.

The Delta Negro is not only appallingly ignorant of the causes, cures, and consequences of venereal diseases, but almost invariably if a white man tries to enlighten him on the subject he will politely listen, regard him as slightly cracked, and leave him to apply his own remedies. A little while ago on the streets of a Delta town I met an old Nego whom I knew. We stopped to chat. He had a bundle under his arm. By way of conversation I asked him where he was going. "Well, suh," he replied, "I'm jes' carryin' dese things to ole brother Williamson. Us b'longs to de same lodge, de Independent Brothers of Charity. He at home down sick wid de runnin' range [gonorrhoea]. I was jes' takin' him some shirts, dese fat-pine knots for a fire, an' a little bit er cawn whisky in dis jug."

I told him that if brother Williamson did not go to a physician he would be down sick with the runnin' range until Gabriel blew his horn; and that corn whisky would have the same effect on the brother's illness that the fat-pine knots would have on his fire. My friend fervently "yassuh'd" everything I said, and he "sho wuz gwine tell brother Williamson." But I knew very well that he would not say anything, and although he regarded me as a fool with good intentions, I was none the less a fool.

The spread of venereal diseases among Delta Negroes is accelerated by their ignorance of or refusal to apply sexual prophylaxis, by their refusal to interrupt sexual activities while infected, and because many of them think that a cure may be had by infecting another person. Most of them feel utterly no social responsibility to the community, and therefore no restraint in spreading these diseases. Some of them are filled with a motive of revenge which can be satisfied only by passing their infection on to unnamed and unknown persons. So common is this practice, that Negroes have created a formula which expresses their feelings. "She gave it to me — he gave it to her — I'm going to give it to somebody else."

The conditions outlined are those which characterize the sexual lives of masses of Negroes in this area. It would be neither fair nor accurate, however, to conclude that there are not many exceptions to the general rule. Hundreds of Negroes as individuals and in family groups lead orderly, correct, and upright lives of the utmost probity sexually as well as in other ways. Their standards are those of sound people everywhere, whether white or black. Their points of view are stable and high-minded. Their conduct is in the best tradition of the good life. They are living examples of rectitude and sanity whom the mass of their brethren might well emulate.

CHAPTER 5

Delta Magic

IDA HUTTER has worked for the Hunt family as cook for more than twenty years. When she was eighteen Mr. Hunt brought her to town from his plantation, where she was in danger of being killed by a jealous lover. She has remained in his employ ever since and is now a woman of over forty.

Ida is dean of the servants of the household; a stern disciplinarian before whom the maids and the chauffeur quail when she regards them with stern glance or calls them to task with sharp tongue. "Don't you know Miss Mary don't 'low no triflin' niggers in dis house?" she screams at a yellow girl who casts her dust-rag at the furniture with dreamy inattention. "Boy, git up offn yo' feets. It's a sin an' a shame how lazy you is," she says to the chauffeur asleep in the kitchen. "You ain't fitten fer nuthin' but a killin'. Gal, is you got de sense of a June bug?" she inquires of a maid. "Dat ain't no way to set a table for white folks. You must 'a' been eatin' off er oilcloth all yo' life."

She is as dark and as fertile and as prolific as the rich soil of the Delta. She has twelve children, and another comes every year. She stays in the kitchen each time until the child is about to be born, and when Mrs. Hunt, alarmed about her condition and fearful for her safety, orders her to go home and rest for two or three weeks before the birth of the child, Ida smiles with great assurance, remains at her work, and makes a time-worn reply: "Miss Mary, I ain't goin' to have no baby. Dat ain't nuthin' but a champagne tumor."

Through years of close association and contact with the Hunts and their friends, Ida has penetrated to their inmost secret hearts. She knows fully their way of living, their hopes and aspirations, and the motivations of their conduct. She has heard their conversations and the conversations of their friends for years. White folks in the Delta speak freely and unguardedly in the presence of Negro servants. They seem to be mobile statues of brown or effigies in black as they wait at table or perform the tasks of the household. Ida knows all that there is to know about the Hunts and their friends.

The two girls of the family have been deeply attached to her since childhood, and she in turn has loved them and watched over them with zealous eyes. It was to Ida to whom they turned when the sorrows and wonders of love began to dawn on them at adolescence. It was Ida who with a scornful phrase or an approving word could dash or raise the hopes of a suitor for the hand of either of the girls. Between servant and employer the years have woven a strong bond of sympathy and affection.

When Ida orders groceries on the telephone she closely imitates Miss Mary's voice. She wears her cast-off clothes and hats, and on the streets walks Miss Mary's walk. When she entertains the ladies of the New Jerusalem and Bethlehem Bible Class in her little home, she affects Miss Mary's mannerisms, and after the meeting serves white folk's refreshments. Ida is a sublimated Hunt in brown.

In her secret heart, however, in the central core of her mind, in the inaccessible recesses of her soul, she treads dark paths which the Hunts can never follow. She thinks thoughts which they could never understand, and dreams dark dreams which their imaginations could never conjure. Ida's children have gone to school, she is an earnest worker in the Baptist church, and she reads the newspapers of the white folks. But in her heart of hearts she believes profoundly deep in the powers and potency of magic; in the might and infallibility of hoodoo; in the efficacy of medicines contained within no pharmacopoeia; in the forces of darkness that prowl forever insatiable and fanatic, seeking whom they may devour. Strange things happen to Ida and to the

members of her household. I put them down here as they were
told to me by her neighbor and confidante, "who washes an'
irons for de bes' white folks in town."

"Ida's husband, Charles Hutter, senior, he works at de white
folks' graveyard doin' gardenin'. Him an' Ida sho loves each
other. All de time dey been together she calls him 'Honey,' an'
ev'y Sadday night he comes straight home wid his money. He
sho don't trifle wid no wimmen an' no drinkin'. Charles is a
mighty good man.

" 'Bout two years ago dey had a neighbor. She was a widder
woman by de name Mrs. Streets, what been married five times
an' she conjured ev'y one of 'em, put spells on 'em, an' dey died.
She got on to Charles 'cause he wuz sich a perfectionate husban'.
She knowed they wa'n't no need to try an' git betwixt Ida an'
Charles, 'cause dey wuz too lovin', so she picked on Nellie Mae,
who wuz dey secon' daughter an' de mawnin' star of Charles's
life.

"One time 'fo' dis somebody had tried to put a conjure on
dat gal, but hit didn' work. Dat was w'en she had de appen-
dictis an' wuz run into by a bicycle. But that wa'n't none er
Mrs. Streets' doin's.

"Den one day Nellie Mae got took down mighty sick an' dey
wuz a breach growin' 'twixt Ida an' Charles. Ida knew hit wa'n't
natchal, 'cause a hoodoo doctor had come th'oo town an' say,
'Miz' Hutter, ef hit wa'n't fer de fact dat you is a two-headed
woman, you'd sho be dead. Dey is de strongest conjure on you
an' yo' family what can be made.' Den he give her a counter-
actin' conjure. But Ida she say, 'Humph, I don't need nuthin'
fum no conjure doctor. All I has to do is set down an' ax my
secon' min'.'

"Dat same night she set down an' axed her secon' mind an'
studied an' studied. Her auntie what rizzed her fum a chile
come to her an' say, 'Ida, dey is puttin' a hoodoo on you an'
Nellie Mae, an' hit's some nigger woman what wants Honey.
In de mawnin' I tells you what you does. You git you some
plain table salt, rub hit in de crown er Honey's haid an' put hit
in de soles er his shoes. You does dat fer three mawnin's.'

"Nex' mawnin' Ida she got up an' say to Hazel Kathereen — dat's one er her daughters — 'Hazel Kathereen, I wants you to go down to de sto' an' git me a dime's worth er salt.' An' Hazel she say, 'Mammy, what you gwine do wid hit?' An' Ida tole her. Den she say, 'Mammy, I done done dat. De sperrits tole me dat las' night. I put dat salt in pappy's shoes de first thing dis mawnin'.'

" 'Bout three days after dat, Charles loved up to Ida good an' got mo' an' mo lovin'-like jes' as he always done, but Nellie Mae she wa'n't gittin' no better. So Ida studied some mo' in her secon' min' and dat night her auntie come to her ag'in. She say, 'Ida, 'cause you is sich a good woman us done 'bout broke up dat conjure, but hit's still workin' on Nellie Mae.

" 'Now I tells you what you does dis time. You git up 'fo' day in de mawnin' an' take dat salt what you got lef'. Den you mops de front po'ch and de back yard wid hit, and out in de back yard you'll sho find a conjure bag. Pick hit up wid sticks. Take hit out in yo' yard an' burn hit. Den you stays home tomorrer an' whoever put dis conjure on you is gwine come to see you like a blusterin' wind.'

"An' sho 'nuf dat widder woman, dat Mrs. Streets, come a-blusterin' th'oo de bushes jes' a-smilin' an' a-sayin': 'How's de sick? How's de sick today? How's Mr. Hutter? How's Nellie Mae?'

"Well, by dat time Charles Hutter, senior, had done got his right senses back. W'en she say to him, 'Mr. Hutter, dey ain't no one in de worl' is as good as you is,' he say, 'I doesn't know 'bout dat, Mrs. Streets. Maybe dey is another somewheres.' He knowed by den dat Mrs. Streets wuz de one what had used de conjure to make trouble 'twixt him an' Ida. But Ida's auntie had done broke de conjure.

"Las' us heerd of Mrs. Streets she had gone off to de country to pick cotton. She knowed den her conjure wa'n't no match fer Ida's secon' min'."

During the entire time that Mrs. Streets, the designing widow woman, was attempting to lure Mr. Charles Hutter, senior, from his hearth and home, Ida, his wife, was deeply and constantly disturbed. But the Hunts were in complete ignorance of the worry and turmoil that had invaded her serene existence. She cooked, scolded, and continued on her way as the beloved and benevolent tyrant of the household. Negroes do not talk to white folks about the beyond-world of magic. White folks have a haughty ignorance which blinds them to anything outside the realm of books. They can see only as far as their noses, and if they would listen, anybody could tell them that that is not far. Negroes know things white folks do not know; they have a wisdom that the white folks have lost. Ida scoured her pans shining clean and kept her troubles to herself.

A few months later fear crawled again in her entrails. Worry wormed like maggots through her brain. The forces of darkness descended upon the Hutter household, threatening the health and happiness of its inmates. Ida worked with heavy heart in the Hunts' kitchen. Great beads of perspiration rolled off the brow of Charles Hutter, senior, as he trimmed the grass in the white folks' graveyard.

"Ida's sister Tillie had a good friend name Ada. One day Tillie an' Ada an' her boy John wuz doin' some washin' fer de white folks. John had excused hisse'f to go outside, an' w'en he come in he say, 'Look at dat great big worm.' Ada say, 'Hersh yo' mouf, boy, an' bring dat worm to me.'

"Tillie say she didn't pay no 'tention ter what dey wuz sayin', but wuz jes a-standin' dere kinder hearin' things in her secon' min'. W'en dey had got th'oo wid de washin' Ada say, 'Tillie, I done cooked you a nice big hoecake.' Tillie she wuz evermo' hongry 'cause she had been workin' all day long. Her pappy had tole her not ter eat nuthin' dey mammy hadn't cooked. You jes' never could tell w'en a person would git aholt er somethin' would pizen 'em. But de hoecake looked so good an' Tillie wuz so hongry dat she et some er hit right den an' dere an' on her way home kep' a-eatin' hit an' th'owin' some ter de dawg.

"W'en she got home her pa say, 'Tillie, what has you been eatin'?' She say, 'I aint et nuthin'.' An' he say, 'Tillie, yes, you is.' Den she tole him dat she had et er little hoecake what Ada had give her. Her pa say, 'Tillie, I done tole you not ter eat nuthin' dat yo' ma didn' cook fer you no matter howsomever hongry you bees. Now you gwine be mighty sick, an' you think you gwine ter die, but you ain't gwine ter die.'

"Dat night dey made Tillie sleep on de y'other side er de house. She got ter feelin' mighty sick an' her little houn'dawg howled all night long. W'en mawnin' come he wuz solid dead. Tillie's pa come to her room an' he say: 'Tillie, you is pizened. Fer sho you is pizened.'

"All th'oo dat day Tillie got sicker 'n' sicker. In de night she got down mighty low an' thought fer sho she wuz gwine ter die. 'Bout de middle er de night here come a little white bird in her room a-circlin' an' a-circlin' 'roun' an' a-roun' her bed. Den he lit at de head er de bed.

"He say: 'Tillie, you is pizened. You mighty sick, but ef you does what I tells you gwine git well.' So Tillie say, 'Little white bird, I'll do anything on earth ter git well.' Den de little white bird he say, 'Tillie, you does jes' what I tells you an' don't let nobody know what you is doin' until you sho dis spell is offn you. Now dis is what you does. You gits you a tomato an' scoops out de middle, jes' leavin' de rind. Den you fills dat wid a little alum, a pinch er red pepper, an' er tennsy-weensy bit er chamber lye. First time you eats it, you gargles an' den you spits. Secon' time you swallows, an' den you spits. You keeps dat up till you has used up de insiders er dat tomato, an' dat sho will make you well, pervidin' you don't tell nobody.'

"So Tillie she pulled herself out de bed, an' by dat time de clawin' an' scratchin' in her th'oat wuz somethin' awful. She fixed up de tomato an', jes' like de little white bird tole her, she gargled an' den she spit. W'en she had done dat she felt like de clawin' wuz er comin' higher in her th'oat. In a little while she swallowed an' den she spit ag'in. Here come a piece er somethin' 'bout dat long an' hit looked roun' an' white like a worm. So Tillie kep' dat piece an' ev'y time she spit come what looked like another link in dat worm. An' w'en hit wa'n't nuthin' lef' in dat tomato 'cept de rind, Tillie she spit ag'in an' up come de haid er dis thing an' hit had roun' beady eyes an' two long horns.

"De little white bird he had a-been settin' dere all de time.

He say: 'Now, Tillie, hit's all gone. Dat's de las' er dat.' Jes' 'bout dat time in come Tille's pa, an' wid him wuz de yerb doctor. He say, 'Tillie, what has you been doin'?' An' Tillie say, 'I ain't done nuthin' 'cept what my secon' min' tole me to do,' an de yerb doctor he say, 'I couldn't have did no better myself.'

"Den Tillie's pa he wanted ter know who had done put dis conjure on Tillie. He say, 'Us sho gwine find out whosomever hit wuz dat pizened you.' Den he took de worm an' put hit in a bottle an' th'owed hit in de river front er dey house. He knowed dat whosomever done dat ter Tillie would have ter foller dat stream fur as hit went an' would never git no res' no mo.'

"Soon in de mawnin' 'bout fo' days after dat here come Ada jes' a-talkin'. She say, 'My son-in-law over in Evenin' Shade done writ fer me ter come over dere and stay wid him an' my daughter fer a while.' Tillie's pa knowed dat wuz a lie, 'cause Ada never had no son-in-law in Evenin' Shade or nowheres else. He was sho den dat hit wuz Ada had done done hit.

"Bless Jesus an' may de good Lawd strike me down right here where I'm standin' at, if Ada didn't take off down dat stream an' las' time us heerd tell er dat ole witch-woman she wuz 'way down in de state er Alabamer."

Thousands of Delta Negroes believe fanatically in the powers of hoodoo. No demonstration of the white man's magic produced by science can sway their belief in the superior might of hoodoo doctors, many of whom secretly practice their black arts throughout this entire area. In particularly difficult cases which do not yield to the ministrations of the local practitioner, and it becomes apparent that a man or a woman is suffering from a charm unusually strong, Negroes go as far afield as New Orleans in search of a master of the arts of magic. There, four hundred miles from the Delta dwell hoodoo doctors of unsurpassed knowledge and technique, who cast baleful spells or remove them as the client may desire. The journey is expensive and the fees of the New Orleans Merlins are high, but Delta Negroes go often to see them and are entirely satisfied that their money has been well and wisely spent.

Often hodoo is the direct cause of crime or is inseparably

interwoven with it. There is a Negro girl serving a sentence for manslaughter in the Mississippi state prison. She is a high-school graduate and well above the average in intelligence. Yet she is as deeply swayed by the powers of darkness as the most illiterate field hand.

"I was married in 1930," she told me, "and me and my husband got along all right for about two years. Then he stopped loving me and started running after other women. I'd cry and beg him to stop, but I couldn't do nothing with him. Then I went to a conjure man and he told me my husband had me fixed and to look under my back doorstep and I'd find some hair.

"I looked, and there was some of my hair 'twixt two silver spoons. I took it to the conjure man and he burnt it and made me a powder. He told me to put it under a loose brick in the fireplace. Then my husband started loving me again, and I started loving other mens because now I had him fixed. He found out about it and started fussing at me and fighting. Then one night he jumped on me and I killed him. That's how come I'm here for seven years. While I was in the jailhouse he come to me and got in bed with me, but he wasn't nothing like when we was married. He had a little body like a dog and a big head. I run him away, though, by saying three times, 'What in the name of the Father, the Son, and the Holy Ghost does you want?' "

Negroes do not consult the doctors of enchantment about the gross and vulgar subjects which prick the imagination of the white man, such as money, business, and worldly success in general. Theirs is a starrier vision, a more tenuous wonder. Their inquiries are usually directed to the vagaries of love. They seek charms and recipes which will enable them to take away the desired person from another man or woman. They endeavor to learn how to keep a loved one in slavish subjection to the holder of a charm. Often they try to cast a spell upon a man or a woman so that he or she will be sexually impotent with everyone save the person who cast the spell.

Sometimes the hoodoo doctor is a woman. Last year Old Lady Parasol, a black and wrinkled enchantress, snatched Willie

Waddy from the embraces of a wicked woman and restored him
to the bosom of his lawful wife, Ethelreeda. They were a happy
couple living in a little house shaded by a chinaberry tree in
Baptist Town, the Negro section of Greenwood, until "dat chock-
lit-colored 'oman come along." Ethelreeda went on:

"I noticed der wuz somethin' come over my husban'. W'en he
come home he wuzn't hongry no mo' like he used ter be. He'd
jes' set at de table an' pick at de vittles an' wouldn't say nuthin'.
I axed him, 'Honey, is you got a misery in yo' haid? Do, I'll go
an' git you some aspereen.' He'd jes' set dere. I'd say, 'How
come you don't eat dem biscuits an' 'lasses?' He'd jes' keep
a-settin'. Dat'd make me mad but I wouldn't say nuthin'. I sho
loved dat man. My backbone would ache sometimes w'en I
looked at him. I knowed dey wuz somethin' mighty wrong, but
hit wa'n't no way to figger out what hit wuz.

"At night w'en us went to bed he wouldn't love up to me none
like he used to do. Seemst lak he didn't have no feelin's fer
me no mo'. Dat keep a-agitatin' my min' an' I went to see Ole
Lady Parasol about hit.

"Soon as I come in de do' she say, 'Ethelreeda, you an' yo'
husban' ain't gittin' 'long. 'Taint no way fer you ter git 'long.
Dat ole mudcat-faced 'oman live out at Minter City got him
fixed.'

"I knowed who de 'oman wuz, all right. Come messin' by my
house an' settin' in front of my fire many a time, playin' friendly
like. 'What I'm gwine do den?' I axed Ole Lady Parasol.

"She say, 'Chile, w'en yo' husban' come home fum de compress
tonight tell him you knows all 'bout him an dat no-'count, triflin'
'oman. She wearin' a white belt wid fifteen knots in hit tied
'bout her wais'. Dat's what she got him fixed wid. Dat's how she
keeps him a-comin' ter her all de time. You says to him, "Willie,
does you know you is bein' hoodooed by dat Minter City 'oman?
Next time you wid her you feels 'bout her wais' an' see what
you feels."'

"Next time he seen her he felt an' he like ter had a fit. After
dat Ole Lady Parasol told me to look in de nawth corner er der
house an' I'd find a ball of pins an' needles wropped in red

flannel and paper. Dat's what dat 'oman had me pinned down wid. I th'owed 'em away an' me an' my husband us start lovin' each other good jes' lak befo'. But somethin' kep' a-troublin' me all de time 'til one day I found a handkerchief dat 'oman had lef' in my house. I th'ew hit in de river one day 'fo' sunup and arter dat us never had no mo' trouble."

In the cases of illness Delta Negroes go frequently to the black hoodoo doctor first, and to the white medical doctor last.

"Las' year my heart pained me so bad I never knew which way to turn. I couldn't do my washin' an' ironin' an' w'en I'd ben' over at de washtub seemst lak my heart'd git stuck in my th'oat. Den I went ter see Aunt Tempe Dixon at Hushpuckana.

"Aunt Tempe say, 'Girl, you has snakes in you.' I say, 'No'm, I bleeves hit's my heart. Does you think you can cyore me?' She say, 'Yas, I can cyore you fer fifty dollars.' So I give her de money — I had ter sell er bale er cotton ter git it — an' she started treatin' me. But I got worser an' worser. Den she say she couldn't do me no good.

"Arter dat I went ter Old Man Joe Ramsey at Alligator Station. He say he could cyore me fer twenty dollars. Didn't, he'd give me de money back. He gimme some medicine, but hit wa'n't no 'count fer nuthin'. Den I went ter de white doctor and he say I had de heart troubles. I tole Aunt Tempe Dixon 'bout hit, an' she say, 'Yas, gal, I knowed hit wuz heart failure all de time, but I didn't want to worry you none by tellin' you.'"

Sometimes Negroes resort to the hoodoo doctor when the medical doctor has failed to effect a cure.

"I went at a dance wid two boys, an' one of 'em give me a drink of whisky, an' I went home jes' as sick as I could be. Mamma she say I had de indigestion and sont fer de white doctor. He come an' give me some medicine, but it didn't do me no good. I didn't git no better an' kep' a-feelin' worser an' worser. So mamma she went over to Slaughter to see de hoodoo doctor.

"She knocked on his do' an' he say, 'Come in. Yo' baby chile is down sick.' Mamma brought him on back to us house wid her. He set me over a tub er boilin' water an' rubbed me hard.

De water in de tub it turned green an' black an' he buried it in
de nawth side er de house. Den he rubbed my chest. A frog
jumped out er my th'oat, run out de house, an' hid under de
steps. After dat I got all right an' never did have no mo' misery
in my chest."

On rare occasions a spell cast upon a Negro is the direct and
traceable cause of his death. During the flood of 1927, a Negro
man became ill in Greenville. He was unable to describe any
symptoms of his illness to his white physician. After thorough
examination the physician found him physically thoroughly
sound. Repeated visits failed to locate the source of the patient's
sickness, and his physician called in his colleagues to examine
the patient. They were completely baffled. The man sank lower
and lower.

Finally one day he told the doctor that a Negro had put a
hoodoo on him which he said would kill him. He gave him the
name of the man who had "conjured" him and search was made
high and low through the watery wastes of the flood for him, so
that he could be compelled to come in and take the conjure off
his victim. He could not be found. The Negro wasted away
and died.

Magic comes on occasion to work its wonders of pacification
when violence has failed. You Doll Perkins cooked for some
rich white folks in Greenville and lived in the servants' quarter
in the rear of their house. Sweetening, a black boy, who was
chauffeur to a neighboring white family, and You Doll were in
love.

You Doll told me: "One night I an' Sweetening an' a gal by
de name er Dora Droe Dennis was settin' in my house, talkin'
an' laughin'. All of a sudden, befo' you could say Jack Roberson,
dat woman pulled a ice-pick an' say, 'Sweetening, come on out
dis house 'fo' I kills you wid dis ice-pick.' He got on up an'
went out de house out on de street wid her. I got me my forty-
five out my trunk an' run out after 'em. I th'owed my gun on
Dora Droe an' say, 'Woman, put dat ice-pick away an' turn
aloose er Sweetening 'fo' I blows yo' brains clean out yo' haid.'
She turned him aloose den an' I an' Sweetening went on back
in de house.

"I wuz tired er dat kind er foolishness, so, soon in de mawnin' as I could I went out to de hoodoo doctor at Elizabeth, ter git me somethin' ter hold Sweetening so dat no other woman could git him away from me. He give me some graveyard dust ground up wid er old dime an tole me to touch it on Sweetening's haid ev'y few days.

"I done dat and den I started doin' his washin', so I could get some suds an' take 'em to de hoodoo doctor. Den I carried him a bottle er Sweetening's bath water, an' us been gittin' 'long good since dat. It ain't a woman come 'roun' my house messin' wid him since den."

These are not isolated incidents. They are typical experiences in the lives of thousands of Delta Negroes. They are carefully hidden and shielded from the skeptical gaze of white folks except when the practice of magic brings the practitioners into the courts or accidentally to the attention of whites. In a white Delta family a young Negro was employed. He became ill in the servants' quarters and would not take food from anyone save the mistress of the houshold, for fear that one of the Negro servants might put something into his food which would "conjure" him. The threat of starvation did not deter him. He would take food from the hands of no one save Miss Celia, and for weeks she was in constant attendance upon her black servant. When he recovered, she fired him and went off to Hot Springs to rest.

A strong belief in hoodoo is common not only to a majority of the older Negroes of the Delta, but also to many of the younger; to those who have attended school and those who have not; to those living in towns and those on remote plantations; to Negroes whose lives are spent almost entirely with their own people and to those whose work brings them in daily contact with whites.

Hoodoo doctors practice in town after town of the Delta. Their profession is barred by law and they are sometimes arrested, but arrests are rare because their clients do not and will not expose them to the white officials. An almost impenetrable veil hangs over the subterranean activities of these workers in the black arts.

Conjures and counteracting conjures are constantly being used by Negroes on each other. Stakes are driven into crossroads at sunrise to keep enemies away. Dimes bearing the year of the wearer's birth are worn in the shoes to bring good luck. Slashes are made in men's coats by women to assure sexual fidelity to the slasher. So common is the practice of women putting nasty concoctions in the food of men in order to make them unattractive to other women, "dat a whole lot er men stirs dey vittles and smells it 'fo' dey eats it." Roots are chewed and spit out on courthouse steps to prevent conviction at a criminal trial. People are paralyzed by sprinkling graveyard dust on paths which they must follow. Red-oak bark is mixed with cornmeal and red pepper to make poultices for driving snakes out of one's body. Charms are hidden in the limbs of trees to produce sexual virility in one who is ardorless.

The white man tries to no avail to stop these practices. He does not know it, but there are things beyond the horizon; beings that one cannot see; hidden forces of evil; ghosts and h'ants. Everybody but white folks know "dere's a heap er stars rolls over yo' haid, but you cain't see 'em all 'cause some is so tiny."

The Delta Negro lives in the modern world. He goes to the moving-picture theaters, rides in automobiles, hears the radio, sees airplanes, and is conversant with the wonders of the white man's medicines. But he moves, too, in a world of his own from which the white is jealously excluded; of which he knows nothing and cannot ever know. His questing mind is impotent to break through its shut windows and barred doors. His penetrating eye is powerless to perceive what is hidden from his untutored vision.

Your Negro cook, quietly reading the newspaper in your kitchen, has a "tobie" in her pocket which she steeps every nine days in whisky lest it die of starvation. Your Negro chauffeur stuck a nail in his foot last week, and there in the oak tree in your yard you see it smeared with hog lard. He is effecting a cure by circling the tree closely twice a day. Seeing him, you smile when you remember how only last week you had boasted of his enlightenment. You are startled when your physician tells you that the best plowhand on your land has an infected eye because he had poured into it by way of cure the urine of a virgin. This practice, almost as old as time, its most famous exponent being Saint Francis of Assisi, now recurs under your startled eyes in the twentieth century.

All around you the black arts of another age flourish in the white light of modernity. You look sadly up and down the gulfs of time. There, many vessels which left the farther shores thousands of years ago are still in midstream, becalmed or vainly beating across in the face of tempestuous winds and stormy seas.

CHAPTER 6

Crime in the Delta

THE STEEL HEADS of a hundred axes describe parabolas of radiance in the bright November sun as they rise from the ground, mount high into the air, and descend with deep bite into logs of wood. A hundred axes rise and a hundred axes fall time after time, hour after hour. The rhythm of their moving becomes a beating into beauty and an enchantment to the eye marking the curvilinear flight of steel from wood to air to wood again, without break, without fault, without pause. Thick wrists liquidly propel heavy axes; powerful torsos bend as to some music of abandon; strong knees flex with silken tiger's ease; slithering muscles drive knotted arms with triphammer strength and dancer's grace. The air rings with the singing of steel and the whirring of chips of wood. It is pungent with the odors of oak and of ash freshly felled. It is troubled with vague, uneasy stirrings. Overtones of death lie on the fields and on the souls of men when the year lays long a-dying in the blood-red sun of Indian summer in Mississippi.

Suddenly a voice is lifted out of nowhere into song. It inquires richly, deeply, plaintively, "Who's gwine buy my high-heel shoes?" Almost instantly the voice becomes a hundred voices that are one voice as all sing:

> "Who's gwine glove my hand?
> Who's gwine kiss my ruby lips?
> Who's gwine be my man?
> Lawd, Lawd,
> Who's gwine be my man?

> Papa's gwine buy my high-heel shoes,
> Mamma's gwine glove my hand.
> Sister's gwine kiss my ruby lips,
> I don't need no man,
> Lawd, Lawd,
> I don't need no man."

The work is never completely interrupted. When one group is at rest another is at labor. Axes swing through their measured rhythm, logs dwindle into firewood, and the music of song moves in and out of the ringing of steel like figures weaving with faultless precision through the steps of an intricate ballet. Sometimes the voices are silent. For a little while there is no sound save the loud bite of steel on wood as it is riven asunder. Then unexpectedly and unaccountably a voice far away is lifted in song, to be joined by another in a distant group, and then another and another, until all the voices merge and blend into one great and splendid voice, and a tall column of song trembles on the air. For crime in Mississippi is expiated to music, and these Negro convicts on the state prison penal farm at Parchman sing at their work until they are released or die.

This prison has no high walls of granite, no stink of foetid humanity, no cages of steel into which human beings are locked like wild animals. Its walls are green trees; its roof is the blue sky; its floor is the rich earth. The prisoners do not eat their hearts out in an endless agony of nothingness. They do not slave at unaccustomed tasks to make articles of commerce for unfair competition with the labor of free men.

On nearly twenty thousand acres of land in the heart of the Delta the convicts raise crops of cotton and corn with the aid of the familiar friendly mule, under conditions of labor closely paralleling those that most of them had known in the "free world." They do the same kind of work, eat the same food, sing the same songs, play the same games of dice and cards, fraternize with their fellows, attend religious services on Sunday mornings and receive visitors on Sunday afternoons. Wives and sweethearts of the prisoners come to see them, and if they indulge in a bit of amorous dalliance by way of softening the rigors of imprisonment, the eyes of the officers are mercifully turned the other way. On the whole, the conditions under which prisoners live in this prison, their occupations and their routine of living, are closer by far to the methods of the large antebellum plantation worked by numbers of slaves than to those of the typical prison.

Negro and white prisoners, male and female, are completely separated in the prison, although they live under the same conditions and receive the same kind of treatment. Its ever-increasing population now consists of nearly 2200 Negroes and 500 whites.

The cardinal characteristic of crime in the Delta is that it is crime of violence. As of March, 1935, 787 Delta prisoners in the state penitentiary were serving terms for the following crimes:

Assault and Battery with Intent to Kill	46
Grand Larceny	69
Burglary and Larceny	70
Burglary	149
Robbery	19
Forgery	8
Arson	3
Attempt to Rape	4
Rape	1
Violating Age of Consent	1
Obtaining Property under False Pretense	3
Attempt to Commit Robbery	2
Aiding Jail Breaks	3
Robbery with Firearms	2
Highway Robbery	5
Possessing Stolen Goods	1
Distilling	1
Counterfeiting	2
Uttering Forgery	2
Manslaughter	92
Murder	304

Crime among Negroes is one of the gravest problems against which the Delta struggles and seemingly in vain. This may be accounted for in part by the fact that Negroes make up the larger part of the population, and on a numerical basis alone it follows that more crime would be committed by them than by the numerically inferior whites. But in this land of paradoxes a Negro criminal often escapes trial and punishment precisely because he is a Negro. The rate of crime is higher than is actually reported because, for reasons which will appear later, many crimes committed by Negroes are never brought even to the attention of police officers. Nowhere are crimes of violence committed with less hesitation than in the Delta. Nowhere do criminals escape with lighter punishment. One must delve below the surface of this society in order to arrive at even an incomplete understanding of the situation.

The Delta is, to begin with, an armed camp. It is common knowledge that almost every person, white or black, carries arms on his person or has them at home. The poorest white and the poorest Negro has usually one or more rifles or shotguns because hunting is the common sport of the country. Both frequently have pistols in addition. The white man's armament ends with these weapons. The Negro's goes far beyond. He still uses the old reliable straight razor with deadly effect in personal combat, and it remains a favorite weapon of a large conservative group. There is a strong tendency, however, among a more modern school to replace the razor with the "crabapple switch" — a knife with a single, long thin blade, instantly released for use by pressure on a spring. Homicides and assaults are committed with axes, hatchets, meat cleavers, butcher's knives, and ax handles, too. The Delta Negro is distinguished by a wide catholicity of taste in his choice of lethal weapons, using whatever readily comes to hand to beat, batter, or maul his foe.

While visiting on a plantation recently one of the Negroes told me that the night before there had been a "ruckus 'twixt two ladies, an' one lady slapped de other lady in de face wid a coal-oil lamp. De doctor had to come an' make six stitches in hit 'fo' de bleedin would stop." When the Negro cannot lay his hands on any weapon, he frequently bites his enemy, snipping an ear off with a sweep of his teeth or tearing a nose into ribbons of bleeding flesh and cartilage. Negroes are often treated by white doctors for bites inflicted on them by other Negroes in fights. These wounds are highly dangerous when not promptly treated, because many Negroes suffer from chronic trench-mouth and convey infection to the victims of their biting.

Nowadays the favorite weapon of Negro women is the ice-pick. They have discovered that this humble instrument of the kitchen, when zealously wielded, is a fear-inspiring, deadly instrument of attack. It is easily concealed, simple to use, effective in action, and never gets out of order. It makes a clean wound having about it an air of craftsmanship and deadly effectiveness which would have been envied by the master stabbers of sixteenth-century Italy.

When I asked the cook of my host on a plantation if she carried an ice-pick, she replied: "Yassuh, I does. But jes' fer show." She wore it with the assured loftiness of a Borgia wearing a poison ring wrought by Cellini. A Negro man-about-town in Clarksdale told me that "w'en us see a cullud lady comin' down de street an' she ain't swinging her arms we don't pay her no mind, b'cause she's sho totin' a ice-pick under dere." And in the annals of the courts it figures frequently as the weapon which brought a Negro to his grave.

Within the Delta, crimes of violence committed by Negroes upon Negroes are so common as to cause little comment among the whites. Shootings, stabbings, and cuttings occur throughout the year, increase usually in the autumn when Negroes have money and leisure, and culminate finally in the time-honored grand climax of the "Christmas killings," occurring just before the Christmas holidays. Violence is a dark flower that grows rankly to prodigious heights under this warm sun and in this rich earth.

The Negro community on the whole is utterly unshocked by crimes committed by its members. Some of the more substantial men of property or position or long residence may deplore the Negro's continued outbursts of violence. The vast majority, however, regard a shooting or a stabbing as merely an untoward incident of daily life, of no moral consequence whatsoever, and regrettable, if at all, only because the white folks are likely to send someone to the penitentiary. And the whites in turn are un-shocked by Negro crime save when it is directed against them-selves. They have lived too long in its midst. They have become accustomed to murders and mutilations, to stabbings and cut-tings, to the severing of heads with axes and the beating out of brains with clubs. Crime is the normal state of being — its ab-sence is the abnormal — and year after year it flourishes and grows without organized protest on the part of the Negroes and with resignation on the part of the whites.

Many homicides are committed out of jealousies. If a Negro woman is sexually vigorous she often arouses in the mind of the man with whom she is living a sense of possession which brooks not the slightest intrusion or interference. "Nigger, ain't you got no sense?" says one plantation Negro to another. "Better stay 'way fum dat 'oman. She's Slim Willis's gal an' he's pussy-pizened fer sho. He'll evermore'n kill if you goes slooin' aroun'." Women, too, are prepared to defend with force and arms their sole rights in their men, and many a Negro woman in the Delta has arrived at an early grave because she insisted on "talking under her clothes" with a forbidden man. Sometimes a Negro Messalina becomes one of the most powerful persons in the com-munity, as a white planter found to his sorrow when he ordered her off his plantation. Many of his male share-croppers threat-ened to go with her, following her with the inevitable compul-sion that marks the swarm in following the nuptial flight of the queen bee.

Last year a Negro was hanged in a Delta county for the love of a woman and his jealousy of her. Despite her pegleg, she was attractive to many plantation bucks, and two of them were ambushed and shot to death by the man with whom she was living, because they had attempted to alienate her affections from him.

The murderer showed no regret for his crime, felt no self-pity, mounted the gallows calmly, and quietly went to his death in the certain and comforting assurance that Jesus was waiting for him with open arms on the other side of the pearly gates.

When the condemned man stood upon the gallows and the black cap had been adjusted over his head and split seconds separated him from eternity, he asked the sheriff if he might have a few minutes to talk with him and his deputy. The request was granted. The black cap was removed. Tobe Henderson looked once more into the face of the sun. The odor of coffee brewing in the jail kitchen came pungently to his nostrils. Corn growing in the jailhouse garden rustled in the strong early-morning breeze. The white ladies' silk dresses used to sound like that years ago when the boss-man's wife gave a house party and he helped wash dishes in the kitchen of the "big house." The whistle of the box-factory far off by the river spoke loudly into the quiet air. It was six o'clock and the box-factory niggers were streaming to their work.

"Mr. Ben an' Cap'n Hugh," Tobe said, "y'all has been mighty good to me an' de other prisoners in de jailhouse. I know y'all is good mens an' I spects to meet you bofe up dere in heaven where I'm fixin to go. Dat's how come I wants to ax y'all to lead Christian lives an' git behin' de blood of Jesus so y'all be sho to git dere. W'en you leaves de jailhouse to arrest folks you can't never tell whether you is comin' back or ain't. You might be settin' at yo' own table in yo' own house an' drap down graveyard dead. You got to be ready to meet King Jesus jes' any ole time. Please, suh, Mr. Ben an' Cap'n Hugh, don't y'all fergit what dis ole nigger tole you. I'm aimin' to see you in heaven. Boss, ef is you ready now, I'm ready."

Negro women in the Delta exhibit a ferocity in crime as bloody and as savage as that exhibited by the men. They stab with deadly effect and shoot with unerring precision. They plunge ice-picks into the hearts of men and women, cut throats with razors, batter heads with axes, and shoot their victims full of holes with pistols. In every county of the Delta, year after year, Negro women commit crimes of violence with deadly weapons. In police circles they are regarded as being more vicious and more dangerous than the males.

Arrests and sentences of Negroes for crime against property are never ending. Constant processions of men, women, and children move through the courts upon charges of petty and grand larceny, burglary and robbery. The victims are more frequently Negroes than whites. Delta Negroes are highly distrustful of one another and take every precaution in their power against theft, yet day after day they suffer losses of money and property at the hands of thieves and robbers of their own race.

Negro women of this section almost universally carry their money in a "nation-sack," a canvas bag suspended on a belt worn next to the body under their underclothing. In Delta stores when a Negro woman makes a purchase she often says to the clerk, "'Scuse me, boss," and modestly turns her back on him while she fishes the necessary money from her nation-sack. It is almost invulnerable against the sneak thief. "Gal," said one Negro girl laughingly to another on Trail Lake plantation, "ef a nigger git yo' money out yo' nation-sack hit's 'cause you never had yo' mind on yo' money." Yet such a robbery occurred recently on this plantation, and threw the women into a panic of fear. The nation-sack has always had about it an unfailing impregnability, and to see this last stronghold of safety violated made them feel that nothing in the world is secure.

Robberies of plantation cabins are common. Thefts of cotton, seed, hogs, money, chickens, and indeed of anything movable, are so frequent as to make constant caution necessary. Crimes against property come to be accepted finally as one of the inevitable hazards attendant upon living in the community.

One of the major reasons for the large amount of crime among Delta Negroes is the attitude of the Negro himself toward the consequences. It is true that the Negro criminal tries with all the skill within his power to escape detection and capture. Once he has been caught, however, he surrenders himself to his fate with utter resignation. He enjoys himself as best he can in the jail and does not for a moment think or worry about the future. Negroes in county jails of the Delta placidly sleep the nights and days away, sing to the accompaniment of guitars, play cards and dice, and on the whole thoroughly enjoy themselves. There is no note of melancholy about a Delta jail filled with Negroes, especially when they are well fed; on the contrary, there is usually an air of great good humor and laughter and song.

These Negroes have an extraordinary adaptability which enables them to endure imprisonment with none of the terrors that it inflicts on the average white man. They have a capacity for living entirely in the moment which completely shuts out of the field of their vision any of the potential horrors or consequences of the morrow.

I visited a Delta jail recently at the moment when Long-Chain Charlie arrived. He is the traveling sergeant of the Mississippi state prison whose duty it is to escort prisoners from the county jails to the prison. He is fat, genial, and competent. It is a tribute to his geniality and his competence that he rarely, if ever, has trouble with his prisoners.

Great excitement prevailed in the jail and all the prisoners stood interestedly and laughingly peering through the bars at the famous and legendary Long-Chain Charlie. The names of those who were to leave were called by the sheriff. His voice rang through the steel corridors.

"Manny Sutton!" he yelled.

"Yas, suh, white folks. I'm ready," a voice cheerfully replied.

"Abe Jones!"

"Comin' up, boss."

"Will Jordan!"

"Got my travelin'-clothes on," Will responded, while the other Negroes laughed.

"Aleck Ball!"

"I heahs you, Cap'n."

Finally all the prisoners were assembled. There were twelve Negro men, three white men, and two Negro girls. One of them could not restrain her giggling. I asked her what she thought about going to prison for two years. She smiled widely. "It ain't no diffunce, white folks," she replied. "I'm got to work wherever I'm is." The procession moved down the stairs to Long-Chain Charlie's waiting bus, which would take them to the prison where years of servitude awaited them. They laughed, joked, and speculated with vast good humor upon the journey ahead of them. The white men scowled and were sullen.

The Negroes who remained in the jail burst into song:

"Way down yonder where I come from
Dey feeds those niggers on hard parched corn.
Niggers gits so big and fat,
Head so big, can't wear no hat.
Big-headed. We shall be free.
Big-headed. We shall be free.
'Cause de good Lawd done set us free."

If the Negro criminal accepts imprisonment with calm and resignation, the Negro who is condemned to die accepts his fate quietly and without fuss. He reads the Bible, talks religion with a visiting minister, sings hymns with his fellow prisoners, and "gits right wid Jesus." When his last day on earth comes he walks quietly to the gallows and goes to his death. There is one unwavering certainty in the life of the Delta Negro. It remains with him unsullied and unchanging from the first moments of his youth when he "gits 'ligion," until his eyes are closed in death. It is that he will surely go to heaven.

The Negro criminal enjoys an invaluable privilege which the white criminal does not have. He suffers no loss of caste, prestige, or reputation in his own community and among his own people, for having committed a crime or served a term in prison. On the contrary, the convict returned to his native place is usually admired by the men and sought after by the women. There is a halo about his head, although he may be recognized as a cold-blooded murderer and feared by his own people as a "bad nigger."

The lot of the Negro imprisoned for homicide is softened because he is rarely a victim to the gnawing pains and terrors of remorse which so often make living a bitter unbearable reality to the white man who has killed a human being. Once a Negro has committed a murder and has begun to serve his sentence the sequence of events which brought about his plight, the death of his victim and the suffering of the victim's family, disappear completely from his mind as "jes' somethin' gone by an' nuthin' can he'p it." The Negro who has killed another usually has only one regret. "Boss, I shot at dat nigger fo' times and didn't hit him but three." They have pride in their marksmanship.

In his criminal relations as in nearly all the other activities of his life the Delta Negro runs afoul of the white man and of the paradoxes of the society which the white man dominates. These paradoxes are at once his refuge and his despair. Because of them one Negro who commits a homicide is hanged and another is not even arrested. One may be guilty of a trivial offense and receive a savage sentence. Another may be guilty of a savage offense and receive a trivial sentence.

Every plantation Negro — and many Negroes of the towns — has his "white folks" to whom he looks for protection when he violates the law. "Whose nigger are you?" is frequently the first question asked by a magistrate when a Negro is brought before him. If he is Mr. Brown's nigger and Mr. Brown is an important man in the community, the Negro may be let off lightly or not be sentenced at all. If he is Mr. Black's nigger and Mr. Black is a man of no importance, the Negro will receive harsher treatment. If he has no white folks at all, his fate is in the lap of the gods. In the Delta these oscillations between severity and leniency are feudal survivals. Elsewhere in the United States they flow out of politics and graft. It is the fate of the poor and the obscure, white and black, everywhere, to pay the penalty of their poverty and obscurity.

It may be safely said that for every Negro in the Delta who is unjustly sent to jail or to prison by white juries or magistrates, another Negro is saved from imprisonment by white influence and protection. It becomes important, therefore, to the Negro to work for or to be attached to white men who are of importance in their communities. If a Negro works for such a man he boasts about it to other Negroes. He thinks of his employer as omnipotent. He is a man who is powerful not only within his Delta town and county, but also all over Mississippi, and all over the world. He makes it clear to his friends that his white folks, Mr. Dick Lyons, is a mighty man who can snap his fingers at the law and get one of "his niggers" out of jail merely by looking cross-eyed at the sheriff, who trembles in his presence.

Some time ago one of my friends drove from Memphis to Vicksburg, a distance of about two hundred and fifty miles, with his Negro chauffeur, Son James. Son had recently migrated to

Memphis from the Delta, where he had lived in a rural community so isolated that "I hadn't never heard a train blow 'til I was fifteen." He brought with him to the city attitudes of the rural Delta Negro which were amusingly illuminated by a little adventure which came to him in Vicksburg.

On the return trip to Memphis my friend asked Son what he had done in Vicksburg. Son said: "Well, suh, w'en I lef' you de other night, I went to git me some vittles. I went at de café an' w'en I come in I heard a rattlin' an' went out in de back. It was a big nigger on de flo' huntin' for a nine. Naw, suh, I didn't git in de game. Dem niggers had too many diffunces [razors].

"I come on out front an' wuz drinkin' me a soda-pop an' talkin' to a cullud lady w'en a white po-liceman come in. He say, 'Nigger, what you doin' here?' I say, 'I come to Vicksburg driving my boss-man.' 'Who is yo' boss-man?' I say it was you, Mr. Sanders, what's at de bank. I say he had shorely heard tell of you. He didn't say no mo', an' I didn't say no mo'. Jes' kep' a-talkin' to de cullud lady.

"One of my foots was kinder 'vanced out in front of de other an' de po-liceman he was spittin' 'baccer juice on it. I kep' on drinking my pop and de po-liceman he kep' a-spittin' an' a-spittin' on my foot." My friend asked him why he had not withdrawn his foot when the deluge started. "Naw, suh," Son replied, "I wasn't goin' to pull in my foot whilst de Law was spittin' on it."

Son assumed as a matter of course that, although his employer was two hundred and fifty miles from home, everybody in Vicksburg, including the policeman, knew that he was an officer of a big bank, had a house on a street in Memphis where the richest white folks live, and a big plantation across the river in Arkansas. He would have made the same assumption had he been with his employer in Norway or China. He would blandly have got into trouble anywhere, believing that his "boss-man" had merely to raise his voice to the officers and Son James would walk out a free man. At the same time he had an almost superstitious reverence for "de Law" in the person of a policeman, one of whose privileges apparently is that of spitting on a Negro's foot.

Negroes are frequently released from jail when an important white man telephones to protest that "you got a nigger of mine in jail there, and I wish you'd let him come on back home and finish picking his crop." That frequently marks the end of the case. It often happens, too, that when a Negro share-cropper shoots or stabs another on the plantation premises, he is never arrested or molested by officers of the law. The planter is not willing to lose the services of a good worker, and in any event, he feels that violence among Negroes is naturally to be expected, is of no moral or social consequence whatsoever, and the whole affair is soon forgotten. Obviously, this encourages crime among Negroes.

The direct causes of Negro crime in the Delta are often dim and obscure. White juries and prosecuting officers try often in vain to dig out of a mass of vague and contradictory evidence the motivations of criminals in cases of homicides or assaults on the person. One of the great difficulties is that when a crime is committed on a plantation, Negroes for miles around are or want to be witnesses for or against the prisoner. This is because each term of the "circus cote" devoted to criminal trials vies in the Negro's eyes in amusement value with baptizings, funerals, fish-fries, and religious revivals. Other important values accrue to the Negro witness. He receives free transportation to and from his residence to the county seat, and a daily fee while in attendance on the court. He has freedom from work while awaiting his call to the witness stand, and the opportunity for loafing with other witnesses around the stove in the winter or under the shade of trees on the courthouse lawn in the summer. In addition to these perquisites, the Delta Negro dearly loves the importance that momentarily attaches to him in the eyes of the crowd when he "teches de Bible," and with eyes piously lifted on high promises to "tell the whole truth, so help you Gawd."

White juries trying Negro criminal cases have great difficulty in arriving at the truth. There are usually two loudly voluble sets of witnesses whose testimony is directly contradictory. Each witness vigorously asserts as he testifies, "dat sho is de truth 'fo Gawd," or "I hopes de Lawd strikes me dead right heah in dis chair if dat ain't de truth." The witness is always free to give full rein to his lush imagination, for there are rarely prosecutions for perjury in the Delta. The Negro's countenance is impassive. His appearance on the witness stand does not betray his inward thoughts. Nor does he flush red or blush — involuntary signals which betray the lying white witness.

White jurymen who have little belief in the veracity of most Negroes, on or off the witness stand, try to guess at the truth as carefully as they can. Gross miscarriages of justice often occur which send innocent Negroes to jail and set guilty Negroes free, because white men in their despair at learning the truth from one Negro about another, end finally by guessing at the truth.

So intense indeed is the desire of plantation Negroes to appear as witnesses or as spectators at criminal trials, and so difficult is it for white planters to frustrate this desire, that scheduled sessions of the criminal courts are often postponed if the crops are in jeopardy and labor is badly needed. Or the schedules are so arranged that the courts meet when little labor is needed on the plantations. This frequently causes the prisoners, guilty and innocent, to remain long months in jail awaiting trial. The Delta has never found a way of escape from this dilemma.

Many crimes of violence among Negroes occur when they gather in numbers at picnics, dances, festivals, and dice games. It does not take a great deal of provocation to start a fight among a group of emotionally unstable people who add to their instability by drinking bad whisky and are armed with knives or guns. Women, too, are present at the gatherings and jealousy flares quickly into a shooting or a stabbing with results fatal to one or more persons. Dances and dice games are flowering places of homicides. Men fight about women, women fight about men, and men fight while they gamble.

One of my Negro friends on a plantation went to a picnic and successfully averted an assault. "Dese is de beatinest niggers 'roun' here I has ever seen. Las' August I was at a picnic in a big pasture back of Wayside station. It wuz a big ole black nigger follerin' a gal wid a pop-bottle in his hand. He kep' a-follerin' her whichever way she went. 'Boy,' I say, 'how come you

keeps atta dat gal wid dat pop-bottle?' He say, 'I'm gwine bus'
her in her haid.' I axed him why he wuz gwine do dat. He say,
''Cause she won't gimme none for thirty cents. She wants fo'
bits an' I ain't got it.' I tole him I would lend him de twenty
cents did he th'ow de bottle away. He say he would. Den him
and de gal went on off."

Out of trivial causes such as this many crimes among Negroes
arise. Another prolific source of shootings and stabbings flows
from what they call "putting 'em in de dozens." This is a form
of Rabelaisian banter engaged in by two or more Negroes. At a
gathering one Negro may begin by saying, "Yo' mammy h'ists her
tail like a cat." The other replies, "Yo' mammy she smell like a
polecat." Aspersion after aspersion is cast by each on the mammy
of the other. Finally a pistol explodes or a knife flashes.

As a general rule Delta juries are inclined to treat the Negro
criminal with lenience rather than severity. The white man has
a deeply grounded belief that it is perfectly normal for Negroes
to commit crime; that they are a childlike people afflicted with
a high degree of emotional instability; and should not, therefore,
be held strictly accountable for their acts.

I was present in an inferior Delta court when the police
officers were searching for papers bearing upon the shooting
of one Negro woman by another. The papers could not be
found. The woman who had done the shooting was in jail. She
could not be brought to trial unless new papers were drawn.
What should they do? After some debate, they decided to let her
out of jail. "Hell," said one officer, "she didn't hurt that woman.
The bullet just grazed her scalp." "Might as well turn her loose,"
said another. "She didn't do any harm, and niggers are bound
to do a little shooting." The woman was released.

It is a common practice, too, in the Delta, when the court in-
structs the jury that it may return one of several verdicts involving a greater or lesser degree of punishment, for the jury to find
the Negro guilty of a lesser crime, as manslaughter instead of
murder.

And when the Negro criminal goes to the state prison he has
an excellent chance of being released by pardon before he has

served his full sentence. The average sentence actually served by persons sent to prison for life is between seven and eight years.

Criminal trials involving whites are tried by Delta juries in the same way on the whole that such trials are held elsewhere. White men guilty of robbery, burglary, assaults, or other crimes are sent without hesitation to prison. Homicides, too, are dealt with in the Delta as they are everywhere, with the exception that defendants who plead the "unwritten law" and bring convincing proof to bear, usually go free. A man who kills another for "breaking up his home" is regarded as being well within his rights, and receives not only his freedom but the plaudits of the community. It does not matter that he assassinated his victim in cold blood.

Cases involving assaults by Negroes upon whites are exceedingly rare in the Delta. Juries trying these cases are swayed inwardly by two considerations above and beyond the evidence adduced before them. The one is that a Negro must not raise his hand against a white man. The other is that the Negro who assaulted a white man must have been driven to do it by the white man himself, and his conduct was therefore justifiable. Sometimes the jury convicts a Negro in these cases, not because he is guilty, but because he is a Negro. And frequently Delta juries acquit Negroes charged with assaulting a white man.

In many Delta communities whites and blacks who offend against the prevailing customs to the extent of making themselves offensive to the general public, suffer extra-legal banishment under the well-known and approved institution of "running him out of town." Homosexuality, for instance, is an offense which lands the offender not in jail, but upon the first train leaving town after his practices have been discovered and he has been notified by an earnest and indignant committee of citizens to leave. If women are guilty of the same offense, nothing is done about it. Gallantry toward women still lives.

So, too, a long-continued series of acts over a period of years may culminate finally in the banishment of a man whose conduct has become intolerable to the community. Such an instance occurred a few years ago in a Delta town. A white lawyer married the daughter of a well-known and beloved judge. He neglected his clients and his wife and remained drunk for weeks at a time. Frequently he beat her. Finally the judge died. At his funeral the son-in-law lawyer, in his drunkenness, fell from the top of the stairs almost into his father-in-law's casket as it lay in the living room of the family home.

After the funeral a number of the most prominent men in the community gathered at a club, sat around and discussed this incident. They recalled the honorable life of the judge and his kindness. They reminded each other of the uprightness and gentleness of his daughter married to the drunken brutal lawyer. The more they talked the angrier they became. They decided finally that they ought to run the lawyer out of town.

A committee was then and there chosen out of their number to call on the lawyer and notify him that he must leave at once. They had no legal authority or sanction whatsoever either to formulate such a decree or to enforce it. But the lawyer, well aware that organized public opinion stood firml· behind the committee, knew that safety lay in flight. He left the town and went to live in another community near-by. After remaining there for a number of years, he was permitted to return from exile, and died in the town from which he had been banished.

A Negro lawyer was disposed of quite as effectively but more picturesquely. An offender against the opinions of the white governing class, he was placed in a skiff with several white men and was rowed out into the midst of some vicious whirlpools in the Mississippi River. At this point he was quietly asked if he would not like to travel and see the world for a few years. He confessed that travel was the obsession of his life. The skiff was thereupon rowed to shore and the lawyer left that night for Chicago.

A feeling of helplessness and hopelessness and profound pathos stirs in the bosom of the onlooker as he contemplates the ceaseless tide of Negro crime in the Delta, against which a small and ill-equipped white minority struggles in vain. Day after day, the shootings, the stabbings and cuttings, go on. Day after day crimes against property are committed. The Negro community is gravely injured and the white community is severely burdened.

Hundreds and thousands of Negroes march in and out of Delta jails and the state prison, sorrowful at their singing and cheerful at their work, patient in misfortune and resigned in tragedy. Year after year the chorus of clanging jail doors and singing Negroes rings on the air of the Delta. Year after year the prisoners change, but the crimes go on. Year after year the same songs are sung by different voices, but all alike are filled with sorrow. They are high and strident and African in the throats of the women, deep and booming and rich in the throats of the men, as convicts pour out their souls with troubling wail:

> "Lawd, I wonder, O I wonder,
> Will I ever get back home.
> Sometimes I'm hungry,
> Sometimes I'm tired,
> Sometimes I sing,
> Sometimes I cry.
> I says I wonder, O Lawd,
> I wonder will I ever get back home alive."

CHAPTER 7

The Share-Cropper System

In 1865, General Hargreaves, late of the Army of Northern Virginia, returned to his plantation home in the Mississippi Delta, to find that he had neither plantation nor home. The land had become a matted tangle of weeds and young trees. The ditches were choked and fallen; the stock scattered and dead; the implements stolen and lost; the slaves freed; the home burned.

The General stayed with friends in the neighborhood and wrote to his family in Kentucky that he would soon have a home ready for them. In a few days some of his former slaves appeared. They had been liberated into poverty. He had been delivered into poverty. Hunger was now their common bond. A partnership was formed: the General would furnish, God knows how, a few mules, implements, and cotton seed. The Negroes would raise the crop. The profits, if any, would be equally divided between them. For food, until money began to come in with the sale of cotton, months later, vegetables could be raised; there were berries and 'coons in the woods, and catfish in the creeks.

In this way the share-cropper system was born. It arose out of necessity and has continued for seventy years because no one has found a better or more workable system to substitute for it.

Critics of the system charge that it is the means through which Southern farmers have kept millions of black and white croppers in a state of slavery or peonage. They say that it is filled with bitter injustices and mediaeval cruelties. The Uncle Tom literature of the system pictures the planter living luxuriously in a white-pillared mansion surrounded by throngs of cringing minions, while the cropper in his hovel, poverty-stricken, disease-ridden, helpless and hopeless, sinks lower and lower in the scale of humanity.

What is the truth?

What follows is not a discussion of share-cropping as it is practiced throughout the South, on all kinds of soils, for all kinds of crops, against many backgrounds, with whites and Negroes as croppers. It is limited to the Mississippi Delta.

In the Delta cotton is the one money crop. Other crops are raised, but the economy of the section is based squarely on cotton and on cotton alone. Here the climate is temperate, the soil rich, the moisture abundant, and the plantations are large. The vast majority of the croppers are Negroes. Nowhere do natural conditions conspire to give them greater opportunities. Nowhere is the soil richer, drought less to be feared, freedom from total crop failures more certain, land easier to cultivate, or cotton more valuable. Delta cotton with its long silky fiber commands a higher price than nearly all other American cottons. Special demands make it marketable usually at a relatively high price when the inferior upland cottons are a drug on the market at any price. And nowhere is the Negro freer from the competition of white labor than here.

If the cropper under these favorable conditions cannot raise his standard of living and rise eventually to the status of landowner, it is clear that he is little likely to succeed under conditions far less favorable. If he must remain at a low economic level on these rich lands, it is not probable that he will rise on the rain-washed, sterile lands of less favored sections. The Delta presents the cropper with the maximum opportunity. Does his failure to rise flow from defects inherent in the system itself? Does he suffer from the one-crop system just as the farmer does? Is he the innocent victim of white exploitation? Or do his own faults of character contribute to some degree in keeping him at a low economic level?

The system in outline is simple. The prospective cropper and his wife present themselves to the farmer, say, in January. They are black, able-bodied, and penniless. Their possessions are few. They own some pots and pans; two cane-back chairs; a Bible and a mail-order catalogue; colored photographs of themselves; a rickety bed; a few "crazy" quilts and a rooster. They stand in all the clothes that they have. They want to make a crop on the farmer's land and he needs their labor. A deal is struck.

The farmer agrees to furnish the croppers with food and clothing in stipulated amounts from January until the following August, when the crop begins to be picked and money comes in. If they become ill, medicines and medicinal services will be provided. These things are at the croppers' expense. They have no money to pay for them, and they are charged against their accounts, to be paid for when the crop has been made and they come into the possession of some money.

The farmer will also provide the croppers, free of charge, with a cabin, water, and firewood. They are now assured of food, shelter, fuel, water, clothing, and medical services for the next nine months. But they cannot make a crop with their bare hands. For that purpose the farmer will supply, without charge, the land, mules, instruments of cultivation, feed for mules, and seed for cotton and corn.

The croppers agree to raise the crops and give half of the cotton, the cotton seed, and the corn raised by them, to the farmer. The remaining half of the crops belongs to them. They agree also to repay the farmer the sums of money already advanced to them in the form of food, clothing, and services.

The homeless and penniless Negroes now move into a plantation cabin. They are assured of complete economic security for the next nine months. At no time do they face the specters of starvation and homelessness. Their living may be meager, but it is secure. They have a humble place in the economic scheme, but they have a hope and a chance of rising. If there is work to be done on the plantation, such as ditching or repairing fences, they are employed at wages of seventy-five cents or a dollar a day, and are paid these wages in cash. It is January and they have little to do on their own account until March. But they are housed, fed, clothed, secure.

What, in essence, is the relationship between cropper and farmer? It is roughly that of partnership. The one partner provides the capital, the other provides the labor, and they agree to divide the profits. But the profits, if any, can be divided only when they have been made, and they cannot be made, if at all, until nine months after the partnership has begun. During that time the cropper must live, and his partner, the farmer, agrees to lend him enough money, in the form of cash or food, to tide him over until the crops come in. The loans will then be repaid to the farmer who has furnished all the capital. And the profits, if any, will then be divided.

It is important to note that this is in effect a partnership in which the cropper agrees to share half the profits, but does not agree to share half the losses. If the crop turns out to be poor and the prices are low, the cropper will get little or no cash. He may even go into debt. The half which he turns over to the farmer according to their agreement is of little value. The half which is his does not yield enough, when sold, to pay his debts to the farmer. Both parties to the contract lose money. Theoretically, the farmer may sue the cropper for the debt. Actually he does not because a judgment against a penniless man is worthless. He cannot hold the cropper on the land by law or by force and try to recoup his losses out of the next year's crop. If the cropper moves, the debt is lost beyond redemption. If he remains, much or all of it is often forgiven, because the farmer does not want the cropper to feel crushed beneath a burden of debt. This attitude is not dictated by charity. It arises from the fact that a debt-crushed cropper with no hope of escaping his burden makes a half-hearted worker.

Let us assume, however, that the crops have been good and the prices high. The cropper in that event, at the end of the season, would have found that he had not only maintained himself during the large part of the year, but would have more or less cash money in the penniless hands that he brought to the plantation.

What risks, then, flow to the cropper and to the farmer out of their relationship? The cropper's risk is that he may not receive, in addition to a living, much money or any money at all. The farmer's risk is that the cropper's half of the produce will not be enough to pay for the sums advanced to him for his subsistence. And certainly not enough to cover the indirect charges of salaries for overseers, interest on money borrowed, taxes, depreciation on stock and tools, and the costs of seed and repairs. These are fixed and inescapable outlays.

The farmer's income to be derived from the cropper can never be even roughly estimated in advance. He does not pay rental in a specified number of dollars. He agrees merely to turn over to the farmer a fixed percentage of an indeterminate quantity of produce worth an indeterminate number of dollars. If he makes ten bales of cotton he gives five to the farmer; if he makes six he gives the farmer three. Cotton may be worth five cents or fifteen cents a pound. In no event can the farmer know how much cotton he is going to get nor how much it will bring in the market. The result is that agriculture, a hazardous enterprise at best, becomes doubly hazardous under the share-cropping system where the farmer takes all the risks and the cropper bears none of the losses. If the cropper loses at all, he loses the time and labor that he spent in making the crop. That is a disadvantage to the cropper, but it is not an advantage to the farmer.

How, then, does the farmer seek to minimize his risks? If prices are low or the crop yield is poor, he has no way to recover money owed to him by the croppers. The natural hazards are high, and the moral risks in his opinion are great. He therefore charges the cropper up to 20 per cent interest per annum on the moneys advanced to him. This practice is denounced by critics of the system as being indefensible and outrageous. But from the farmer's viewpoint it is not.

In the first place, he himself must pay 6 to 8 per cent interest on money borrowed to make the crop. Delta plantations, on the whole, year after year, are operated on borrowed money. The farmer incurs high risks in the share-cropper relationship, and where the business man incurs high risks he expects and demands a greater interest return upon his money.

When you buy the bond of a government you are in effect lending your money to that government. You may demand 8 per cent from Peru, but only 3 per cent from Canada. You feel that you are more likely to receive interest regularly and be paid your principal at maturity if you lend to Canada instead of to Peru, and because of a higher degree of security you are willing to accept a lower rate of interest. You are free to lend or not to lend to governments, as you see fit. The farmer has no choice. He must lend to his croppers in order that they may live and work. He charges a high rate of interest because he feels that he incurs high risks. He must make large profits in the prosperous years to tide him and his croppers over the disastrous years from which the cotton economy is never free. Sometimes he collects his 20 per cent interest. At other times he loses both interest and principal. The average Delta farmer would be glad if he could earn 6 per cent net on his investment year after year.

The majority of farmers in this area do not give their croppers cash money with which to buy their food and clothing. They give them, instead, a coupon book usable as money at the plantation store or commissary. This is seen by critics of the system as another fiendish device by which the farmer grinds down the helpless cropper. It is regarded as a scheme to make him pay the farmer an exorbitant profit on everything he buys, and to enforce a monopoly of his purchases. It is viewed as part of the general method of keeping the cropper bound to the land in a state of peonage.

Essentially the farmer is in the farming business — not the grocery business — and he looks to farm profits, not grocery profits, to support him. He gives the croppers coupon books instead of cash not primarily to squeeze a profit out of them — although it is true that he makes a reasonable profit on groceries — but in order to prevent them from squandering their money. Long experience has shown that where the cropper received cash at the first of the month with which to supply himself and his family with food and clothing for the next thirty days, he would be likely to squander it on women, whisky, gambling, gasoline, and other pleasures. Once the money was gone the cropper and his family would still need food. He knew that the farmer would be compelled to give it to him because the farmer depended upon his labor. And the farmer always did, under the compulsion of necessity. Such extra advances made the farmer's investment higher and his risk greater, as well as causing the cropper's debt to mount. They were beneficial ultimately to neither. This practice was terminated through the use of coupon books. It is significant that their use has been praised and supported by the wives of croppers, who feel that their men now have no opportunity to throw away money badly needed for their subsistence.

The farmer defends the economics of share-cropping from the cropper's viewpoint on many grounds. Under no other system in America, he says, can a penniless man of no proved ability, with nothing to offer save his labor, enter into a partnership relation to furnish his labor, divide the profits, and, in effect, share in none of the losses. And if, at worst, and through the fault of neither farmer nor cropper, there are no profits, the cropper has inevitably gained to the extent that he has had a living throughout the greater portion of the year. If, on the other hand, there are profits, the cropper may take them and in a relatively short while, provided that he is thrifty, he may rise to the higher economic status of a renter or a landowner.

There is one inescapable risk which both partners to the relationship suffer. The farmer may be an incapable farmer. In that event, through no fault of his own, the cropper suffers because there will be little or no profit to divide. The cropper, on the other hand, may be lazy and shiftless, and through the play of these qualities will cause a loss to the farmer. These risks are inherent in any partnership. Success for both sides depends upon hard work and fair play upon the part of each toward the other. If eventually neither one profits, or the farmer profits at the expense of the cropper, it is not because there is anything inherently unfair in the system, but because of a breakdown of the human factors of fair play that are involved.

Both cropper and farmer, of course, are subject to the hazards of agriculture and of the market. If crops are poor, both suffer. If prices are disastrously low, both suffer.

Many of the evils of share-cropping flow not from the economics involved, but from the workings of human factors on both sides. It is obvious that the cropping contract is worth neither more nor less than the worth of the moral integrity of the parties to it. It is undoubtedly true that some farmers in the Delta exploit their croppers. They are poor, usually ignorant and illiterate, the white man's word is law, and resort to the courts is a dubious enterprise. Once there, the bias is in the Negro's favor — not against him. But Delta Negroes do not like to sue white folks, however just their claims. Croppers, therefore, represent a rich field for exploitation, and some Delta farmers have exploited them as ruthlessly as possible.

It is true, too, that some coal-miners in Pennsylvania and West Virginia exploit their miners. Some textile mills in New England and the Carolinas pay starvation wages to their mill hands. Some chain stores miserably underpay their clerks. Exploitation of labor is, unfortunately, a phenomenon common to American life. It is applied to no one group of workers, limited to no one section of the country, restricted to no one phase of industry or of agriculture. It would be strange indeed, therefore, if some of the farmers of the Delta did not exploit their croppers, and a mockery of the truth to deny that a number of them grind down the croppers wherever possible.

It is at the same time true that the majority of the farmers of this section deal honestly with the Negroes on their lands. As men of integrity they treat their croppers with every consideration of justice and fairness, and render to them what is their due. The records of their dealings with their croppers are written upon their ledgers for all to read. Their reputations are known to their neighbors, and in a rural community no man can hide from his neighbor what he is doing when his actions touch the lives of hundreds of croppers.

One of the paradoxes of share-cropping in the Delta is this. The cropper renders no greater service or loyalty to the honest farmer than he does to the cut-throat farmer. He works no harder, exercises no greater degree of care over his stock and tools, forms no greater attachment to his land or to his person, and is filled with no higher measure of gratitude. It is common knowledge in the Delta that Negroes who well know that a certain farmer is a ruthless exploiter will flock to him with offers of their services, and work as hard and as loyally for him as they would for a farmer who is known to be just to croppers.

In endeavoring to understand the reasons for this seemingly inexplicable conduct, I went to the Negroes themselves for answer, and they freely gave it to me. It is this. Every Negro, with, of course, some exceptions, is profoundly convinced that every white man will rob and exploit him without heart and without limit. No matter what the white man's conduct toward him actually is or seems to be, the Negro is deeply suspicious of it and mistrustful of the motives. If he receives one dollar or one thousand dollars for his share of the crop, he feels that he has not received his just share. He believes that the white man's success is solely and always at his expense, that he gets richer and richer out of the stolen fruits of the Negro's labor, and he clings to this belief although almost every farmer in the Delta has been in difficult financial straits during the past few years, or at various times in the past, and dozens of them have lost their lands, their money, their health, and sometimes their lives in a desperate effort to hold their farms.

Was this attitude of suspicion toward the white man fostered in the Negro's mind out of the conditions under which he has lived in America first as slave and then as freedman? And if it was, were not these conditions dictated and enforced by the stronger whites? Then must we not conclude that the Negro's suspicion of the white man was seared deep into his mind by the whites themselves? Would it not seem true, in conclusion, therefore, that the mind of the Negro has been poisoned at its central core against the whites by the whites? And that the whites have only themselves to blame?

These conclusions seem to be true. But examination reveals that the causes of the Negro's suspicion of the white man go far deeper. The fact is that the Negro cropper distrusts the Negro landowner as much as he distrusts the white landowner. In addition, he is enormously jealous of the prosperity of his fellow

Negro. He feels that the white man has enriched himself at his expense, but he is not envious of his wealth, nor is he resentful because he possesses it. But he hates to see his fellow Negro succeed. He prefers, indeed, wherever possible, to work for the white man rather than the Negro, feeling that he will be treated more fairly. And Negro landowners, in turn, complain bitterly of the shiftlessness and unreliability of their Negro croppers.

Croppers stand, therefore, without faith in the whites and without faith in landowners of their own race. They are always on guard against chicanery in others, and often busied with counterschemes of chicanery of their own.

The Negro's suspicion of the white man can be accounted for in part on several grounds. It is a remnant of slavery persisting in freedom, of a time when the slave was actually owned by the white man solely for the white man's benefit. It is perfectly sound for the Negro to believe that the white man will still try to avail himself of the fruits of the Negro's labors with none of the responsibilities of slave-holding accruing to him. So, too, there has been some exploitation of croppers, and the victims spread the news of their misfortune throughout the community, so that every Negro comes to believe that every white man will exploit him if he has the opportunity. In addition, the average Delta Negro is illiterate and unsystematic. He may draw rations or money throughout the growing season, and when repayment is asked by the farmer, he has forgotten that he ever drew money, and concludes that the farmer is exploiting him. So, too, if his accounts are settled on the basis of cotton at, say, ten cents a pound, nothing will convince him that cotton is not at that moment twelve cents a pound. A glance at the newspaper market reports would convince him of the truth or error of the planter's statements on the price of cotton, but he does not read the newspapers at all, or if he did, he would find the market reports too complicated to decipher. The suspicions of the illiterate fester in his mind, and he concludes that he is the victim of the white man's greed.

If the cropper is on the land of a Negro he thinks that he is being exploited more bitterly than if he were on the land of a white man. The only difference is that he feels freer to express his views to the Negro than to the white man, and the Negro landowner has greater difficulty proving to his cropper that he has given him a square deal.

This attitude has a number of far-reaching and unfortunate results affecting alike both cropper and owner. The cropper who believes that he will invariably be robbed of the fruits of his labors naturally regards his relationship with the farmer as makeshift and transitory. It follows humanly that he will put as little into it and try to get as much out of it as he can. What, then, does it matter if he loafs on the job? Or mistreats the farmer's stock and leaves his tools in the rain? Or if he steals a few sacks of cotton or corn and sells them to a neighbor? It is against the law to steal, but it is not wrong morally. Essentially these things belong to him, and what the white man calls stealing is merely a form of insurance, a wise precaution against his rapacity.

With this viewpoint deeply imbedded in his mind, if the cropper finds in June or July that because of an impending low yield of cotton, or low price, he will not be likely to receive much money at the end of the season, he often deserts the farm without warning. On one plantation the owner saw a large family of croppers working in the fields at sundown, and discovered their cabin emptied of its occupants and their possessions at sunrise. When this happens the farmer loses all the money that he has advanced to the croppers for their subsistence, and must hire additional labor at added expense to complete the abandoned crop. But the financial loss is not the greatest loss. The reckless breaking of written or oral contracts strengthens the white man's conviction that the Negro is utterly unreliable and completely irresponsible. And the Negro's equally strong belief that the white man is always seeking to exploit him adds immeasurably to the difficulties of many men and women in the Delta who are deeply interested in improving the Negro's lot.

When the honest and well-meaning farmer sees that his earnest efforts on behalf of his croppers evoke in them no response of loyalty or of gratitude; when they desert him at the end of a season and move to a neighboring plantation where every Negro knows that he will be exploited; when they leave him without warning in the middle of a season, thinking that the game is no longer worth the candle, he becomes profoundly discouraged. And when he becomes convinced that his croppers think that he is robbing them, although in fact he is treating them with scrupulous fairness, he often in a revulsion of feeling himself joins the ranks of the exploiters.

In America, on the whole, there is not the slightest vestige of sentiment in the mind of the employer toward the employee. But the Delta still has many farmers who, out of reasons of religion, paternalism, and affection, feel a deep interest in the welfare of Negroes on their plantations, and are strongly affected when croppers do not treat them with the fairness with which they are treated. And slowly, painfully, and surely their minds are being drained of tenderness and kindliness toward the Negro, to be replaced by that detachment which measures all effort in terms of dollars expended and services received, quite oblivious of the human values involved.

The financial condition of the vast mass of rural Negroes in the Delta today, as for many years past, is that of poverty. It does not matter that this section has paid them millions of dollars when crops were good and prices were high, nor very little when crops were poor and prices were low. The croppers remain poor. They got the money. What did they do with it?

In some years, croppers on plantations have been paid sums of money equal to the value of the plantations themselves. It is a commonplace throughout this area that if Negroes saved their money they would own the land and everything on it. Yet they remain poor year after year. Why?

The blight and scourge of the Delta Negro is his incredible improvidence. It is an improvidence so fantastic, so deep-rooted, so absurd as to appear impossible to anyone who has not lived among these people. Shortly before the great flood of 1927, when it seemed certain that the whole area of the Delta would soon be under water, a Negro walked into a store. "Boss," he said, "I wants me a Stutson hat." He paid five dollars for it.

Then he said, "Dere's another Stutson I'd sho lak to have. Dat brin'le-brown one. I ain't got but ten dollars an' I wants me bofe dem hats so I has 'em w'en de flood come. Does you gimme a dime to git me somethin' t' eat, I'll take 'em." The clerk gave him a dime. He went out of the store happy but penniless, with two hats to wear during the flood which would probably be of long duration.

At "settling time" in the autumn, when croppers are finally paid for their share of the crop and accounts are squared, they are usually earnestly exhorted by the farmer or his overseer to spend some part of their money for groceries and essential clothing to tide them over the idle period of the winter. The croppers say, "Yassuh," and, "I'm sho gwine do dat, Boss," to these exhortations. Some of them do spend part of their money for necessary food and clothing which they put away for the winter. But many others squander the greater part of it with wild recklessness on whisky, gambling, women, and automobiles. It has been not uncommon for Delta plantations to pay tens of thousands of dollars to their croppers in October and November, and be compelled to furnish them rations for their mere subsistence before the Christmas holidays.

On one plantation this autumn a Negro received $150 in the morning in settlement of his account. By night of the same day he was back in the plantation manager's office, trying to buy some groceries on credit with five or six penniless months ahead of him. "Cap'n," he told him, "a low-down yaller woman stole all my money." Another who received $75 spent all of it on an ancient automobile. He had no money left either for a license or for gasoline. He borrowed a few cents each day from his friends, and drove the automobile on the muddy plantation lanes. In the yards of hundreds of croppers' cabins in the Delta are the abandoned wrecks of automobiles upon which were spent the proceeds of a year's labor. Among the peasantry of France or Italy ownership of automobiles is rare. Among the Negro croppers of the Delta such ownership is common. But in the long run the French or Italian peasant is more likely to own the land he tills and to have money in the bank.

It is not an unusual sight to see Negro women working at strenuous tasks in high-heel shoes and silk stockings. If they have no money for shoes, they work quite unconcernedly barefoot. One often sees them walking in the rain wearing silk dresses, or riding to town through the hot sun and dust in a slow-moving wagon, dressed in expensive clothes. The French peasant woman may have a pair of silk stockings, and does have a silk dress or two. But they are carefully handled on the rare occasions when they are used at all, and are carefully put away when not in use. But the French peasant woman and her husband are more likely through thrift to reach a state of economic independence than the Delta Negro woman and her cropper husband.

Firewood is free for the gathering to every cropper on a plantation, and there is plenty of time for gathering it. Yet often they do not have a stick of wood in their cabins until the cold days of winter are upon them. The Delta Negro does not like cold. So he sometimes burns his furniture. And he commonly throws into the fireplace in the autumn the fence rails that he split in the spring to fence his garden.

The Delta Negro is almost always lacking in foresight. He does not plan far ahead. Usually he concerns himself only with the affairs of today. The one great exception is his preparation for burial. He religiously prepares during his lifetime for the disposing of his body after death, through insurance or burial societies to which he pays monthly dues. Many of the larger plantations have burial societies of their own for the sole use of croppers and laborers on these plantations, and membership in them is at a rate much lower than in outside societies. Every Negro on the plantation is a member, and his contentment of mind is deepened by the knowledge that he will have a splendid funeral when he dies.

The besetting sin of the Delta Negro is his uncurbed, headlong extravagance. Yet thrift is the only means through which he can ever hope to rise. The Negro cropper without mules, plows, feed, and seed is a "half-hand," and gets only one-half of the crop. The Negro with these things immediately advances to the higher status of renter whose share of the crop is in some places two-thirds, and in other places three-fourths. The next step is to land ownership and economic freedom. But none of these steps can be taken without money. Money can be accumulated only by thrift, and the average Delta Negro has no thrift. The vast majority of croppers remain, therefore, in the status of half-hands, or may sink to the even lower level of day-hands employed by the day at fixed wages and dischargeable at will.

America was built out of the savings of its people, millions of whom have progressed from poverty to economic independence through the wise employment of thrift. The world is familiar with the spectacle of the millions of dollars which have annually been sent abroad by immigrants. This money represented the savings of the Chinese laundryman, the Italian laborer, the Polish miner, the Scandinavian farmhand, the Jewish merchant, and the labor in general of men of a hundred nationalities. But the Negro cropper of the Delta, dowered with opportunities which would make a European peasantry wealthy within a few years, is poor now, has always been poor, and unless he mends his ways will always be poor.

What are the opportunities of the Delta cropper or renter? His shelter, water, and fuel are free. Clothing and food are at his expense, but he can raise much of his food. He must buy certain things which the land will not produce — coffee, rice, sugar, tobacco, wheat flour, and minor items of diet. He may raise dozens of vegetables, and industry in the garden will provide him with fresh and canned vegetables throughout the year. He prefers corn bread to wheat bread. He may raise his own corn and have it ground into meal. He may grow sorghum and have it made into molasses. He may have chickens and eggs, a cow and milk and butter. He may raise a hog or two for meat and render his own lard for cooking. He may, indeed, at little cost save that of his own labor, not only live on the fruits of his industry but have a varied, health-sustaining, palatable diet. But what does he actually do?

The greater number of Negro share-croppers live on meat, meal, and molasses obtained at the plantation store on credit.

They may vary this diet with imported foods — sweet potatoes canned in Tennessee, white potatoes grown in Maine and molasses produced in Louisiana. This indeed was almost the invariable diet of Delta Negroes until a few years ago when farmers began to force them to raise some food of their own.

Here is land so rich that it will grow almost anything with little effort, a climate so warm and yet so temperate that it will produce an astounding variety of products, yet the vast majority of its people remain at or below the level of poverty. They live, it is true, without starvation or actual want, but they do not live well. Some of them suffer from diseases arising from lack of a balanced diet upon a land that will grow almost anything from peanuts to pumpkins merely for the scratching of the soil. Contrast the opportunity before these people with that presented to the Vermont or New Hampshire farmer wrestling with the stones and cold of New England, or the farmers of the hot, arid west coaxing life-giving water to their carefully tilled acres. Compare their chances for economic advancement and a full life with the Japanese farmer wringing a living out of a tiny plot scarcely larger than the Negro cropper's garden. Compare their lack of variety of food and their cooking with the food and cooking of a French peasant family who derive a sound and independent living from a few acres.

What is the white man's attitude toward this lack of industry on the Negro's part? He has always observed it and wondered at it. He has preached to the Negro and threatened to drive him to do things for himself, and when his preachings were of no avail he decided to let the Negro shift for himself. Time after time he has given his croppers vegetable seeds and a patch of ground in which to plant them. He found that often the seeds were not planted at all, or, if planted, the cropper let grass and weeds overrun the garden. In the exceptional case he might cultivate it during the early spring, gather the vegetables, and plant no more to care for his needs during the long summer and autumn.

The cropper felt no imperative necessity to grow his own food because he relied upon the long-established tradition that the farmer who needed his labor would not let him starve. He would under any circumstances be supplied with meat, meal, and molasses, and with these he was content. In the last few years this tradition has gone out of the window. The farmer, faced with the desperate task of making both ends meet, has literally compelled the croppers to raise some of their own food. Because of this they have paradoxically had more to eat and a greater variety of foods during the depression than during the so-called years of plenty. For once they had called upon the earth and the earth had responded. But this revolution was brought about almost at pistol point. No white farmer thinks that the Negro has learned a lesson in self-support or that he will continue in these ways when the white man's discipline is relaxed. To a man, they feel that with the coming of higher prices for cotton, and a lessening of white pressure, the Negro will revert again to meat, meal, and molasses bought on credit.

The Negro cropper of the Delta has not only wide opportunities for economic advancement, but has, probably, more leisure than any class of people in America who work for their living. The number of days worked by the average cropper on a Delta plantation is not more than 120 to 130. If the farmer employs him on work outside of his own crop he is paid extra for it. The average workingman in America who is so fortunate as to have steady employment works about 300 days a year. He works twice as many days as the Negro cropper. No other people are able to gain even the most meager livelihood with so little effort.

The cropper does not use his leisure wisely. He wastes it. He attempts no form of self-improvement. He works at no craft. He does not attempt to make his cabin more comfortable or its yard more attractive. He does nothing to improve his condition in any way. His prodigal leisure is spent in sleeping, in loafing at country stores or in the little towns, in wandering aimlessly about the countryside, in going to picnics or dances, in gambling or pursuing women, or just sitting on his front porch gazing vacantly into space.

Critics of the share-cropper system say that he does not try to improve the condition of his cabin because it is not a fit habitation for a human being. It is true that many cabins in the Delta are hovels. Some of them are scarcely good enough to be nests for migratory birds. But it is also true that within the past few years thousands of better-type cabins have been erected and are being erected by farmers who are financially able to build them. On run-down plantations dwindling to physical and financial ruin there are cabins of the old-style, one-room type which are not fit for human habitation. But on the plantations which are in better financial condition the old-style cabin is rapidly giving way to the new.

This, however, remains to be said, and while it is no defense and is not meant to be a defense of indefensibly bad housing, it is true that even the poorest cabins of croppers compare favorably in light, comfort, and sanitation with the dark, stinking rooms occupied by workers in the slums of many of the richest cities of America. The tendency of the Delta is to build better cabins, and as the financial condition of this section improves, it is likely that the old-style cabins will give way entirely to the new.

The farmer who provides his croppers with better housing or better living conditions is frequently discouraged by their disregard for property which does not belong to them. Recently, because of a recurrence of malaria, thousands of Delta cabins were screened by the farmers. They carefully explained the reasons for screens to the Negroes, who listened to the explanations with every evidence of interest and gratitude. Shortly after the screens had been installed, farmers on many plantations found that the screen on the front door of a cabin had a great hole in it, and the screen on the kitchen window had been ripped wide open. The screen on the front door had been torn so that the dog might have a way of entering the house. The screen on the kitchen window had been ripped so that the wife might have an opening through which to throw the slops. These actions naturally do not increase the farmer's enthusiasm for making improvements on croppers' cabins.

There is no air of permanency about a cropper's cabin because he does not usually expect to stay long in one place. He is afflicted with a nomadic instinct. He is constantly moving about from plantation to plantation. Sometimes he remains in one place three or four years before moving; then he goes away for a few years; finally he returns to the plantation from which he started. This pattern is repeated over and over again throughout his life. Usually he remains in his wanderings within the Delta, but occasionally he goes as far afield as Louisiana or Arkansas.

When he announces to the farmer that he intends to leave, the farmer is not surprised. When he appears again on the farmer's premises after an absence of a few years, the farmer regards the cropper's return as a matter of course and they take up again their relationship as though it had never been broken. The cropper does not return in a prosperous condition. Usually he is in desperate financial straits, and returns, so to speak, to his first love whose failings he has forgotten and whose virtues glow now like stars in a sky of velvety black.

The white farmer finds the migratory instinct of the Negro beyond his understanding. He feels that a sensible man will stay in one place if he is prospering, and will remove to another only out of carefully calculated self-interest. Not so the Negro cropper. He moves often when he prospers and remains when he does not.

This is a typical case which occurs over and over again on Delta plantations. A penniless cropper begins as a half-hand on a plantation. Within two or three years he acquires enough money to buy mules, plows, and other things necessary to advance to the higher status of renter. He remains a year or two longer and accumulates some cash as well as property. The Negro, during the days of his rise, counseled with the farmer and took his advice, which events proved to be sound. Now, however, that he is prosperous, he appears suddenly one day before the farmer and announces that he is going to move. This is an old and oft-told tale. The farmer does not urge the Negro to remain on his land. He merely tells him that he will have a cabin ready for him when he returns. Long experience has taught him that nine times out of ten the Negro will go to a plantation where he will be exploited, and will soon come back and start over again where he began as a half-hand five or six years before.

In seeking to account for this extraordinary behavior I questioned dozens of white men who had spent their lives among Negroes. Their answers were not only unrevealing and unsatisfactory, but they illustrated also the complexities and difficulties that arise when peoples of widely differing mentalities and capabilities live and work side by side. They said that you can never know what a Negro will or will not do under any given set of circumstances; that he is subject to an incurable migratory instinct which runs counter to self-interest.

I went then to the Negroes for answer. Their replies revealed how far apart the races are in mutual understanding; how intricate are the motivations which move Negroes; how difficult it is to find a common meeting-ground for Negroes and whites.

They said that Negroes move away from plantations where they prosper for a number of reasons. A cropper may have some real or fancied grievance against the owner of the plantation. He is afraid to air his grievance, and rather than run the risk of arousing the white man's displeasure he prefers to move away. Others move because there is a woman on another plantation irresistibly attractive to the cropper. Or the cropper's wife wants to be near her relatives on another plantation and persuades her husband to move. And many move for another and quite extraordinary reason.

Often a cropper or a renter buys mules, wagons, and other farm gear through loans from the farmer, who retains a chattel mortgage. Eventually the Negro pays off the loans and the mortgage is in fact discharged. An unscrupulous farmer might, however, still seek to enforce it against the Negro if he attempted to move. In most instances, the farmer does not make such an attempt. But the Negro is suspicious of all white men, good or bad. Moving then becomes for him a test of ownership of things for which he has paid in full. If the white man does not attempt to seize them and he is permitted to take them away, he knows that they belong to him. He leaves the place, therefore, where he has prospered, in order to determine whether the fruits of his prosperity are really his.

Negroes gave me other reasons for the moving about of croppers from one plantation to another. They felt that many were undoubtedly afflicted with the migratory spirit which made them restless and unhappy if they remained too long in one place. Others moved because the hogs looked fatter and the corn grew taller on the other side of the road.

Many croppers leave their plantations because of the allurements dangled before their eyes by "decoy niggers." The decoy Negro is the tool of an unscrupulous white farmer who exploits his croppers. He lavishes money or favors on one or two of his cropper families, whom he sends out to other plantations to visit with the Negroes, and by the example of their own prosperity induce them to leave at the end of the season and join them on their plantation flowing with milk and honey.

Is there any hope for the Delta share-cropper? Are the cards so stacked against him that he can never rise? Is he condemned always to live at or below the level of poverty? Is the sharecropping system as applied in the Delta a trap from which the cropper can never hope to escape?

The answers to these questions are written in the land records of the courthouses of the Delta. There is abundant hope for the share-cropper. He does rise. Thousands of acres of rich Delta land are owned by Negroes who began as penniless sharecroppers. In some places there are whole colonies of Negro landowners, composed of 75 to 100 families, each of whom owns farms ranging in size from 40 to 240 acres. Throughout the whole area of the Delta, in almost every section, are found Negro landowners who started at the bottom as day laborers or half-hands and worked their way by industry and thrift to the status of landowners. During the past few years many of these Negroes, in common with many of the best-equipped white farmers, have lost their lands by reason of disastrously low prices for cotton. They had, however, demonstrated that they could rise from the share-cropper status.

Negro landowners are the exceptional and relatively rare members of their people who combine thrift and industry. They own their homes, their land, their mules, their tools, and everything needed to run a farm. They have cows, chickens, fruit trees, and gardens. They are well housed, well fed, happy, and prosperous. They are among the best and most respected persons in the communities in which they live. They rose through their own efforts, aided often by white men who like to help the hard-working, home-loving, thrifty Negro. The Negro landowners of the Delta are a credit to their race, an example to their fellows, and a living refutation of the assertion that the cropper has no chance to rise in the economic scale.

It is impossible to discuss the ramifications of share-cropping within the limits of a single chapter. I have, therefore, narrowed this discussion to a partial consideration of the human factors involved. These have the aspect of permanency and will continue to function under any system. No system of business or of law is free from the faults and failures of human beings who must administer the system or enforce the law. So long as men are less than gods wrongs will be done and injustices committed. Human ingenuity has not yet been able to set up a system of economics or of law which is proof against the chicaneries of administrators. Share-cropping is no exception.

It is not a perfect system. It offers opportunities for injustice on the part of both farmer and cropper. If, however, both parties to the cropping contract show good faith, it affords a far greater chance to the penniless cropper to rise than he would have if he worked for small day wages and was responsible for his own shelter and subsistence. It seems certain that more and more croppers would rise to land ownership if they were more industrious, if they helped themselves without the never-ending compulsion of the white man, if they employed their abundant leisure profitably, if they saved their money and had the ambition and the will to rise. Negroes who have these qualities can always get a helping hand in the Delta, and the thousands of acres which they now own prove that fact beyond dispute.

The Negro's ultimate success in the Delta as an agriculturist is largely in his own hands. And the key to it is the unfailing combination of thrift and industry which moves mountains.

CHAPTER 8

The White Man's Point of View

THE point of view of the Delta white man about the Negro varies sharply with his origin and breeding. At one extreme of attitude stand the descendants of the early settlers of the Delta. At the other extreme stand the poor whites who have lately come to the Delta from the hills of Mississippi. In between are masses of people who have no sharply defined points of view about the Negro. They take his presence and his status for granted. He is a member of an inferior race, and they are members of a superior race. The Negro is here, he belongs in a certain category, a definite code of etiquette governs the races in their contacts with one another, and that is all there is to it.

The upper-class whites still retain, although in a denatured form, the spirit of paternalism which has come down to them from their slave-holding ancestors. The obligations of *noblesse oblige,* somewhat weakened by time and changing conditions, continue to influence their actions toward Negroes. They regard the Negro with affection and sentiment. They have not only tolerance for him, but often a friendly intimacy with him. Many whites of this class maintain life-long friendships with Negroes, watching over them, protecting them, helping them, sheltering them, lavishing upon them love and affection. These relationships are the despair of the student who seeks to untangle the raveled skeins of Negro-white association in the Delta, and interpret them for the benefit of the outsider. Yet they are basic and strong and deeply interpenetrate the structure of this society.

142

Whites of this group may always be found fighting for justice for the Negro in and out of the courts. They oppose lynchings. They frequently rescue Negroes from the clutches of thieving white men. Some years ago thousands of ignorant Delta Negroes fell into the hands of a group of white loan-sharks. They paid huge rates of interest upon loans which were never discharged, and were faced with a lifetime of grinding debt. Aroused by this injustice, a white lawyer of the Delta called a great mass-meeting of Negroes on the lawn of the courthouse of a Delta town. He told them to pay no more money to the loan-sharks, and if they were haled to court he would defend every case without charge. The loan-sharks threatened his life and tried to organize community opinion against him on the ground that he was "protecting niggers against a white man." The community stood with the lawyer, and the Negroes were freed from the slavery of debt.

Upper-class whites in the Delta perform innumerable acts of spontaneous kindness for friendless and poverty-stricken blacks. They feel a personal sense of humiliation and shame when the community or members of it inflict some brutal injustice upon a Negro. It was one of their number who first advocated common-school education for Negroes in this area, "because the Negro who knows arithmetic can prevent the unscrupulous white man from cheating him."

They show Negroes, however humble, the same courtesy which they show to their white friends. They do not, in their own conversations, talk about "niggers," but about Negroes. And the Negro in turn, lightning-quick to perceive social distinction and breeding in the white man, prefers to work for and be associated with people of this kind whom he classifies as "quality." Yet these men, with all their instinct for fairness and justice to the Negro, have a clear-eyed perception of the difficulties that weigh upon the members of two widely differing races living together in intimate daily contact.

The poor white is distinguished by his blind hatred of Negroes. Many of them came to the Delta from counties or communities where no Negro was permitted to live at all, or only upon terms of the most abject sufferance. Some of their towns are adorned with signs reading: NIGGER READ AND RUN. IF YOU CAN'T READ RUN ANYWAY. Or, NIGGER DON'T LET THE SUN GO DOWN ON YOUR HEAD IN EXVILLE. To these people the Negro is a subhuman creature without rights, without virtues, without feeling. Painfully conscious of their inferiority to the aristocratic whites of the community, whom they hate with a hate just a trifle less bitter than the hate which they reserve for Negroes, they demonstrate their superiority as white men by acts of brutality or injustice to Negroes. And even when they rise in the world, when they learn to wear shoes, to give up snuff, to eat wheat bread, to drink iced tea, to quit spitting through their teeth; even when in a generation or two they have become landowners and hold public offices, when they have been to schools and colleges, they continue to hate the Negro. They will not surrender the luxury of having someone to whom they can hold themselves superior. They will not deprive themselves of the fine sense of superiority by occasionally being wantonly cruel to a Negro. They must, from the low eminence upon which they stand, have a man farther down.

Fortunately for the Negro in the Delta, the poor white is numerically and politically without influence, although his numbers are growing and he may yet prove to be a dangerous enemy of the Negro in this section.

There are certain points of view upon which all the whites of the Delta of whatever class agree. These go to the heart of the problem and are unchanging from generation to genereation.

Intermarriage between a white person and a Negro, or between a white person and "a Mongolian person who shall have one-eighth or more of Mongolian blood," is forbidden by law in Mississippi. The state sanctions any mixture of white bloods or sects. A Greek may marry a Jew. An Italian may marry a Russian. A Catholic may marry a Baptist. But color marriages are taboo.

This law has behind it the sanction and approval of the entire white community. It represents the iron determination of the white people that they shall not amalgamate by marriage with

Negroes. It crystallizes their profound belief that the Negro race is inferior to the white race. It illustrates Anglo-Saxon abhorrence of racial mixing with black or yellow peoples. It is an ineradicable line which no white or Negro in this state may ever cross. And the purpose in part of this law is constantly flouted by miscegenation.

While intermarriage is forbidden by law, the associations which normally lead to marriage are sternly forbidden by custom. Marriage flows usually from propinquity. Propinquity is an aspect of social equality. It is a part of the free and unrestricted mingling of men and women without barriers of law or of custom. There must be a social equality in this sense before there can be marriage on a wide scale between the members of any groups. Such equality does not exist in Mississippi. A white person who attempted to receive Negroes socially would be banished from the community. A Negro seeking to mingle with whites on a level of social equality would be "run out of town." This is a taboo which no man may violate save at his peril.

Any person — white or black — publicly and openly advocating social equality between the races would be in grave danger of losing his life. At best he would run the risk of being fined and sent to jail. A statute of the State of Mississippi provides that:

> Any person, firm or corporation who shall be guilty of printing, publishing or circulating printed, typewritten or written matter urging or presenting for public acceptance or general information, arguments or suggestions in favor of social equality or of intermarriage between whites and negroes, shall be guilty of a misdemeanor and subject to a fine not exceeding five hundred dollars or imprisonment not exceeding six months or both fine and imprisonment in the discretion of the court (Section 1103, Mississippi Statutes, 1930).

The white man of the Delta lives side by side with a race of people whom he will not assimilate by marriage. If it were attempted to force assimilation upon him, the bloodiest war that can be imagined would not bring it about. Yet this is the method that has often been advocated as the way to end the Negro problem.

While the Civil War was still in progress, there was published in New York a book which advocated intermarriage between the members of the races not only as a way of eliminating a difficult problem, but also as a source of regeneration for the impoverished blood of the whites:

> All that is needed to make us the finest race on earth is to engraft upon our stock the Negro element, which Providence has placed by our side on this continent. Of all the rich treasures of blood vouchsafed to us, that of the Negro is the most precious because it is the most unlike any other that enters into the composition of national life.
>
> Let the war go on, until church and state and society recognize not only the propriety but the necessity of the marriage of white and black . . . in short, until the great truth shall be declared in our public documents and announced in the messages of our Presidents, that it is desirable that the white man shall marry the black woman and the white woman the black man. (*Miscegenation,* by D. G. Croly and others, New York, 1864.)

Not even the fanatics of the era of Reconstruction were mad enough to press such a conclusion. Federal soldiers left their mulatto progeny in the South, and the carpet-baggers who followed them cohabited with Negro women. No one, however, attempted to force racial intermarriage upon the defeated South. Yet the disappearance of the American Negro through assimilation with the whites remains the dream of many Negroes. Professor Kelly Miller, who has spoken frequently for his people, puts the case as succinctly as anyone:

> Amalgamation of all the diverse elements of our cosmopolitan population would indeed be the surest and most expeditious means of solving the race problem. If physical dissimilarities disappeared, race prejudice would have no visible means of support. In the long run it might, indeed, be wisest for the Anglo-Saxon to adopt this method of getting rid of a troublesome and complicated situation. (*Negro Year Book,* p. 75, 1931–32.)

Professor Miller's reasoning is impeccable. Amalgamation of the races would indeed cause the American Negro to disappear, because there are only about 12 or 13 millions of Negroes in the United States as against 115 millions of whites. With the

Negro's disappearance would go the Negro problem. There is only one stumbling-block. The white people of the country will not adopt the proposed solution. They will not intermarry with Negroes for the sake of "getting rid of a troublesome and complicated situation." And the very statement of the proposed solution of the problem in these terms causes the Negro to sink lower in the esteem of the white man of the Delta.

He is driven to feel that the Negro is utterly without pride of race or hope for posterity. He sees him as lacking in spiritual stamina and integrity of soul. He observes the strange spectacle of more than twelve million people clamoring for their own racial extinction. And in essence he notes that the expressed points of view of Negro leaders are either hypocritical or false.

These leaders are at constant pains to point out the extraordinary progress which Negroes have made in many fields in America since slavery. Negro publications recite constantly and with obvious and justified pride the achievements of Negro artists, athletes, actors, professional and business men. They boast that they have given a music to unmusical America. They show the constantly growing roster of Negro graduates of white and Negro universities and colleges. They deny that the aptitude of the Negro for education is less than that of the white man. They deny that his intellectual potentialities are feebler, and declare that, given the white man's opportunity, the Negro is his match in any and all fields.

Pride of race may or may not be a good thing for the world. Yet it is human to be proud of achievements within the bosom of one's own family or one's own group. It is undeniable that the Negro has made extraordinary progress in America in the short space of years that separate him from slavery. If, then, it be true that mentally he is in no way inferior to the white, if indeed his progress under grave difficulties has been without parallel, if he has piled up his achievements within so few years, what miracles may he not accomplish in the next century or two?

In the face of these facts which the Negro himself asserts to be true, the white man of the Delta poses certain questions. If you are genuinely proud of your achievements, he says, if indeed you have the capabilities that you assert, why do you not want to continue on your way as a people hugging fiercely to your breast the burning facts of miracles accomplished in the face of almost insuperable difficulties? If you have a distinctive Negro contribution to make to white civilization, why do you not want to make it, so that it will stand for all time an immemorial refutation of the slander that you are inferior to the whites? Why do you seek for extinction? Why do you clamor for obliteration? Is it because your lot as a Negro is hard in America and you would take the easy way of committing race suicide by plunging into the vast sea of whites who surround you? Other minorities have suffered as bitterly as you ever have, yet they have persisted and have survived and become stronger and have preserved their integrity and their souls. Surely you are not less strong of spirit than they, or less tough of mind? And if you are, what then have you to give to the whites in return for assimilation with you? Perhaps the glory of life lies in struggle. Who knows? And it may be that down the centuries, if you keep yourselves whole, this will be your immortal contribution to white civilization — that you preserved whole and clean the unassailable temple of your own integrity as a people.

The *average white man* of the Delta sees the Negro as a human being with a soul, but of a definitely lower order than the whites. God put him on earth as He put all other creatures. There is a place for him in the world, hope of happiness here, and of immortality in heaven, but it is clear on the testimony of the Bible that God did not intend the Negro to be the equal of the white man. As against these convictions, all the evidence of the anthropologists to the contrary is as the chattering of jaybirds.

If the argument is advanced that the Negro in America has not yet had the time or the opportunity to demonstrate his capabilities for advancement and for making definite contributions to white culture, the white man of this region is unimpressed. He points to Africa. There the Negro has lived for centuries in a free society of his own making under his own tribal systems.

But he created no culture which affected the outside world. He evolved no codes of laws which were adopted by other people. He erected no monuments of importance, painted no pictures, made no sculpture save wood sculpture of which the world has only recently become aware. The African Negro built no great cities; made no contributions to exploration, no long sea voyages of discovery or of commerce to distant lands. Each African tribe had, it is true, a culture which was suited to the needs of a rude society. But they did not succeed even in bending the prodigal resources of nature to their own needs. It was only with the coming of the white man that the natural riches of the continent began to be used.

Yet while the Negroes of Africa dreamed away the uncounted centuries, great contemporary cultures rose and fell not only in widely separated parts of the world, but in lands near to them. The Cretan, the Babylonian, the Greek, the Egyptian, the Persian, the Roman, the Maya, and the Inca civilizations rose to their heights and collapsed while Africa slumbered through time. The evidences of their activities are everywhere. The ruins of their buildings and temples are all over the earth; their art is gathered in museums; their writings and laws are collected in books. Mankind has been enormously enriched because they lived. But the Negro in his jungle home died and was born again and again in his children through thousands of years, and left no imperishable traces of his going or coming. And this because, in the opinion of the Delta white man, he was incapable of accomplishing more than the ordering of a rude society at a low state of intellectual and artistic development.

In the Delta the Negro is regarded as not only mentally inferior to the white man, but also as morally inferior. He is thought of as lacking in those basic qualities which distinguish the higher order of man. The keystone of modern civilization is the family. Implicit in the concept of family life are certain deep-rooted, powerful feelings: loyalty, self-sacrifice, sympathy, foresight, responsibility, and affection. Family life in the sense that the white man understands it does not, on the whole, exist among Delta Negroes. The absorbing interest of white mankind, which is the proper rearing of children who are the result of a lifelong union between one man and one woman, is an interest not shared by the vast mass of Delta Negroes. And the white man feels that a people lacking in this most essential element of his civilization is not yet even prepared to set out upon the long road which leads to the culture which he has erected and of which he is proud.

When the Deltan regards the position and status of the Negro in the North his convictions are strengthened. He sees that essentially his viewpoint toward the Negro is that of the Northern white man, although there may be superficial differences of treatment and conduct.

Intermarriage between Negroes and whites, for instance, is permitted by law in the North. Massachusetts and New York are seats of alleged liberalism toward the Negro. They have no Jim Crow laws. The two races attend or may attend common schools and share common facilities of tranportation. Negroes vote, serve on juries, sit as judges and as legislators. Numerically they constitute a tiny fraction of the population of these states. And they may intermarry with whites. The fact is, however, that these marriages are rare. And when a white man or a white woman marries a Negro he or she is usually of the lowest stratum of white society.

The theory is that racial minorities tend to become absorbed by racial majorities where no insuperable obstacles are placed in the way of amalgamation. The Negroes of New York and New England are a definite racial minority. No obstacles to intermarriage are placed in their way by law. They are willing, even eager, to intermarry.. But they do not because white men and white women willing to marry them can rarely be found. Absorption of the minority may proceed at a snail's pace by illicit relations on the fringes of the races. It does not proceed frontally and quickly by way of legal marriage. The white man of the Delta concludes, therefore, that intermarriage with Negroes is as repugnant to the whites of the North as it is to him.

When he regards other activities of the Negro in the North, he sees that there the Negro is actually the victim of as many restrictions and prejudices as he is in the Delta. No Negro in this section would dream of trying to put up at any hotel save one which caters exclusively to Negroes. He would not try to get a meal save in a Negro restaurant. In New York a Negro may theoretically get a room in any hotel of the city and dine where he pleases. But he does not and cannot.

The great hotels and restaurants of New York always find it possible to deny rooms to the Negro whether he be of high or low degree. The Negro does not stop at the Waldorf. He does not take cocktails with his white or Negro friends at the Ritz bar. He neither gives luncheons nor attends them at the Plaza. He may be thoroughly presentable, well-behaved, able and willing to pay. Under the laws of the state governing inns and hotels he is entitled upon these premises to use the facilities of the hotels and restaurants of New York. But he cannot actually use them at all, or only upon terms of severe humiliation. It is made clear to him that he is not wanted. It is true that the aversion to his presence is not exhibited with the brutal frankness of the Delta; it is manifested more subtly and more cruelly with a thousand evasions and excuses. The result is the same in both places: the Negro is excluded.

In the theaters and motion-picture houses of the Delta the whites sit on the lower floor and the Negroes in the gallery. The custom is clearly defined and no member of either race ever thinks of flouting it. In New York there is no such custom, nor does the law provide for separate seating of the races. Yet the New York Negro who attempts to buy theater tickets often runs into difficulties. He is told that none are available, or that when they are available he will be notified. If he secures seats by the stratagem of buying them through a white man, he is often made to feel uncomfortable once he has sat down. His white neighbors are likely to make it clear by their actions and their glances that they resent his presence in their midst.

When the Negro goes into court because of discriminations against him in theaters and other places open to the public, he usually wins his suit. The laws of the state give him certain rights which the people of the state are constantly at pains to deny him. Ingenious schemes have therefore been evolved by theater-owners which enable them to exclude a Negro without giving him grounds for an action against them. One owner found that his orchestra chairs could be made to collapse by removing two pins from them. He arranged to have a few chairs made ready for instant collapse, and Negroes were sold seats to these chairs. When the inevitable fall occurred, the management apologized, regretted that it had no more seats for the evening, returned the patron's money, and the Negroes left the theater before the curtain went up. The Delta is free at least of that kind of hypocrisy and chicanery.

In this area Negroes live in definitely segregated parts of the towns to which they give picturesque names. The Negro section of one town is called "Balance Jew," because the lots on which they erected houses were bought on deferred payments and they were busy for a long time paying the balance due. In another town the Negroes live in "Lick Skillet"; in still another they dwell in "New Africa"; and they have given a name almost metaphysical to the Negro section of a small town, "Spot Without a Wrinkle."

No Negro in the Delta would attempt to buy or rent a house in a white neighborhood. In New York Negroes are free theoretically to live where they please. Actually the majority of them live in one or more segregated areas. Bitter conflicts between the races have been caused in the North because Negroes have rented or bought property in white neighborhoods. If, for instance, a Negro tried to acquire a house in Sutton Place, and there is no reason in the law why he should not, a loud howl would go up from every white owner in that section. If he succeeded in making the purchase, real estate values would drop and there would be general consternation in the neighborhood. Why?

A bloody civil war was fought to free the Negro from slavery. The army and navy are federal establishments. Yet there have been extraordinarily few Negro cadets at West Point, and no Negro graduates of Annapolis. In the regular army there have been a handful of Negro officers; in the navy the Negro is welcome only as a messboy or cook. When there is a Republican administration in the saddle at Washington a few federal jobs and appointments are thrown to Negroes as a sop for the Negro vote; but generally they are not wanted or welcomed on their own by any administration. In the federal judiciary no Negro has ever sat as judge. In the Diplomatic Corps Negroes have never had a place except as minister to the Negro republic of Liberia. In the very seat of the federal government, under the dome of the Capitol, the Negro is excluded from dining in the Senate restaurant, although he is welcome there as waiter. Why?

Shall the Negro have even the right to live? Shall he be permitted to earn his bread and butter and support those dependent upon him? The Delta believes that he has not only the right to live, but gives him every opportunity to pursue that right. No Negro starves here. No Negro goes homeless. He finds employment in industry and on the land. Certain avenues of employment are, however, closed to him, and he is meeting with keener competition in every field from whites. He is not hired by the stores, banks, and corporations of the Delta as clerk, accountant, cashier, or typist.

The same kinds of work are, however, usually denied him in New York. You will look in vain for a Negro clerk in the great department stores of that city. You will not find Negro typists or accountants in the offices of corporations. They are not employed as ushers or ticket-takers in the theaters and moving picture-houses, nor as waiters or elevator operators or as bellboys in the great majority of hotels and restaurants. They do not find employment even as guards, conductors, or motormen on the transportation systems; they do not drive buses. In the beauty shops there are no Negro women workers, except maids.

The New York Negro, unless he is a professional man or the owner of an independent business, finds employment usually as a domestic servant or in the lower and more disagreeable forms of menial labor. Yet there are any number of Negroes in New York who could successfully hold positions in many fields which are closed to them. The available jobs are always given to the whites. Why?

The white man of the Delta visiting New York sees that there is some social fraternizing between whites and Negroes. He finds that this usually occurs among two classes of whites — the lower and the upper. The great middle class is aloof from associations of this kind. Its members who have not reached the definitely marked position to which they aspire and are socially insecure are fearful of the stigma which may come to them through associating with Negroes, and therefore refrain. The lower-class whites who have no social position to lose feel free to fraternize with Negroes. And the upper class whites who are so secure in their social position that they cannot lose it feel equally free.

The mingling of Negroes socially with the lowest stratum of whites sets no precedent for other whites and opens the door of social equality no wider. In America the masses take their cues and their clothes from the classes. Nor does the association of a few Negroes with a few upper-class whites have any effect upon the opinion of the vast majority of the white population in general, nor upon the body of the upper-class whites in particular. These relationships are usually damned and distorted because they are not free and frank. Sometimes they are plainly sexual. But it is deeply rooted in the American tradition of serio-comic humor that sexual relations do not constitute an introduction to society. The gulf still yawns between the bedroom and the drawing room. Sometimes the relationships between whites and Negroes are intellectual or pseudo-intellectual. But they are warped and circumscribed so far as social equality is concerned.

There cannot be a mingling of peoples on terms of complete social equality free from condescension and studied tolerance, unless the persons concerned are willing to grant even theoretically the logical consequences which flow or may flow from the free meeting of social equals of both sexes — marriage. That is a consequence which the upper class New Yorker is not willing to grant even theoretically. The men will not contemplate the possibilities of marrying Negro women, nor will the women consider marrying Negro men, save in the most extraordinarily rare instances. This in turn precludes all those associations which occur between equals: dining and dancing in common in public places; attending theater together; going on journeys together; or indulging in sports.

In New York, as elsewhere, a great deal of entertaining is done in hotels and restaurants and night clubs. The whites, however, who receive Negroes socially invariably entertain them in their homes and apartments at dinner or at cocktail parties. Southerners and Latins regard it as a compliment to be entertained in the homes of their hosts rather than in hotels or restaurants open to the public. The white man of the Delta wonders whether New York whites who receive Negroes only in their homes do this because they wish to lay this token of hospitality at their feet graciously, or have they other and more subtle reasons?

How then and in what manner is the Negro received socially in New York? If he is an intellectual he is regarded somewhat patronizingly as a phenomenon, a specimen of exotica, a biological sport who is an enchanting deviation from the norm. If he is a singer or a pianist he pays for his entertainment by singing or playing the piano. Whatever his accomplishments may be, he is often regarded by his white hosts and their friends with the naïve wonder with which a child might regard a parrot reciting poetry. And a Negro of the most meager artistic or intellectual ability is often invited to white homes where white men of the same caliber would not be asked at all. This is an advantage which flows to the thicker-skinned Negro who is anxious for white associations. But to the more sensitive Negro it is an insulting attitude to be invited to white gatherings not as a man but as a rare zoological specimen.

Negroes themselves are frequently aware of this inverted form of white condescension; some of them use it for their own purposes; others scorn it. A Negro student of literature to whom I talked a little while ago was keenly conscious of the dubious advantage that the Negro writer enjoys not primarily as an artist but as a Negro. "The truth is," he said to me, "that any number of books by Negroes would not have been published had they been written by whites. They were published only because they were written by Negroes. And they were bought and read by whites because it afforded them a pleasant sense of condescension mixed with wonder."

The white visitor to New York from the Delta concludes that essentially the same discriminations that run against the Negro in the Delta run against him in New York. And he wonders how much wider and deeper these discriminations would be if the racial percentages of the two areas were reversed. What would be the white man's attitude and conduct toward the Negro in New York if 70 per cent of the population were Negro?

The prophetic voice of Abraham Lincoln comes down through the years. In 1862 he said to a delegation of Negroes who called on him: "You and we are different races. . . . But even when you cease to be slaves you are yet far removed from being placed on an equality with the white race. . . . The aspiration of men is to enjoy equality with the best when free, but on this continent not a single man of your race is made the equal of a single man of ours. . . . Go where you are treated best, and the ban is still upon you."

The Anglo-Saxon bitterly hates, and prevents wherever possible, the marriage of his kind with black or yellow peoples. There are separate schools for Chinese in Mississippi, because by statute they are not permitted to attend white schools. Chinese took this law to the Supreme Court of Mississippi, where it was upheld.

In this case one glimpses again the extraordinary delicacy and complexity of the whole color problem in this area. There are many Chinese in the Delta. They are successful merchants. Some of them live with their Chinese wives; others have Negro mistresses and families of half-breed children. To the casual eye these children are often indistinguishable from full-blooded Chinese. The fear arose in the white community that if Chinese children were permitted to attend the public schools these Chinese-Negro half-breeds would go along. The result was that separate schools for the Chinese, at the expense of the community, were provided for by law. Theoretically these schools are of the same quality as the white schools. Actually it is impossible to make them of the same quality without prohibitive expense. Chinese children, therefore, do not enjoy the same facilities for education that are open to white children.

The leaders of the Chinese, knowing the real reason for the exclusion of their children from the public schools, hope one day to have the barriers removed. To this end they are insisting that their men shall refrain from having Negro mistresses, and no half-breed children. When they feel that they can prove to the satisfaction of the white community that the children whom they present for admittance to the white schools are racially pure Chinese, they may attempt to have the statute repealed. If they succeed, no people will have arrived at equal opportunities for education through stranger means.

The minds of the Delta Chinese, already confused by the complexities and contradictions of the alien civilization in which they live, are thrown into utter confusion by the fact that their children who are denied access to the white schools are eagerly received by the white churches. The public-school superintendent views them with a fishy eye. But the Sunday-school leader welcomes them warmly. They stand before God in equality with white children on Sunday, but on Monday they cannot stand together before the same blackboard.

The whole program and plan of Negro education in the Delta is haphazard and sketchy. The whites do not advocate classical or purely cultural education for Negroes. They believe, first of all, that the Negro should be taught to work with his hands; that it is more important for him to know how to earn a living than to be able to conjugate Latin verbs. They think that education of this kind tends to unbalance him mentally and to lose a sense of the realities about him; or in plain Delta language, to "get out of his place." The Negro's place is the status and deportment ordained for him by the white man. He must be content to remain within that status or leave the community.

Despite these beliefs, Negro education in the Delta is roughly of the same texture as that offered to the whites. The plan is not prepared with cold logic. It is not organized with an eye to the conditions under which the Negro must live when he leaves the schoolroom. The whites are being prepared either to enter college or to embark upon a way of life widely different from that open to Negroes in this area, yet both receive roughly the same kind of education. And the Negroes themselves, not content with an education of strict utilitarianism, demand and get curricula with a definite classical or cultural tinge. The blackboards of their high schools are filled with diagrams of the Peloponnesian wars; they prattle of Pericles and of Crete.

Thus it is that anticipations are being aroused in the Negro's breast which he can never hope to realize so long as he lives in the section where he was born. Demands are being created in his mind which the dominant whites will never grant within any ascertainable future; hopes are budding which can never come to fruition. A sense of frustration and bitterness must inevitably grow in the Negro's heart, and with it an increased suspicion and hatred of the whites. This in turn will deepen white suspicion and hatred of the Negro. Conditions of living for both races will be made more difficult and more intolerable. In the long run, however, it will be the weaker Negro who must pay the penalty for white muddling with education.

An education program to be worthy of the name or to be effective must have a definite aim. That aim may be to prepare the student to earn his living. Or it may have for its goal the spiritual enrichment of the student through learning for its own sake. But this is a luxury which the Delta Negro can ill afford even if he were fully prepared to receive it. In no event can any program of education in this area be fair or just to the Negro which does not contemplate his ultimate welfare, bearing in mind always the limitations which are placed upon him in this white-dominated society.

The present program prepares the Negro for the white world from which he is debarred by the whites. He finds, therefore, on leaving school, that he has been given a vision of a land whose gates are closed against him; of water with which he cannot quench his thirst; of food with which he cannot satisfy his hunger. The end is pain and confusion and bitterness.

I asked this question frequently of white men in the Delta. Let us assume that overnight your towns were emptied of all

their Negroes and their houses. In the morning there would be
a new Negro population. The men and women would be university graduates. Their manners would be your manners. Their
dress your dress. Their speech your speech. Their homes and
furnishings your home and furnishings. In every respect their
way of life would closely approximate your way of life. Would
there be more race prejudice against these Negroes than those
who now live here, or less? The answer was — more.

It follows, therefore, that if the Negro is to continue to live
in this area, all programs for the betterment of his condition must
be prepared with an eye to the cold realities of the actual situation. There is room and welcome in the Delta only for the Negro
who "stays in his place." Negroes of the kind whom I projected
in my question would not be likely to bow uncomplainingly and
silently to the will of the whites, and eventually they would be
brought into catastrophic conflict with the dominant race. The
present relatively untutored Negro of the Delta harbors no
feelings of resentment or bitterness or revenge against the whites
unless the disabilities under which he labors are too cruelly
pressed upon him. If he is able to earn a living and seek happiness among his own people, he is content. And in turn the whites
not only tolerate him, but have affection for him. The delicate
balance of harmony between the races rests squarely upon this
basis. If it is lightly disturbed without first preparing a counter-
equilibrium, both races may suffer grievously.

The Delta is fearful, too, that the vague generalities of numerous interracial groups functioning in the South may eventually
lead to difficulties. Many whites want to "do something for the
Negro" without stating definitely or knowing precisely what they
want to do. Sometimes they meet with Negroes amid sweet-
scented clouds of sentimentality and soar for a week on wings
of fancy. When they go home, both whites and Negroes realize
that they had neither the common sense nor the cold courage
to come to grips with the naked facts. The Delta has a high
disdain for many white professional workers among Negroes who
hold secure positions and receive substantial pay for their services. It feels that these men, like professional Chinese mourners,

are prepared to weep for anyone who employs them. Today they wail by the waters of Babylon for the Negroes; tomorrow they would wear sackcloth and ashes for the Armenians for a ten per cent increase in pay; and the next day their fluent eyes would run with tears for the Mohammedans of Tadjikistan if presented with sufficient tear-compelling cash. But this region has a sincere and deep respect for that minority of white men and white women everywhere who quietly and without material recompense have labored for years to improve the lot of the Negro.

All plans for the betterment of the Negro, in the opinion of the Delta white man, must be futile and sterile unless their object is to fit the Negro harmoniously into the white man's society. Nothing can be honestly promised him which the whites are not prepared to grant. And the dim generalizations of interracial committees are likely to be sheer cruelty toward him unless they are more sharply defined. It is far kinder to be brutally frank. So, too, many Negroes who are realists, freely express their disgust for their fellows and for whites who sit at round tables at endless meetings, merely to talk about belling the cat.

The vast mass of Negroes in the Delta do not vote. In order to qualify as a voter in Mississippi one must, when challenged, be able to understand and interpret to the satisfaction of an official, a section of the constitution of the state when it is read to him. If the applicant is a Negro, it is not likely that he will be able, however intelligent or learned, to satisfy the clerk that his interpretation is correct.

The Delta Negro does not serve on grand or petit juries. In one of the counties, however, Issaqueena, he does serve. Nothing more strikingly illustrates the enormous preponderance of the Negro population in this area, than the fact that there are so few whites in this county that it is often impossible to assemble a jury of twelve white men. Negroes then are called in to serve to satisfy the legal requirement that there must be twelve persons on a jury. They exercise, however, no discretion or judgment; they vote in accordance with the instructions of the white jurors.

The white man of the Delta says to the world beyond his gates: I live with my family among an overwhelming mass of

Negroes. We are Anglo-Saxon. Nowhere in the world do we intermarry with Negroes. Nowhere do we receive them on terms of social equality. Our blood cries out against it. We are determined that it shall not happen within the span certainly of our own lives. We must, therefore, although we are as kind and as just as the generality of mankind, enforce certain repressions and discriminations.

We do not give the Negro civic equality because we are fearful that this will lead in turn to demands for social equality. And social equality will tend toward what we will never grant — the right of equal marriage. As a corollary to these propositions we enforce racial separation and segregation. If certain of our men cohabit with Negro women and produce hybrid children, that is regrettable but humanly understandable. If some of us exploit Negroes, you must remember that we are merely men. If some of us are brutal in our treatment of Negroes, you will recall that in the little group of twelve who gathered about Jesus there was one who betrayed Him.

Most of us have a deep and abiding affection for the Negro. Our paternalism is not designed to enslave him. It is in our blood. The Negroes on our plantations are both our partners and our wards. Now, as in slavery, some of these plantations are filled with happy, well-treated Negroes, and some contain discontented, badly-treated blacks. So much depends and must depend upon the character of the man who runs a business. As we understand it, workers in mines, mills, stores, and factories all over the United States are frequently at the mercy of the owners of these enterprises. This situation is not peculiar to the Delta.

We do not feel that it is our duty — even if we had the wisdom and the strength — to solve the race problem of the Negro. We are primarily engaged, as are all other men, in conducting our own affairs and earning a livelihood for our wives and children. We should be glad to see the Negro improve his standard of living both for his sake and for ours. We prosper or fail to prosper together.

It is difficult to explain to you, who do not live here, the strange and enduring bonds which unite so many of us and so many Negroes in lifetime friendships in the Delta. Sometimes we are frightfully irritated with the brother in black. We wish that he had never come here. At other times we are sure that we could not live happily without him. Perhaps we are his cross, too. We distort the Negro's life. We cause aberrations in his character. And he in turn has set up grievous stresses and strains in us. His presence has sharply changed our spiritual visage. We wonder sometimes what we would be if the Negro had never come among us.

We go on living year after year in peace with thousands of Negroes. Their inner and personal lives are profound mysteries to us. They know us inwardly and outwardly. By the unfailing use of tact on both sides we get on exceedingly well. The Negro, fortunately, is master of the art of exquisite discretion. We feel, indeed, when we regard the conduct of the white and the Negro in the North toward each other, that both the blacks and the whites of the Delta have succeeded admirably in retaining a sense of proportion.

We are at all events as just and as fair as it is given to us to be. We live among tens of thousands of Negroes. You who live far from the Delta live among whites. You may meet an occasional Negro. Your life is not bound up with them as are our lives. Your economy does not rest upon their shoulders. You do not see them morning, noon, and night. We spend all our days with Negroes and yet we know them so little. Is it possible for you to know them better?

And when from the distance of an alien civilization you attempt to formulate rules of conduct for us, we beg of you to remember that necessity has its iron laws which transcend all others. It was Paul who said, "All things are lawful for me; but not all things are expedient."

CHAPTER 9

Eva Mae in Boston

Eva Mae Brown is a young Negro girl of twenty-four. She was born in Memphis, but has spent nearly all of her life in the heart of the Delta. In appearance, points of view, aspirations, and attitudes she resembles thousands of other Negro women in this section. She has no white blood so far as she knows, and indeed appears to be a full-blooded Negro. Her skin is brown, her nose squat, her forehead markedly recessive, and her kinky hair is tortured into a resemblance of straightness by the liberal and unremitting application of greasy oils. She is gay, smiling, pleasure-loving, utterly irresponsible, artlessly engaging, and usually happy.

She stopped school in the ninth grade and since that time has been employed in various capacities in the homes of white people. Despite a succession of men in her life, and a marked aptitude for love, she has recently married and, temporarily at least, retired from the world. Her husband is "a man who gets $9.20 a week driving an ice-truck. We gets along on that all right. I pays $1.25 a week for rent, and groceries don't never cost us more than $3 a week."

Eva Mae had never been beyond the borders of the Delta until "some rich white folks took me to Boston." Her account of what happened to her on her journey from the Delta to Boston, her thoughts while on the way, the effect on her mind of what she saw, and her actions while there sharply illuminate the mentality of an average Negro of this section. Despite the fact that she

163

found it pleasant and novel, if a bit frightening, to go to beer gardens "with white mens" and to teas with white servants, she preferred to return to the Delta.

In Boston, she told me, "if you gets sick, don't nobody, neither white or colored, care whether you dies or not. Down here a whole lot of white people are mean to the colored, but it's a whole lot of white folks will take care of they colored people. If I want me a dress an' I'm workin' for a white lady she will get me a dress. If I get down sick I know she'll get me a doctor.

"White people up Nawth will give you your wages and that's all. If they advertises for what they calls a personal maid they expects you to know a whole lot about it, and they won't take no time to teach you like they will here. It's many a colored girl maid right in Greenville don't hardly know how to do nothing 'cept sweep a room with a broom and make a bed. Boston ladies wouldn't take up no time with 'em. I had to look over my mind a whole lots 'cause I coulda got me a job up there, but then I figgered I'd be better off here if I got in trouble or got down. So I come on home."

Eva Mae, who prides herself on her ability to write, wrote this account of her journey from the Delta to Boston, and her life while there. I set it down here just as she gave it to me.

Once upon a time I was working for a dr an' his wife who live in Greenville, Mississippi, on Broadway St. I work for them three months are better. They was well please with me in every way. So they had to go to Boston for a year on Biseness. They left an was gone a month an wrote back to me asking if I would like to come up there an work for them. I wrote them I would.

So they got ready an all set and send for me which was on 5th of October 1934 when I riceved my first letter giving me full instructions what to do an how to come. first I washed my Blankets an sheets. Pack my box. I riceved my money. A white lady friend of the one I work for went to the Bus Station with me. Bought my ticket Sunday 4 o'clock, October 15th 1934.

My first stop was Leland a small town. The next was Rosedale. I was well acquainted with it. I stop an git a small drink to keep my worry down after being on such a long trip leaving my Peoples behind to go 1700 miles to work for the Peoples who had offered me such a good opertunity to earn good an see a lots of the world.

The bus arrived in Clarksdale at 8 something. I had left an pass all the relitives I had except my Aunt and Cousin who live at my home in Memphis. I knew then everything I had was left behind even to my Boy friend. On my way to a new world to meet new People see new things an make new friends.

Our next stop was Nashville Tennessee. I new no other there at all. Now my life began. The bus was there 15 minits. Went at a Cafe an Bought my Breakfast. Got back on the Bus. Left out for Knoxville Tennessee. Such a different. Got acquainted with a boy who worked at the Bus Station. He taken me out for a good time since my Bus didn't leave till 4 hours.

We went to a flat an got a private room. Drink Played Cards. Sent out an order our supper on a tray an Beer also Cigarets. Those 4 hours seem to be going very fast. We dance By the radio then came back to the station 5 minits before my Bus leave out. All the way from Knoxville to New York I had something to think about.

Now I had to stop in Philadelfa for my Breakfest next morning. The Bus was there about 20 minutes. I walked into a Druggest and Lunchon all to-gether. I saw no Colored Peoples at all. Nothing but white. We all had to go to the same rest Room which I was not use to. I was afraid they might Scold at me for useing the same Room the white Ladies did. But I got up nerves an went to it. I came out all right there.

I told the Clerk I wanted a ham sanwich. He asked me if I wanted my Bread Toasted. I look at him very hard because I wasen use to such kind words an such a pleasant face. I ancered him: You may Toasted it on one side. Please he asked me if I would except Butter on it. I say Yes Sir. When it was all Ready I asked him would he wrap it up for me. He did. I went and got on the Bus an when it left I began eating my sanwich.

When we got to New York I had to exchange Bus again an wait till the Bus got ready to leave out that next morning for Boston. While setting in the waiting room it come to me my Lady I was going to work for told me to phone her from New York so I ask a Bus Station Boy who was a Colored Boy jest about how much would it cost me to make a Telephone call from New York to Boston. He said girl it will cost you about 75¢ I am sure. So I gave him a long look as tho I didn't Belive him an said thank you.

I didn't no how to use those kind of phones they had so he saw I didn't an ask me would I like for him to make the call for me. I told him no an turn away. From him I walk over to the white ticket officer an ask him how much would it cost me to call from there to Boston. He turn an look at me quick and said Go over there an ask that Colored Boy. He no know how much it is. He will call up for you. I say Yes Sir.

I turn an walk Back cheaple an set down. So the boy went out of the room an stayed a little while an come back to the door an call me. He say Girl come here a minute. I walk to the door. He said Where are you from. I told him Memphis Tennessee. He asked if there was my home. I said yes. Well have you ever been here before. I said No. He said Well where are you going? I told him to Boston. He reply Why don't you stay over a day or so an let me give you a good time. I told him I could not. Then he ask me why so. I explain why I had to hurry. He gave a smiling look and said, Oh I understand. Then give me your address I will drop you a card. So I did.

When we had finished talking I asked him would he mine making this call to Boston for me. He said Oh no I don't mine. I gave him the Ladys name an Phone number. He walk over to the Phone and Put his finger in a little hole. Pick up the receiver started to caring that little hole around and around then started to talk.

I got close up where I could here the Lady talking. After he had finished he called back to the operated asking how much was the call. I heard her say 75¢. So I gave him 75¢ an thank him. He reply forget about it an smile. Went out again and come back and set down beside of me and ask was I very tired. I said not so much. He said maybe if you had a little smile it would help you some. I reply I am sure it would. Then come go outside with me as far as the door. I walk out there with him. He out with a full pint. His boy friend walk up and we all Three drink.

It was about 4:45 then and By that time all my embaresment had left me, the way I had spoke to him about the phone calling. He went away then and told me good by and good luck hoping he would meet me again. Maybe I would be afraid to trust him an laugh. I felt very cheap again.

I set there two more hours. Then I went an order 2 eggs an bacon an a glass of milk costed me 35¢. When my bus got ready it was 7:45 an I was sleepy and tired. The Bus then stop at a place called Lake Providence, Mass. Everybody left the Bus for dinner and I followed the crowd. All went into a big Cafateria with a long counter on one side an the other side was full of peoples. They got there trays one by one an I watch them. The Clerk ask me was it something for me. I ancered In a minute. I pick up a tray and walk up closter to the counter put it up there. The Lady who waited on the trays put me a knife and fork an spoon on my tray. I ask her for a bowl of soup and she put the soup on the tray with a slick of butter on a little butter plate.

I helt my tray an look all around. I didn't see no place to set down. Every table was full. Only 2 or 3 had one Person at them an they was white. So I walk over very slow and ease down in a chair at a table where a white man was eating. Drink up my soup an ate my Bread but left the butter. I was almost afraid Because I was the only colored person in the whole big Cafateria. Finely I got up. Everybody was ready to leave.

I got back on the Bus Hungry as ever. I didn't get enough to eat because I didn't no what to do. Now our next stop was Boston. I felt better.

The Lady who I was to work for was not at the Station when my Bus got there so I got one of the Bus Station boys to phone her. She came in about 20 minutes all white an fair looking an had gain some Pounds since those last 6 weeks had pass. She came in pick up my large suit case an started to walk off with it. Her husband which was a Dr came in an pick up my Big Bundle of quilts an blankets. I follow them out. Everybodys eyes was on me seems like as we all walked out to a small one seated coupe of an old Model.

The Streets was crowded with Peoples. Such a sight to be seen. In the Place of the Peoples stopping for the cars to pass the cars had to stop for the peoples. Passing by the schools white and colored childrens was playing all to-gether. We had about 9 miles to go to a place called Newton Centre Mass where nothing but rich peoples live. Every house had from 1 to 2 to 4 maids and they was white.

Now I often wonder why they had sent way to Mississippi to get me to work. Whether it was because she had promised me in the spring are what. So finely I found out because it was cheaper to get me to work than it was to hire a girl up there. But I didn't mind it at all since I had a chance to have such a good time an did.

I stayed in my room every evening I got off. No place to go an no one to talk to. Nothing to do but walk from my Bath Room to my bed Room. My salary was $7.50 a week an Room an Boad. My days off was Saturday afternoon an Sunday evening.

One night finely a maid who was a French girl an a old maid who hadnt Never been married come to the bottom of the stairs in my peoples house an called me asking me to come down an set with her for a while. So I powdered up my face an fix my hair an went down.

She had two more girls setting on the sleeping porch knitting something I haden seen for years. One was knitting a sweater an the other a pair of mittens. Something I wore when I was a girl. The maid who was a old maid and haden ever been married interduced me to the other girls. I didn't do much talking. Jest set an look an smile. I set with them from about 7 o'clock to 9:30 an ask them to ex-cuse me I was a little tired. So they did.

I went up an got my ready for my Bed an went to crying thinkin about home. I finely went to sleep.

One night a white maid she ask me to go out an take tea with her. I fix up an we went out. 3 more maids joined us. We was all going to the same place, but I still was the only colored one along. We didn't have very far to go an when we all walk in 4 are 5 more maids was there. They was white to. The one who invited us start telling jokes an a few more jokes was told. I laugh along with them but how different I felt.

They talk to me a while asking me where did I come from. I told them. A little later tea was serve. We had hot tea Cookies and Cheese and Baker Bread. I watch everybody. Did as they did. We stay there until 12 o'clock since the maids white people was out of town visiting. We had snow there over 2 feets deep at the time But it made no difference. They was about snow there like we are about rain in Mississippi.

One night I walked out to catch the bus. I haden been no-where. While standing there a fish man come along in a truck an pick me up ask me how far was I going. I told him to town an he taken me there. I walk the streets awhile an bought my Boss man a paper. Got on street car and wrode it awhile then got off. I ask a man to show me where Brookline Village was at. So he did. I got my bus for Chestnut hill an walk a mile from there to home.

The next time I went out to Boston I had me on my new fur coat. I was jest a twitching walking down the street. Somebody come up an put his arm around me. I look up an it was a white man. I was scared to death. He say Girl are you accompanit. I say No Sir. He say May I come along. I say Yes Sir. He say where are you going. I told him to the beer garden. I was fritened walking that way with a white man but I got up my nerves and never let on. We had a good time drinking beer. Then he stopped at a drug store on the way home and got a pint of whiskey an I went to his flat. He was mighty nice to me after that. He was a big blonde looking man that worked for a oil company.

A colored boy who work at the Bus Station come out one Sunday about a month later. He had talk to me the day I came to Boston. He call me one Saturday an ask for a date. I was glad to give him one so I could go out in town again. We walk awhile then rode the street cars awhile then we went to a Picture Show. I injoyed it very much since they last 2 hours longer than the ones down South. When we come out he ask if I wish for supper so I except the offer. We walk into a cafateria all decorated with pretty blue an yellow lights an nice clean white tables. Everyone had a Bill of Fare in the center of them.

I look the Bill of Fare over an choose spagetti an meat ball an lemon pie. So did my Boy friend. When we had finish he walk out with me an seen me on a street car strate home. The worst part of it was I didn't like this Boy so much But jest for the first time an first date I went on out with him.

Now I new the town a little so I stayed at home for a long time until I had made me enough money to dress like the other peoples I had seen. One night I went to a big store an bought myself a coupla dresses an a new winter coat.

Then I started going about. My first Boy friend I had met I really liked got jealous an threatened to kill me so I quit him an started out with another bunch of boys an girls. Finely one day this boy I had quit new that I went to a beauty shop on Saturday. So he caught me outside and tried to cut my throat with a sharp meat knife. I run inside a grocery store an slammed the door. The police got the boy. They give him six months in the jailhouse for that an 4 more years when they found out he had jumped his parole. I know a colored girl right here in Greenville that killed another girl about a man. They didn't give her but one year in jail. White folks in the north is tough on you when they catch you in trouble. They easier in that way in Mississippi.

I began to be afraid of the Boston boys an I stay at home for a long time. Finely a good looking boy who work on a ship come along. I fell for him. He had lots of good looking close an so did I. He started caring me out to dances.

My first dance was at the Big State Ball Room where Cab Calloway played for us. We also had a big spot light to shower down on us. That was something I was not use to. How thrill an excited I was when I first seen one. Of course the thrill come in on me because I was all Dress up in a silver evening gown with silver slippers to match with my hair all Marcell an my good looking wrist watch. My face all made up. My Boy friend was wearing a light gray suit also a pair of gray suedes shoes to match. He was tall light ginger cake color with good hair.

I seemst to be having the best time I ever had in my life. He also induce me to a lot of his friends who I was Proud to meet an they all would ask me where did I come from. He told them from Tennessee. So the next time they meet me they call me

Tennessee. I didn't mine that a bit jest so long as I could keep it hid I was from Mississippi. Everybody up there seem to be afraid of Mississippi. You seldom heard that name mention.

I was up there 9 months. My white people was ready to leave an come back South. All the boys an girls tried so hard to keep me from leaving But I had to come back to see my people. So my last 2 weeks I made all the Partys an Dances also Picture Shows I could with diffrent ones. An my last night with my boy friend.

CHAPTER 10

Preachers, Deacons, and Undertakers

On a Saturday, as the evening sun goes down on the wide flat lands of Trail Lake plantation, and the illimitable horizon flames suddenly red beyond the borders of the world, mules and tools are placed in the barns, and the people of the plantation go home to put on their Sunday clothes for a bit of gayety after a week of labor. Usually Negroes do not work on Saturday afternoons, but there has been much rain and the cotton is in the grass. For six days, men, women, children, and mules have stood sweat-drenched in the fields, going out in the cool darkness before the sun has risen, and going home again with the coming of darkness. Weeklong, plows stirred the rich earth; weeklong, hoes flashed in the sun. Now the fields run endlessly to the horizon swept clean of grass; cotton plants heavy-fruited stand solidly rooted to the earth in their abundant fatness; tall corn thick-clustering sways slowly in the evening breeze. Crops are good, Saturday night is at hand, tomorrow will be Sunday, and the Negroes of the plantation are happy.

Long before the last bird has settled to roost in the trees along the banks of the Bogue Phalia, Negroes begin to stream in groups of twos and threes toward the local point of life and living in the little community — the plantation store. They come slowly across the fields, but even in the dim distance one knows that they are Negroes. They move with a curious shuffling walk that brings them liquidly and leisurely to their destination. The young women sway on their hips with a grace born partly of

carrying burdens on their heads, partly of their proud consciousness of sex, lusty, free, and unashamed. The men — especially
the younger men — strut or stroll with free-swinging arms and a
certain rolling of the torso that white men never achieve. The
spaces are wide on Delta plantations. The skies are high. Time
is long. Life is to be enjoyed in the present moment. "It ain't
no need to hurry, 'cause de Lawd he gwine gether you in when
He ready, don't keer what you does."

With the coming of darkness the air grows suddenly soft and
the sky swarms with stars. In front of the store a single naked
electric bulb casts a dim circle of light. Under it two small black
boys work furiously at the task of polishing the shoes of two
dark languid gentlemen, who stand on one foot in attitudes of
lordly ease, hats tilted far back on their heads, smoking "Two
Orphans segars" and greeting their friends with loud cries of
delight. "Hi-di there, Clabber," one of them yells. "What you
say, nigger?" "Howdy, Tylertown. How you gittin' 'long on de
deadenin'?" "Boy, where you come from? I sho thought you
wuz in de jailhouse."

The boys in the meanwhile whip their polishing cloths into
jazz tempos on the shoes of the customers, make them pop with
loud reports, smear on paste with rhythmical up-and-down movements of their hands, and conclude the job finally with two or
three loud bangs. It is a point of pride with them — a mark of
careful craftsmanship and a lightening of tasks — not only to
cause shoes to shine like mirrors, but also make music with their
polishing rags as they work. Later when they are grown they
will soften with song the rigors of labor.

Before the gentlemen step down from the boxes on which their
shoes are growing to a brighter brown, a plantation beauty
flutters mincingly up to one of them with diminutive gait. Her
free-swinging stride is sadly diminished by the painful tightness
of Sunday shoes upon feet that have been free all week of fetters.

"Manny," she says, "is you gwine care me to de dance?"

"Gal," he replies, "I ain't stud'in' 'bout car'in' you to no dance.
Heah you is doin' ugly all de time wid dat sloo-footed nigger
from over on Triumph and won't give nobody else none, den

you comes axin' me to care you to de dance. They's three or fo'
wimmens right heah right now dat's runnin' me down like they
was barnyard roosters."

"Ain't you heered de news?" she inquires. "Me and Bubber
done split up. An' hit wuz 'bout you. I been lovin' you a long
time. I say to Adaleen jes' fo' I lef' de house tonight, 'Adaleen,
does you reckon dat's a blind nigger I been makin' dem eyes at?'
Manny, I sho could love you good. Come on care me to de dance."

"Ne' mine all dat 'bout dem eyes. You meets me by de gin-
house in 'bout ten minutes. Den us'll see 'bout goin' to de dance."

A Negro man stumbles over the feet of a woman in the crowd
in front of the store. He immediately says, "Ex-cuse me," and
she replies, "Youse 'scusable." Plantation Negroes have good
manners, and a rough, rustic grace. They have not yet arrived at
the so-called civilization of some white people, among whom by
an inversion of values, rudeness has become a virtue, and pro-
fanity an evidence of virility.

Suddenly a wagon rumbles up out of the darkness, dripping
water. The driver jumps down from his seat, lights two or three
lanterns, and in a loud sing-song cries his wares:

"De catfish man is here. De catfish man is here. Bolivar Lake
catfish. Boliver Lake catfish. Spoonbill cats from Bolivar Lake.
An' channels fum de river."

At the sound of his voice he is surrounded by a crowd. The
catfish man brings out his scales and does a flourishing business.
A mass of people press closely around him, clamoring to be
served, fearful that all the fish will be sold before their turn
comes. Negroes and discerning whites know that the catfish is
one of the most delicious of God's gifts to man. The fish-seller,
busied with making change, weighing fish, and putting strings
through their gills so that they can be dragged along by his customers, bursts into song:

> "I got yellow cat and the white cat,
> Got everything but the tom cat,
> And he's on the inside.
> If you believe I'm lying
> Buy one and try him.
> Take him home
> And then you fry him."

In a short while the fish are sold and the catfish man whips up his mules and moves out into the darkness from which he came. Three journeymen barbers now come and prepare to do business under the dim light in front of the store. During the week they till the fields: on Saturday nights they become hairdressers and ministrants of beauty. Each brings his kit of instruments and a soda-pop case on which his customers sit. Their work is simplified because only one style of hair trimming is in vogue and no man who makes the slightest pretense of fashion would tolerate any other kind. Most of the scalp is cleanly shaved, leaving a fringe of hair sticking sharply upward from the forehead. This is called, with the superb grandiloquence of the plantation Negro, the "high English," or the "English brush-back."

The crowd swirls about the barbers unmindful of the arcs of their shears or the parabolas of their razors. Often one of them stops his work to talk or swap jokes with passing friends, disappears in the darkness to fill his shaving-cup with water from a near-by pump, or reassures a timid customer with the cheerful guarantee, "Does I cut yo' th'oat I gives yo' money back."

Inside, the store is close-packed with Negroes, asking for "A nickel's worth of them cheese, Boss"; "Is you got any Sunday stockings for a lady, Mister George?" "Cap'n, please, suh, reach me a can of snuff," and "White folks, gimme a sack of meal." A little black child, the whites of his eyes large in the dim light, shyly places five cents on the counter, points to something in the showcase, and receives in his outstretched hand a "stage-plank" — a ginger cake covered with pink icing, the shape roughly of the stage planks of Mississippi river boats. Next to the child stands a tall youth digging "sardine-fish" out of a can with his pocketknife, and a brown woman buying a length of gingham for a dress. A black field hand who complains to the clerks of a "misery in my stomach," purchases a box of "Cannon Balls," a famous purgative, while his companion looks lovingly at a shining guitar hanging from the ceiling.

The clerks rush from one end of the store to the other, crowding the activities of a week into the few short hours of Saturday night. They sell flour, alarm clocks, kerosene, fish-hooks, underwear, raisins, axle grease, stick candy, lard, medicines, salt, meat, hair-straighteners, and cake-flavorings. The plantation store is all things to all people. It is the rural Negro's place of clearance for his business; his postoffice; his club; his point of contact with the outside world.

Preachers, elders, deacons, sisters, plain "pul-pit hands" and officers of burial societies mingle with the crowd and are cordially received by everyone. Death and dying are omnipresent in the minds of Delta Negroes; burial and the grave occupy a place in the forefront of their thoughts; and those who have to do with them are important persons in the community.

The majority of Negroes in this area are Baptists. White Baptist missionaries were among the earliest in the field when the slaves came to America, and, largely as a result of their efforts, more Negroes are members of this denomination than of any other. There are also Negro Methodists, Episcopalians, and Roman Catholics.

Doctrinally the Negro's religion is simple. It is merely a belief in the existence of a powerful God, and in the divinity and overflowing love of Jesus for sinful mortals on earth. Religion is a source of enormous and unending solace to him, an emotional outlet of great importance, and a personal possession of his own upon which the white man cannot and does not intrude.

There is no doubt in the Negro's mind of the existence of God or the quality and nature of His being. The Bible says there is one God, Jesus is His Son, the earth, and the moon, and the stars, are his handiwork, and he manifests Himself every day to all save fools blinded with ignorance and with pride. God rules the heavens and the earth, whips the devil, and on Judgment morning will lift up and preserve for a life immortal all those who have repented, believed, and been baptized.

When the Negro prays to God he does not pray to some dim gaseous spirit wandering wraithlike in space. He talks directly to God as a child talks to his parent, or as a comrade talks to his comrade. God is a "natchel man," with the eyes and face and figure of a man, and he talks and acts like a man. Strangely enough, He is a white man. The Negro feels close to God. If he wants something, he asks Him for it. If he receives it he thanks Him, quite simply and naturally, as one expresses one's thanks to a friend for a gift. The Negro addresses God spontaneously, and on simple occasions as well as great. "Lawd, put some sense in dis jug-headed mule," an exasperated plowman says when his mule balks. "Gawd, jes' lemme lay dese hands on dat no-'count woman so I can bus' her brains out," prays a man whose woman has deserted him. "Thank you, Lawd," is uttered by a woman when she bends over and picks up a dollar bill lost by someone on the road. The Negro walks and talks with God all the days of his life.

Jesus is the lamb of God. He is filled with an ineffable sweetness. His is the power and the willingness to forgive. It is He who, sitting at the right hand of God, tones down His stern and righteous wrath with a glance of his gentle soft eyes. In His bosom all the creatures of the earth find compassion and warmth. From Him blessings flow as sweet waters gush from the oases of the desert. In his great heart there is room for white folks and for Negroes. And through all the days of eternity the humblest may pillow his head upon the bosom of the Son of God.

Negro churches, in the town and in the country, are used far more than white churches. The church is not only a place of worship, but it is also a social center and a place of amusement. Here neighbor meets neighbor, friend meets friend, there is singing and conversation, swapping of gossip and fraternizing. Young people make engagements to meet at church, and when services are over they stroll out under the stars.

In rural Negro churches the hours of services are indefinite, but apparently the longer the services last the more pleased is the congregation. It is a not uncommon sight in summer to find a Negro church, close-packed with sweltering humanity under the dimly burning kerosene lamps, ringing to the voices of preachers and of songs long after midnight. White folks, enchanted by the singing, stop their automobiles to listen. Fragments of song and of sermon come to them on the still air.

"You don't need no candles in heaven, 'cause dere de candles will be shinin' 'long as de Lawd Gawd lives, and He don't never die. . . . De Bible tells you to love yo' neighbor like yo'self. It ain't no love for nobody when people goes about a hollerin' and a-shoutin' 'bout what dey neighbors doin' and stirrin' up ruckuses wherever dey can. Don't nothing hurt a wild duck but his mouf. A hunter wouldn't know where he was at if he didn't holler and flap his wings. . . . One of dese days dis heah earth will be burnt up to a cinder and drap plum down into a bottomless pit. A thousand years us gwine stay dere. Den Gabriel gwine blow his hawn like seven claps of thunder, and us gwine rise, and come back as saints and live wid Jesus, our Captain, in a place which He has prepared for us." The preacher's voice is lost as the congregation sings:

> "When de saints come marchin' in,
> O when de saints come marchin' in,
> Lawd, I wants to be in dat number,
> When de saints come marchin' in.
>
> "And when de sun refuse to shine,
> O when de sun refuse to shine,
> Lawd, I wants to be in dat number,
> When de sun refuse to shine.
>
> "And when de moon drops down in blood,
> O when de moon drops down in blood,
> Lawd, I wants to be in dat number,
> When de moon drops down in blood.
>
> "And when de gates, O when de gates,
> When de pearly gates swing wide,
> Lawd, I wants to be in dat number,
> When de pearly gates swing wide."

The white folks start their automobiles and drive homeward through the moonlight, silent and sad and vaguely troubled in their hearts.

In every Negro community the preacher is the leading figure. No Negro ever deliberately enters the church as a career. He must first "see the light and hear the call," as Paul heard and saw upon the road to Damascus. Thereafter he is free to attend a theological school or to read the Scriptures himself and prepare for ordination.

The rural Negro preacher of the Delta makes no attempt to appeal to the reason or the intellect of his congregation. Those who do find themselves without churches or with small congregations. In one of the largest towns of the Delta there is an intelligent Negro preacher whose church building is by far the finest in town. But it has only a handful of members. "I can't get people to come to my church," he told me, "because I try to conduct my services with sense and they don't want that. They insist on having the old-time religion."

Some time ago I stood upon a bridge above a lake, watching my friends fishing. A Negro man stood next to me, a briefcase resting upon the floor of the bridge at his side. I asked him if he preached. It was a safe guess, because usually in the Delta the only Negroes who carry briefcases are preachers. And in any event, almost any Negro is either a preacher, an elder, or a deacon, or in some way is officially connected with a church. "Yas, suh, I does," he replied. "I'm gwine preach tonight over at Scotts." "How are the collections?" I asked. "Collections is turrible. I don't know what's de matter wid dese people. I can't git nuthin' outen 'em."

Suddenly a voice came from under the bridge, and a little Negro boy, whom neither of us had seen and who had been overhearing the conversation, crawled through the railing and stood beside us. "Reverend Threadgill," he said, "you ain't never gwine do no good for yo'self till you starts shoutin' an' squallin'. You don't do enough squallin'. People like to fall out. I heerd a heap er sisters say dat 'bout you."

"Huh," said the Reverend Threadgill, contemptuously. "Sisters. You can't git ahead er no sisters. De Lawd fixed dat. He give de wimmens 209 bones and de mens didn't git but 208. Ever since dat time w'en a man mess wid a woman de woman th'ow him every time." He looked at his watch and started sadly out to walk eight miles to Scotts through the dust and the hot sun, meditating upon the painful necessity of squalling when he arrived at his destination.

The Reverend Burr is one of the most eminent and successful preachers in the Delta. He toils mightily not only for the Lord, but also for himself, thereby storing up treasure for himself in heaven and on earth. He has a large congregation in a large town — "1100 members at fo' bits a head a month," and "pastors" six other congregations scattered over a wide area. He is black, fat, amiable, well fed, eloquent, shrewd, and diplomatic. If one of his colleagues had taken his advice he would still be the pastor of a large church at a big salary.

"It was this a-way," the Reverend said. "We bofe had big congregations. I was married, but he wa'n't. My wife she's mighty sharp, but she ain't never goin' to ketch up wid me. Well, I was kinder messin' 'bout wid three or four sisters in my corngregation, and he was messin' 'bout wid four or five ladies in his corngregation. One day I say, 'Brother, let's git dis straight. I tell you what le's do. You carry on wid de sisters in my corngregation and I'll carry on wid de sisters in yo' corngregation. Dat way won't neither one of us git in no trouble.'

"Well, suh, do you know, dat ign'ant nigger wouldn't pay me no min'. He kep' a-messin' about wid de sisters. Den he goes up St. Louis and marries him a woman. He brought her back here and de sisters th'ew him clean out de church."

One day I attended funeral services for a member of another church, that of the Reverend Scott. Sister Rosie, the deceased, lay in a beautiful dove-gray, flower-covered casket, near the altar. Her relatives and family, in deep black, sat on the "mourner's bench," in a front-row pew. Her friends occupied every seat in the church. She had been a power for good in the community; a toiler in the vineyard of the Lord; a midwife of enviable reputation; an earnest worker for the church; a recording secretary of the Lady Knights of Love. The pulpit was crowded with elders, deacons, preachers, and prominent laymen and lay sisters. A good woman had departed from the earth and was about to be committed to the dust from which she came.

A preacher of reputation and importance rarely begins the services in a Negro church. He leaves this lesser duty to an elder or a deacon or a visiting preacher, who first brings the congregation almost to the point of frenzy. Then the Lord's anointed takes charge of the services and scores an easy emotional victory over the already trembling nerves of the people before him. So it was on this day. Some of the sisters were ripe for "falling out" when the Kid began to preach.

"O my brethren and my sistern, we are gethered here today to say our last good-bye to Sister Rosie Fuller. All the days of her life she was a good woman. [Voices in the congregation: "Dat's de truth."] She praised Jesus wid de last breath lef' in her body. ["Amen."] She trusted in de Lawd who was her Maker. She paid her burial dues on de dot and wasn't never behin' in her church work. She was like a rose of Sharon. Like a lily of de valley. Like a rainbow in de sky. She was one of Gawd's chillun and now He done come and called her home. ["Lawd, have mercy."]

"I 'member de day Sister Rosie got sick. I 'member how she went on downtown to see de doctor. He examined her in his big office. He looked th'oo her wid de X-rays. He put her blood under a glass. 'Rosie,' he say, 'you got to go de horspital. You has to have a operation.' Rosie went. Dey laid her out on de table. She screamed w'en de knife struck her ["Save us, Jesus."] Den she died. ["O Lawd!"]

"Rosie done lef' her good husban' behin' her an' de chillun. Dey misses dey good mammy, an' he done los' a noble wife. But be ye of good cheer, for she has gone to a better lan' where dere ain't no pain or sorrow, no work or no worriment. Right now she's resting in de arms of sweet Jesus an' He's breshin' away her tears.

"Far as dat's concerned, of co'se don't nobody lak to die. Once when I was a little boy my mammy said to me, 'Kid, de preacher's gwine be here for Sunday dinner. Now you go out dere and pen up dat dominecker rooster, an' I'm gwine cook him up wid dumplin's.' My mammy always believed in feedin' de preacher. Well, I went out dat night 'bout sundown an' looked for dat rooster, an' he wasn't nowheres to be found. I looked de nex' day and de nex'. Finally when it was too late to kill him for Sunday dinner dere he was roostin' in his tree. Now dat proves don't nobody like to die, and w'en it gits aroun' to me, well, I'm willing to wait right here on Third and Oak street 'til Gabriel blow his hawn."

The congregation, including the mourners, were vastly amused by this and other drolleries of their minister, and smiled broadly in sheer good humor. The Reverend Scott gave way to another preacher, and sat among the elders and the deacons with whom he engaged in conversation, or swapped jokes with the undertaker.

Suddenly an usher "got 'ligion," and loped wildly up an aisle, striking at people in the pews, who dodged with alacrity born of long practice, and was finally subdued and thrown moaning, shouting, and sobbing onto an empty bench in the rear of the church. The ushers were large, fat, black sisters, clad in white, wearing hats the shape roughly of a chef's hat with this legend embroidered on them in red thread: Progressive Lady Ushers of the True Vine Baptist Church. It was part of their duty to subdue ladies in the congregation who "fell out," but, unfortunately, they themselves were the first to succumb to the emotional excitement of the old-time religion, and the brothers present had to hurl themselves upon three lady ushers and hold them down until they became quiet again.

Soon the church was in pandemonium as the Reverend Scott's successor moaned, shouted, sang, flailed his arms about, painted the horrors of sin, the pleasures of repentance, and the golden reward in store for those who believed and were baptized. Suddenly a sister, her eyes rolling wildly in her head, shouting, "Jesus, save me," over and over again, threw herself into the lap of a little man seated next to her, almost smothering him in her onslaught. She tore convulsively at her clothes, shrieking and kicking, while he vainly tried to force her leaden weight off his sagging body, and was relieved of her only when three men came to his assistance and removed the sister by force.

When all the congregation had been worked up to an almost unbearable pitch of excitement, Reverend Scott, calm, collected and smiling, resumed. He stood for a moment or two leaning upon the altar, fingering the massive gold watch chain that extended across the length of his ample waist. The tension in the church began to lessen. The Kid was the very picture of well-fed worldly prosperity. He looked solid and durable. It was inconceivable that his imposing bulk would ever be prey to the worms of the grave. Perhaps he would be here on Third and Oak Streets until Gabriel blew his horn. Services had begun at noon. Now the slanting rays of the setting sun touched to a darker gray the covering of Sister Rosie's casket. The undertaker moved smilingly about, trying carefully to hide his impatience. Sister Rosie would be buried in Arkansas, and he must take the casket to the Rock Island station to catch the 7:45 train.

The Reverend Scott began to speak. "My friends," he said, "there is just one mo' thing to say to y'all before we turn the casket over to Brother Dave Willis to take to de depot. Many of y'all as can I hope will be dere to give Sister Rosie a good send-off. She was a woman dat tried to improve herself; to git her a good education an' put mo' sense in her haid. Dat's what I want every one of you to do. Improve yo'self. Study over yo' min.' What do de min' do? What do de min, do, I say to each and every one of you. I'll tell you what de min, do.

"Suppose we was to have a train dat could start right here in dis church on Third and Oak Street and run clean th'oo to New Yawk City widout a stop in five minutes. Dat's goin' fast, ain't it? Well, dere's plenty of things goes fast in this worl'. Lindbergh he got in his airplane, an' flew in no time straight to Paris. Dat's fast, ain't it? ["Sho is."] Dere's faster things dan dat. De other day I wanted to talk to a friend of mine in Duncan, Mississippi, forty miles away. I picked up de receiver of de telephone. I rung de bell. I say, 'Central, give me Duncan, Mississippi.' 'Bout three minutes later dere I was talkin' forty miles away. Dat's sho fast. ["Hit's de truth."]

"Well, de min' of man is faster dan dat. Here I am standing on dis pulpit. I say, 'Min', carry me to Chicago and let me feel dem sweet evening breezes,' and fo' you know it, dere I am setting by de great Lake Michigan. I ain't satisfied wid dat, so I jumps 'way over yonder into Canada. Den I come back down to de Gulf of Mexico where New Orleans is at. Den I looks up at de sky, clean up th'oo de clouds, an' I say, 'Min', carry me up dere where de Lawd's settin' on this throne,' an' I rises straight up to glory and comes on back. ["Well, suh!"] I pulls out my watch. It ain't hardly took me two minutes to travel all about de worl' and dat fast train dat don't take but five minutes to go to New Yawk City from here, ain't got dere yet. ["Dat's right."]

"Now you take de President of de Nunited States. He got bad laigs, but dat don't make no diffunce. He takes a gravel, crack it on his desk, and forty-eight governors comes a-runnin' to ax him what does he want dem to do. If he lost bofe his laigs, dat wouldn't make no diffunce. If he lost bofe his arms, dat wouldn't make no diffunce. If he lost bofe his eyes an' his ears, dat wouldn't make no diffunce. But if he lost his min', de Vice would have to take de gravel away from him an' tell dem governors what to do. ["Hit's de gospel truth."]

"Education is like a sucker on a pump. You sho can't git no water widout it. It's like de polish on a shoe. You can git anything you wants wid education. Jes' suppose Henry Ford was settin' in his room. In come his wife. 'Henry,' she say, 'us is down to us las' slice of meat an' de meal in de bar'l is gittin' low.' Do dat worry him? Naw, dat don't concern him at all. What do he do? He reach for his checkbook an' write out a check. Dat's what education is.

"Now I has one announcement to make. Sunday mawnin' us goin' to have a whole barbecued hawg in de basement of dis church. Tickets ain't goin' to be but ten cents. I know dere ain't nary one amongst you can't git a dime's worth when you's turned loose on a hawg."

The congregation filed slowly out of the church into the setting sun. Reverend Kid Scott stood upon the pulpit, surrounded by a circle of admiring women. Two deacons discussed the Baptist convention soon to be held at Lake Village, Arkansas. Sister Rosie's casket melted softly into the gathering shadows.

The preacher is the most important man in the rural Negro community, and his importance is seldom overshadowed by anyone in the small towns of the Delta. He is the one leader of Negroes who might be a power for good. Yet it is the testimony of interested observers among both whites and blacks that the preacher is often an influence for evil.

Many Negro preachers in the Delta are ignorant and super-stitious, and at the same time, shrewd and calculating. They know the weaknesses and credulousness of their congregations, and how to play upon them for their own material benefit. Some of them are merely lewd and lecherous money-grabbers, batten-ing upon the ignorance and simple faith of their people.

Negro women are pre-eminent in the church. It is they who raise the money to pay the preacher, maintain church structures, and erect new ones. They have the power to hire or fire preach-ers. Without their aid no preacher can be successful.

The Negro preacher must have charm for the women and strongly marked sex appeal, in addition to the ability of arousing his congregation to emotional heights, if he would succeed. If the women like him and he has lusty manhood, he is sure to be well fed, well clothed, well housed, and well paid. Asceticism is a quality incomprehensible and unknown to Delta Negroes. I asked a successful rural preacher what were the qualities that brought him success. "Cap'n," he said, "a nigger preacher ain't got to have but two things — a bass voice an' make de bedsprings moan."

Given appealing voice tones and the unquenchable ardors of satyriasis, the successful Negro preacher makes his position impregnable by appointing each sister to a definite place of labor in the vineyard of the Lord. Innumerable committees are invented and every woman, however poor or humble, has her pride titillated and her sense of importance increased by being made a member.

Many Negro preachers are rustic Machiavellis. In an effort to reconcile doctrine with behavior, I put this question to an eminent minister. "Elder," I said, "how can you mess about with the sisters all week long, and be a Christian man in the pulpit on Sunday?" "Well, I tell you how dat is," he replied without hesitation. "If a Christian man goes to bed wid a Christian lady dat's just like rubbing two clean sheets together: dey can't soil each other."

When the fame of a preacher spreads, he gets calls from many congregations, and usually accepts as many of them as he can possibly "pastor" by going on circuit. Some years ago a Delta preacher became so famous, and the demands for his services were so great, that he administered to the spiritual needs of congregations scattered over an enormous area from Dayton, Ohio, to New Orleans. He became very rich, had a secretary who traveled with him, was revered by thousands of Negroes, and at his death had the greatest "turn out" ever known in Mississippi.

His body was embalmed and taken from town to town where he had had congregations. In each town, services were held by day and the casket containing the remains traveled by night to the next stop. In quite the same manner the ancient Scythians buried their great chiefs, placing the body upon a wagon and driving about the steppes until each tribe had looked upon it, before it was interred in the earth.

A friend of this great Negro minister told me that the "Reverend Doctor B. H. Perkins was a noble man. Dey kept him out of de ground for thirty days. His funeral cost $1100."

The Negro church in the Delta is a sharp financial drain upon the people, and an utterly ineffective instrument as far as their ultimate welfare is concerned. Churches are constantly being formed and erected out of groups who have split off from other churches. Factions within each church are frequently at odds with another group, and peace is finally achieved only when one or the other departs and organizes a new church. Preachers are often not satisfied with the material offerings which come to them from one church, and they foment dissatisfaction until they get the backing of an influential group, and go out to build a new structure with a new memberhip.

The result of this is that there are far more Negro churches in the Delta than the people can reasonably afford to support, and the limited funds of the members of the congregation are dissipated in erecting and maintaining buildings, and in supporting an army of preachers and hangers-on. In many towns of this section there are seven to ten times as many Negro churches as white churches, although the disparity between the populations of the two groups is not nearly so great.

If the preacher has failed as a conscientious, disinterested leader of his people, if he has shown no tendency to lead them in ways that will improve their lot and, so far as possible, reconstruct their lives, there is little evidence in the Delta that other Negroes who could assume leadership have any desire for this responsibility.

Leadership could be of two kinds. An internal leadership which should undertake to decrease the rate of crime among Negroes, inculcate in them a sense of responsibility toward their own group, develop a better family life and a love of home, and instruct them generally in those qualities which would raise their whole level. In addition to this, there could be, so to speak, an external leadership. Leaders who undertook this responsibility would be unofficial ambassadors to the whites — a strangely pressing need in this area — who might forestall difficulties and racial friction by anticipatory conferences with white leaders. There was a time in the Delta when deans of the Negro community who had acquired the confidence of the whites achieved notable results for their people. In latter years, because of constantly increasing suspicion on the part of Negroes toward whites, relations of this kind have almost completely broken down and the seeds of trouble are being permitted to grow unhindered.

I have discussed this lack of Negro leadership with many Negroes in the Delta. They say that it arises from two causes. "One nigger ain't gwine trust another. Jes' las' night I attended a business meeting of de Independent Sons and Daughters of Treasury. We had seventy-five dollars in de bank an' fourteen dollars in de treasury. One nigger got up an' made a big speech. He say, 'Brothers, us has a whole lot er money in de bank an' in de treasury. Now I been studyin' somethin' over in my min' fer a long time what to do wid dat money. I been makin' up plans fer a Y. and M.C.A. building. Y'all jes' put dis money where I can git it an' I'll go ahaid.'

"Den I got up. I say, 'Mr. President, I heered what de constituated brother said. He have always been one of my most intimated friends and preadventually we always will be, jes' like

we was when both er us was senior daycons in de Old Jerusalem
Baptist church. I'm a min'-reader and I studies opinion. Th'owin'
away money is a eatin' cancer dat we has got to stop. Now de
prerogative of my min' sho ain't evil, but I'll fight dis proposition
till Shiloh come. Dat dog he talkin' 'bout ain't gwine hunt.' De
lodge voted to keep de money where it was at, and if dey hadn't
dat nigger sho would a-took it on off."

When Negro lodges and other organizations send money to be
deposited in the banks, frequently all or most of the officers go
with it in a body. No one trusts the other. And when money is
to be withdrawn by check, as many as three or four officers must
sign and countersign. Sad experience has made them cautious.

In many towns of the Delta there are intelligent Negro business men and professional men who possess means, have the
respect and good will of the white community, and who could
be of invaluable service to their less fortunate fellows in many
ways. I asked why these men made no effort to lift their hands
or their voices in behalf of their people. My informant said, "I
see you don't know nuthin' 'bout niggers." I regretted that my
information was lamentably incomplete. "De truth is dis. When
a nigger git rich an' rise in de worl' he jes' stays off to hisself and
don't have nuthin' to do wid no niggers 'cept dem what is fixed
like him."

In nearly every town of the Delta the Negro undertaker is
one of the most important men in the community, and usually
one of the wealthiest. The poorest Negro is sure to be a member
of a burial society, so that he will be assured of a befitting
funeral when he dies. Until relatively recently the Negro undertaker enjoyed a complete monopoly of this lucrative field. Now,
however, he is meeting with competition from white burial
societies who provide a casket, Negro preacher, and all the trap-
pings of an impressive funeral. The Negro undertaker, however,
is always employed to prepare the body for burial and deliver it
to the church and to the cemetery.

Recently a curious case was aired in the Delta courts, back of
which lay facts and implications that violently shook the foundations of Negro rural society. A member of a burial society in

Cleveland, Mississippi, died suddenly in a near-by town, and the undertaker, under the terms of the society's agreement, sent a hearse to fetch the body. The family of the deceased bought a new suit of clothes to be placed upon the body and delivered it to the undertaker.

The body was brought to the late residence of the dead man in a sealed casket, and the undertaker would not open it to permit the family to have a last glance at it, on the ground that it had decomposed. The family protested in vain and finally consented to have the burial without opening the casket.

When they returned to their home after the funeral, the relatives of the deceased began to wonder why the casket had been sealed, contrary to all custom, and they concluded finally that it was because the undertaker had stolen the new suit of clothes which they had sent him. This charge he vigorously denied. The relatives continued to wonder and to worry. They were enormously disturbed because, if their suspicions were justified, the corpse would be unclothed, and "Eddie sho couldn't face de lady angels nekkid."

They then went to the cemetery. Here they disinterred the body and found Eddie lying there clad only in his skin. They left Eddie as they had found him, and hastened to hire a lawyer. In the meanwhile, the news of their actions had come to the undertaker, and he secretly hastened to the cemetery and placed the suit of clothes at the feet of the corpse.

The next day when the irate relatives descended upon him, he blandly denied their accusations, and suggested that they disinter the body. The whole group went back to the cemetery, and the undertaker was completely vindicated. "What did I tell you niggers?" he inquired with righteous indignation. "Dere is Eddie's suit right at his feet, so he won't have far to reach when Gabriel blows his hawn."

Despite the fact that there are nearly 300,000 Negroes in the Delta, they conduct almost no businesses of even the most negligible importance in any fields save of those of undertaking and insurance. They own and control no firms of any consequence that deal exclusively with whites, exclusively with Negroes, or with members of both groups. There are no Negro dairies, no butcher shops, no dry-goods stores, no junk dealers, no professional truck gardeners or poultrymen, and no banks. They transact some business in groceries, in restaurants, in dry cleaning, in hotels, and in trucking. But on the whole, all of the business of the Delta of whatever kind, is owned and controlled by whites and Chinese.

In Greenville, the largest town of the Delta, Negroes buy their groceries largely from the fifty or more Chinese stores scattered throughout the Negro sections of the town. It is obvious that their patronage could support fifty or more Negro-owned stores and a large number of employees, instead of the handful of stores which Negroes now conduct. This would benefit the entire Negro community and would be a source of inspiration to ambitious young Negroes who might aspire to a business career.

Negroes here ascribe the lack of Negro business in the Delta to many causes. First among them is lack of capital. It is true that few Negroes have much capital with which to begin a business. It is also true that many white men and Chinese have started in business with but little money and have eventually built successful firms and won economic independence for themselves. Some of the best merchants in this area started their careers as peddlers with packs on their backs, trudging laboriously from house to house, through roads muddy in winter and dusty in summer. Today the peddler of the Delta is an Italian with a horse-drawn wagon going slowly about the countryside, selling trinkets and clothes to Negroes. Many of them acquire a competence and retire or go to a neighboring town and open a place of business. Their capital at the beginning has always been a pitifully limited sum which thousands of Negroes of this section could raise as well as they, yet there has rarely, if ever, been a Negro peddler in the Delta.

As a corollary to lack of capital, perhaps, Negroes assert that the Negro cannot meet white competition. It is undeniably true that this competition is severe, yet the independent white merchant who deals, say, in groceries, meets with sharp competition from the giant chains. Those who are competent survive; those who are incompetent perish. As for the Chinese, they flourish in the midst of the competition of the superior-capitalized white independent merchants and white-owned chain stores.

It cannot be fairly asked of the Negro consumer that he trade merely because of race pride or for the sake of race solidarity with Negroes. There is ultimately no patriotism of purse among Negroes or whites. The white housewife does not trade with the white grocer unless he can meet the competition of the chains, despite the fact that he is her friend and neighbor, a fellow-member of her church, and was liberal in extending credit to her when she badly needed it. She buys when and where she buys for less. All the appeals to her patronizing home merchants, to "keep your money at home," to "spend with those who spend with you," are lost on the air. If potatoes are two cents a pound cheaper at the Big Chain than at Joe Ford's, The Family Grocer for Forty Years, she buys potatoes at the Big Chain.

The Negro merchant therefore, if he hopes to win and retain the patronage of Negroes, must be able to meet competition on all sides. Unfortunately for him, his troubles are not ended even when he is able to sell merchandise as cheaply as the other fellow. Negroes and whites pay cash to the chain stores. But Negroes trading with other Negroes are often unwilling to pay cash and insist upon unlimited terms of credit. They feel that because the merchant is a Negro he ought, as a matter of blood fellowship, give them credit. But, conversely, they do not feel that because the merchant is a Negro they ought to support him without end. This unreasonable demand, therefore, makes it difficult even for the competent Negro merchant to succeed in the Delta.

The Negro merchant here is faced with another serious difficulty. He finds it almost impossible to hire honest employees. Many Negroes have no compunction whatsoever about stealing from their Negro employers, and many small firms have had to close because of this quirk of Negro character.

The average Delta Negro has but a dimly defined sense of financial responsibility, and the volume of credit extended to Negroes here, save share-croppers, is negligible. With their gift of precision in language, Negroes often illuminate their own attitudes more sharply in a single sentence than a white man could in a chapter. I was in a plantation store when a Negro approached the manager and skillfully began a conversation on the delicate subject of "credick." He needed some shoes, some flour, some shirts, and other things. He would pay the merchant "soon's I gin." The skeptical merchant recommended a policy of cash to his would-be debtor as a means of keeping himself out of financial trouble and free from worry.

"White folks," the Negro said, "you don't understan'. It ain't what I owe dat worries me. It's *gittin'* to owe dat worries me."

It is an axiom of the Delta that the Negro will buy anything on credit. It does not matter that the things offered for sale are utterly useless or wildly improbable or hopelessly luxurious; they can be sold in the Delta to Negroes on credit at the blink of an eye. They will buy anything from giraffes to second-hand iron safes; from porcelain bathtubs to grand pianos; from velvet curtains to gold teeth. And if crops are good and they make money, they will pay their debts to the limit of their ability.

The Delta Negro's financial irresponsibility is not generally rooted in dishonesty. They are not dead-beats save in some instances. It is merely that they have only the vaguest ideas about money and their capacity to pay. They will cheerfully contract debts which in the aggregate constitute more than their earnings for ten years, and when they find themselves unable to pay they do not worry, but merely say to their creditors in the most artless way: "Boss, I jes' ain't got it."

It is an axiom, too, of the Delta, that the Negro can get almost anything from the white man that he desires. As a result of slavery, when the Negro's whole life and happiness were at the whim of his master, and as a condition of living in a white-dominated community where the Negro's welfare and prosperity largely depend upon the good will of one or more white men, the Negro has learned to be a master of tact. As part of tact he has cultivated an almost Oriental patience which enables him to wait and to contain himself until the right moment to make a request has arrived. He has learned, too, out of sheer necessity, to become an expert analyst of white character. He quickly estimates the qualities of white men for whom he works, and immediately determines their strength and their weakness, whether they are kind or cruel, firm or flabby, determined or vacillating. The Negro is in many ways more subtle than the white man, more sensitive, and more skilled in the use of discretion.

The Delta Negro knows, too, how with the use of a word or a smile or a gesture, not only to turn away the white man's wrath, but to win favor for himself.

Last year a big black Negro who answered to the name of Bear was employed on a plantation by a friend of mine. When Bear came to him he asked him where he had worked before.

"Boss," he said, "I used to work fer de Lowrance brothers. Dey's levee contractors an' de meanest white folks I ever seen in my life. Dey'd kill a nigger sho as you bawn out on de levee ev'y Monday mawnin', run de graders over him an' bury him right dere. I ain't never been 'roun' no white folks what was tough on niggers like dey was."

The planter, who knew that the Lowrance brothers were not at all unkind to Negroes, was amused.

"Bear," he asked, "which of the brothers was the meanest?"

"Mr. Cholly Lowrance," Bear replied. "He'd kill a nigger jes' like you'd stomp a snake in de ground."

The interview came to an end, nothing more was heard of the Lowrance brothers, and Bear went to work on the plantation.

Months later the planter was sitting one day on his porch when an automobile came to an abrupt stop on the road in front of his house. He went out to find that the driver of the car was Charles Lowrance, who had had to stop because of a flat tire. No one was in sight to repair it save Bear, who was plowing in a near-by field. He was summoned and began to change the tire.

The planter winked at Lowrance and turned to Bear.

"Bear," he said, "what was the name of those white folks you told me you used to work for?"

"De Lowrance brothers. Dey was de meanest white folks in Arkansas. Dey'd kill a nigger ev'y Monday mawnin' and bury him right dere in de levee."

"Who was the meanest brother?"

"Mr. Cholly Lowrance. He'd kill a nigger like he squashin' mosquitoes."

Both the white men were enormously amused, and when Bear had finished the job Mr. Cholly gave him $1.50, a fabulous tip in this land. The planter turned again to Bear.

"Bear," he said, "do you know this white gentleman you have been fixing the tire for?"

"Naw, suh," said Bear. "I ain't never seen him in my life."

"Well," said the planter, "he's Mr. Charles Lowrance."

The white men stared at Bear, wondering how he would extricate himself from the trap into which he had fallen. With lightning rapidity Bear turned a wide and gleaming smile upon the planter and "de meanest white folks in Arkansas."

"Mr. Lowrance," he said, "you is lookin' at de lyin'est nigger in Arkansas."

Bear is still on the plantation and in all probability will remain there the rest of his life. The planter likes him and he has a new friend and protector — Mr. Cholly.

The white Delta, a relatively poor community and markedly inferior in numbers to the Negroes, finds it impossible to handle adequately the grave and pressing problem of Negro health and hospitalization. Despite the fact that there are nearly 300,000 Negroes in this area, there are pitifully few hospital beds available to them in Negro hospitals within the Delta, and the charity hospitals of the state are utterly unable to care for them. These hospitals are 50 to 150 miles distant from the Delta, so that a Negro in need of an emergency operation is likely to die before he reaches them. And when he does, and succeeds in entering, they cannot, because of their limited resources, give him the kind of treatment that should be administered.

In one instance, related to me by a planter, a Negro woman on his plantation needed an emergency operation. He converted a truck into an ambulance, sent another woman along with the patient as a nurse, and directed the driver to go to a charity hospital, 125 miles away. When he arrived at his destination the patient was refused entrance because there was no room for her.

With the woman in pain and dying, the truck lumbered on to another, 50 miles distant. Here, too, entrance was denied because the hospital was already overcrowded. The woman died. The truck brought her dead body back to the plantation.

Lack of hospital facilities is undoubtedly responsible for many preventable deaths among Delta Negroes. The problem is far too great to be solved by the Delta alone and unaided, and both whites and Negroes are injured ultimately because of the community's failure to provide hospitals for approximately 70 per cent of the population.

The state of Mississippi, by its system of issuing permits to midwives, and instructing them through county boards of health, has done much to lower the rate of infant mortality and of infection and mortality among mothers. Midwives are carefully instructed in sanitation, in the advice that they shall give to pregnant women, and in the delivery of children.

Meetings are called constantly by the county physicians at which the midwives are drilled in technique and kept up to date in their work. This is of vast importance to Negro health because the overwhelming majority of Negro children born in this area are now and have always been delivered by midwives. They have organized themselves into Midwives Clubs and with characteristic Negro gusto sing *The Song of the Midwives,* to the tune of *As We Go Marching On,* at every meeting:

> "We aim to be good midwives of the state,
> We try hard to be up to date,
> To be on time to meetings, and never be late,
> As we go marching on.
>
> *Chorus:*
> "Glory, glory, hallelujah,
> Glory, glory, hallelujah,
> Glory, glory, hallelujah,
> As we go marching on.
>
> "We put drops in the baby's eyes,
> Whether the mother laughs or cries,
> The state for us the eye drops buys,
> As we go marching on."

Negroes of the Delta, in the towns and on the remote plantations of the country, go on from year to year treading with great skill the labryinthine ways of white civilization into which they have been thrust. Laughter is the shepherd's crook upon which they lean when they are weary and heavy-laden. "When troubles come a-pilin' up I jes' rares back my head an' laughs, an' long's I can do dat can't nothin' tech me." Religion is the asylum to which they retreat when the woes of the world press heavily upon them, and comfort is to be had only in the eyes of God, and surcease in the bosom of Jesus. Patience is the faithful companion with whom they walk quietly down the long corridors of time. Humility is the cloak of invisibility protecting them from a myriad of foes.

Joy of living is the Negroes', and song, and the capacity for extracting pleasure from the simplest things. They have survived and multiplied incredibly amid a host of ills, some of their own making and some of the making of others, that would have shattered a race less adaptable, a race less humble, a race gifted with a lesser degree of almost passive non-resistance. It has been their strange fate to be cast among an alien people irreconcilably different from themselves. And it has been the fate of those among whom they were cast sometimes to lose their souls in the Negro's presence and sometimes to gain their souls because of him.

CHAPTER 11

The Last Stand of Noblesse Oblige

UNDER the heading "A Mississippi Rascal in Kentucky," the Greenville, Mississippi, *Times*, of December 16, 1876, contained the following news item:

We had not heard of Bill Gray, ex-Radical State Senator from our County, ex-Brigadier-General of Ames' militia, and Color-Sergeant of the Nonpareil Brigade of Grand Rascals for some time, but we knew that William's light would shine somewhere. His genius for villainy is bound to be recognized, go where he may. We were trembling from apprehension that some penitentiary had engulfed him, but the following from the Lexington, Kentucky, *Press* shows that the Reverend Bill is still on PREYING ground.

"Reverend William Gray (colored), elder of the Independent Baptist Church of this city, was arrested yesterday on a warrant sworn out by the trustees of his church, charging him with appropriating to his own use the funds of the church."

Bill don't make any bones about going through the collection box. About three years ago the Negroes down here collected about $3000 for church purposes, and Bill, who was then a high buck in these parts, got his paws on it, and it was "Farewell, Brother Crawford," with that collection! How that nigger has lived through all his impudence and rascality down here is a blistering shame to all good shooting people.

Thus the *Times* jubilantly registered its exultation over the arrest of a Negro who had been prominent in the local politics of the Reconstruction era. Negroes were then actually in possession of or were struggling for the control of many of the municipal and county offices of the Delta; they swarmed in the state legislature; and Mississippi was represented in the United States Senate by a Negro.

The whites waged a bitter warfare, by fair means and foul, to regain complete control of local and state politics and to oust the Negro entirely from public office. So long as he could vote his numbers made him formidable in elections, and the whites moved therefore to emasculate him politically by way of disfranchisement.

On June 2, 1883, the Greenville, Mississippi, *Republican,* an organ of the Reconstructionists, raised its voice in weak protest at the success of the local whites in their struggle to oust the Negro from politics:

> For six years the colored man has been at the mercy of the Democratic will, and they have borne it meekly, never failing to lend a hand since 1875 in all their schemes. We believe that there are about 600,000 colored to 400,000 white people in this state, and of this vast number of colored people there is not one holding a single state office and very few holding county offices. . . . We are American citizens and as such we demand representation and we will have it.

A few days later the Greenville *Times* made reply to this threat and this demand in a few words:

> You have tasted just enough of the "juice" of office to spoil your palate for your fitting vocation, and that is what is the matter.

For many years following Reconstruction, local and state politicians ran upon platforms of white supremacy, involving the complete elimination of the Negro from public office and his disfranchisement as a voter. The Negro is now no longer a political issue in the Delta or in the state of Mississippi, around whose figure rival politicians battle for office. Reconstruction belongs to history. Its bitterness and it battles are vague memories gained by the present generation at second and third hand from those who fought them. Few are now alive who remember it personally. The Negro holds public office nowhere in the state. His vote is negligible and of no political importance whatsoever. White supremacy is no longer a political issue in Mississippi, save when its rotting corpse is sometimes disinterred by a desperate politician and futile efforts are made to blow the breath of life into it. Politically the Negro is as dead as the Indian.

Local politicians in the Delta have no platforms, no programs, and no issues upon which to run for office. There is no party division, because the vast majority of the people are Democrats, and the handful of Republicans go into political hibernation when their party is ousted from control of the administration at Washington. Strangely enough, and contrary to legend, candidates for local offices rarely if ever make public speeches. They solicit votes in the solid old-fashioned way of calling upon the voters in their homes, at their offices and stores, and on their plantations. They join lodges of all kinds and are on terms of peace and contentment and understanding with a varied fauna ranging from elk to beaver. They hand around cards bearing their names and the title of the office they seek, together with a stereotyped formula of gratitude: "John Jones will appreciate your support." Sometimes the candidate lists his real or fancied qualifications on the back of the card, with the inevitable assurance that "if elected I will treat all alike without fear or favor," proving that the divine indifference of the gods sometimes descends upon a humble court clerk.

For months before an election local politicians are indefatigable in going to the remotest parts of the counties, in visiting the sick and acting as pallbearers at funerals, in seeing and being seen. They become overnight spiritual brothers to Catholics, Protestants, and Jews, achieving the metamorphosis smoothly and without apparent mental dislocations. Their pre-election manners combine the informal dignity of the Prince of Wales receiving a gift of seashells from the Boy Scouts of Brighton, and the slightly obsequious bearing of a floorwalker assuring a customer that roller skates may be found on the third floor, first aisle to the left.

The voters have no criteria by which to measure candidates for office. They do not consider whether they are fitted by training, temperament, or experience, for what is called the "high trust of public office." One quality, however, the candidate must possess in order to be successful at the polls — he must be a "nice fellow." If he has this primary qualification his chances of being elected are enormously increased by his having a large family and such incompetence in private life that he cannot support it. Incompetence and amiability thus become touchstones to success in public life.

The ideal candidate would therefore appear to be the hotel clerk. He is richly endowed by nature and training to seek office. He has a keen memory for names, a property smile, and a capacity for unending small talk. His hands slap backs with the accuracy and swiftness of a semaphore arm of a train signal automatically rising or falling as the limited flashes by. He has just enough ability to master the minutiae of his job. If in addition to these invaluable qualities the hotel clerk should have a wife, nine children, two crippled spinster sisters, and an aged grandfather, there is little reason why he should not be able to rise to any office in the land. Strangely enough, he remains the country's most neglected potential political figure.

This is a pure and a true democracy. There is no qualification of property or of mental attainment for the franchise of voting. One need be only free, white, and twenty-one. Yet the voter may not vote unless he pays his poll tax of a dollar or two. Frequently he does not have the money or is unwilling to spend it for the nebulous privilege of voting. But politicians may always be found who are willing to assume this onerous burden for him, and what is more natural than that he in a burst of gratitude should vote for the benefactor who has made it possible for him to register his voice in government? Democracy, after all, is a device for expressing the free will at the polls of all the people.

The Delta pays more taxes into the state treasury than any other section of Mississippi. But its influence in state politics is painfully limited. It has not sent one of its citizens to the United States Senate or the governor's chair in twenty years. There is a sharp division politically between the Delta and the rest of the state. It is a division roughly of hill people and of

Delta people; of large landowners and of small owners; of an area predominantly Negro in population and of an area dominantly white in many of its counties.

The small hill farmers of Mississippi scratching the sterile soil of their lands have no love for the large planters of the Delta tilling their fat acres. They have no affection for the lingering aristocratic tradition of the Delta. They hate the Negro or barely tolerate him at best. Their lands are largely worked by the labor of their own hands. The plantations of this area are almost entirely worked by Negroes. Numerically the whites beyond the Delta far exceed the whites within the Delta. And they vote almost solidly against this section in state and national elections.

This cleavage between two classes of whites within the state has become sharper with the passing years, and political control in the larger affairs of Mississippi is now vested in the hands of the non-Delta people. There are less than one hundred thousand whites within this area; there are more than nine hundred thousand whites beyond it. And the large Negro population of the Delta does not vote.

That this situation would some day arise was anticipated long ago by some of the clearer-thinking members of the old régime of the Delta, and by other men outside of this section, who belonged by birth and tradition to that régime. One of their leaders, at the constitutional convention of 1890, suggested that the Negro be enfranchised. His theory was that the enfranchised Negro would always follow politically in the orbit of the upper-class whites; that the hatred of the poor whites for Negroes would always keep them apart. It was clear, then, that if the Negro voted, his numbers would assure victory to the whites of the old régime. This bold and revolutionary suggestion never came to a vote.

Even within the Delta itself political control is rapidly flowing out of the hands of descendants of the early settlers into the hands of newcomers to this section; it is passing from the planters and townsmen of the pioneer tradition to white share-croppers and white farmers owning small tracts of land; from the few industrialists to their mill and factory workers.

In one county of the Delta largely occupied by big plantations, there has been a marked infiltration within recent years of poor whites from the hills of Mississippi. They have served notice with brutal frankness upon the planters who bear the brunt of taxation, that they will freely vote for roads and other public improvements of any kind whatsoever, regardless of the ability of the planters to pay the taxes. They know that they themselves will not be burdened by taxation because they own little or no property. They have from their point of view everything to gain and nothing to lose. And in addition they may taste the delights of putting unbearable loads upon the shoulders of a class whom they cordially dislike.

This threat, if carried out, must result eventually in the breakup of large plantations, in an economic anarchy, and the collapse of local government, with inevitable repercussions upon state government. This is a war of the classes without guns or bayonets. It is a symptom of mass irresponsibility gone mad. It demonstrates clearly that a democracy may be an ordered form of government expressing the will of the people, or the disordered stampede of a majority trampling a minority into the earth, and rushing without program or plan or principle, hate-envenomed, to the destruction of that minority.

The coming of the hill whites to the Delta in large numbers to work on the plantations and in the factories must inevitably remove the last vestiges of influence in public affairs which still remain to the small number of men in each community who cling to the traditions of *noblesse oblige*. It must drive the Negroes from the Delta if not from the South, because white labor will displace Negro labor, and the hatred of poor whites for Negroes will make their position precarious if not impossible. The whole character of this civilization will be completely altered; its racial and social habits changed; its pride trailed in the dust; its memories erased and its flickering dreams of a better way of life extinguished.

One of the tragedies of the Delta is the position of the small minority of men whose forefathers settled the country, who cherish an intense love for it and a passionate desire to make it a land both beautiful and just. They want their country to be honored, to be able to hold its head high in any concert of civilized communities, to administer even-handed justice in and out of the courts to high and to low, to struggle away from darkness toward the light. Some of them strive lifelong to lead their communities in the ways of beauty and of truth; others in their despair migrate elsewhere or advise their sons and daughters to migrate. Those who remain are frequently misunderstood, are lost, or are dismissed as quixotic.

Men of this group were in the forefront of the fight against the Ku Klux Klan in the Delta nearly fifteen years ago. They walked undaunted when the sultry twilight of that period of hate threatened to dim forever the light of the sun of reason. They fought the insanities and inanities of the Klan with every weapon at their disposal, until the bed-sheets of the Klansmen became the shrouds in which bigotry and hatred were consigned to an ignominious grave.

These men see that the presence here of large masses of Negroes among a minority of whites may produce strange maladies of the soul among their fellows, leading eventually to spiritual degradation and to complete weakening of the whole man. It is impossible, they think, for a community to nurture a high civilization and justify its position as a superior race, if the Negroes, who are utterly dependent upon it in so many ways, are allowed to sink into bottomless pits of despair and disappointment. It is difficult, they believe, for a community to avoid paying the ultimate penalty for its neglect of the Negroes, in the form finally of callousness toward one another. It is absurd, in their opinion, for a community to believe that it may condone crimes and injustices on the part of some of its members toward a weaker people, without finally having the same crimes and injustices directed toward themselves. It is reasonable to believe, they say, that the petty criminal who begins his career as a pickpocket, emboldened by his success and greedy for gain, will become a thief in the night, a robber or a burglar, and that in the committing of a major crime he will not hesitate to kill. Degeneration proceeds subtly, slowly, and often without the knowledge of the person in whom it is proliferating. Its roots spread slowly and wide like the roots of a flowering cancer, reaching deeply and painlessly into the vitals of his victim, until there is no recourse save to the desperate remedy of the surgeon's knife or the grave.

Once there was in the Delta, as in the South, the fact and the ideal of the white man's responsibility toward the Negro. It is true that he was emancipated from slavery. But he was not emancipated from the white man, nor the white man from him. The stronger race remained the stronger. The weaker race remained the weaker. Knowledge was the white man's portion, and ignorance was the Negro's. The doors of hope and of opportunity were wide open to the whites; the Negro might enter only through their sufferance. The freed slave was no longer in bondage, but the force of economic circumstances held him still in servitude. And the former masters, the stronger, the more knowing, the unassertively superior whites, extended to the Negro a kind and generous paternalism. If, say these men, the whites of the Delta wish to enjoy the rights and privileges that flow to them as members of the dominant race they must be willing to assume those responsibilities which are inseparably attached to enlightened privilege and justified right.

The problem before them is a difficult and delicate one. It is to raise the Negro's standards in every phase of his life without disturbing the equilibrium of racial relations, and the *status quo* of the white man's dominance socially and politically. It involves a profound comprehension of the deep-rooted prejudices of both the white and the Negro community, of the infinite complexity of the racial situation here, of the functioning in peace and contentment side by side of two widely differing peoples. The risks of attacking the problem wrongly are not that the protagonists of a certain plan shall be eliminated from having a voice in community affairs, but that the Negroes whom they are trying to help shall be pushed nearer the abyss.

The risks, on the other hand, of doing nothing are also great. There is the ever-present danger of the moral degeneration of a whole group of people. There is the failure to perform a duty

— a failure attended with complete spiritual obliquity — on the part of a stronger race toward a weaker. There is the fear that the emancipated but underprivileged Negro may eventually prove to be as much an economic illusion for the welfare of the Delta as Southerners were beginning to discover the slave was shortly prior to the Civil War.

Consider, for instance, the state of Negro health in the Delta. Literally tens of thousands of Negro men, women, and children are reeking and rotting with venereal diseases. They are a fruitful field for the diseases of filth; their tuberculosis rate is far higher than among the whites. If one disregards all concepts of humanitarianism it is still clear that people of this kind must be a severe economic drain upon the whites who own or control practically all the lands and business of this section.

The losses caused by the Negro who cannot plow his fields because of syphilis, who cannot work in a lumbermill because of tuberculosis, who is an intermittent laborer in the intervals of malaria attacks, and who is committed to an asylum for the insane, must ultimately come out of the pockets of the people of the Delta or of the state. The underpaid Negro whose standard of living is kept at a low level is an economic loss to the majority of persons in the community and ultimately to the community itself. He cannot buy, and therefore cannot consume, beyond his extremely meager purchasing power. He is an almost meaningless cipher to the merchant and to the manufacturer. He can never hope to become a property-owner and a taxpayer. Trembling always on the verge of poverty, illness or misfortune or the loss of a job throws him immediately upon public or private charity. It follows, therefore, that if the three hundred thousand Negroes of the Delta had more money to spend and to save annually, the one hundred thousand whites of the area would benefit enormously. They control practically all the business and pay the larger part of the taxes.

So, too, the white community pays enormously for Negro crime which is permitted to rage almost unheeded. The costs of jails and prisons, of days lost from labor, of courts and trials, of officers and the whole paraphernalia and personnel for the detection and imprisonment of Negro criminals, comes out of the pockets of the taxpaying whites.

In fine, say the visionaries of the Delta, perhaps the boasted cheap labor of the Delta is not so cheap, after all, if you add the high indirect costs to the low direct wages. The wages that we pay, while low, are yet not coolie wages, and our labor supply, while large, is not an inexhaustible labor supply, although for the moment it is more than abundant. It seems to be docile and contented, but may that not be because the Negro of the Delta has nowhere to go in business-depressed America?

It is certain, they maintain, that we neither want nor welcome white labor in our fields. The whites are less tractable, more belligerent, far less sympathetic to us, and in no wise more efficient. We do not understand them and they do not understand us. With all our crimes of omission and commission we still retain a marked affection for the Negro. It is inconceivable to us that we should ever be without him. Yet our memories cannot be so short that we fail to remember how only a few years ago thousands of Negroes streamed out of the Delta in endless processions of trains bound for Chicago, Detroit, and St. Louis. By preference and of necessity we have committed ourselves so far as possible to a policy of all-Negro labor. Is it not wise, then, within the limits imposed by economic necessity, to raise that labor to the highest possible level of excellence, of earnings, and of contentment? Does a man in the presence of an oncoming flood burn his boat and take to a tree?

These men of the Delta who love their country and do not want to see her dishonored, desire to preserve the best of the old South and engraft it upon the new. They clearly realize that the task of rehabilitation to which they would set themselves is far beyond the slender resources of this section. They know how very many ills from which the Negro suffers are of his own making. They understand that if the whites can do much for the Negro, the Negro must do much for himself. And above all, while they are moved by unselfish humanitarian impulses to help him, they are more strongly moved by the fear that the temptation of his presence may cause the whites to lose their own souls.

The earth of the Delta is a violent earth. Its flat black fields cry out for fruition under the blazing sun of summer; they are fecund to the touch of the plow; they writhe with life longing to be released. Heat stands upon the Delta during long days and nights; it pours as from a giant furnace an unending stream of white dazzling light upon the earth; it stings the flesh and opens cracks in the fields; it drains the minds of men and wearies their bodies. A clear sky suddenly blackens with clouds, rolls with thunder, crackles with lightning, and the sudden, warm tumultuous rains of the Delta flood the steaming earth. Then they are gone and the dust-stained trees shine again with their rich green; the gray-white bodies of mules gleam black; the furrows of the fields run with water and the ditches gurgle with rain. In an hour or two the earth is dry again, cumulus clouds of virgin white float high in the sky, jaybirds shriek from thorn trees, buzzards float high up against the blue, and mules tread again the endless cotton rows of the Delta.

Against this background, variable, shifting, uncertain, and heat-tortured; amid swamps dark and mysterious and lost; in the presence of the mighty and eternal river rolling onward like some creature of despair forever haunted and forever at bay; under sudden suns and swarming stars; never far from Negro speech and the Negro singing; within America and yet withdrawn — white men fight for their souls and for the souls of those about them, so that they may be free forever and the country they love forever fair.

CHAPTER 12

How Long, O Lawd?

THE TREE-CLAD CLIFFS of Natchez look down from their heights upon the thick-coiled yellow waters of the Mississippi. They gaze with unsleeping vision across its width to the shores of Louisiana, flat and palely green in the white sunshine. The river comes slowly and gracefully to Natchez, moving through an immense crescent to the north of the town until it straightens itself out at its feet, and then with quickened speed hurries its homing waters to the distant sea.

Upstream the washed blueness of the sky is smudged with the black smoke of dredges. Pygmy men pit their pygmy strength and logical minds against the herculean powers of the unpredictable river. Downstream in the glare of the hot morning sun, fishermen in their skiffs seem to stand waist-deep in the molten waters as they draw in their trot-lines heavy with catfish the color of blue and of pearl, with dignified whiskers, and mouths pursed in righteous indignation. Across the river little shantyboats burn cool white in the shadows of green willows. Overhead seas of clouds drift eternally in tumbled confusion.

The town lies drowsing in the anaesthesia of overwhelming heat. Upon the bluffs there is little sound save the droning of bees in the honeysuckle, the far-off, uncertain coughing of a motorboat breasting the swift current, and the whine of a saw in the lumber-mill far below muted by distance to a tiny querulous wail. Upon the land and upon the water the July sun of the deep South imposes silence, and where there is movement it is the dream-movement of sleep-walkers.

It was here, two hundred and fifty years ago, that La Salle paused to visit with the Natchez Indians — no people, brown or red or yellow or black, is so remote as to escape the curse of the white man's presence — while his king, Louis XIV, the Grand Monarque, sat amid the mirrored magnificence of Versailles and dreamed of a world-wide Holy Roman Empire. The flag of France flapped in the alien breezes of the Natchez bluffs until the English came with Protestantism, the common law, and the cutlery of Sheffield, to be succeeded in turn by the Spanish bringing Catholicism and the wines of Jerez. At the turn of the nineteenth century the Americans of the new republic arrived, ("Oh, say, can you see?") spreading out over the wilderness with the relentless flow of a river in flood.

And it was here that I met Henry. Henry is a stricken giant who left the Delta in his youth to become a roustabout on the steamboats that plied the Mississippi, the Ouachita, and the Black. He stands six feet two, although stooped now with toil and pain. The muscles of his powerful arms still dart like aroused blacksnakes against the sudden whiteness of his tattered shirt. His eyes are liquid with pain and sorrow and remembrance. They are wide with troubled bewilderment. His voice is low and wistful and sad. His hands seem folded always in attitudes of profound resignation.

That noontime when I met him he was seated on the ground with his back against an oak tree of the bluffs, looking down upon his beloved river, dreaming of his hot lost youth when he would have matched his strength against the might of a donkey engine, and his prowess with women with any "ramrodding" buck of the land. One night at Greenville, as they were loading cotton on the *Tennessee Belle*, in the darkness and the rain, and the pace became swifter and ever swifter ("O Lawdie, is you boys gittin' weak?"), a bale came tumbling down upon Henry, crushing his ribs, twisting his back, thrusting him into darkness and sudden old age.

"Den," he said, "I seed de Lawd. I walked in dere an' dere He wuz settin' to an altar wid a desk to His side. He had gray eyes an' a white face jes' like a natchal man, an' He talked in a low voice so's a man could un'erstan'.

"De Lawd looked up when He seed me an' said, 'Henry, has you got heah at las'?' I said, 'Yas, Lawd.' Den I seed a rack what looked like a hatrack an' on hit wuz a lot er robes. De Lawd said, 'Henry, dere's yo' robe. Try hit on.' I tried hit on an' de Lawd said, 'Henry, dere's yo' crown.' I said, 'Lawd, lemme try hit on.' Den I seed a golden wais'ban' an' golden slippers an' I put dem on.

"I said, 'Lawd, lemme walk about in dese golden things.' An' de Lawd said, 'Walk, little one, walk.' Den I said, 'Lawd, lemme go fum heah wid dese glory robes.' De Lawd leaned back an' jes' smiled quiet-like. Den He said, 'No, Henry, you has to go back where you come fum, do what yo' father an yo' mother tells you, an' some day dese things will be yo's.' I said, 'Yas, Lawd.'

'An' w'en I lef' out f'm dere I looked back an' de Lawd's long hair which came clean down to his waist was all lit up wid colored lights jes' like de lights on a floatin' palace."

Henry lay long pain-wracked weeks in the hospital where the doctors marveled at his strength and the capacity of his crushed body to cling to life. He was pleased with them and with himself when they said, "Henry, you are a hard nigger to kill," and he was grateful when with the strange ways of white folks they drove away the demons of pain with the prick of a needle. Once the flame of his life burned very low.

"Den," said Henry, "I seed de Lawd in a white chariot wid white horses, an' I said, 'Lawd, I wants to ride in dat chariot wid you.' De Lawd lemme git in wid Him an' He turned aroun' to me an' said, 'Henry, ef a person axes fer a thing in his heart, de Lawd will grant hit to him in grace.'"

Henry's "white folks" came to see him in the hospital, bringing gifts of money and little things for his comfort. His companions of the river, when the *Belle* was tied up at the Natchez landing, brought him the news of the world, and said, "Nigger, you is gittin' so lazy an' fat layin' up heah in dis bed you ain't gwine be fitten fur nuthin' 'cep' killin' lak a Christmas hawg." An elder of the Sanctified Church of the Living God came one day with vague ideas of converting Henry to the true faith. Henry was

glad to see him because he liked to talk to strangers, and had a
reverence for the officers of any church. He himself "wa'n't
nuthin' but a pulpit hand. W'en you rousts you jes' can't rise."
But the Sanctified elder could not bring him within the bosom
of his church, although he labored mightily with subtle innuendo.

Slowly Henry recovered and walked out at last to warm his
broken, sun-yearning body in the bright sunshine. Back to the
river he went, hoping to work once more as a roustabout on the
Mississippi, the Ouachita, or the Black, where "all de white folks
knows I'se a cotton-snatchin' nigger." There was no work for
him. He was crippled. Henry received the blow dazedly. He
could not bring himself to believe that it had fallen. In his own
mind he had endowed his body with an immortality of strength
on earth, even as de good Lawd would endow his soul with immortality in heaven. Surely no one could say that Henry's
strength had been exhausted until that far day when his brothers
and sisters of the Bright Morning Star Baptist Church should
gather about his coffin and sing:

> "De blood done sot me free,
> De blood done sot me free,
> Oh, don't you see what de blood done done,
> De blood done sot me free,
> Hallelujah, hallelujah,
> De blood done sot me free."

Henry pleaded in vain for another chance on the boats. His
body ached for sweat-drenched nights and days of labor; for
the excitement of arriving at and departing from strange-familiar
river towns; for high-piled plates of corn bread, cabbage, hog
meat, cowpeas, and molasses; but most of all for payday and time
ashore with money in the pockets of his Sunday clothes. Then
he could boast to the weakling "town niggers" of his prodigious
strength. Henry felt that he was still almost the equal of the
fabulous Green Runner, "who wuz de strongest man I ever
heered tell of on de river. He'd eat half a bar'l er flour an' a
middle er meat at one meal, wid a bar'l er greens an' a water-
bucket full er syrup. Den w'en he had et dat he stretch an'
say to de Cap'n, 'Cap'n, turn off fo' er dese niggers an' I does dey

work.' An' de Cap'n he turned off fo' mens." Ashore, Henry
bought presents in the five-and-ten-cent stores and the fleeting
favors of bright-skinned girls. "Some niggers say de blacker de
meat de sweeter de bone, but I doesn't bleeve dat." He sat in
the catfish-scented dining-room of the Rooster Café, "settin' 'em
up to de ladies," showed his gold teeth bought on Canal Street
in New Orleans in bursts of wide-mouthed laughter, got a "English brush-back haircut" in the barber shop next door, and finally
at nightfall swaggered down Walnut Street ("I rams as I walks
along"), and over the levee to the waiting *Belle*.

The white cap'ns and the white mates who had known Henry
in the days of his glory listened patiently to his pleas for work
because they liked him. They were sorry for him and vaguely
troubled by the little pinpoints of light which near-starvation
caused to dance in his soft eyes. But they gave him instead of
a job a little money. Then he went ashore and up the hill to
sit under the shade of the trees on the bluff, as he watched his
former comrades load and unload the boat, starring their work
with song as they toiled up and down the steep embankments,
heavy-laden.

And when the boat at last departed Henry watched it move
slowly up the river, its paddle-wheel throwing cascades of dia-
monds into the bright sun, until it disappeared around Giles
Bend, bound for fabulous ports a hundred miles away, where
dice rattle in the night, banjos play, and bright-skinned girls sit
on the laps of dark-skinned men, drinking "mule" out of the
same bottle and making love.

Day after day, like a man enchanted, Henry sits in the shade
of the trees high above the river. He watches with sorrowful
restless eyes the movement upon its bosom; the insect passage
of the ferry from Natchez to Vidalia; the rafts of logs shepherded
by squat tugboats; the swift launches of government engineers
going to Glasscock Island, and skiffs of fishermen dancing in the
shimmering heat.

Sometimes Henry dozes and his head drops to his bosom.
Then the muddy river runs high above him, staining the clean
softness of the heavens, while the sky flows pale blue flecked

with the white of clouds in the brown abandoned bed of the river. The banks both sides are lined with sinners in robes of black. Henry stands on a tall mast far above the golden decks of a steamboat shining with gold, holding his right arm aloft, because "w'en I got 'ligion de Lawd placed seven burnin' candles in my right hand an' tole me to hold my light high so de sinners could follow an' take my gospel an' spread hit everywhere."

And sometimes King Jesus Himself bends over Henry as he dozes in the shade of the trees of the river. He whispers to him so softly that only Henry can hear. So softly and with such sweetness of tone that His voice is one with the soughing of the wind in the trees, with the singing of birds in the wild honeysuckle that clings to the bluffs, with the rich voices of Negroes chattering near-by, and the mournful, lost wail of a steamboat's whistle as it struggles slowly around a bend in the far distance.

Part Two
1947

CHAPTER 1

Greenville Revisited

Y ESSUH, the best way to get to know the folks is to work a local freight." The brakeman of the Cannon Ball and I were chatting as the train clanked along its one-track route from Memphis, the Tennessee capital of Mississippi, to Greenville, the small metropolis of the Mississippi Delta. A desire to know more about the art of travel prompted me to ask why.

"Well, I'll tell you," he said. "A few years ago when I was working the local freight out of Greenville, we noticed a couple of kids — a boy and girl — cleaning up a piece of woods. Every day we'd see 'em cutting down trees, lopping off the limbs, stacking the logs. They worked hard all the time, and we got interested in 'em because most kids nowadays ain't worth the powder to blow 'em up with. First we got to waving to 'em when we went by. Then we started dropping the *Commercial Appeal* so's they'd have something to read. When it got real hot, we'd slow down and hand 'em fifty pounds of ice. Those kids just never did stop hitting the ball. Almost before you could say Jack Roberson, they had built a little ole log cabin and started making a crop. We watched 'em like they was ours and in a way they was because we kinda adopted 'em. We'd bring 'em things they needed — especially groceries. Now you take the conductor sitting there. I know he gave 'em over $200 worth of groceries of himself. We watched that couple work themselves out of the woods into a nice house, pay off their land, and start on their way to be somebody. That's what I mean by saying the best way to get to know the folks is to work a local freight."

The brakeman, a rough-hewn man who, although he sat hunched in his seat and ate peanuts while he talked, yet suggested the massiveness of Michelangelo's David, had hound-dog soft brown eyes and a manner of speech like the somnolent whisperings of summer cottonwoods. He recited the American idyll in which he had participated so artlessly that it seemed an everyday occurrence for a freight-train crew to mother youngsters struggling with the forest; not at all unusual for pioneers to be putting up a log cabin in Mississippi in 1941, even if the first of its kind had been erected by Swedes along the Delaware early in the eighteenth century; while as long ago as 1890, the Census Bureau had announced that the frontier was forever closed. By these tokens of spontaneous kindness, arcadian simplicity, and pioneering in the day of the airplane and the skinless frankfurter of synthetic meat, I knew I was back in the Mississippi Delta.

As, in the Shellyean phrase, life stains with its radiance the white dome of eternity, so is a man forever stained by his childhood environment. Childhood and its memories — that incandescence which grows brighter as the fuel diminishes upon which it feeds — is the glowing element in the private edition of time, space, and beauty that each man takes everywhere with him. It is his secret wood, his world lost and found, his comforting infant's thumb. It is the day you sailed down a wide river, green-wooded both sides, until, its mouth reached at nightfall, the lights of land astern, the all-enveloping darkness about you, you first felt the surge and thrust of ocean and knew that henceforth you would be forever ocean-borne on an ocean forever surging. It is the split second in the darkened theater auditorium when the babble is stilled, the proscenium glows with light, and you are about to glide from the sentient world into the world of make-believe: the illusion never sundered, the mist never dissipated. It is the youth dreaming of recreating the life of humanity, and the child suffering the pangs of bellyache from eating stolen plums.

Going home again is bitter-sweet. It was therefore with a warming melancholy that I awaited the departure of the Cannon

Ball in the Illinois Central station in Memphis; the well-remem-
bered train that would take me back to the town where I was
born and raised. This station through which I had passed so
often in my youth was to me an architectural miracle when it
was built. It is true that, when I came to know them, the Grand
Central and Pennsylvania stations in New York — the latter
fashioned after the Roman baths of Caracalla — did seem somewhat larger and had huge marble halls and stars that shone in
lofty ceilings. But the Illinois Central station had its own wonders. It was taller even than the Washington County courthouse
to whose soaring tower, impeded by fright and pigeon droppings,
a child had once clambered. One entered its central hall by stairs
with a magnificent sweep. Here were hordes of people awaiting
their trains, and a perpetual air of carnival gaiety that prevailed
in Greenville only when Barnum & Bailey's circus came to town
during cotton-picking time and celebrant country folks spent
their "circus money." Passengers took long and ardent farewells
of friends and relatives for, as one later learned, among the
people of the Delta, as in Provence, Sicily, Tahiti, every parting,
however brief, is excuse for a mild emotional orgy and every reunion an exercise in delighted surprise. "Now, Mary, you be
sure and write me." "Take care of yourself, Jack." "Reverum
Wilson gwine be there the third Sunday. You and Cooter be
shore to come."

There were kissings, embracings, handshakings, long leave-
takings. The station was redolent of the mingled odors of ham
biscuits, fried chicken, and bananas which passengers had in
their lunch shoeboxes. Children carried little glass replicas of
pistols and railroad lanterns filled with multicolored jellybeans.
Their elders struggled with parcels. Memphis is the shopping
center for a tremendous area and, their trading done, people
were taking home the luxuries of metropolis. Occasionally an
incoming train discharged its stream of passengers to breast for
a moment the stream of the outward bound, but the particles
quickly separated and the intense life of the waiting room was
resumed with steady, throbbing beat. Punctuating the confusion
and giving it a sense of imminent crisis was the high voice of

the Negro train crier: the American muezzin calling his train-intoxicated countrymen to take their places in the cars as his Moslem counterpart calls the faithful to worship. "Train fur Lulu, Tunica, Clarksdale, Alligator, Shelby, Leland, Greenville, Rollin' Fawk, Vicksburg, an' New Ahluns. A .. ll a .. boa'd. . . . ."

Outside in the trainshed were giant locomotives, their wheels taller than a man, smoke flowing turbidly from their stacks. These were the monsters that would take you to such far places as Chicago or St. Louis where your elders had on occasion gone, but which you had not visited nor were likely to visit. Whistles wailed, bells rang, the floor of the waiting room trembled as the Rock Island Flyer arrived, and you suddenly found yourself walking toward the train that would take you on your first long journey.

Three months later, at Christmastime, you came this way again, a freshman homeward bound for the holidays. Returning home that year, you ran into Simon Levy. A clerk in Greenville, Simon was usually out of a job except during the fall. Then Negroes had a little money, white folks a little more, and there was a feverish flurry of business. Simon was a poor salesman. If a man asked him for shoelaces he did not try to sell him a pair of shoes but, his demand satisfied, dismissed him with elaborate courtesy. Vague and dreaming, the one passion of his life seemed to be wildflowers; and so ardent was this passion that a wag nicknamed him "Willie Wildflower" after a zany comic who had appeared at the Grand Opera House. Everybody liked Simon although nobody knew much about him except that he had come over from the old country when he was a boy and had drifted down to Mississippi. But nobody would give him a job until the fall came, and it is hard to make enough money in three months as a clerk to keep yourself for the rest of the year.

This Christmastime he stood at an intersection of busy streets near the Illinois Central station in Memphis. Hatless, topcoatless, shivering in a thin suit, he had by his side his stock in trade — garish lithographs of Christ: the pearly halo, the bleeding heart in the marbleized bosom, the sorrowful face. Simon had set up for business in an area given over to cheap stores and eating joints patronized by poor whites and Negroes. But even here the gaiety of the season was evident while all of us must be thankful that the poor are always with us at Christmas so that once a year we may shed our love and last year's garments upon them together with a pound of mixed nuts. Cold-driven crowds hurried past. Men carried Christmas trees and wavering pyramids of parcels. The Salvation Army's dinner bells tinkled with thin music. There was a hint of snow in the air. Perhaps, rarety of rareties, there would be a white Christmas in the Deep South.

Nobody bought Simon's wares nor did he offer them for sale. He just stood there with his long, crooked nose, his clear blue eyes, his serene forehead, his tortured mouth uncertainly shaped as though it had been fashioned by a little child. Simon stood there while the crowds hurried by, the Salvation Army's bells tinkled ever more icily on the frostier air, automobile horns honked, an occasional firecracker exploded, and the fried-pork-chop warmth inside a retaurant meeting the outside cold set up a mist that almost obscured the legend — FOR COLORED ONLY — painted on its shadows. It was Christmastime and Simon Levy stood at the busy street intersection near the railroad station exposing for sale wares that nobody wanted.

Years later I came back to Greenville by the same train which I gained by the same street intersection leading to the same station. This time I brought with me Jacob Epstein's "Mask of Christ." I lent it to my friend William Alexander Percy. He put it on the mantelpiece in his library, and sitting there with him I often looked at it. I saw its long, crooked nose, its deepset eyes, its serene forehead, and the tortured mouth uncertainly shaped as though it had been fashioned by a little child. I did not talk of it — not even to Will Percy who understood almost everything — but just sat and looked at it while friends drifted in and out of that most hospitable of living rooms in the home of that most generous of men.

A few months ago, I took my place in the last car of the three-car Cannon Ball. One car is for white folks, another for Negroes, the third for baggage and mail. Unlike the old days, the passenger cars were identical in their appointments thereby adding another dimension to the Negro saying — compounded of weariness and the irony to which Negroes are seldom given — that "niggers is as good as white folks in two places — the bed and the graveyard." There were other changes. The cars, by contrast with the past, were shining clean. The red plush of the chairs — once itchy and a corporate-endowed refuge for wild insect life — was covered with white cotton crash. About one-fourth of the car was partitioned from the remainder by latticework suggestive of a similar arrangement in Moslem palaces where ladies of the household, seeing but unseen, look upon the world forbidden to them. Behind the screen sat the smokers. It is a curious thing that Americans, more garrulous and bathroom-obsessed than any other people, yet squeamish about the public or semi-public exercise of the natural functions, should have decreed the toilets of trains as their smokingrooms. But now after years of planning by railroad officials, the toilet of the Cannon Ball had lost its function as a smokeroom forum.

There was air-conditioning, but this aspect of progress, like progress in general, has its price. A child can no longer stick his head out of the car window as the train slowly rounds a long curve and experience the almost unbearable pleasure of peering nearly into the locomotive's cab where that most enviable of men, the engineer, was visible for a moment, hand on throttle and eyes, you knew, on mysterious gauges. Nor can you, as formerly when the train stopped at a little station, holler to a friend in a field a quarter of a mile away. When he hollered back, you could ask him when was he going to send that rooster and, distance retarding the conversation, carry on for five or ten minutes while the engineer, privy to it all as was the adjacent countryside, held the train until your business had been settled.

I secretly exulted, however, to observe that in a changing world the Cannon Ball had not essentially changed. Outwardly transformed, inwardly it was what it had always been. Theoretically it was the creature of a rigid schedule by which it was supposed to go from Memphis to Greenville — a distance of one hundred fifty miles — in five hours. But the schedule is obviously a transparent device to satisfy the demanding but unimaginative Interstate Commerce Commission. The train moved as it had always moved: in accord with the dictates of its inner life. And if some progress-bitten maniac — a traveling salesman, a young Deltan coming home from a sales conference in New York, a fashionable clergyman — should protest that an airplane had taken him a distance of one thousand miles in five hours while the Cannon Ball takes as long to go a fraction of this distance, the trainmen would be unmoved by so alien and novel a speculation. Persons who harbor such subversive thoughts are plainly dangerous radicals; at worst, they might even be Republicans.

The Cannon Ball is a triumph, not of speed, but of persistence. Yet, unlike men who are corroded by this dreary virtue, there is nothing stolid about it. Occasionally and without warning, like a long retired dancer arising from his chair and doing a furious jig to the delight of his grandchildren, it burst into intemperate speed. Telegraph poles shot by. The water cooler rattled in its stanchions. Passengers looked quizzically at one another. Then capriciously, the train would slow down almost to a walk and you could leisurely observe the life of the countryside.

There were few passengers on the train. In the old days it had been crowded. The reason for its present condition was evident: the paved highway parallel to the railroad track along which ran buses and cars. The United States has been the most backward of the great western nations in road building. Mississippi, the poorest and most backward of the states, was one of the last to come out of the mud. As it emerged, the glory of the Cannon Ball declined. Hence it now moves as though by the dictate of an imperative psychological compulsion; or as the last exemplar of a lost cause. The roads have come and the Delta's isolation which preserved its peculiar flavor has gone. Westward-bound tourists stop fleetingly in its little towns. They are good people, earnest people, worthy people; as incapable of letting you down as of lifting you up. They spread their insidious doctrines of the importance of bank clearings, going after business, staying on the job. Missionaries to a man, they are spiritual carpetbaggers more destructive than the small-scale looters who went South in the wake of the Yankee armies. After they pass, carrots are cultivated where hollyhocks once grew. In their presence the provincial passions wither and die, to be succeeded, alas, by the passion for uniformity.

The morning ran its course. One by one the towns along its route were ticked off by the Cannon Ball. At midafternoon I descended from it in Greenville. Waiting at the station for a tardy friend, I spoke to a white taxicab driver and found myself catapulted into the complexities of the race question.

There are two groups of white-driver cabs, as well as Negro-driver cabs, in Greenville. One group does take them. Negro-Negro passengers. The other group does take them. Negro-driver cabs haul members of both races indiscriminately. But, said my informant, "A lot of white people around here take a Negro cab when they don't want anybody to know what they're up to." By these tokens, also, I knew that I was back in the Delta.

Greenville is a fast growing and changing town. This was made clear to me on the day of my arrival when I asked the telephone operator to connect me with the home of an old citizen. Much to my surprise she said, "I'll give you Information." Ten years ago "Central" would have connected me at once. Fifteen years ago, if she could not have found my friend at home, she might have added that he was probably at the hospital where his wife, Miss Eugenie, was momentarily expecting the arrival of a baby.

In the last decade Greenville's population has increased from fifteen thousand to twenty-one thousand, and is now estimated to be close to thirty thousand. One can no longer walk down Washington Avenue and know nearly everybody by name or repute. The gray anonymity which the city dweller likes and the small townsman abhors, has crept upon it like a river fog. Old citizens, bewildered by the town's growth and displeased with some of the changes it has brought, cannot account for it. Greenville is off the main line of the Illinois Central. It does not throb with industry, nor is it a playground for tourists. Unlike Natchez, it has no past to sell. Neither oil nor gold has been found under its adjacent cottonfields. Yet Greenville Grows, as the town-proud *Democrat* used to say twenty years ago, whenever a dynamic citizen put up a new cowshed.

The town has an energetic Chamber of Commerce composed of farsighted citizens and much of its growth is undoubtedly traceable to the activities of this sagacious organization. But luck has also had its way here. This is no untoward reflection upon the abilities of the citizenry for, as beauty is an aspect of genius in a woman, so is luck an aspect of genius in the affairs of a man or a town. Shielding her face as this golden vixen often does, luck came to Greenville in the form of the disastrous river flood of 1927. Once the waters had subsided, the Red Cross and fraternal organizations assisted the flood's victims to their feet. The Army Corps of Engineers engaged in great works of repair and flood prevention along the river near Greenville. It released millions of dollars which largely served to carry the town through the blackest years of the depression of the nineteen-thirties, while similar towns so unfortunate as not to have been submerged by the river lived on whippoorwill peas and cornbread.

Greenville was then, and still chiefly is, a cotton town. It is an appendage of its surrounding plantations. Yet here where the soil is rich most of the people have always been poor, and they were growing poorer when in 1930 Congress passed the Triple A with the warm approval of Delta farmers. They were paid for not growing cotton and corn, our ingenuity as a nation having reached the point where we could produce wealth to the extent that we did not produce it. Farmers clung to their mortgaged lands and embraced the new dogma; the more fervently perhaps because men fight fiercely for dogmas in which they no longer believe. When the Triple A was ruled out by the Supreme Court, Congress passed the Soil Conservation Act which subsidized the production of cotton. The "noble, independent farmer," as he was called in the eighteen-thirties; the vehement states-right farmer; the farmer whose individualism is summed up in his maxim "Hoe your own row" — all these prospered as they were wet-nursed by the federal government. But the more they prospered, the louder they cussed the Government. The more they emerged from near-bankruptcy, the sharper their denunciation of the agricultural decrees that had snatched them from the abyss. They called President Roosevelt a dictator; took all the handouts they could get; asked for more while asserting their fierce independence in the same breath; and voted the straight Democratic ticket when they went to the polls. The while Greenville, center of a large and prospering agricultural area, grew.

The hard times of the early nineteen-thirties forced white and Negro farmers into a straitjacket of economy they had never known. How hard were the times was indicated to me by a Negro, who, years afterward, said: "Boss, I et so much okra I jes' slid out of bed." Banks no longer turned over to the farmer-borrower the entire proceeds of the loan he got to make a crop. He might use much of it to buy jewels for his wife; to be kind to a hard-pressed lady in Memphis; or indulge in a poker game. He was given so much money each month, and had to produce a budget showing how he was spending it. Thus many Delta farmers, for the first time, were compelled to use business-like methods and to profit from them, while Greenville, the metropolis of the area, profited along with them.

Federal aid for roads enabled the Delta to come out of the mud. A government loan helped to throw a bridge across the Mississippi below Greenville and so bring within its reach hitherto untapped trade areas in Arkansas and Louisiana. Two large local industries, based upon forest products, grew larger as the country prospered. Their payrolls contributed greatly to the town's growth. But the industries were unionized. Their wage scales were higher than those enjoyed by the non-union labor in the community. This angered some of its middle-class group, although they were the direct and indirect beneficiaries of the mills' payrolls. Burdened by antique processes of thinking, they are spiritual refugees from the Civil War. They like to sell the land's cotton high. But they are not averse to selling the land's people cheap. It does not move them that high-wage areas else-

where have prospered, while the low-wage South has worn overalls and eaten fatback. They are unwitting enemies of their
region. The shares of unionized mills operating in Greenville
are not owned there, in Mississippi, or in the South. One can
understand, in terms of human greed, that Deltans might exploit
their neighbors for their own benefit. It is difficult to understand
why they should want them exploited for the benefit of absentee
shareholders. The while the mill workers spent their money
locally; the economic middle class grumbled; and Greenville
grew.

There came our entry into the Second World War. War is
like the once wandering Mississippi. It might enrich one man's
lands and ruin another's. War came to Greenville in the form
of a large air forces base. Thousands of men and millions of
dollars poured into the community. Huge sums were sent to the
dependents of soldiers. Farm products went at high prices. The
town prospered mightily.

As an added increment, with romantic overtones, its belles
were snapped up in marriage — Greenville's own youths being
away at war — by young men with alien accents hailing from
such outlandish places as Skaneateles, New York. Even slightly
shelfworn girls, to their delighted amazement, found themselves
saying "I do" in Church, while the organ pealed *O Promise Me*
and the bride's mother, tearful in a ladylike way, wore (according to the local press) a "Halliday model in heavenly blue." War
hath its victories no less renowned than those of peace.

Prosperity is not an unmitigated blessing. Old citizens of
Greenville who used to sit on their porches and watch the
familiar folk go by, with many a hearty "hey" on both sides of
the fence, have given up the struggle. Swamped by newcomers,
they have sold their houses; sold them at prices they never
dreamed of getting and retired to new houses in new suburban
areas where they are making their last stand against the out-
landers. Here, with nice actuarial accuracy, they live and estimate
that their jerrybuilt dwellings with Arkansas gas piped into their
chicken-coop rooms will last just as long as they last. Genteelly
unhappy in their belated prosperity, with newcomers swarming

about them like summer gnats, theirs is a sad fate. It is as though Saint Anthony of Padua, retired to a hermit's cell in the desert, was visited by a plague of bobby-soxers clamoring for his autograph.

Older Negro citizens of the town are perhaps more confused than their white counterparts by the abrupt changes of a society in turbulent transition toward a final form which no man can foretell. They once enjoyed a certain prestige among members of both races. It derived from their continuity of residence, their stability and relative prosperity, a tradition of and reputation for respectability and responsibility, a friendship with the older and more influential white families which gave them a position as arbitrators of race conflicts. But the younger generation of Negroes is sharply at odds with their elders. If the latter suggest moderation in racial points of view; if they say that the world cannot be changed in a day, younger Negroes are likely to dismiss them contemptuously as "handkerchief heads" or "Uncle Toms" — epithets taken from the Northern Negro press whose often reckless and irresponsible outpourings they avidly read.

Sometimes an old Negro, incensed by such taunts, may say to a young man, "Boy, you ain't nothin' but one of them walk-off folks." And when the young one does not know what this means, he is told a tale which illuminates the point:

'Way back yonder in the beginnin' of the world, Ole Adam an' Miss Eve was livin' on fawty acres of good bottom land the Lawd had give 'em. They didn't have no boll weevil nor neither high water an' they made a good crop every year. They had 'em two good cows; a heap of shoats an' sheeps, an' they et they own fryin' chickens because it wa'nt no preachers there to eat 'em. They had a fine garden full o' mustard greens an' rosenears an' a house which didn't never leak. Ole Adam had the best mules in the county; two bran'-new Studebaker wagons; an' a pack of fine rabbit dawgs.

Miss Eve, she he'ped Ole Adam make the crop. She done the cookin', washin', an' ironin', an' they got along mighty good. Hit wa'nt but one thing twixt 'em. Ole Adam he was a man that liked to hunt an' fish, and ever'time he could sneak off, there he was chasin' rabbits, or lookin' after his trotlines. But that vexed Miss Eve 'cause when Ole Adam was away she got kin o' lonesome, it not bein' no folks for her to talk to. So one day she say, "Adam, don't you git some folks for me to talk to whilst you 'way, I ain't gwine let you hunt an' fish."

Ole Adam he didn't like that 'cause he loved to hunt an' fish mo' than anything in the world. So he went off down the big road studdin' what could he do 'bout hit, when here come the Lawd. The Lawd he give Adam hi-dy, and Adam he give the Lawd hi-dy.

"Lawd," say Ole Adam, "You sho been good to me. You gi'e me fawty acres of good bottom lan' an' us makes a good crop all the time. You gi'e me Miss Eve and she sho is a good woman. She he'ps make the crop, an' does all the cookin', ironin', an' washin'. But, Lawd, you knows I'm a man that'd druther hunt an' fish than anything in this world o' yourn, but Miss Eve say don't I git some folks for her to talk to whilst I'm 'way, she ain't gwine lemme hunt an' fish. Lawd, please suh, can't you make some folks to keep that woman company?"

The Lawd say, "Adam, when does you want them folks made?" and Ole Adam he say, "Please suh, could you make 'em this evenin'?" So the Lawd got out his almanac — the one with the quarterin's of the moon in it — to see did he have anything to do that evenin', and when he see he didn't, he tole Ole Adam to meet him twarge sundown by the creek that got that good clay bank an' he would make the folks.

Well, Ole Adam he was right there when the Lawd come up on his good saddlehorse, got off, and hitched him to a little persimmon tree. Adam handed the Lawd a heap o' clay. He started kneadin' it to make the folks, and Ole Adam he cut some fresh green saplings for the framin' work. The Lawd he made some Hebrew chillun an' some Christian chillun, some white chillun an' some colored chillun, some A-rabs an' some Chinermens. Then he put 'em all up by the fence rail an' say, "Now, Adam, you meet me right here soon after sun-up in the mawnin'. I'll be back then to put the brains in these folks."

Old Adam he was right there at first day. But it wa'nt nothin' there. All them folks had already walked off before the Lawd come back, an' they been multiplyin' an' replenishin' the earth ever since.

Nothing, however, bridges the gulf between the generations. Younger and older Negroes, as whites often do, substitute the hurling of epithets for a resort to reason. As a white man who advocates simple justice for Negroes may be called a "nigger lover" by other white men, so a Negro who suggests gradualism rather than revolution as the way to ultimate emancipation, may be called a "white man's nigger" by other Negroes. The counsel of Negro elders is rarely sought by the young, and is regarded with scant respect when volunteered. The elders can seldom turn, as they once did, to members of older white families for remedy or alleviation of their people's wrongs. They are largely dead. With them has died almost the last vestiges of *noblesse oblige*. Their children, tiring of the unceasing struggle, have either moved away, or, remaining at home, devote themselves solely to their own affairs. Their voices, in any event, are lost in the shouts of newcomers many of whom are poor whites filled with a venomous hatred of Negroes. The taxicab driver cannot now take you undirected to Mr. Percy's house; not even when you tell him it is on Percy Street near the Oil Mill. He has never heard of Mr. Cholly Williams, or his wife, Miss Adah. He does not know the names of the old families who were contemporaneous with the mud roads and plank walks of the community; yellow fever and malaria; Reconstruction and the coming of the first railroad. He certainly could not understand these people who, lacking the versatility as well as the boorishness of many of their successors, had only the same manners whether for Negroes or for whites.

Hence the older Negroes of Greenville are lost in a world they do not comprehend. Some of them join their children in New York or Chicago. Others remain, talking as old people talk, of other days and other ways. It won't be long before death comes riding on his white horse.

A little town in process of becoming a big little town, loses in some respects as it gains in others. So the child grown adolescent loses its sense of wonder; and the adolescent become adult sheds his hair with his starry faith. Thus growing Greenville has lost something. Its provincial charm has gone. The tux has become the dinner jacket. It is no longer good form to shop at the Piggly-Wiggly with bobby pins still in your hair after a visit to the beauty parlor. Freud and Elizabeth Arden, that unlikely pair who have transformed America, have come to Greenville as to every other town: the libido faintly redolent of all-purpose face cream. Appetizers, through the sorceries of refinement, have been transmuted into *hors d'oeuvres*. The doctor's wife is no longer "Mrs. Doctor." In the columns of the *Democrat-Times*, people are not now "pleasantly located on Popular Street," but merely live at such and such an address. Yet, thanks to the stand made in the name of the old regime by the society editor of the newspaper, food served at parties remains "delicious refreshments."

The town's streetcars long ago gave way to buses. These conductorless cars ran on the honor system. Passengers put their fares into a cigar box nailed near the entrance doorway. The motorman, intimately acquainted with his patrons, dropped them at points most convenient to their homes. Often he stopped his car to let a passenger pick up a bottle of Durkee's salad dressing, or a loaf of bread. Nobody protested because there was no hurry. There were the obligations of courtesy. What was done for others would also be done for you. Time had not yet become money. All this was part of the long Indian summer of the community — before the coming of such miracles as the self-serve grocery store, nylon stockings, and Williamsburg antiques.

Finally, as evidence of convulsive change, The War is no longer The War Between the States. It is the first World War or the last. Few persons remain such as the old, unreconstructed Confederate lady who, in her tearful anxiety, not only for the Confederacy and Southerners but also for the United States and Yankees, said to me: "How on earth are we ever going to have unity in this country when *Life* magazine prints whole pages of photographs of Mr. Lincoln?"

No one can foretell the ultimate shape of Greenville, and only the mentally arthritic would lament its growth, or hark vainly back to the past. Nowadays, for example, it has police radio cars. One cannot expect a metropolitan chief of police to behave in the manner of Mr. McClain, once Greenville's Falstaffian chief of police (*circa* 1914) who commanded a force of five men awake, asleep, or dozing. Mr. McClain, in whose person the Law lost none of its awful majesty or order any of its austerity, for all that he, their guardian, had an oceanic belly and a gentle face upon which smiles constantly rippled as waters pour from an ever-swelling spring; who wheezed when he walked, and overflowed the buggy in which he rode. Any nimble-footed thief could easily have escaped him, for his whistle could scarcely have summoned in time his scattered lieutenants as one sat eating a hamburger in the Olympia Café at the East End, and another dreamily watched the drift of locust blossoms on O'Hea Street. But nonetheless, the majesty of the Law was unsullied, order reigned, good humor marched everywhere with Chief McClain and, one later realized, he was animated by that passion for intellectual inquiry which moves men to weigh the stars and peer into the mountains of the moon.

This was strikingly demonstrated on an occasion when Hagenbeck's Wild Animal Circus came to town. In its company was a group of Philippine Islands Igorrotes. Savages they were who went half-naked and — horror of horrors — ate dogs! What a sensation Chief McClain caused in Greenville when, ambling around the circus grounds, he came upon a group of them stewing dogs in a huge pot. Dwarfing the Igorrotes as an elephant dwarfs a mouse, he pointed to the pot and made chewing motions with his jaws. Lawyer Hazelwood Farish, one of the lucky bystanders, said that the savages smiled upon the Chief and gave him a drumstick which he immediately ate with every gesture of delight. The news of his fearful act spread quickly through the town. We youngsters expected him to die. Our elders thought he was a little crazy, although some said that dog might not be so bad if you did not know what you were eating. None of us realized that the Chief's spirit was what had made America great; that, conversely, we shall be on our way out as a nation when Americans are no longer willing to take a chance.

Mr. McClain is dead. Dead, too, are his lieutenants who once walked the streets of a little leafy town. Their successors have radio cars and the Bertillon system of fingerprinting. Some of them have attended the FBI school in Washington where they were taught "scientific methods of crime detection." In this way, too, the majesty of the Law is upheld and the austerity of order.

Greenville, with the coming of paved roads and cars, has become a considerable medical center for a large territory. The old fashioned, small-town doctor has almost disappeared. Once he was Dr. J. D. Smythe who practiced with his brother, Dr. Emmett. He was Dr. A. G. Payne, or, with his superb Dickensian name, Dr. Shivers. An aura of wonder, together with a faint odor of anaesthetics, hung about these men. They were Hope. Hope, handsome and hearty in the person of the black-bearded, brown-eyed, Dr. J. D. Smythe, gaunt and sad-eyed, in the slight figure of Dr. Shivers who got tuberculosis and had to leave town. They were Faith. And, nine times in ten, they were Charity.

They wrestled mysteriously with the Angel of Death. Sometimes they lost. This always seemed incredible on a May morning. Then the heavens gave forth their light and the sun its warmth and the earth its flowers. Daffodils blew yellow in the front yard of the house of the dead. Birds made nuptial music in their mating time. Children walking by to school loudly squealed for joy of living. Negroes on their way to work laughed their golden laughter. The milkman came and the breadman and the postman and the boy delivering newspapers. All was as before. But was it? You did not seem to know.

Neighbors gathered early at the house of the dead. The women in crisp, white, dotted swisses, come to dress the small children of the deceased and get breakfast for the family. The men, looking grave in their oyster-white linens, arriving to offer their sympathy and their services. When the doctor emerged, haggard and worn, the little group of people gathered on the porch made way for him to pass. Going out he might meet priest, preacher, or rabbi, coming in to offer the consolations of his office. Yet this old-fashioned doctor was in many ways priest, preacher, rabbi. Often he knew the awful secrets of soul as well as the ills of body that afflicted his patient. Sometimes in the dreadful marches of the interminable night, he was more confessor than healer. For him alone in the community was vanity abandoned, pride dropped, and the breath-clouded mirror made clear.

But the small-town doctor has had to transform himself in order to compete with city practitioners now easily accessible to his car-driving patients. Once they had been satisfied with his services, but when they could motor to Memphis or New Orleans where, it was assumed, the best doctors lived, they tended more and more to patronize the local doctor only when they had a bellyache or sore throat. They went to the city for treatment of the fancier and more costly ailments, leaving the local physician with only the low-profit or charity trade, and so drove him to put himself into another category.

In the city, meanwhile, many physicians no longer practiced individually, but corporatively or collectively as clinics. There is something reassuringly learned and comforting about the word "clinic." It suggests the infallible pooled wisdom of many men rather than the fallible judgment of one man. We are a people, moreover, as enchanted by the pseudo-scientific as savages are by an alarm clock. Nowadays anyone who eats merely because he likes to eat, is either a fool or an outdated romantic. "Science" and advertisers dictate that you eat only what is "good" for you. Our vocabulary is corroded by psychiatric jargon. Children list the words and their elders roll them richly upon their tongues: inferiority complex, conditioned, inhibited. As some Negroes become drunken with words and phrases whose meaning escapes them, so do white folks; the distinction being that theirs is a poetical debauch often deliciously absurd, while ours is merely dull and pretentious.

Noting all this, the small-town doctor began his transformation from an individual into a clinic. He left town and went to the

Mayo Brothers' Hospital, or even to Vienna for further study or to "specialize." His departure, and the object of his quest, was noted in the local newspaper, and after a while he came home. But he was no longer the same man.

J. W. Wilson, M.D., had disappeared and re-emerged as Dr. Wilson's clinic. Associated with him were Dr. Hartman (eye, ear, nose, throat); Dr. Woodbury (gynecology and obstetrics); Dr. Poffenburger (genitourinary); Dr. Safley (roentgenology and pathology); Dr. Powdermaker (pediatrics); and, of course, Dr. Wilson himself. Assisting them were two pretty nurses: Miss Willa Snavely (graduate, Northwestern University Hospital), and Miss Melba Dubbs (graduate, Touro Infirmary).

A receptionist sat in the outer office of the clinic. One saw the doctors by appointment only, or at the brief, crowded office hours five days a week. Waiting patients observed the impressive-looking diplomas of the doctors (some of them in Latin) upon the anteroom walls, and felt that where there was so much accumulated knowledge there must be infallible powers of healing. The old, familiar, homey touch was retained by Dr. Wilson's presence. As you passed from his benign hands into those of his associates, whatever uncertainty you may have experienced was dissipated as they exposed your body to ingenious machines that seemed to peer into your secret soul. There were no hit-or-miss methods as in the old days. If then you had got a thorn in your foot and had gone to Dr. J. D. Smythe's office, he would have washed the wound with alcohol, cut out the splinter while you winced and sweated, daubed the spot with iodine, affixed a bandage, and talked all the while about crops or local affairs. He himself owned a plantation and it was meet, therefore, that there should be cotton samples on the case containing his surgical instruments; a copy of the annual report of the Department of Agriculture next to his Gray's *Anatomy*; and a sack of pecans under the lithograph of Ambroise Paré amputating a man's leg in the early days of French surgery.

At the Clinic, in a similar case, things were done better and more suavely. First, a doctor took your case history and noted the minutiae on a card. Second, a nurse gave you a Wassermann test. You blushed because you had never had anything of that kind, yet you were pleased that science was on your side. Then your chest was thumped. Your liver and lights were examined. Your heart was spied upon. A day or two later when the data had been compiled, the thorn was removed.

These processes bred confidence in the patient. They were more costly than the old methods. Often you had to pay on the spot or within thirty days by contrast with other times when the doctor's bill was the last to be paid — if ever. But this seems reasonable because, for occult reasons which have not been explored, we willingly render to the corporation that which we give grudgingly, or deny, to the individual. Yet there was no longer doubt that Greenville's doctors were as skillful as those to be found in Memphis. And as patients of the clinic spread the news of its miracles, others came from distant points. Thus Greenville has become a medical center for a large area; a factor of importance in the health of the region and the welfare of the town.

In the western world there has long been a universality of tenderness in healing which the organized religions, in their professions of universal tenderness, have rarely equaled in practice. All are one within the compassionate bosom of medicine. Politics and prejudices end at the door of the sickroom. This is the high tradition of medicine. But such are the darknesses of the color question, that sometimes there is no room within the bosom of the universal mother medicine, even for a man sick unto death.

Some time ago a young American-born Chinese, who is a leader of Greenville's Chinese colony, applied for admission to the King's Daughters' Hospital. Bent over with appendicitis pains, he was in need of emergency surgery. But he was denied admission. The institution does not take Chinese patients. It does take Chinese money donations. (The father of the patient in question had once given it a contribution of five hundred dollars.) The sick man then went to the Negro King's Daughters' Hospital. There — such are the complexities of the color problem — he was assigned a private room so that he would not have to share quarters with a Negro. And there a white surgeon attended him.

Somewhat later the King's Daughters' Hospital was confronted with a more complicated case. A Chinese brought his white wife to the institution for her accouchement. She, being white, was admitted. This necessarily gave admittance to her unborn, half-white child. But its Chinese father was not permitted entrance to the hospital even to see his offspring.

One might assume, then, that white people of the Delta are incapable of making adjustments, however small, in their attitudes toward non-whites. The cases I have cited — and one does not attempt to defend them upon their merits — might provide fuel for sermons by the self-righteous elsewhere; sermons dealing with the allegedly barbarity of Southerners. (The truly intolerant Southerner is matched only by the South-lecturing Northerner who is forever at odds with himself as he tries to harmonize his condescending tolerance toward the Negro with his disciplined hostility toward him.) Yet the whites of the Delta, as noble and as ignoble as other Americans, do make racial adjustments, if slowly, and here the record is clear. In one important matter such an adjustment has recently been made.

The Greenville School Board now permits Chinese children to attend white schools although this is expressly forbidden by the Constitution of Mississippi. Unable to change the law, the local community flouts it in its local application. Obviously there are grave dangers in such a course however beneficent the motive. Yet even in this case a condition, indicative of the complex race relations of the Delta, was attached to the admission of Chinese children to white schools. It is that the Chinese themselves must see to it that no children of Chinese-Negro blood apply through their community. The status of this tiny minority in the Delta is indeed peculiar:

(*a*) They are American citizens and citizens therefore of Mississippi.

(*b*) They may not, however, intermarry with whites or (legally) attend white schools.

(*c*) They are welcomed into white churches; principally Methodist, Baptist, Presbyterian.

(*d*) They are excluded as patients from the Delta's largest hospital.

It is impossible to reconcile the irreconcilable phases of the status of Chinese-Americans in the Delta. The case is important, however, as a demonstration of the manner in which a white majority, struggling against ancient color prejudices, attempts to do essential justice to a colored minority. Hypersensitive in all that concerns color, the local community has taken decisions in this case which have the wholehearted approbation of the group and are therefore soundly rooted.

It is evidence of salutary change in Greenville and the Delta, that the community sees its own shortcomings and is deterred neither by false pride nor a sense of inferiority — attributes which long handicapped the progress of the whole South — from bringing them out into the open. One notes, in this context, the following editorial in the Greenville *Democrat-Times* (October 10, 1945):

> In a recent talk, Mayor Ed Gray commented that from 40 to 50 per cent of the Greenville residential districts could be properly described as slum areas. . . . It is improbable that many areas in the South or East could equal this unenviable record. . . .
>
> We have become used to slums, and don't think of them as slums. They're part of the scenery. They are principally the hovels in which much of our Negro population lives, because they're the best that are available for the money which they can allot for rent. But there are also many white hovels — if it takes a difference in color to make you aware of the relationship between squalor, on the one hand, and crime, disease and other social maladjustments on the other.
>
> It is too easy to dismiss our slums on the basis that they are better than no housing at all, and that they are all that the sub-marginal population of our town can afford. . . . There are white people and Negroes in Greenville whose small earnings are still large enough to pay for better housing than they now have. In considerable measure, this housing shortage and these slums exist because of the virtual cessation of building during the war. But there is also an apathy in respect to decent housing.

The editorial continuing, says that "the low income standards of a large segment of the population makes decent housing for many a remote dream." Yet there are those in the community who clamor for "still lower wages, and a return to prewar levels," without considering the relationship between "sub-standard income and crime, juvenile delinquency, and disease. If Greenville, and all of the South, is to progress in human as well as economic terms, ways must be found to provide jobs at better than bare subsistence pay, and housing in keeping with that pay. . . ."

The editor, dealing with a complex question, states much of the case concerning Negro housing in his town, but not all of it. Since, however, the South (and Greenville) must not, in Ellen Glasgow's phrase, "be a section slipping through life without looking it in the face," it may be well to pause for observation even if it is not the pause that refreshes.

Slums are a dark patch upon the whole American earth. They are a disgrace to this richest and allegedly most humane of nations. They are common to our greatest cities as well as to Greenville. Even within the shadow of the nation's capitol in Washington, men live in squalor comparable to that of the pigs of a poor, bedridden widow. New York is the world's richest city. It is also the largest Negro city on earth. Its Negroes live mainly in the multicellular cesspool called Harlem. Here, segregated as though they were lepers, tens of thousands of Negroes exist in dark, stinking, disease-breeding rooms. (Compare them with the superb living quarters occupied in the Bronx Zoo by baboons with sky-blue behinds.) Here a whole great section of the world's richest city is a fearful racket from which both police and landlords benefit.

This, in any event, is the opinion of Channing H. Tobias, a Negro resident of Harlem, and a director of the Phelps-Stokes Fund. His address to the Cooper Union Forum in New York (November 20, 1946) was reported by the New York *Times*. He said that the crime situation in Harlem is "alarmingly bad" and "an expression of lawlessness that neither police authorities nor community leaders are able to cope with successfully."

(Thus New York, the seat of the United Nations, cannot keep order within its own precincts.) Harlem residents must "stumble over drunks and assignation-house habitués every time they walk down the streets." Harlem real-estate owners "make income their sole interest." They oppose new housing projects by whomever built. Dr. Tobias condemned segregation as partly responsible for Harlem's high rate of juvenile delinquency and asked the city to "rid the community of houses of prostitution," and "restrict the licensing of saloons. . . ."

This is the nation's metropolis in its treatment of five hundred thousand of its Negro citizens. This is the city of stupendous riches, universities, great newspapers, cathedrals, and Park Avenue liberals as thick as wild greens along a springtime Delta levee. It is also the New York where, as Will Percy put it, "too much is said too loudly."

Chicago, the nation's second largest city, is the heaven to which many Southern Negroes aspire. How does this center of light, this midcontinent repository of civilization, house its Negroes? The answer is given by St. Clair Drake and Horace R. Cayton in *Black Metropolis, A Study of Negro Life in a Northern City*.

These authorities state that Chicago's Negroes live in a "black ghetto," in such a "state of congestion that Negroes are living ninety thousand to the square mile as compared with twenty thousand to the square mile in adjacent white apartment-house areas. . . ." There is little or no chance of escape from this ghetto. "Black Metropolis," say its authors, "has become a permanent enclave within the city's blighted area. The impecunious [white] immigrant, once he gets on his feet, may . . . move into an area of second-settlement. Even the vice lord or gangster . . . may lose himself in a respectable neighborhood. Negroes . . . wear the badge of color. They are expected to stay in the Black Belt. Here the Negro tuberculosis rate is five times the white rate. . . ."

It would appear, then, that North as well as South, the Negro is segregated, and Northern segregation is not the less restrictive and humiliating to him because it has a hypocritical overlay of theoretical freedom (mobility). Since Negroes must shop for iving quarters in an area where the demand is greater than the supply, landlords who dominate the area fully exploit their monopolistic position. Thus nearly everywhere in America, including Greenville, Negro housing is an immensely profitable white man's racket. This is not to say that the South, and Greenville, are without white landlords who treat Negro tenants equitably. Numerically, however, men being what they are, such landlords in proportion to those who gouge their tenants, are as saints and sinners.

Many Greenville Negroes pay rentals which consume a large fraction of their incomes. These rentals, in relation to the amenities of the shacks occupied, are monstrously exorbitant. Who, visiting the "nigger districts" of Southern towns would not agree that they are among the worst of America's slums? The long rows of crazy hovels perched uncertainly on cement blocks along creeks or drainage ditches; often intersected by railroad tracks and divided by gullies; lighted by coal-oil lamps; usually without toilet facilities except for a multi-family privy; lacking screens, running water, or access to a fire plug; the whole area in darkness or semidarkness at night because of a complete lack, or an inadequate supply of, municipal lighting. Here where land is cheap and limitless the shacks are placed so close together that tenants live in an airless way. Each is of necessity conscious of the other's domestic affairs, the squallings of his children, the barkings of his dog, the contents of his kitchen pot.

"Nigger property" is regarded as a prime investment by its owners. Capital outlay for each unit is small. Thus aspirant landlords may start on the shadow of a frayed shoestring. Tax assessments are low because the shacks cost little to build and stand on graveyard-narrow plots of cheap ground. They are also low because the white community, going upon the mistaken assumption that Negroes pay little or no taxes, provides Negro districts with only the scantiest municipal services. The shacks are seldom painted, and usually are repaired only when they are about to blow away. Yet rentals are based neither upon the facilities offered nor a fair capital return. They are whatever the tenant can be made to pay. Landlords frequently make upward of twenty per cent per annum upon their investment, and one finds men who own a hundred or more "nigger houses." Occasionally, in the *grand seigneur* manner of an English slums owning Duke, such houses are made part of a bride's dowry.

Who pays the bills in this case? Negroes pay in misery, disease adult crime, juvenile delinquency, and lowered efficiency as workers. Whites, as the wealthier, governing element of the community, must pay for the treatment of diseased Negroes and criminality flowing from slum conditions of living. As the employing group, it pays also for the lowered efficiency of Negro labor. Those who sell goods or services to Negroes who constitute at least half of the population, also pay for "nigger property." Since Negroes spend disproportionate fractions of their low incomes for rent, by so much must they buy less food, clothing, amusements, medical and dental care. The tax-paying whites go far toward subsidizing owners of Negro slums. They bear most of the tax burden of the community which recovers few taxes from slum landlords. The benefits of "nigger property" accrue, therefore, to a tiny group, while the penalties are borne by the whole community.

The question involved here transcends, however, all that pertains to the ill effects wrought upon both Negroes and whites by Negro slums. It concerns deeply the conscience and mores of the white group. That group insists upon race segregation. This being so, a heavy moral obligation rests upon it to prevent segregation from becoming an instrument of exploitation in the hands of white landlords. Certainly no Delta sportsman, when rising river waters have driven deer out of the woods onto mounds, would club to death the defenceless animals.

Greenville is suffering those growing pains and undergoing those changes that effect towns in like estate elsewhere. The business man who once went home for a leisurely midday dinner, now takes a snack in a restaurant. He formerly communicated with his employees by hollering at them through an open door. Today he is likely to address them through an intercommunications machine. His relations with labor tend to become more formal than in the past whether they lead to good will or to good-bye. At the time of the sit-down strikes in 1937, a local employer came back to his shop after dinner to find his labor force of two Negroes sitting down. Asked why they were not at work, one of them said, "Boss, us on a set-down strike." "Well, goddam it," shouted the industrialist, "y'all go outside and sit down." "Yassuh," said the strikers, as they wearily arose and went out to sit on the grass in the sunshine.

For several decades, Deltans, in common with other Southerners, merely grumbled about their colonial status in the national economy. But as Hindus and Nigerians have long been going to the London School of Economics to study the methodology of their colonial masters, so the sons of Delta business men now go to the Harvard School of Business Administration or the Wharton School of Finance of the University of Pennsylvania to ferret out the secrets of Yankee dominance of American business. They do not indulge in the unprofitable pursuit of damning Yankees. They try instead to outtrade them.

The Yankees have nonetheless successfully invaded Greenville. Its home-owned grocery stores have almost entirely disappeared, with the exception of those run by Chinese whose ancestors imperturbably sipped their tea in Soochow straight through the siege of Vicksburg. They have been succeeded by branches of corporations whose operations are gigantic and nationwide; anonymous, impersonal, irresistible. Other absentee corporations, vendors of drygoods, bakers of bread, distributors of gasoline, have also come to town. Our corporations are sometimes pioneers overseas, but never at home. Here they let the natives do the dirty work of clearing the land, controlling the rivers, exterminating malaria, creating relative prosperity. Then only do they move in. As they come, the local merchant tends to go. His sons will become employees of stores owned by men whom they will never know; of whose names, even, they will remain ignorant. They will be standardized, easily replaceable parts of a complicated machine whose workings will forever elude them. Statistics embalmed in the files of a New York tower. Fractional digits in the ephemeral annals of trade. As such they will be one with millions of their fellows elsewhere in the United States.

Self-service grocery stores doubtless have their virtues. But where now, in Greenville, can one find such a store as that operated by L. Vormus when the town was tiny and its wealth negligible? Mr. Vormus was a Frenchman of Alsace. He brought with him into the then pioneer community of Greenville his own French love of food, and his passionate conviction that food ought to nourish soul as well as body. On his shelves were French *pâtés,* tinned snails, the sardines of Amieux Frères (*"toujours amieux"*), the *foie gras* of Strasbourg, the mustards of Dijon, the plum puddings of England, the *lebkuchen* of Nuremburg. Mr. Vormus was friend-counselor to his patrons as well as merchant. They did not, as do today's shoppers, wander directionless in a wilderness of tin cans and cellophane. They consulted lovingly with him about food; as the Englishman confers with his wine merchant, and the Frenchman, dining out, with his waiter.

Mr. Vormus prospered modestly. He read Mérimée and Balzac and *Le Temps* which came months late from Paris. He dreamed, among his piccalilli and *truffes de Périgord,* of the day when the fair provinces of Alsace-Lorraine, torn from France by Germany, should be restored to her. His customers enjoyed the felicities of the table. They agreed with Mr. Vormus that a meal without wine is like a day without sun. And all this ended only when the epicurean grocer was forced into retirement by illness. He has had no successor, and it is unlikely that he will have one in this dark era of gulp-and-gallop which has overwhelmed Greenville as it has the rest of the country.

Yet not all the lights of the old town have gone out. Greenville retains its ancient tolerance toward "foreigners"; those who come to it from another state of the union or from overseas. It still has a tinge of cosmopolitanism, rare in Deep South small towns, by virtue of its population, not only those of Anglo-Saxon descent and Negroes, but also those of Italian, Greek, Jewish, Syrian, and Chinese descent. Thousands of miles from that hyacinthine sea, one comes upon a bit of the Mediterranean brought into a Mississippi town by a Syrian resident. In the rear of his store there is a tiny garden. Here grow grapevines, pomegranates, and a fig tree. There is trellised shade from the hot sun and the music of a tiny fountain.

The town keeps its bemused hospitality to eccentrics, cranks, and noncomformists at least in their romantic attitudes. It patiently drinks the bad whiskey it must buy from bootleggers, and thanks heaven on those rare occasions when it comes by a bottle of sound bourbon. It attends church but is by no means fanatically committed to the oldtime religion of hell, brimstone, and eternal punishment, so common in Mississippi. It amiably forgives the shortcomings even of crass sinners, and reserves a place in its secret heart for those who sin with grace. In its theology, a lady can do no wrong, while it would be boorish indeed to hold it against a gentleman that he was tempted beyond his strength.

If the continuance of tradition is in some cases heartening, a breaking with it may be equally heartening. It is perhaps too much to say that Greenville's clergy have broken away from the Southern Protestant church tradition which silenced them in nearly all that pertained to social program in the community. Yet there is strong evidence that the town's clergy — some of them young, broadly informed, vigorous men — are more and more concerning themselves with the profound realities of the community's life. Their great influence is being used positively for its betterment rather than negatively, as so often in the past, by denunciation of "sin." Sin was usually some innocent pastime which gave people pleasure: cardplaying, dancing, drinking, having fun on Sunday.

It seems impossible that Greenville could ever have another burning at the stake such as occurred a few years ago. On this memorable occasion, the minister of one of the local churches asked the members of his congregation to go down on their knees and pray for Sister So and So. She had put her immortal soul in jeopardy, and it would take wholesale praying to save her from the pits of hell. Her sin incarnadine was that she had attended a performance by the Denishawn Dancers in the high-school auditorium! The congregation knelt and prayed for her soul and, it is assumed, she has been saved from the burning. But the denouement, such being the slyness of Ole Satan, was extraordinary and anticlimactic. Only a few days after the errant sister's martyrdom, her minister was found to be human, all too human, in his relations with a lady of the choir, and left town.

The minister in Greenville (and the South), more than elsewhere in the United States, is omnipresent in the community's life. On nearly all public occasions, at meetings of luncheon clubs, testimonial dinners, lodge banquets, and even at groundbreaking ceremonies for the erection of a factory, he is on hand. The *Democrat-Times* published this item in July, 1946:

> . . . While a near-score . . . civic leaders looked on, D. L. Beach, president of Delta Bread Company, yesterday afternoon laid the cornerstone for a building . . . which will become the company's $250,000 plant. . . .
>
> "Oh God . . . we beseech thee to grant our petitions that this undertaking which is begun this day, may . . . be brought to a prosperous conclusion," the Rev. Albert C. Morris . . . said in prayer as the assembly stood with bowed heads.

The relations of the Protestant clergy to the community is a factor of great importance. For, as Howard W. Odum has pointed out in his *Southern Regions,* the South "reflects a greater influence of the church than other regions; a greater place for religion in the ideology of the people; a greater influence of ministers; a greater protestantism, especially of Baptists and Methodists; a greater influence in education and politics and race. From the viewpoint of regional planning and analysis, however, the church and religion assume more nearly the role of natural cultural evolution, the modifications of which are brought about indirectly through the incidence of other agencies and influences. The church has done little with reference to the tenant and the laborer in the way of programs; the tenant and the laborer have played a small part in the life of the church whose fortunes will fluctuate with the prevailing culture of the region. With all its mighty influence the power of the church has been in its ideologies and conditioning attitudes and not in its program."

There are many signs that the Protestant church in Greenville is now concerned with more than "ideologies and conditioning attitude." Some of its clergy, quietly, earnestly, and effectively, are working toward a program. Their influence is great. The work they are doing must beneficially affect the local community. Their doctrines will spread to adjacent areas, and so subject to influences civilizing and enlightening, large segments of the population who could be reached in no other way.

Among Greenville's recent accessions is what might be called a literary renaissance. In the past it was not given, any more than similar towns, to an excess of book reading, although a respectable number of its older citizens were conversant with letters — an aberration patiently endured by the letterless. Their leavening effect was such that when Mike Conner ran for governor of Mississippi, he did not have to apologize to Greenville audiences because in his misguided youth he had got a degree from Yale University; although this blemish upon his otherwise spotless character caused him embarrassment, and lost him votes, elsewhere in the state.

Thirty years ago, long before the town had a municipal library, and long before there were book-of-the-month clubs, some of Greenville's citizens had their own book-of-the-month club. They were a tiny group whose position was such that they did not have to be secret readers. They could openly display their infirmity without loss of prestige. Each of the twenty members of the Coppée Book Club bought one book a month. Each book, as read, was circulated among the members. Thus each could read two hundred and forty books a year, although each bought only twelve books. Then when all the books had made the rounds, every member got back for his own library those he had originally chosen.

Now Greenville not only reads books avidly, but, far worse, it writes them. It has a number of practicing writers disproportionate to the size of its literate population. It is awash with aspirant authors of every kind. Yet, as a striking departure from the past, there is not among them a poetess of the Confederacy or a genealogist of the genteel. Apparently there is a thesaurus under every bed in the community; a novel simmering with every housewife's soup. More sober citizens, however, alarmed by this lush literary renaissance, are fearful of its dangers. If this thing goes on, they ask, who will do the useful work of the town: cooking, laundering, standing behind counters of the stores? But the movement shows no signs of abating. It has, on the contrary, received official encouragement. The City Council, reckless of the perils involved, appropriated ten thousand dollars recently for the upkeep of the town's library; the largest appropriation in that institution's short history.

In another field, the manners of another day continue unabated. Young ladies of Greenville and the Delta are outwardly indistinguishable from their sisters elsewhere. They are given to the same froufrous and scents, hair-dos and clothes, as other American girls. But in one respect they are quite unlike their Northern counterparts. They avoid the disabilities of the higher education as they avoid dishpan hands. They conceal their brains from men, not to mystify, but to beguile. And by so doing they achieve a happiness marred only by suffering those agreeable fatigues incident to an excess of male gallantry. Even in these changing times, they see no reason to disagree with the soundness of advice given young ladies in *Miss Leslie's Behavior Book* published in 1860:

> Generally speaking it is a mistake for ladies to attempt arguing with gentlemen on political or financial topics. All the information that a woman can possibly acquire or remember on these subjects is so small . . . that the discussion will not elevate them in the opinion of masculine minds. . . . Men are very intolerant towards women who are prone to contradiction and contention when the talk is out of their sphere; but very indulgent towards a modest and attentive listener who only asks questions for the sake of information. Men like to dispense knowledge, but few of them believe that in departments exclusively their own, they profit much by the suggestions of women. . . .

Delta girls are modestly content, therefore, that this should be a man's world, asking only to run the men who run it. These size-twelve realists in Molyneux copies, at once poetic and pragmatic, have always known what businessmen have only lately come to realize. It is not the ownership of property that counts; it is the control. So, too, in their relations with men, they knew, long before Dr. Rhine's experiments at Duke University, that mind influences matter. Careful to avoid pedantry, they do not utterly reject formal education, for many of them attend those academies where it is meet to put a pretty restraint upon their natural feminine capacity for the excessive. It is, rather, that they prefer a crown of honeysuckle to one of laurel. The results of such a course are sometimes astonishing.

If civilization is, from one point of view, the bending of the resources of nature to the uses of man, then Mary Alice Whitcomb of Deep Snow Plantation, Dundee, Mississippi, is highly civilized.

A little while ago, dining with her and her husband in their East River (New York) apartment with its dramatic view of the stream, we remarked that fifteen years had passed since they came to a cocktail party I had given while living in New York. It remains vividly in Mary Alice's mind because it was there that she first met John. I remember it vividly because I witnessed then an exquisite demonstration of the triumph of mind over matter.

Most of the girls who came to that party long ago were admirably educated. But Mary Alice is not precisely bookish. Her sole skirmish with the monster of learning consisted in attending Ward-Belmont College, where she took art appreciation for six months. Then she left for a chaperoned tour of Europe with six other girls and returned with some "cute hand-painted place cards hand-painted in Switzerland," which she used at dinners in her plantation home. Ve'y Suthun at home and twice as Suthun in New Yawk, Mary Alice while still in the nursery determined both her sex and her role in life. Since then she has marched with tiny steps toward her goal without once making the error, so commonly committed, of causing one to suspect that she conceals a field marshal's baton beneath her gossamer nightgown.

Late in the afternoon of my party, there appeared several Wall Street bachelors looking Savile Rowish in their English-made clothes, masculinely competent and, two or three of them, including John, quite handsome. They are the kind of men who are described in women's magazine fiction — for the titillation of astringently virtuous housewives — as having about them "the man-smell of tweeds and pipe tobacco and shaving lotion." But John said little to Mary Alice when he met her. Then she took the situation in hand.

Vaguely she had heard something about a hotly debated issue of the day: whether or no the United States ought to go off the gold standard. Looking fragile and helpless, turning her eyes up to John's as though they were morning-drowsy flowers being slowly awakened by the voluptuous sun, her voice drenched with midnight magnolia, she said: "Would you please tell me something about the gold standard everybody is talking about? I just can't understand it."

For twenty minutes he told her; learnedly, simply, enthusiastically. Mary Alice looked adoringly at him, although she had not the faintest understanding of his words and was oblivious to the black looks cast at her by the other girls present. They understood the gold standard. They also knew that John was one of its glittering exemplars and clearly saw what was happening to him. It was inevitable, since he did all the talking, that he should conclude, as men nearly always do in such a case, that the girl listening was superlatively intelligent, while Mary Alice, looking ever so little-girlish, appealed at the same time to his male protective instincts so that he was wooed as he was persuaded.

They dined together that night. Three months later they were married. Mary Alice has ever since lived on the gold standard, leaving it to her husband and his friends to argue about a dogma hopelessly discredited. She takes no part in these discussions because for her, as for other sensible women, lost causes, so appealing to men, are at best nothing more than pretty exercises in flower arrangement.

Every little while I run across some of the other girls who were at my party. Most of them have remained single. In the interval between the wars they went in for Near East Relief, and could tell you offhand the infant mortality rate in Cettinje or the

incidence of rickets in Xanthe. Sometimes they crossed to
Europe on the *Aquitania* with Mother, parked her at Barbizon,
and spent the summer in Italian hill towns. During the winter
they presided at the more fashionable charities. Now they indulge in other good works whose emotional content is equal to
that contained in a Christmas card from an old beau long married, almost forgotten, living in Spokane, Washington.

It is not without reason, therefore, that Delta girls take the
higher education *diminuendo*.

Growing Greenville has been wise enough to preserve its
superb trees. Birds still sing from its magnolias. Squirrels fling
themselves, in anti-Newtonian acrobatics, from limb to limb of
tall water oaks. Weeping willows are cascades of tender green
in springtime. Crepe myrtles in full bloom run through the
streets with cloudy fire in their branches. The fruit of cottonwoods drifts white in summer. There is an instinctive love of
beauty here and of trees which inform it.

All that has happened anywhere in any town since men first
began to build towns, happens daily in Greenville from dawn
to dawn. It is clear, then, that some of its young men who went
to war will come home no more. It is equally clear that its old
citizens become more and more a part of the majestic harmony
of growing cemeteries. The night goes, the sun rises, the day
comes. One asks: "What time is it?" One tells him. It is another
time on the seven hills of Rome, and still another by the green
lagoon of Bora-Bora, and no one knows what time it is. But
Greenville arises at the arbitrary symbol and goes to work and
loves and marries and begets children and is noble and ignoble
and happy and wretched and mean and generous and repetitive
in its pattern one generation after the other. In all these respects
it is one with Sidon and Tyre, and Petra of the red-rose walls.

A link in the historical continuity of man, it is also part of the
present. As such, perhaps, all might be for the best in the best
of all possible worlds, if only one could know the answers to
gnawing questions. What is cotton's future? Will it survive on
its own? Will industry come to supplant it entirely, or largely

take its place? What will happen if Negroes should leave the community in large numbers? What will happen if they should remain? How can the town, without sharply increasing taxes, supply the needed new schools and municipal services for a greatly augmented population? And sometimes there arises the most anxiety-ridden question of all if it is seldom asked aloud: Is Greenville overbuilt?

The answer to such inquiries must necessarily await the future. In the interim, pity the poor white man searching for a security that does not exist. Sing a sweetly sad little song for him who fails to live fully today because he is morbidly concerned with the morrow. Make opiate music for him who, even when he has pillowed his head on the voluptuous bosom of life insurance, hears disturbing voices in the night.

CHAPTER 2

Mistuh Bones, Santa Claus, and the Pore Widder Lady

THE RELATIONS of individual whites and Negroes in the Delta often defy analysis, and sometimes challenge probability. They temper the austerities of racial codes; transcend the rigidities of the established order; cause men to do individually what the group might oppose collectively. Their mellowing social effect, operative over wide areas, is large.

A case in point is education. Many whites still oppose education for Negroes; especially the higher education. So, outwardly, does Mr. Harry Vinson whose Kentucky ancestors founded a Delta cotton plantation and named it Trafalgar out of their admiration for Lord Nelson.

Elderly statesman of his community, an authority on bourbon whiskey and mixer of the best toddies in the county, a former wing-shot of renown, perennial introducer of distinguished speakers at political gatherings, courtly in the presence of ladies and manly with men, Mr. Harry is a splendid representative of the old order. Yet he is wont to growl when the question of Negro education sometimes arises in his living room after dinner, "Damn niggers don't need any education. Ruins 'em. Makes 'em unhappy."

It so happens, however, that perhaps his greatest devotion, except for the memory of his wife, is to Ike Haley — a Negro. Ike was born on Trafalgar. He and Mr. Harry played, hunted, and fished together when they were boys. When Mr. Harry finished his schooling at Princeton and returned to the plantation, Ike, already raising an annual crop of cotton and children, was there to lend him counsel. A few years later he was raised to the eminence of straw boss; a position he has since occupied. The two men have grown closer as they have grown older. Upon only one occasion was their friendship even fleetingly marred by the shadow of a shadow.

For forty years Ike has been coming to Mr. Harry's house on Christmas morning to "drink Christmas" with him. Nothing is permitted to interrupt this ceremony which neither time nor circumstance stales. During the long period of prohibition, however, Mr. Harry's precious stock of bourbon dwindled alarmingly. He would not defile his own palate with local corn whiskey, or offer it to his friends. He called upon the bishops of the Episcopal church to start a holy war against Protestant sects who stood for prohibition, "that foul invention of the thrice-damned — may they lead apes in hell through flames everlasting." But prohibition persisted, his bourbon was near the vanishing point, and Ike would soon appear for the ancient rite.

When he came on Christmas morning and had been seated near the log fire, Mr. Harry left the room and solemnly returned. He came tenderly cradling a bottle of whiskey as though it were the infant Moses just retrieved from the bulrushes. "Ike," he said, "this is the last bottle of whiskey in the house. It was aged for fifteen years in the wood near Frankfurt, Kentucky. It has been bottled for twenty years. Now it is just half our age. It's the oldest whiskey in Mississippi and the best. In fact, it is a liqueur whiskey, and ought to be served only after dinner as a brandy."

"Yassuh," said Ike.

Mr. Harry reverently poured a drink for his guest and one for himself. It was a far smaller quantity than was usual on this occasion. "Merry Christmas, Ike," said Mr. Harry, holding his glass aloft. "Merry Christmas, Mr. Harry," said Ike. "But before I dreens this glass, I jes' wants to ax you one question. How come this here whiskey can be so old, and be so little?" Ike then tossed off his drink. Mr. Harry smiled the smile of the defeated, and reached for his last bottle of precious bourbon to refill his friend's glass.

Ike had a passel of chillun. The brightest of the lot was Ezekiel, nicknamed Pud, because he always deviling his Ma to make cornstarch pudding. He got good grades at school, worked hard around the plantation in summer, and these achievements, plus the fact that he was Ike's son, endeared him to Mr. Harry. When Pud was big enough to do a good day's work, Ike wanted him to leave school and start "gittin' some sense in his haid." But Mr. Harry would not hear of it. "Now, Ike, you let Pud alone," he would say. "He is doing all right."

Mr. Harry put Pud through Fisk University. After his graduation, he got him a job teaching school. He hopes eventually to get him an appointment as county superintendent of Negro schools. But when the question of Negro education arises around his fireside, he is likely to growl: "Damn niggers don't need any education. Education ruins 'em. Makes 'em unhappy."

There have been many Mr. Harrys in the Delta, and females of the species as well. They have been a beneficent influence in the lives of many Negroes. If they are fewer in number today than they once were, the tribe still persists, and it gains recruits in the most unexpected places. There is no record of their activities, for compassion keeps no ledgers. Students of the Negro question deplore their existence on the ground that they deprive Negroes of initiative and hamper their ability to stand on their own feet. When this point of view is mentioned in the Delta, it draws a brief, definitive, unanswerable retort: "Aw, shucks."

Sometimes a white man, through the workings of a subtle alchemy whose effects he perceives but whose source he cannot penetrate, is moved, step by step, to become the friend, protector, partner, confidant, and financial mainstay of a Negro who may have come only yesterday into his ken. An excellent example is the relationship between Bones Barcroft of Greenville and W. P.

It never occurred to Bones when W. P., a small, nondescript, graveyard-black Negro, ambled into his yard one summer afternoon, that it could mark the beginning of an association between them that would last a year, cost him considerable sums of money, and almost cause his wife to leave him. Prospectively, the development of such a situation would seem impossible. Retrospectively, it seems wholly improbable. Yet I have had the story from Bones. His townsmen have amplified it for me. His wife has commented upon it with the neatest blending of objectivity and faint derogation of masculine intelligence.

Rarely have sorcerer and bewitched been more unlike. Mistuh Bones, as he is known to Delta Negroes, is a tall, kindly, middle-aged man. His Scotch ancestry is so strong upon him that his sandy hair seems touched with heather; his pipe and tweeds as much a part of him as his eyes and ears. He is a capable businessman. Decimals do his bidding as swiftly as his setters in bird season, and he is no stranger to the sound Aberdeenshire precept that a shilling, like your wife, wants time for the knowing. A member of Rotary he is also, by way of other soul-side, a vestryman of St. James's; a respected, well-liked citizen of the flourishing river town in which he lives.

W. P., on the other hand, is a pint-size sideways-walking man of obscure origins and undeterminable ways of living. Even the records of local Negro historians are scant with respect to him. It is known that he has often "taken up" with ladies from whom he severed ties by that caprice which befits a truly free spirit, rather than through the laborious processes of the law which enchains so many whites and Negroes. He has numerous progeny. Sometimes he regards them with touching paternal devotion; occasionally with lordly indifference. At other times he refuses to recognize them in any manner because a man jes' can't 'member everything that happens in his life. Leisure early singled him out for her own, and he responded with feverish sublimation of all else in his personality, as another man might respond to the genius of music or painting burning within him. From childhood, he manifested a precocious aversion to labor. In his maturity he became a living protest against the decadence of his neighbors who rejected the high estate of loafing for the ignoble condition of toiling. These things are known of W. P., but that is all.

W. P. was unfortunately born out of his time. At another period in the Delta, before the serpent of progress came into that whilom Eden, hardening the hearts of people and making them almost one with Yankees who never did know enough to keep from working, W. P. might have been supported in honor by the community. His aristocratic disdain of labor alone, to say nothing of his other engaging attributes, would, in that far-off time, have brought him into harmony with the quality white folks. They would have recognized him as an ornament of the society which they themselves ornamented; an upholder of the gracious order which even then was being threatened by coarse pushers. He would have been attached to their entourage as a keeper of bird dogs, a mixer of toddies, an exerciser of horses. These are tasks which befit a man of cultivated tastes who unhappily has to earn a living; but they are not too burden- some and they distinguish the man who performs them from common Negroes or common white folks.

But, alas, times have changed. Delta life is now corroded by the bleak concept of the *quid quo pro*. Contrary to hallowed custom, it is required of every man that he earn his living in the sweat of his face. Ingenious machines, moreover, measure the work which you do by machine, and this involves a chilling paradox, for while you could fool white folks who do have some sense, you just can't fool a machine which has no sense at all. More and more, W. P. found himself living out of his time. His point of view was circumscribed by a changing society. Chang- ing codes had converted the once honorable into the dishonor- able. He was pushed into an airless way where he could not freely breathe or spread his wings. Saddest of all, the gentleman of leisure had given way to the man of toil, credit to cash, while promise and performance were made to match. Under these lamentable circumstances, W. P. was forced to sell his soul in the labor market and, as many a man before him, turned to the bucolic pursuit of mowing the grass of the white folks' yards in the fecund summertime.

It was at this low point of his fortunes that he came upon Mistuh Bones, who was sitting on his porch in the cool of the evening after a hot day at his office, slowly savoring his ice-tinkling highball and thinking those thoughts that become a vestryman of St. James's. Out of the nowhere appeared W. P., pushing a ramshackle cart containing a battered lawnmower and a few rusty garden tools. The grass in Mustuh Bones's yard was thick and rank. The flower beds were iron hard. The hollyhocks leaned tiredly on their tall stems like footsore Delta girls at the end of a long evening of dancing. Even the morning glories, hardiest of flowers, seemed exhausted. It was a bad moment for W. P., for if, unfortunately, he got the job that was apparently within his grasp, it would be a tough one. He therefore hesitated to speak to Mistuh Bones and he, in turn, was in no hurry to address W. P. He knew that the work would cost more if he should ask it to be done than it would if W. P. asked for work.

For a brief interval the men remained in a state of suspension. Then they slowly gravitated toward one another. Mistuh Bones asked W. P. what he would charge to mow the grass, work the flower beds, and trim a few shrubs to which he pointed. "Boss, I doesn't know," said W. P., "but us ain't gwine fall out 'bout dat. I does de work and you pays me whatever you think hits wuth." Mistuh Bones, being a businessman, demurred. He said that this was strictly a business deal. Unless he knew exactly what the work would cost, everything was off. W. P., a smooth-mouthed man, replied: "Dat sho is satisfaction. Like I tells the ladies, hit ain't nothin' like a man knowin' where you stands all de time. I does it for six-bits."

The deal was struck. Mistuh Bones retired to the porch to drink his highball and think his high Episcopalian thoughts. W. P. made a few zigzag paths through the grass with his lawnmower. Then he stopped to pet a stray dog for a while. "Dog, you sho favors a ole pup I onct had," he said. "I wonder is you any kin to him." A few more rounds were followed by an interval of discussion with the passing hot-tamale man who was going home to get ready for his evening's work. When he left, a fellow grass-cutter appeared. He and W. P. talked a long time. Then W. P. walked up to Mistuh Bones and said, "White folks, this boy got him a bran' new twelve-dollar mower. Say he'll sell hit for fo' dollars on account of him going to Dee-troit. If you 'vances me the money, I'll leave hit in yo' garage an' cut hit out." After being assured that W. P.'s old lawnmower was "no 'count," Mistuh Bones put up the money.

Then, as slitheringly as the serpent moved through the bells and grass of Eden, W. P. smilingly uttered a few words whose implications were lost upon the already bewitched Mistuh Bones. "Boss," he said, "now *us* got *us* two lawnmowers." This obviously meant that the two men had become partners. Thereafter they would engage in enterprises of large dimensions. The profits, if any, would go to W. P. The inevitable losses would be borne by Mistuh Bones. By this time the sun was going down. W. P., content with his labors, put the firm's lawnmowers in us garage, said good night to his partner, and went home.

The next morning, as Mistuh Bones was leaving his house, W. P. told him he needed a broom with which to sweep up the grass. Us could git us a good broom for fo-bits at Mistuh Wetherbees. W. P. got the money and walked slowly through the soft morning to the hardware store, an establishment which by the merest chance is just across the street from Will Hardin's catfish parlor. It may be that, as the Book says, man cometh up and is cut down like a flower. But you needs a heap o' tools when you's workin' in the white folks' yard and garden. When Mistuh Bones came home for dinner, W. P. told him he needed a sickle to cut the tall grass in the backyard, and large shears for the shrubs. He got the money for them and the working member of the firm proudly said, "Us gwine have plenty of tools befo' us through."

For two whole days thereafter W. P. worked furiously. The grass was being brought under control. The hollyhocks were beginning to breathe again. The shrubs were trimmed. Mistuh Bones's investment was yielding dividends, and the investor was able to tell his wife, Miss Mary Nell, whose opinion of W. P. was less than exalted, that she had maligned a good man. It was therefore with a light heart that the next morning at breakfast he left his grits and bacon and the cotton quotations in the *Commercial Appeal,* to go to the kitchen where, his cook told him,

"W. P. say could he see you, suh." The grasscutter, it appeared, was low sick. He had a misery in his head. His back jes ached him so bad. His th'oat felt like hit was a bullfrog in hit. But did Mistuh Bones give him an order to Dr. Scruggs, he'd get fixed up and would work out the bill.

A few hours later the Doctor telephoned. "Bones," he said, "in all my twenty years' practice, I've never seen a case like W. P.'s. He's got acute malaria, acute appendicitis, and both the v.d's. I don't know what to tackle first, or whether you want me to go ahead at all. What shall I do?"

For a long moment there was silence. Mistuh Bones saw himself saddled with endless bills for W. P.'s treatment. He groaned and twisted in his chair to the alarm of his secretary whose former employer had exhibited similar manifestations just before dropping dead. Finally, he said weakly, "Go ahead, Doc."

At supper that night, Miss Mary Nell told her husband that W. P. had not turned up all day. This did not disturb him because he knew that his faithful partner was taking medical treatment, although he had not seen fit to mention this item of news to his wife. Then she added that anybody who had sense enough to pour water out of a dipper could see that W. P. wasn't worth killing. This remark aroused Mistuh Bones because no man is willing to admit that his wife's intuition is superior to his intelligence. He thereupon launched into a somewhat incoherent recital of W. P.'s sterling qualities, and was going into a devastating climax when the telephone rang. "Sounds like long distance," said Miss Mary Nell. It was long distance. A collect call from Shreveport, Louisiana, two hundred miles away. Mistuh Bones would accept the charges. His wife, of course, would listen to the conversation.

"Dis W. P.," said the voice at the other end of the line. "Where the hell are you?" roared Mistuh Bones his mind befuddled by indignation because he had just been told where W. P. was, and his anger made sulphurous by his wife's presence at this wretched moment. Both she and W. P. were making a fool of him.

"Ise in Shreveports," said the voice. "Hit was a boy drivin' a truck right after I lef' out from de doctor's office, and he say did I 'company him, he wouldn't charge me nothin' to ride. Nawsuh, he ain't comin' back. He gwine to a place call Fernwood or somethin' like dat, where his Papa stay inginerally but he ain't there right now. Boss man, I sho wants to come back home, so does you send me fo' dollars by the Western Nunion, I'll be yonder tomorrow." Mistuh Bones looked at his wife. Then he said, venomously, "W. P., you're the most no-account scoundrel I've ever seen, and I've got a mind to let you stay right there until you rot." He slammed down the receiver to be met with a didn't-I-tell-you-so look in his wife's eyes.

An hour later he told Miss Mary Nell that he had some work to do in his office, drove to the Western Union, and sent five dollars to W. P. Two days afterward Miss Mary Nell came upon W. P. in the garden. He was tying up her sweet peas and handling each plant as though it was imperial jade. She has perhaps the best sweet peas in town, and is quietly proud of them. It is a favorite thesis of hers that no man can be hopelessly bad who loves flowers. W. P. worked lovingly among the flowers for several days. Miss Mary Nell's suspicions of him were temporarily lulled, while the neglected grass grew even higher, thus assuring W. P. of work, if he wanted it, for an indefinite period.

During all of this time, however, he had drawn little cash since he was working out his tools. It was understandable, therefore, that Mistuh Bones should buy him a sack of flour and some canned simon-fish; a bottle of tonic for his wife who had chills and fever; give him six-bits to pay off a boy who was worryin' him; and ninety cents to get his shoes half-soled. After a number of these transactions, Mistuh Bones, finding himself as bewildered as an owner of shares in a labyrinthine holding company, suggested that the members of the firm have a settlement and get on a cash basis. This seemed unreasonable to W. P. A conservative fanatically dedicated to the *status quo*, he was for keeping things as they were. "Lawd Gawd, Boss," he said, "hit ain't no tellin' how us stands. Jes lemme have fo-bits mo' for my Burial 'Sociation dues an' us'll settle nex' time."

This was the last that Mistuh Bones saw of W. P. for a month. He next heard from him at two o'clock one morning when his

telephone rang and an excited voice said, "Dis W. P. Ise shot."
He was asked where he was shot and where he was talking from.
W. P. said he was shot on Blanton Street and was talking from a
café near the C & G depot. "Goddam it," roared Mistuh Bones,
"I didn't ask you what part of town you were shot in, but what
part of your body." After so long W. P. said he had been shot
in the leg and had walked to the depot. Mistuh Bones told him
that if he had walked that far he wasn't hurt much, and to wait
until morning or go to a doctor, and stop waking him up in the
middle of the night. "Yassuh," said W. P.

Fifteen minutes later he was knocking on Mistuh Bones's
back door. Miss Mary Nell was for calling the police and having
him put in jail. "Mistuh Bones," explained W. P., "I wants to
show you where I was shot at. Nawsuh, I doesn't know how
come innybody would shoot me. I was jes' walkin' home 'tendin'
to my business when boom! Ise shot. Please, suh, loan me a
dollar. Doc Sellers, he takes out bullets for a dollar." He got
four dollars and left, and Miss Mary Nell said that if her husband could throw away so much money on that worthless Negro
she might as well buy the Venetian blinds whose purchase she
had been putting off so long.

Casual inquiries by Mistuh Bones the next day revealed that
W. P. had been shot while messin' 'roun' with another man's
wife, and that he had spent the four dollars on whiskey. But he
bought W. P. some antiseptic and bandages for dressing his
wound, and paid for his groceries during his convalescence.
Then W. P. disappeared. The grass grew higher in Mistuh
Bones's yard, and his wife talked darkly of returning to her
mother if that scoundrel came upon their premises while she
lived.

Mistuh Bones had given up hope of ever seeing his partner-
protégé again, when one morning he was awakened by the
noises of a lawnmower under his bedroom window. W. P. was
making the grass fly. "Where the hell you been?" Mistuh Bones
yelled. W. P. had had a hard time. It appeared that he was
walking on the Leland road, when a car with three white men
in it stopped right by him. One of them said, "That's him. Get

in, boy." W. P. got in the car. It flew down the road. The men said they were glad they had got him at last for murdering their friend, and when he denied it they slapped him 'side the head with pistols. They took him a long way and threw him into jail in Birmingham, Alabama, but he was no sooner in a cell than a ole white gemmun with white whiskers looked at him and said, "That ain't the boy," and turned him out. "I had to walk all the way home, an' fo' Gawd, hit's three hunnerd miles."

W. P.'s partner waited patiently until he had told his story. Then he began cussing him. He cussed the slavers who had first gone to Africa; the man who thought of bringing slaves to this country; and the Yankees who freed them once they were here. He cussed the day his eyes had fallen upon W. P. He reflected somewhat indelicately upon his ancestry, maternal and paternal, and all his relatives whether by consanguinity or affinity; he accused him of every crime in the catalog of crimes from treason to incest; compared him unfavorably with every vile bird of the air and every skulking beast of the jungle; and concluded by threatening to have him run out of Mississippi if he didn't reform. W. P. bowed his head. He looked mournful and repentant. The more terrible the accusations made against him by Mistuh Bones and the more awful his rage, the more W. P. yassuhed him and soothed him with honeyed words. "Boss, you's layin' hit on yo' po' ole W. P. but he knows you's doin' hit jes' to he'p him out."

As soon as Mistuh Bones had smoked a cigarette and cooled off — W. P. making a touching display of his poverty and humility by picking up the butt and putting it in his pocket — the return began to yesterday. W. P. said didn't he care a piece of meat home his wife would "sho slap the taste out of my mouth. You knows how ladies can vex a man's mind," he added slyly. In order to prevent this domestic tragedy and the breakup perhaps of a happy home — an event harmful both to the state and the parties involved — it was obviously up to Mistuh Bones to give W. P. some money and so he did.

The summer passed, autumn came, and Mistuh Bones saw nothing of W. P. During the early winter he went hunting in

Louisiana and was amazed to learn on his return home that although he had not seen W. P. for a long time that servant of his, faithful unto death, had saved his life although by so doing he had placed his own in great peril. It appeared, according to the tale W. P. had told around town, that the two men had become inseparable friends. "Nawsuh, Mistuh Bones wouldn't go nowhere widout me to brang him his toddy." The friends, so the story ran, had driven a giant bear into a hollow log from which it would not emerge. Whereupon Mistuh Bones ordered his brave and devoted servant to go into the log and drive out the bear. This he unhesitatingly did. Mistuh Bones shot the bear seven times but it kep' on 'vancin' twarge him and was jes' about to strike him down, when W. P. snatched the rifle from his friend's hands, clubbed the ole bear 'bout de haid, and drove him clean to the woods. Naturally, concluded W. P., as he recited his unselfish deed, Mistuh Bones was so grateful to him that he had told all the high white folks in town he was always going to take care of W. P., no matter did he live to be nine hunnerd years old like Methusaleh.

W. P. spent most of that winter sitting by the stove in the E-Light Barber Shop and Poolroom Combined. All sensible folks, in the cold wintertime, sit by the stove drinking whiskey, when they can get it, and talking religion. On occasion, W. P. would stir out and pass by Mistuh Bones's office to ax him how was he and Miss Mary Nell getting along and quite incidentally borrow small sums from him. This, however, his manner, indicated, was more by way of maintaining the continuity of their friendship and permitting Mistuh Bones to do something for his benefactor, than necessity. The size of the loans and the nature of their intended uses bear out this theme: two-bits for some Cannon Ball pills to cure the heartburn; $7.50 to he'p a friend pay his fine and knock off the days he hadn't served; $2 to get back his 'cordeen he had pawned. There is no doubt that W. P. was a generous man with a delicate sense of the amenities of living, while he revealed himself to Mistuh Bones in their last meeting in the novel role of a moralist.

This meeting occurred upon W. P.'s return from a trip to

Chicago. He had gone there, he told Mistuh Bones, to attend the funerals of two uncles. They had died at the same time, and he felt it imperative to go because he had never before laid eyes upon these relatives. How did he get to Chicago? "I was fixin' to let you send me, but I talked a cullud boy into a trade." This remark made Mistuh Bones flinch. After all that he had done for W. P., it seemed ingratitude that he should now let newcomers barge in upon the business of doing him favors. "I tole that boy did he pay my 'spenses up yonder, us'd divide my uncles' es-tate. But hit wa'n't no es-tate, so he's jes' out $17." How did he get back to Greenville? "Hit was a cousin of mine there from Atlanta, so I borrowed enough from him to come on back."

How did he expect to repay the loan? W. P.'s reply illuminates the character of a much misunderstood man. He had borrowed the money, it seems, to teach the lender the salutary lesson that it does not pay to lend money. "Nawsuh, I ain't got no idee o' sendin' that boy that money. Its like the Book say: Him that lendeth money to a stranger will sho smart for it. Folks ain't got no business lendin' money to strangers nor neither they kinfolks, and this'll learn that boy a lesson."

The lamentable circumstances of Mistuh Bones's last dealings with W. P. were such as to prevent their meeting. One morning his wife telephoned him to say that W. P. had called him. He was in jail — probably for teaching a moral lesson and suffering the fate of a reformer — and wanted Mistuh Bones to get him out. But, said Miss Mary Nell, "If you do, I'll divorce you before sundown."

He did not go to the jailhouse, but sent $13.80 to pay W. P.'s fine. With it went a note instructing him to stay away from his house for ten days so that Miss Mary Nell would think he had served his time.

Mistuh Bones has never again seen W. P. who disappeared from town. He misses him and wistfully hopes that he will turn up once more. Sometimes at the dinner table, Miss Mary Nell asks with a quizzical smile, "Bones, whatever became of W. P.?" "Well, he wasn't as bad as you thought he was," her husband replies. Whereupon Miss Mary Nell, wise and compassionate, changes the painful subject. "Oh, honey," she may say, "I forgot to tell you. Broadie Crump called and wants you to go bird hunting Saturday." "What did you say, dear?" Mistuh Bones asks, affectionate reminiscence suddenly dying in his eyes.

The student of the Delta, observing its application of the criminal laws, is inclined to agree with Negroes that it jes' ain't no telling what white folks will do. Sometimes its judges will severely penalize a Negro for, say, stealing a cow, and let a white man off lightly for committing the same offense. At other times, a Negro will be let off lightly, but a white man guilty of the same crime will be severely penalized; while now, as always, a Negro guilty of homicide may be sent to prison for years or not be brought into court at all.

In a Delta town, where I spent some months, there was a great deal of petty thieving, especially in the summer when the white folks would go out in their cars in the evening and access to their houses through open door or window was easy. This troubled the town not only because it had always been law-abiding, but also because, contrary to Delta custom, it was troublesome to lock up the house before going out. The town's police were worried because they rarely caught anybody, and had been severely rebuked by its police court judge for throwing out a dragnet and hauling in men and women who were obviously innocent. The force consisted of three patrolmen and a chief, all of whom had been accustomed to dozing through the summer months. Yet here they were forced into superhuman activity during the hottest period of the year, and were the butt of the town's jokes for their ineptness.

The chief was a fat, slow-going man of about fifty. His natural gift for sleuthing had been enlarged by taking a correspondence course in crime detection from a Kansas City school of detective training. Yet the outburst of thievery in the town, largely undetected, was imperiling both his reputation and his job, while the constant reiteration of his friends, "Jack, you don't look so well," was beginning to affect his health.

The criminals who matched their acumen against that of the chief had an insuperable advantage over him, and none were caught while I was in the town. One of my Negro friends told me the secret of their success, and the reason for the chief's failure to catch them. "Mistuh Jack," he said, "got him a colored lady a few months ago, and when the people sees his car parked in front of her house they goes to thievin' all over town."

During these troubled days, I often went to see the chief in his police station. I was weighed down by a trust which I could not betray, while the cause of the chief's difficulties was of such a delicate nature that I could not even hint at it, and although I yearned to deliver him from his purgatory, my hands were tied. Deeply fatigued by his failure as a detective, he fell into long periods of melancholic abstraction. These were unfortunate for the prisoners in his care who were kept in cells adjoining his office: petty offenders against the peace and dignity of the town whose penance was usually ten days in the calaboose. The chief had no written records of his prisoners' sentences. He just kept track of things in his mind, and his mind had been otherwhere for weeks.

One day, as I sat at his desk, he awoke from his reverie and tiredly called "Mistuh Willis" to the policeman in the next room. "Mistuh Willis," the chief asked," how long was Bertha supposed to stay here?" "The judge said ten days, Mistuh Jack." "Well, go in yonder and get her," ordered the chief.

Bertha, a long, tall, black girl, shuffled into the room on her "coppit" slippers. "How much time did you get, Bertha?" asked the chief. "The judge say ten days, I believe." "Well, doggone it, you been here seventeen days. Now get your things and go on home." "Yassuh," replied the woman.

One of the horrors of the administration of American justice, common to much of America as it is to the Delta, is the Justice of the Peace court. The jurist who presides over these courts is nearly always ignorant and often bigoted. But even if he were learned and enlightened, the pressure upon him to find defendants guilty is almost intolerable. His livelihood is derived from a percentage of the fines assessed against those who appear before him, and these are usually the poor and the obscure who cannot hire a lawyer and are without political influence. The result is that legalized outrages are daily committed in the name of justice against the weak and the helpless.

The Delta Justice of the Peace, in addition to sharing the ignorance and callousness of his brethren elsewhere, is often a poor white whose position enables him to make his hatred of Negroes profitable. Sometimes trials in his court are marked by a sadism refined in its cruelty.

In Mistuh Jack's town there was such a JP. He was an old, bent, wizened man whose mean and narrow life had been deeply embittered because the quality white folks of the town had never paid any attention to him. All his accumulated hatreds, treasured as a miser might treasure bits of string and paper, were poured out upon the heads of Negroes who came before him. His court was located in an old-fashioned "office"; a weatherbeaten shack facing a forlorn, rutted street. Only a part of it was given over to the administering of justice. The rest of it was devoted to his peanut-roasting business. The air was heavy with the odor of roasting peanuts. The floor was littered with peanut shells and the droppings of mice. The Justice sold his peanuts through Negro boy vendors, and sometimes he would interrupt a trial as a boy came in and counted out a small stack of nickels before loading his basket to go out again. Justice, fortunately for her, is blindfolded. God help her if she had visited this court and witnessed what was done in her name.

This jurist had read about the lie detector in a magazine, and decided to rig up one of his own. It consisted of a rounded glass paperweight and a featherweight writing pen. The inventor explained the working of his device to me. Before court began, he balanced pen upon paperweight so delicately that it would oscillate when he blew the slightest breath upon it, and he arranged it before him in such a manner that the prisoner would not know that the pen's oscillations were caused by the judge's breathings.

When a Negro appeared before him, the Judge would first ask several routine questions: his name, address, occupation. He would then explain that he had a lie detector on his desk. If a lie was told the pen would move. In winter this explanation would be preceded by an order to the defendant to pull up his vest or unbutton his coat, "so's I can aim the lie detector at your belly." Little more was needed to throw ordinary Negroes into terror and befuddlement, for so many of them are familiar with the dark uses of hoodoo and here was hoodoo in a sinister form manipulated by the Law.

These proceedings were a cruel form of third degree administered while a so-called trial was in progress: an exercise in vicious sadism. And as the pen oscillated, it is safe to say that many defendants pleaded guilty however innocent they may have been, to escape its inhuman gyrations, just as other innocent men pleaded guilty under Nazi torture.

Sometimes as I sat in this court, I could see townsfolk pass in their cars. They were, on the whole, a kindly and just people. They would have been horrified had they known what was happening inside the weatherbeaten shack on the forlorn, rutted street. But the businessmen were too busy to find out what was done to poor Negroes and whites in a Justice of the Peace court. Their wives were too busy arranging charity dances and teas whose proceeds were destined for missionary work in China. The preachers were preoccupied with visiting their flock and preparing sermons against sin.

I have observed elsewhere that a lack of local leaders is a deterrent to Negro progress in the Delta. Negroes are rightfully proud that they have produced contemporary figures distinguished in the arts and sciences — persons such as George Washington Carver and Marian Anderson. But in the day to day life of the community, it is not these figures who influence the white mind in its attitudes toward Negroes, but the conduct of the generality of local Negroes. Here local Negro leadership could be invaluable. This was forcibly brought home to me in Natchez.

Some years ago, Judge Patterson of that town sought to introduce me to a local Negro called Santa Claus, but he could not be found. Time passed, and I forgot the matter. One day I sat in Patterson's Police Court when he had before him a Negro man charged with drunkenness and beating his wife. He was an habitual drunkard and wifebeater and the usually even-tempered Judge flew into a rage. He told the defendant he regretted that he could not send him to prison for life, but unhappily he could do no more under the law than to commit him to jail for sixty days.

As I listened to the trial, Patterson stopped for a moment to call out to me, "There he is," and pointed to a door. In the door stood a policeman. By his side, ashen-gray with fear, was a white-haired, pop-eyed Negro. I felt that he must be Santa Claus and so he was. Santa Claus, at the Judge's words, looked at me. As a stranger he knew that I could not be the local Law, and must therefore be one of Uncle Sam's mens — the Law in its most terrifying form. He did not know that Judge Patterson, unable to locate him in any other way, had sent a policeman to find him so that he and I could have a chat.

I rushed out and immediately assured him that I had nothing to do with the law, and we went to a near-by room to talk. This was the first of numerous meetings between us.

Santa Claus had for many years been a street salesman of hot peanuts and it was from this genial occupation that he derived his fanciful name; the only name by which he was known to most of the whites and Negroes of Natchez. Laden with a basket of freshly roasted peanuts, he would go along the streets crying to the white children: "Heah come Ole Santa Claus! Heah come Ole Santa Claus! Git yo' hot roasted pinders fum Ole Santa Claus!" His cries, his infectious good humor, his outpouring kindliness, endeared him to the children. They bought his peanuts and so did their children in turn.

But Ole Satan, who switches his tail everywhere, got a-holt of Santa Claus one day, whispered to him, and inflamed him with ambition — that drug which has been the downfall of so many men. Santa Claus decided to branch out and make more money. He decided, he said, "to sell jes' a little whiskey." In so doing, he sold a pint of whiskey to a boy "fum the Jefferson Millinery

College. He got drunk, told the commander where he got the ruckus juice, and "the police come and put me in jail."

A Circuit Court jury found him guilty. Then, said Santa Claus, the Judge spoke. "Green Smith," he said, "stand up." "I say, suh?" The Judge say, "You ain't deef. It is the sentence of the cote that you are to pay a three hundred dollar fine and serve sixty days in the county jail."

Santa Claus soon got out on light bail. "I got me some mo' pinders," he said, "and whenever the white ladies slowed down in they car, I'd say, 'Please, ma'am, gimme a little somethin' to pay twarge my fine.' The ladies they would gimme two-bits, fo'-bits, an' sometimes as much as a dollar. They all knowed me, an' some of 'em had bought pinders from me when they was chillun. Well, suh, it wa'n't no time 'fo' I had collected three hunnerd dollars to pay my fine, and the white folks lemme off the days."

This was his first and last encounter with the law. It did not strike him as odd that he, a convicted prisoner out on bail, could escape the penalties imposed upon him by going out on the streets of Natchez and collecting money to "pay twarge my fine." Nor would he have believed it, if he had been told that he might have met with less success in such efforts in Lynn, Massachusetts, or Concord, New Hampshire. He could not conceive of white folks who would not give a Negro something to pay twarge his fine.

One day, discussing Negro affairs in Natchez with Santa Claus and several of his friends, I brought up the case of the habitual wifebeater and drunkard. I said that most of the Negroes of the town were law-abiding, but this was a man who constantly disturbed the peace of the Negro community and, while it was unfair, many whites would judge Negroes by a few constant offenders rather than by the generality whose conduct was good. I asked why Negroes did not themelves take this kind of thing in hand through a committee of their own which should, so to speak, police the Negro community. When it found an incorrigible person, as the wifebeater, it might ask the white folks to run him out of town for the sake of better relations all around. Then

I suggested as chairman of such a committee, an intelligent, well-to-do, respected Negro.

My friends smiled indulgently. One of them said, "You don't understand niggers. When a nigger rise in the world, he don't want to have nothing to do with the rest of us. He jes' has his own friends, and don't care whether the other niggers lives or dies."

This, it seems to me, approximates the truth of Negro leadership in the Delta. It is understandable in terms of human conduct, but it is also lamentable, because good local leadership by their own people could do much for the welfare of Negroes. In the absence of such leaders, the task is assumed — even monopolized — by rural and smalltown preachers and this is an almost unmitigated misfortune for their flocks.

White and Negro students of the question agree that preacher leadership is unfortunate. He is nearly always a man of much native charm; smooth-mouthed; plausible; and exerting great power as a toiler in the vineyards of the Lord. He is also, however, addicted to the fleshpots; mighty at the board and in the bed; and, seeking to retain or enlarge his perquisites, he is forever scheming. Among Negroes, as whites, the most ardent churchgoers are the ladies, and the Negro preacher, for reasons lay and secular, carefully cultivates their friendship. For one thing, he sees that every lady member of the congregation is appointed upon a committee and when all of the ordinary committees have been filled, a toilet committee is sometimes organized. The duty of its members is to show new communicants where the toilet is.

During a discussion of this question with Dr. T. R. M. Howard, the capable Negro chief of the Taborian Hospital at Mound Bayou, he said that he had gone to a rural Negro church to urge the congregation to avail themselves of inoculations and vaccinations against disease. He spoke just before time for passing the collection plate. But, he said, the preacher was so fearful the minds of his flock would be taken off the collection, he got up after the doctor sat down. "Now that's all right 'bout dem 'noculations, but don't you git behind the blood of Jesus, don't you repent, believe, and be baptized, dem 'noculations an' vaccinations sho ain't gonna save you."

The visitor to a Delta town is surprised by the many Negro churches he sees, far outnumbering those of the whites. They are not necessarily proof, however, of that faith in God which led medieval Europe to rear lofty cathedrals. They are often the result of wranglings in the congregational body which end in "splitting-off." These rows, born of doctrinal disputes, the pastor's personal life, or either reasons mundane as well as spiritual, divide the group against itself. When the quarrel becomes irreconcilable, the preacher may leave his church and, taking part of the congregation with him, start another. The process frequently repeated results in a multiplicity of pastors and churches.

Ten years ago, for example, Greenville's population of twenty thousand was almost equally divided between whites and Negroes. The town's numerous white Baptists had only one church. But its Negro Baptists, because of splitting-off, had nearly fifty churches, and this does not take into account churches of other Negro Protestant sects.

At this time, a delegation of Negro Baptist pastors and laymen called upon Will Percy. They wanted to enlist his aid in getting the white people of Greenville to build a Negro Y.M.C.A. Needing time to think it over, he asked the delegation to see him one week later.

Upon their return, he told them he thought the project they had suggested entirely worthy. He felt, however, that it was harmful to Negro development to shrink from assuming communal responsibilities, and let the whites shoulder burdens rightfully theirs. He had found, he said, that Negro churches, particularly those of the Baptists, far outnumbered those of the whites. The maintenance of so many pastors and churches was a heavy drain upon the Negro community. He would urge the white people, upon a certain condition, to build a fine, large Negro Baptist church, and adjoining it a community center with a library, dance hall, pool room, and other facilities where members could enjoy themselves in wholesome surroundings. But this only upon the condition that the Baptists close their fifty-odd churches. They would then have to maintain only one structure and one pastor; they would have a fine church and the features of a Y.M.C.A.; while because of the savings, they themselves could bear half of the burden.

The delegation listened in stony silence. Its members would see Mr. Percy again. But he never heard from them thereafter. The power of the preachers was so great that the condition he had attached to the building of a church and community center made the project impossible of realization.

Magic and hoodoo are constants of Negro life now as they have always been. There is, for example, Galley, the hostler on Tralake Plantation. One morning when Galley was in the stable lot, a strange Negro came up to him and said, "Good mawnin', Galley." "You'se a stranger to me," replied the hostler, "how come you knows my name?" "Ise a two-headed man," said the stranger. "I knows everything and everybody straight from Adam an' Eve up to right this minute when us is standin' here talkin'." "If you's a two-headed man," asked Galley, "how come you wearin' overhalls like a common nigger?" "I wears 'em," replied the man, "so the white folks won't know who I is. Did they know I'm a two-headed man, they'd run me off."

Galley and the worker of magic fell into conversation for some time. Then the man who had seen all and knew all asked the hostler whether he had any money in his pocket. He replied that he had five dollars. "Well, I tell you what you does," said the wizard. "You gimme that money and I'm gonna work a conjure on Mr. Mac so's when you go to the sto' tonight, soon's you go thoo de do', he gonna say, 'Galley, does you want twenty-five dollars in cash, or does you want hit in groceries?'"

The money changed hands. Galley spent the day impatiently at his tasks, trying hard to make up his mind whether he would rather have twenty-five dollars in cash or its equivalent in groceries. If he took it in cash, would he rather have it all in two-bit pieces, fo'-bit pieces, silver dollars, or have some silver and the rest folding money? If he chose groceries instead, how much of it would he take in tobacco, meat, meal, flour, baking powder, dried apples for pies, molasses, Vienna sausage, cheese, potted ham, bananas? Galley's mouth watered. His mind ached with the pains of indecision. Time dragged. It was nearly seven o'clock before the mules had been returned to the stable lot, and Galley could go to the store.

He briskly entered and said good evening to Mr. Mac who was busy weighing up sugar and coffee for the next day's business on Saturday. On this evening, Mr. Mac, a polite man, did not reply to Galley's greetings, but worked scales and scoop as though he did not exist. The hostler leaned against the counter; shifted from foot to foot; and scratched his head while waiting for the two-headed man's conjure to take effect on Mr. Mac. But nothing happened. Mr. Mac continued about his tasks. Mr. Coleman, his assistant, totted up accounts. The hands of the big clock at the back of the door crept inexorably toward the figure of nine. When they got to that point, Galley knew, the two white gentlemen would close the store.

About eight-fifteen the hostler, weary with waiting and fearful that the white folks had a conjure more powerful than that of the two-headed man, bought a can of sardine-fish and a bottle of pop from Mr. Coleman. He opened the can with his pocket knife, skeeted some pepper sauce on the sardines, put them on crackers and slowly began to eat, all the while keeping a watchful eye on Mr. Mac who with frozen deliberation continued to weigh up coffee and sugar. As the fish dwindled in the tin, Galley ate more and more slowly. After each drink of pop, he would shake the bottle to make the contents foam, thereby giving him "more" pop, so that the drink would last longer. The clock at the back of the store ticked with horrible loudness. Its hands, black against the white face, crept on and on. Still Mr. Mac did not say a word. At nine o'clock, he straightened his back, rose from a sugar barrel and said, "Galley, close the back door. We're fixing to leave here." "Yassuh," said the hostler.

He walked slowly and sadly down the dusty road in the moonlight toward his house. He felt in the pocket of his overalls where a five-dollar bill had snugly nested in the morning. "Well, I be doggone," he repeated over and over.

Practitioners of magic in the Delta retain their numbers, their undiminished prestige, and their power. One of them a hoodoo lady, lives on Percy Street not far from the former home of Will Percy. She specializes largely in delicate problems of the heart, and she toldd me how she had handled a perhaps typical case. The problem presented on this occasion is one not unknown to more exalted circles than those from which her clients are drawn.

"This lady," said the hoodoo woman of her client, "come to me an' say she had been living for about a year with a man which loved her good enough to live with her but not good enough to marry her. She wanted something to make that man marry her. I told her to go at the dime store and buy a pocket knife. I said when she got home to break off one blade and th'ow it over her left shoulder out on the street. Then to stick the handle with the blade in it in her front do' step where that man had to pass when he come to see her so it would cut his objections. It wasn't three weeks after that that nigger up and married the lady."

Magic, in some form, is availed of by Americans both white and Negro, especially in the field of divination. Thus astrology has an enormous vogue extending to millions of people. Bankers, businessmen, professional men and women, resort to astrologers, many of whom earn large fees. The shopgirl often has her fortune read in the tea leaves at lunch; she may wear a good luck anklet; or study an astrology magazine. For many Delta Negroes, as much as for primitive Africans, belief in witchcraft is real and logical. The Negro's fears, which the white man or the educated Negro may scoff at, are to him real and living fears; so, too, are the evil spirits which he actually sees and hears. He is obsessed with fears of many kinds and he turns to the hoodoo man, in whom he has complete confidence, to exorcise the evil spirits through his supernatural powers, or, in other cases, to give him dominance over a man or woman through aligning the spirits on his side. Educated people find it almost impossible to view the world through the eyes of the superstitious, fear-ridden, spirits-haunted Delta Negro; they cannot grasp what goes in the mind of one whose ways of thinking and acting are so remote from their own. Yet it is to the credit of the Delta that although its law does not, and cannot, make a distinction between a crime committed by a civilized man and one committed by a magic-enchanted, almost primitive man, the region often, as I have before indicated, makes allowances for crimes perpetrated in the name of magic.

Sometimes the practice of hoodoo leads to a tragedy. In one case the tragedy was of a kind which somberly illuminates the strange, complex relations of whites and Negroes in the Delta. This tragedy had the quality of high tragedy: inevitability. Given the existing circumstances, and the status of the persons concerned, it could end only with the destruction of the protagonist.

The facts are simple. On a plantation near Greenville, there lived a few years ago, a planter with his wife and young daughter. They had as houseboy, gardener, and man-of-all-work, a young Negro named Zed Jackson. Polite, cleanly, industrious, of pleasant personality and cheerful manner, he had come to the family as a boy of fifteen, had worked about the house and garden for ten years, and had won the respect and affection of his employers. His reputation in the community for sobriety and industry was excellent, while his habits were so exemplary that his contemporaries mockingly called him "preacher."

One evening, the planter's daughter, sitting on her bed for a moment preparatory to disrobing for the night, heard a noise underneath her. She was not startled until, looking desultorily under the bed, she saw the family's Negro houseboy naked except for his drawers. She frantically screamed, Zed ran out of the house, and her father, hearing her screams, came running in, pistol in hand. The man of the house immediately summoned his neighbors, bloodhounds were obtained from a near-by prison, and intensive search for Zed was made throughout the night. No trace of him was discovered. But in the morning, he was found stark, raving mad, groaning and writhing in the mud and manure of the stable lot. He was not harmed but was taken off and put in jail.

At breakfast, after the heat and passion of the man hunt, the planter and his neighbors tried to account for what had happened. The precise occurrence was not only without parallel in their experience, but they found it difficult to believe that the exemplary Zed, devoted to his employers as they were to him, would attempt to commit a horrible crime. Their speculations left them in darkness, until they concluded to question the plantation's Negroes about the case.

Then they understood and were able to reconstruct what had occurred. The Negroes said that for over a year Zed had gone about in terror of his life because a man had put a conjure on him which would kill him. Negroes rarely, however, mention hoodoo to white folks and Zed's employers, seeing him going calmly about his tasks, could not know that he was haunted by fear of death; death inevitable unless he could find a hoodoo man with a conjure more powerful than the one in the possession of his enemy. Reconstructing the events of the night, it appeared that Zed, in his own cabin, had stripped himself down to his drawers preparatory to getting into bed, when someone appeared at the window making cabalistic signs at him. In his overwhelming terror he fled instinctively to the one place where he felt he might be inviolate — "his white folks'" house. But once there, in his drawers, he was overcome by another terror not less overwhelming and, like a wounded animal, crept under a bed.

On that dark night everyone concerned acted instinctively. It was instinctive of Zed to fly terror-stricken from the hoodoo man to his employer's home and, once there, to crawl under the bed in his double terror. It was instinctive of the planter's daughter to scream when she found him. No one stops, at such a moment, to make psychological inquiries into the mentality of the man under the bed. It was instinctive of the planter, hearing his daughter scream, to appear with his gun. And for Zed there was but one way out — the mercifulness of insanity precluding the violent death that would otherwise have been his lot.

It is a genial delusion of white Deltans — of nearly all white Southerners — that, because they live among masses of Negroes, employ Negro cooks, maids, nurses, washerwomen, they intimately understand Negro life. The truth is, in my opinion, that most Southern whites have only the faintest comprehension of the inner lives of Negroes which remain forever secret and alien to them. This is strikingly apparent even in the field of humor.

Hospitable Deltans are wont to regale their guests with a variety of so-called Negro stories. Many of these stories — especially those depending for their effect upon malapropisms or the usage of grandiloquent phrases — are white folks' concepts of Negro humor. Often they are staples of the old vaudeville stage or of minstrels long vanished. They are about as accurate in mood as are the music and lyrics of Gershwin's *Porgy and Bess*; or the lovely, but psychologically false, "Ol' Man River" of Kern's *Showboat*. (The showboat was always known in Greenville, far more poetically, as the "floatin' palace.")

Numbers of stories — dreary and mirthless — concern the Negro's amorous adventures and misadventures and nowhere is the difference between white and Negro humor more marked than in this category. The borderline story at best tends to be dull but the white man's stories in this field are almost invariably lewd, lecherous, and mephitic as well as dreary. They are self-conscious and have about them something of the false bravado of the small boy scrawling naughty words on the fence. Here the Negro's humor is warm, vigorous, picturesque, and lusty, and would have been readily comprehensible to the Elizabethans whose Christopher Marlowe wrote:

> Madam, shall I undress you for the fight?
> The wars are naked that you wage tonight,
> In a bed as broad as a battlefield.

It is difficult to get from the lips of most white folks an authentic Negro story — a story, which in its background, development, language, and climax is as much a part of the people as the soil on which they live; a story which could not proceed from any other people or environment in this country.

Perhaps I can illustrate my thesis by such a story.

Elzida Davis, a settled widder lady who ran a rooming house

in Vicksburg, was arrested for shooting at a colored man who came to her door. Her landlord — Mr. Eubanks — visited her in jail. He was told the circumstances of the alleged shooting, and knowing Elzida's propensity for "overtalking" gave her strict instructions to keep her mouth shut in court and to say no more than was necessary. She solemnly swore she would keep quiet.

At the trial, her first witness was Mr. Eubanks. He said that Elzida was a noble woman of great righteousness; a good mother and a pillar of the church; a person who paid her rent on the dot; and one quite incapable of behaving coarsely with a pistol. Other white folks testified to the same effect and then, after she had held up her right hand and had sworn to tell the truth, "s'elp you Gawd," Elzida took the stand. Without having been asked a single question, without the slightest prompting from anybody, she launched into a nonstop flight of narrative and oratory:

"Judge, I aims to tell you the truth an' nothin' but the truth an' if I doesn't I hopes Gawd will strike me dead right heah in this chair where I'm sittin'. Everybody in Vicksburg knows I'm a pore widder lady that works hard an' stays out of devilment, an' if you ask Mr. Eubanks what's out yonder in de cote-room wid the other white folks, he'll tell you I haven't missed nair Sadday payin' my rent the six years I been livin' in his house. I'm a pore widder lady wid five head o' chillun but I keeps shoes on they feet and somethin' t'eat in they stomachs an' don't ask no he'p from the Red Cross lady or anybody else, an' the white folks in town will tell you I'm a hard-workin' woman that don't do no dead-beatin', an' if that ain't the truth I hopes Gawd will strike me dead right heah in this chair. But, Judge, you knows hits wrong to cheat a pore widder lady like that no-'count dead-beat that come at my house, rented my bes' room, used up might' nigh all my wood an' kindlin', then run off 'thout payin' me a cent of rent. So I was settin' there studdin' how could I get my rent money when it come to me that ole deadbeat had lef' his trunk and maybe it was somethin' in it would he'p pay the rent.

"Well, suh, I opened that trunk but hit wa'n't nothin' in it 'cept some trashy ole papers an' a pistol. I say, Lawd, what is I'm gwine do to keep my chillun from gittin' a-holt of this pistol and hurtin' theyself, and I was jes a-studdin' when they come a knockin' an' a poundin' at de front do'.

"It was a terrible knockin' an' poundin' so I hollers out, I says: 'Stop dat knockin' an' poundin'.' He kep' it up not payin' me no mind, so I hollers again, I says: 'Stop that knockin' an poundin'. You breakin' down the white folks' do'.' But he kep' on, so I gits up to keep him from breakin' down the white folks' do', an' 'fo Gawd, Judge, when I opened that do' that pistol jes' went off in my face."

The Judge, gallant toward ladies in distress and having a wide experience of miraculous manifestations in the lives of Negroes who come before him, is not inclined to ask too much of flesh and blood. He therefore dismissed Elzida, who with queenly majesty stalked out into the street where Henry, her gentleman friend who drays on the town, was waiting with his lopsided wagon to take her home. There she was met by her landlord, Mr. Eubanks.

"Elzida," he said sternly, "we had a hard time keeping you out of jail today. Now don't you ever let me hear of you again taking your pistol and shooting at anybody because Judge Moss told me the next time you shoot at anybody he's going to send you up for a long time."

"Nawsuh," replied Elzida demurely. "I'm ain't. Nex' time one of them no-'count deadbeats don't pay me my rent, I'm gonna get me fifteen cents wuth o' cocaine an' a dime's wuth o' gin an' jes' cut his head off with my razor."

Pleased that she had been vindicated by the law, sure that she had found a way of circumventing it in the future if the need should arise, and knowing that her prestige had been enhanced in the community, Elzida mounted serenely to the rickety seat of the wagon. "Giddap, mule," said Henry, and the wagon rolled slowly downhill carrying the honest widder lady to her house and her five head o' chillun back of the Vicksburg National Park.

CHAPTER 3

The Gulf Between

WHILE GATHERING the data that went into the first part of this book, I spent an afternoon discussing the race question with a Memphis Negro. A graduate of a great university, he was an intelligent, thoughtful, deeply embittered man. He courteously regretted that his foot which lay bandaged on a stool before him, did not permit him to rise and greet his visitor. "But," he said, his eyes blazing with indignation, "I'm thankful for this injury. Except for that I'd have to be in Atlanta tomorrow for a meeting of an interracial commission. Its proceedings are lies and frauds. Everybody present is overpolite in a strained way. The whites are hell-bent upon being broadminded. The Negroes affect to take it all as a matter of course. But nobody present ever dares speak the blunt truth. They drift on clouds of sentimentality. They pass meaningless resolutions. Then they go home. That's why I'm glad I don't have to go through another of those sessions tomorrow."

A little later, I had a confirmation of this point of view while lunching in Memphis with a white man who had abandoned the ministry to devote his life to race relations. He works hard in his chosen field; believes devoutly in the worth of his activities; and is apparently a dedicated man. Throughout lunch he alternately dripped sweetness and light, or dilated angrily upon discriminations against Southern Negroes. Then, over coffee, he said, almost hysterically, "But there is one thing I cannot stand. When I go to Chicago I cannot bear the sight of Negro men dancing with white women."

There is nothing new in all this, but much that is significant. In 1904, when Booker T. Washington dined at the White House as the guest of President Theodore Roosevelt, a roar of anger went up from the South. "White men of the South, how do you like it?" asked the New Orleans *Times-Democrat*. The Memphis *Scimitar* said that the President had perpetrated "the most damnable outrage ever." The Richmond *Times,* though more hysterical perhaps than other Southern newspapers, more nearly expressed the subconscious Southern mind. It pictured the President as believing that white women should receive attentions from Negro men and that members of the two races might intermarry.

Here we come to the heart of the problem. I submit that our understanding of it depends upon three candid acknowledgments. The first is that the Negro question is insoluble; as are nearly all complex social questions. It is insoluble in the sense that no cure-all may be applied which would immediately dispose of it in its numerous ramifications. (This is not to say, however, that today's truth may not be tomorrow's falsehood.) Yet it is part of our naïvete as a people to believe, or profess to believe, that complex social questions can not only be solved but solved out of hand. Every American has in him something of the missionary and of Kublai Khan. He wants to make over the world and decree its making over. Such attitudes may be disastrous. For when we find, as we must find, that this is impossible, we tend either to become childishly petulant and back away from the question, or, in our adolescent frustration, we irrationally adopt measures that increase its complexities and make even amelioration more difficult. Thus as a people we cling to our patent-medicine attitudes in social questions, although no individual believes that he can solve all the problems arising from his relations with God, parents, wife, children; nor are his illusions shaken even when he sees that his failures do not necessarily keep him from leading a happy, useful life.

Second, we must acknowledge that the race question is primarily insoluble because, in the conscious or unconscious minds of Southern whites, it is a blood or sexual question. Today, as yesterday, their laws prohibit intermarriage between the races. There are Southerners who advocate the relaxation of Jim Crow ordinances, and those who believe that the Negro should vote. But there is none to say that the ban of interracial marriage should be lifted.

Today, as in the past, the iron taboo remains in force nearly everywhere in the South. It is that no white woman may voluntarily have sexual relations with a Negro except upon the penalty, if discovered, of death for both parties, or, at best, banishment of the woman from the community.

A recent case drawn from the annals of a Delta town will serve as illustration of the pitiless sternness of this taboo. So all-pervasive is the taboo, and so fraught with dreadful consequences is its violation, that the slightest evidence of a budding relationship between a white woman and a Negro man, may become a matter of police attention. In the case in question, the police learned that a white girl was having a flirtation with a Negro man. He was a middle-aged, skilled craftsman, who enjoyed an excellent reputation in the white community for industry and sobriety. Fearful that trouble might ensue, two white men who knew of the flirtation pleaded with the Negro's employer to suggest to the man that it might be wise for him to leave town. No attention was paid to their warning. Shortly afterward, a policeman found him and the girl together near a railroad embankment. He shot the Negro to death. His action, shocking to the sensibilities of the town's whites, nonetheless had their approval. The girl was sent away by her parents and will never return to her home.

These are the remorseless facts of the situation. Unless there should come a revolution which would completely change the American way of life, it will never be possible, within foreseeable time, to appeal from them with any hope of success. Under these circumstances there cannot be "social equality" among the races. This is impossible in any event without the willingness to grant intermarriage. Nor is this all. There cannot even be forms of physical propinquity that smack of social equality, open or clandestine, between the races. It follows, therefore, that there must inevitably be physical and social segregation of whites and Negroes.

If marriage flows from propinquity, the way to prevent marriage with members of a prohibited group, is to keep them from propinquity with members of your own group. It may be illuminating, in this context, to note observations of the Delta by one who has spent his life outside the area. He is Dr. John Dollard, Research Associate in Sociology, Yale Institute of Human Relations, who, in 1937, published his *Caste and Class in a Southern Town*. It is, says the author, "an attempt to give a dynamic view of social life in the deep South." The town, judging from statistical, geographical, and other evidences, is situated about twenty-five miles from Greenville. It is a "typical" Delta town. Speaking of the taboos of the community, Dollard says:

> The commonest of these taboos are those against eating at the table with Negroes, having them in the parlor of one's house as guests, sitting with them on the front porch of one's home, and the like. Any of these acts would imply social equality instead of social inferiority for the Negro. *The white-caste view on this matter is simple and logically consistent. . . .* This is probably no delusion. After all, our traditional techniques of courtship center around the dining table, the parlor, and the front porch, as well as freedom of access by the front parlor and the front door. (My italics.)
>
> One who cannot share these privileges can hardly expect to court the daughter of the house. . . . From the life-history material comes an interesting line of confirmation on this point. The dreams of middle-class Negroes, at least, suggest that eating together with white people in the dream is symbolic of marriage and sex relations. One does not begin to discourage an unwanted suitor from sex relations when he is already married to one's daughter; one begins long before by denying him his house. The white people seem to feel about this matter in the same way and are quite as direct in their statements about it. . . .

It is useless to tell white Southerners, as they are often told, that Negroes make no claims to "social equality" and intermarriage; that their fears on this score are groundless; and that, therefore, they could relax some of the more stringent ordinances of segregation without weakening their social-equality-intermarriage taboo. This the whites will not do. They fear and believe that once a small crack is made in the walls of social segregation, the walls will eventually be breached. As evidence of their impassioned feelings in this respect, Mrs. Franklin D. Roosevelt, by a strange hate-transference, has become the most hated woman in the South since Harriet Beecher Stowe, because she is looked upon as an advocate of social equality between the races.

Southerners reason, moreover, that Negroes must want social equality and intermarriage not only because their denial condemns Negroes to a permanent status of inferiority, but also because granting them would automatically erase the repressions which now run against the group, since, if there were intermarriage, the whites would remove discriminations out of familial self-interest. The steel-hard rigidities of the matter remain the same, however, whether its bases are logical or illogical, reasonable or unreasonable. Here we are dealing with the subconscious as well as the conscious mind. We are stumbling along the darkest trails of the jungle of the human mind. In their shadows lurk blood-chilling monsters and howling furies and spiders as big as bladders. Certainly if sex is the most profound and driving of human instincts, sex fears are capable of evoking demoniac passions and searing hatreds against which reason, love, logic, are as thistles driven against battleship armor.

That sex fears and consequent racial segregation are the heart of the race problem, is clearly recognized by Gunnar Myrdal in his monumental *An American Dilemma*. These factors, he notes, strongest in the South, are common to all the United States. The Swedish sociologist says:

> This brings us to the point where we shall attempt to sketch . . . the social mechanisms by which the anti-amalgamation maxim determines race relations. This mechanism is observed by nearly everybody in America, but most clearly in the South. Almost unanimously white Americans have communicated to the author the following logic of the caste situation which we shall call the "white man's theory of color caste."

Myrdal then enumerates the items that compose the color caste theory:

> (1) The concern for "race purity" is basic in the whole issue; the primary and essential demand is to prevent amalgamation.
> (2) Rejection of "social equality" is to be understood as a precaution to hinder miscegenation and particularly intermarriage.
> (3) The danger of miscegenation is so tremendous that the segregation and discrimination inherent in the refusal of "social equality" must be extended to nearly all spheres of life. . . .

As for white Southerners specifically, when they are asked, says Myrdal, to "rank, in order of importance, types of discrimination, they consistently present a list in which these types are ranked according to the degree of closeness of their relation to the amalgamation doctrine. The rank order held nearly unanimously is the following:

> *Rank 1.* Highest in order stands the bar against intermarriage and sexual intercourse involving white women.
> *Rank 2.* Next come those inequalities and discriminations which specifically concern behavior in personal relations. These are the barriers against dancing, bathing, eating, drinking together, and social intercourse generally.
> *Rank 3.* Thereafter follow the segregation and discriminations in use of public facilities such as schools, churches, and means of conveyance.
> *Rank 4.* Next comes political disfranchisement.
> *Rank 5.* Thereafter come discriminations in law courts, by the police and by other public servants.
> *Rank 6.* Finally come the discriminations in securing land, credit, jobs, and other means of earning a living, and discriminations in public relief and other social welfare activities.

Myrdal draws the inescapable conclusion from these attitudes:

> . . . It should be noted that the rank order is very apparently determined by the factors of sex and social status, so that the closer the association of a type of interracial behavior is to sexual and social intercourse on an equalitarian basis, the higher it ranks among the forbidden things. . . .

The case is not bettered when, as sometimes happens, the Delta's fears are given point. A Delta plantation Negro recently went to Chicago and remained some months. On his return, his employer asked him why he had gone away. "Well, Mr. Ed," he said, "if you won't git mad, I'll tell you." Mr. Ed, as it happens, is an aristocrat. His informant would not have spoken so frankly to a member of the white middle class since this, considering the nature of his revelations and the mores of the community, would be to court bodily harm. Told to go on and talk, the Negro said that he went to Chicago because he wanted to sleep with a white woman. Continuing, he said that his aspiration, shared by others, had enabled Chicago Negro slickers to organize a profitable racket based upon it. They meet trains from the South and ask Southern Negroes, most of them entering the city for the first time, if they would like to sleep with a white woman. The slickers, upon being told yes, take their victims to an isolated spot, slug them, and rob them.

This form of crime has made its appearance in the newspapers. Under a New Haven, Connecticut, dateline the New York *Times* (November 1, 1946) says:

> State Attorney A. S. Ulman announced today that he would move for trial on Dec. 3 of Robert Bradley, 36, one of two Negroes indicted yesterday for first degree murder in connection with the deaths of three other Negroes whose bodies were found buried in the East Haven woods recently.
> . . . These victims, police say, were lured individually to a secluded section of East Haven on the pretext of meeting with white women, and then murdered. . . .

Such is the fierceness of the white Southerner's sex taboo, and so deeply does it pervade his personality, that he took it overseas with him during the last war as he did in the First World War. He could not, for obvious reasons, enforce it. But he often tried although this was to risk death, maiming, imprisonment. It is unlikely that the Army will ever make public a record of conflicts between white and Negro soldiers over white women in nearly every part of the world. The facts, however, are known to thousands of service men of both races; some are buried in foreign graves because of it. Clashes between these groups, especially in England where the soldiers remained nearly two years before D-Day, were frequent and deadly. Sometimes they assumed the scale of small engagements involving a hundred or more men who used rifles, grenades, clubs. These lethal quarrelings were a source of great trouble to the Army high command, and to the British who were our hosts. A palliative was found by permitting Negro soldiers to go to an English village on one day, and whites the next day. But wherever the troops went, the problem went with them. It was never settled to the satisfaction of all concerned, and it ended only with the disembarkation on American soil of most of our soldiers.

If it be said, on the other hand, that the Southern white man, allegedly zealous for the purity of his blood, has not hesitated to have physical relations with Negro women, the charge is irrefutable. Historically this has always occurred, as we have noted before, when there was a master and slave relationship between peoples; when the aftermath of slavery was the degradation of marriage, the weakening of family ties, the sundering of children from parents; when the richer race could buy women of the poorer race, or the powerful could command consent of the weak. The fact is nonetheless indefensible. It is shameful to a people holding themselves superior to another, but its recognition leads to no solution of the issues involved.

It is worth noting, however, that by the testimony of members of both races, sexual relationships between white men and Negro women in the Delta have long been decreasing. It may be that this has been brought about in part by an awakened conscience on the score; that such relationships now belong in the category of things not done. It may also be because, as Delta Negroes say, "White folks have come down to our level"; indicating thereby a sharp relaxation in their sexual standards as elsewhere in the nation. Whatever the reason, the fact is nonetheless certain.

The manner in which one white man was converted to the true faith, was the subject of a story told me by a Delta resident, as he apparently got it from his troubled, repentant friend. It is illuminating not only of the attitudes of certain whites, but also of those Negroes who deeply feel that white men ought to let Negro women alone. This is how the tale was told to me. The names and places mentioned are, of course, fictitious.

Ed Blank, one of our leading citizens, was a man that liked to get his loving in the dark o' the moon. He couldn't any more keep away from the high-yaller gals of Bogue Bend than he could keep from asking on a July day whether it was hot enough for you.

People talked about Ed a good deal on and off. Once in a while some of the old-timers said that years ago when he was a young man and had just moved to town from Willow Lake — long before he married Miss Clara Belle — he'd drive his buggy out Cottonwood Street on dark nights, and disappear inside a Nigra shack. Then about midnight, just before number fifteen pulled out for Memphis, he'd clatter down Jefferson — our first paved street — and eat him a hamburger at the Acropolis before going home. Well suh, as time passed colored folks out in Dahomey saw Ed's Stanley Steamer, then his Apperson Jack Rabbit, his Stutz Bearcat, and the Packard he's driving now. But you don't see his car parked any more in front of Hattie Henry's house, and people reckon he's gone and got too old to do ugly any more.

I'm here to tell you he didn't get over it none too soon. Long's his kids were little, people said it was a sin and a shame for a man like Ed Blank to be carrying on like that. At least, that's what the ladyfolks said. The men they just kept quiet. But when Mary Elizabeth and Ed Junior got to going off to college up North and bringing back visitors in the summer, lots of people said it was time for old man Blank to get some sense in his head if he ever was going to have any. One day it come mighty near a showdown and it wouldn't have surprised me if a committee had waited on him and told him he'd have to cut out his monkeyshines or leave town even if he was one of our leading citizens. It come up like this.

Carolyn Summers, Maggie Bart, and Mary Withers — three of Mrs. Blank's closest friends that have been together in Bible Circle Number Two ever since it was started fifteen years ago — were shopping in Wolf's Store. And who should come in dressed finer than any white lady in town and looking like she owned the place but this Hattie Henry, while, like my wife said when she heard about it, Clara Belle Blank hadn't had a stitch of clothes so long she looked plum tacky. Well, suh, that made the ladies so mad they left the store and went over to Hartman's Icecream Parlor to get 'em a drink to cool off with. Carolyn and Mary, who don't bite their tongues for nobody no matter who they are, wanted to go right on up to Ed's office in the Wilkins Building and give him a piece of their mind about him, a married man with a fine wife and two fine children, carrying on like he was. But Maggie Bart says, No. It wouldn't be ladylike talking to a man about a thing like that. Ed Blank would get his reward up there — pointing to the ceiling where there's a picture of an Eskimo spearing a walrus for the Bogue Bend Coal and Ice Company, Makers of Colder Ice. Anyhow the ladies got pretty hot under the collar, and I reckon they'd a-finally laid the law down if this thing hadn't come up that I'm fixing to tell you.

I suppose Ed would still be chasing high-yallers or would a-got into a peck o' trouble, if it hadn't been for Alonzo Henderson, the Nigra that ran the Nigra paper called *Jubilee's Harp*. He drifted into town a few years ago and got a-hold of the *Harp* when it didn't have nothing much in it except a few hair-straightener ads and church news. He graduated from that school over in Tuscaloosa but there was nothing biggity about him like there is about some educated Nigras, and he got the co-operation of the better element of the white people when they saw he wasn't smart-alecky and started printing the right kind of editorials. Anyhow he was a good Nigra respected by both white and colored.

One night when Ed was having his carburetor adjusted at Grimes's Garage, he saw Alonzo's light burning in his office over the B.B. Undertaking Parlor, and thought he'd go up there a minute just to kill time and encourage him in the good work he was doing. Alonzo told him to come right in, suh, pulled him up a chair, turned on the fan, and asked him did he want a Coca-Cola to cool off with, it was so hot.

Ed said, no, thank you, he didn't have much time and was just getting his carburetor adjusted account the mixture was too rich, but he'd sit down a minute. Yes, replied Alonzo, he liked Bogue Bend fine. It had about the best white people in the state and they treated colored folks right. Ed said the two races always did get on well there, and there was good and bad amongst all kinds of people. Alonzo told him that was certainly right and he was going to do all he could to get colored people in town to copy the better class of white folks, like you, Mister Ed, instead of poor white trash. About that time Joe Grimes he hollers up that Ed's car is ready, and when he got up to go Alonzo said he'd better lead the way because the light is busted and you might fall and hurt yourself on the steps, so he went on ahead. Just when they hit the sidewalk, two high-yaller girls come by and said good evening to Alonzo. Ed watched 'em go on down the street, winked at Alonzo, and said, "You certainly got mighty pretty girl friends." Alonzo didn't say anything, so Ed hung around a minute and went to get his car.

Well, suh, about two weeks after that, Ed dropped in Alonzo's office again one night and said he was waiting for his car it looked like they didn't make cars as good as they used to and he certainly was tired of taking it to the shop every time he went out. Alonzo said he was mighty glad to have Mister Ed or any of his good white folks friends come to see him, they were always welcome. Then he asked did Mister Ed reckon cotton ever would bring a good price again, and Ed said he thought it would if those smart alecks in Washington who had never met a payroll in their life would let it alone and be ruled by the law of supply and demand like God intended it to. Alonzo said yessir, fifteen-cent cotton and thirty-cent meat makes it mighty tough on folks, but Ed didn't say any more about that. He pulled out a cigar, cut off the end of it with that gold clipper that the Bogue Bend ballteam gave him for being the most loyal rooter when they won the pennant, took him a puff, and asked Alonzo did he think he could fix him up a date with one of those girls that had passed by that night when he was in his office.

Alonzo said, "Mister Ed, I can answer that question by telling you a story if you won't get mad at me." Ed said he wouldn't get mad, go ahead.

"I don't know if you know it, Mister Ed, but during the

world's war I was a second lieutenant in France. One time when I was stationed near a town called Metz I got leave and went there. Not having anything particular on my mind and not knowing anybody around there, I just walked around town until I come to a place where some music was being played by a French army band.

"I was standing there listening when all of a sudden I smelled some mighty fine cologne it looked to me like right under my nose. So I whirled around to see where it was coming from and standing not as far as I am from you was a fine-looking, blonde, white lady. She said good morning and I said good morning. She asked me was I stationed in Metz and I said no, ma'm, that I was stationed about thirty kilometers away. She certainly was a pretty lady, but the way she talked to me at first I suspicioned she was a pleasure lady — there's a lots of them in France — but you could tell by the way she talked she wasn't anything like that. She asked me was I spending some time in Metz and I told her no, ma'm, I was just there for the day and night. Right then I looked over to the other side of the bandstand and who did I see but my Colonel eyeing me hard. He was from Alabama like I was and I knew he didn't want to see me talking to a white lady, and I didn't want him to see me either. So I eased on around to the other side of the stand where I wouldn't be near the white lady.

"I had no sooner got over there than there she was and asked me did I have a place to spend the night and I told her no, ma'm, I didn't yet. So she says, you can spend the night at my house. My husband is away and you'll be welcome. So I cut my eye around to see where the Colonel was at, but he wasn't anywheres around, and I told her I'd be glad to accept her invitation and we started on walking to her house.

"I reckon we walked about fifteen minutes before we got to her house and I was feeling mighty funny because I never had been treated by a white lady like that. When we did get to her house the lady told me go on upstairs and wash up and meet her in the garden. I hopped up those steps like a cat and hopped down 'em in a hurry to join the lady in the garden."

Right there Alonzo stopped. You couldn't hear a sound in that room except kids in their cars parked downstairs to drink cokes. Ed sat there like the bank had just shut down on him that morning and his family had died of lockjaw in the evening.

Then Alonzo said: "Mister Ed, I've been watching you close. You been getting pale like all the blood had left your heart. You been biting your cigar, leaning on the edge of your chair, and looking like you'd like to cut my throat. You can't stand the idea of me, a Nigra man, being with a white lady. I suspicioned you would ask me fix you up a date with one those colored girls ever since that time you winked at me when they passed by and you said how pretty they were, so I made up this story to tell you if it ever came to that and see how you would feel if the shoe was on the other foot. Now some of us colored people feel the same way about white men and colored women, and I believe you ought to know it."

Ed got up, said good night, went on over to the garage, got in his car and drove straight home. And as far as anybody in town knows, that's where he's been every night since.

The Delta, as we have seen, erects a sex taboo whose violation may result in death. Yet by its own actions it tends to bring it dangerously into contempt in the minds of its highly suggestible Negroes. What was said in this respect of the whole South by W. J. Cash, a North Carolinian, in 1941, applies presently to the Delta:

> . . . Once the suppression of red-light districts and the streetwalker had turned most Southern hotels into public stews . . . Negro bellboys . . . acquired a virtual monopoly of the trade of pander and pimp, and demanded and secured from the white prostitutes they served all the traditional prerogatives of the pimp, including not only a large share of their earnings but also and above all the right of sexual intercourse. . . .
>
> The result was the rise of a horde of raffish blacks, full of secret, contemptuous knowledge of the split in the psyche of the shamefaced Southern whites, the gulf between their Puritanical professions and their hedonistic practices — scarcely troubling to hide their grinning contempt for their clients under

the thinnest veil of subservient politeness and, in the case of bell-boys, hugging to themselves with cackling joy their knowledge of the white man's women. And this has drifted out to infect large numbers of other Negroes. (*The Mind of the South,* Alfred A. Knopf, Inc.)

It is no secret that you can easily buy whiskey and women in many Delta hotels. The peripatetic prostitute does not, as in other days, cater largely to the traveling salesman trade. These gentry, moving by automobile, find it easy to go home at frequent intervals. She caters to those who once went to the now closed red-light district: local businessmen, clerks, farmers, high-school boys. They make their contact with the prostitute through the bellboys, all of whom are Negroes. They are the indispensable middlemen of hotel prostitution. Sometimes they may suggest the traffic to an incoming guest — "Boss, does you want a woman?" Or the guest may say, "Boy, get me a woman."

No hotel prostitute may ply her trade, under these circumstances, without the good will of the bellboy. He is in a position, therefore, to demand all that the traffic will bear. In his mind, given the mores of the area, the prostitute is an anomalous creature. She is, on the one hand, a whore. But she is also, on the other hand, a white lady. As a whore, the bellboy naturally looks upon her as such. But as a white lady, she is the inaccessible female untouchable except upon penalty of death. Yet she is accessible through the manner in which she earns her living. She is made pliant, even if she were otherwise resistant, because she cannot earn her living without the bellboy's good will.

Sometimes the relationship between bellboy and prostitute client ends tragically. In one case, the bellboy demanding that the woman submit to him as the price of his services, got into a quarrel with her which resulted in blows between them being traded. The woman told her white lover who shared her earnings. He got together a group of hoodlum friends and when the bellboy left the hotel at midnight, they seized him and threw him into an automobile. The car was driven to a lonely place where the white men castrated the Negro.

Professional prostitution in small hotels is inevitably known to the hotel management. The manager knows, or must know, that its effect is to bring into contempt the stern sex taboo of the community. It is a taboo which admits of no exceptions whatever the quality of the white woman. The men who run Delta hotels, and those who resort to hotel prostitutes, would not hesitate to enforce the taboo, if violated, although this means death to the violator. Yet the management, for the sake of revenue, and the clientele, for the sake of their sexual gratification, debase their own taboo, sharply lower white pretensions in Negro minds, and damage their whole social structure.

It would be an oversimplification to say that the blood or sexual element hitherto discussed constitutes the whole measure of the race problem. There are other factors. It is the sexual factor, however, from which social and physical segregation grows. It is segregation which Negroes find most humiliating and crippling in their aspirations, such as entrance to white schools. It is segregation which throws a heavy burden upon the white South in providing dual facilities for the races in education, transportation, hospitals, jails, and nearly everywhere that the two groups may meet. Yet whatever may be the disabilities worked upon Negroes and whites by segregation; whether the fears that provoke it are reasonable or unreasonable; whether it is anti-democratic, anti-constitutional, or anti-Christian, there is little chance, in my opinion, that it will be obliterated within foreseeable time. He who evades, beclouds, or challenges the issue may do great harm to the whole American society. He who does not take segregation as the starting point for an exploration of the possibilities that may lead to a betterment of the race question will find himself lost in a haunted wood.

Since the deep-seated mores of a people cannot be changed by law, and since segregation is the most deep-seated and pervasive of the Southern white mores, it is evident that he who attempts to abolish it by law runs risks of incalculable gravity. There are nonetheless whites and Negroes who would break down segregation by Federal fiat. Let them beware. I have little doubt that in such a case the country would find itself nearing civil war.

Writing five years ago in the Louisville *Courier-Journal,* Mark Ethridge, the publisher of that newspaper, said:

> He (the Negro) must realize that there is no power in the world . . . which could now force the Southern white people to abandon the principle of social segregation. It is a cruel disillusionment, bearing the germs of strife and perhaps tragedy, for any of their leaders to tell them that they can expect it as the price of their participation in the war.

This, it seems to me, is a statement of indubitable fact, yet Mr. Ethridge was denounced by the Negro press and Northern white liberals as a fascist, a Ku Kluxer, and, anticlamatically, a scoundrel.

Let us turn to another source of opinion on this all-important matter. Hodding Carter, publisher and editor of the Greenville (Mississippi) *Democrat-Times* was awarded the Pulitzer Prize in 1946 for editorials on racial and religious tolerance. He has consistently and courageously stood for essential justice to Negroes; he has strongly advocated practical measures for their educational, health, and economic betterment; and has been in general a salutary influence in the area where his newspaper circulates. For these reasons he has been called everything from a "nigger lover" to a communist, and has become a controversial figure throughout Mississippi.

Yet these are the words of this alleged firebrand when he addressed students of the University of Mississippi in December, 1946:

> As Southerners our great challenge is to lift the economic, health and education standards of the Negro together with our own. . . . But I want to make it clear . . . that I consider any program which would end the segregation of races in the South as unrealistic and dangerous to the hope of progress in race relations. . . .

It is not surprising, then, that when the President's Committee on Civil Rights issued its report on November 1, 1947, sharply criticizing racial segregation, it was savagely denounced in Mississippi. There is indeed ground to suppose that had the report been issued two months earlier, it might have resulted in

the election of Congressman John Rankin to the United States
Senate, instead of his abysmal defeat at the hands of Judge John
Stennis who never once injected "white supremacy" into his
campaign speeches.

I come now to the third acknowledgment concerning the race
question. If it is insoluble in the sense hitherto discussed —
namely, finding a universal remedy for all its ills — the issue is
confused and harm is done to the relations of the races when
leaders of both sides, out of sentimentality, hypocrisy, or refusal
to face the fact, pretend that somehow it is capable of solution.
Such make-believe tends nowhere. It is simply a malefic maw-
kishness. But it does not follow that a question which cannot
be solved may not be ameliorated.

No notable improvement of race relations can be achieved,
in my opinion, except by employing the utmost toughness of
mind. Little can be done unless it is granted that abstract justice
and right are qualities, not of this world, but of an ideal world;
one that so far has eluded us. Men are what they are. They
are, among other things, a little lower than the angels. If the
distance between them is often no more than a gallow's drop,
is the gulf still not fatal? If it can be bridged, will it yield to
less than a heavenly calculus? And is not the South somewhat
comparable to the Supreme Court in the view of Mr. Justice
Holmes? "It is very quiet there," he said, "but it is the quiet of a
storm center."

White Deltans, insisting upon race segregation, are being expedient; that is, pragmatic. Truth and right, by this norm, are
what are expedient today. Tomorrow, it may be, when they are
no longer expedient they will cease to be true and right; when,
especially, truth has lost its power to "work." The marked
progress made by the Delta Negro during the past half-century
has been made under the drab banner of pragmatism; not, however much his white neighbor may delude himself, under the
rose- and lily-embroidered banner of absolute ethical standards.

Consequently the permanent betterment of race relations cannot be brought about unless the ground is cleared by a recog-

nition by members of both races that (*a*) the problem will not yield to a cure-all solution, and (*b*) the explosive issue of segregation must not be called into question. The progress of the Delta Negro since the turn of the century and the constant improvement of his position which, measured relatively, is astonishing, make it reasonable to believe that upon the premises stated almost all of the differences between the races — except only that of social segregation — may be gradually adjusted or removed through the exercise of patience, wisdom, and good will on both sides.

If the races made this pragmatic approach to the problem, and ruled out the one thing that brings it into the realm of the emotional, not only would many of the difficulties between them be brought within the possibility of healing amelioration, but the burden would then rest upon the whites to do for the Negro what they have often not done at all, or only in part. This would mean giving him his political rights; extending to him complete protection in his person and property; treating him to equal justice in the courts; distributing to him a fair share of tax monies for education, health, and public services. It would mean giving him the right to earn a living, to be paid according to his worth and not his color, to be protected in his practice of the professions and the skills. And, not less important, he would be asked to assume his fair share of the burdens of the whole community.

Let us not delude ourselves. This is obviously less than democracy. It is merely a step toward democracy. It squares neither with the nation's Christianity nor its constitutionalism. It is expediency; the philosophy that most of us live by however highflown our pretensions. And let us bear in mind that there has never been a government — indeed, no organized religion — which has not at some time compromised with the logic of its own institutions. Yet one does not reject democracy because it is less than perfect, any more than one rejects other institutions for that reason.

So far I have largely discussed the Negro question as though it were a Delta, or Southern, question. It is, of course, a national question since it concerns nearly fourteen million persons who make up one-tenth of the nation's population. More than three million Negroes live outside the South. Others are constantly emigrating. But wherever they live, almost the same repressions run against them as in the South, except that elsewhere they are often sicklied over with a revolting hypocrisy. This is especially true of social segregation. In terms of the South, however, both races need the sympathetic understanding of others; not their unreasoned recriminations or pious homilies. They need it deeply at a period when misguided counsel may take the question out of the hands of decent whites and Negroes and deliver it into the talons of demagogues; to the irreparable harm of the Negro and the detriment of the whole American social order.

Both races are caught in a tragic dilemma. No one can view the position of the American Negro without a sore heart, a troubled conscience, and a deep compassion. Nor can one view the position of Southern whites without sympathy. They are the sum of their inheritances and environment and behave according to their lights. Whites and Negroes alike will each have to yield much to the other if American democracy is to survive in the long run, and each will have to yield out of conviction rather than compulsion. Those who would attempt to solve the race question by legal fiat will do well to heed the words of the sagacious sociologist, Doctor Robert E. Park:

"We do not know what we ought to do until we know what we can do; and we certainly should consider what men can do before we pass laws prescribing what they should do."

CHAPTER 4

Vanishing Mules and Men

One day, ten years ago, I visited the folks in the blacksmith shop of Tralake Plantation. It is an amiable place for all that it is sooty, clamorous often with the ringing of metal upon metal, acrid with the scent of toasted hooves of mules being shod. Its recesses are hung with the intricate lace of spider's webs, their gossamer filaments soot-stained tern-gray and silvery-black. Its darkened rafters lost against the darkened ceiling, the whole structure seems suspended in space. Light and shadow gambol endlessly with one another for the most part in slow grace, but furiously moving as to a mad music when the bellows blow or the red eye of hot iron gazes balefully into the gloom until it is extinguished hissing in cold water. If it is, as one suspects, the haunt of fire-enchanted fairies, it is also a place of work, and here strangely, there is respite from the glare and heat outside despite the flames inside.

Work is performed in ordered but leisurely discipline, its rigors tempered as the smith gossips with the man whose plow-point he is sharpening. The shop is, among other things, a rural forum, and on the day I visited it there were two Negroes come to fetch tools. They talked about what the white folks might be expected to do the next year in the matter of mules or tractors. "Boy," said one, "the white folks done got so tired o' niggers treatin' mules bad, they gwine put tractors heah." "Does dey do dat," said the other, "I'd sho feel bad. I'd druther have a mule fartin' in my face all day long walkin' de turnrow than dem durned tractors." "Nawsuh, not me," said the first speaker. "I loves to ride a tractor. Heap easier'n walkin'."

So spoke advocates of the Mule Age and the coming Machine Age. The mule had always been the prime motor factor of the farm. Patient, enduring, strong, able to work in fierce heat, he seemed one with the land he plowed. Without him the Delta might have been developed less rapidly, for the workhorse, common elsewhere, does not flourish under the sun of the cotton country. There was even a breaking-point for the mule, and so there arose the practice of "shadin' the mule." At midmorning in hot summer, he was taken out of the plow for an hour or two and rested under a tree.

The mule is a creature of singular distinctions. He has more mother wit than the horse. He will never, as the horse often does when permitted, founder himself upon his own oats. Despite his stolid appearance, he has an acute sense of humor, while his inability to reproduce himself delivers him from those absurd posturings common to the stallion (and all other males), and permits him to concentrate his energies upon his inner life. He is a thoroughgoing individualist. He cannot be forced to assume burdens beyond the limitations he imposes upon himself. He is given to moods of exaltation, depression, and the exercise of strange caprices. White men of the Delta never succeeded in penetrating the mysteries of his soul. Negroes only, it was believed, understood the mule.

He affected the language of the people. "Stubborn as a mule," "strong as a mule," indicated a man's qualities. His biological origins often were used by a politician in telling off an opponent: "There he stands like a mule, without pride of ancestry or hope of posterity." His property value was such that if a man was unlawfully deprived of his services by another, the killing of the thief, it was held in a once famous Delta case, would be regarded by the courts as justifiable homicide.

In Tallahatchie county there were two Negro neighbors living at a distance of a mile apart. One of them, J. D. Pitts, was a simple rustic who, as his friends said, "didn't had no mo' sense than the law 'lowed." He cultivated a few acres of land with the aid of an ancient, swaybacked, almost blind, mule. The other man, Stump Wheeler, also cultivated a small tract. But his mule had died and, having neither cash nor credicks with which to buy another, his prospects were dark. Stump, however, was a rural slicker. He had once worked in a Beale Street saloon in Memphis. He knew city ways and was no stranger to guile. After thinking things over in his second mind, he decided he could get J. D.'s mule, and went to see him.

Stump found his neighbor in his lean-to stable smearing axle grease on a wound in the mule's leg, and after talking religion for a long time, he got down to business. "J. D." he asked, "how much does you want for that mule?" It had never occurred to J. D. that anybody would ever want to buy his mule, and in his confusion he mentioned the first sum that came to mind — the astronomical sum of $150, the animal being worth no more than $25. "Nigger, you's crazy!" snorted Stump. "Dat ain't no rabbit mule. Dat's a levee-camp mule if ever I has seen one. It ain't a better mule in Tallahatchie county."

Stump praised the qualities of J. D.'s mule. He insisted that he would not buy it for the ridiculously low price of $150, for this would be to profit by J. D.'s ignorance of the true value of this pearl among mules. After hours of persistence Stump, the buyer, succeeded in forcing the selling price of the mule up to $400. "Fo' hunnerd dollars," whispered J. D. dazedly. He had never had so much money in his life. He became lost in visions of a rich. leisurely existence stretching into infinity. The deal was struck. Then came the delicate, hitherto ignored, question of payment for the animal.

"J. D.," I tell you what you does," said Stump in his brisk, confidence-breeding manner. "You bring dat mule over to my place an' you can work him out at fo' dollars a day." Fo' hunnerd dollars. . . . Fo' dollars a day. . . . The dazzling figures went around and around in J. D.'s mind, emitting stars like the pinwheels folks light at Christmas. He couldn't quite understand it. But nee-mine 'bout dat. Fo' hunnerd dollars. . . . Fo' dollars a day. . . .

Every day J. D. plowed Stump's land with the little mule.

Every day Stump went to town and came home twarge sundown. J. D. studied and studied as he went up and down the turn-rows. Fo' hunnerd dollars. . . . Fo' dollars a day. . . .

After thinking hard for two weeks, J. D. saw the light. According to the terms of his deal with Stump, if he worked his mule for one hundred days on Stump's land, it would then belong to him. The next morning J. D. shot Stump through the head with his Winchester, got on his mule, and rode home to await the coming of the Law. After he had told his story in Judge Wilson's Justice of the Peace court, the court held that his action was justifiable homicide and dismissed him. J. D. walked out into the street a free man, scratching his head in bewilderment. Fo' hunnerd dollars. . . . Fo' dollars a day. . . .

From its beginnings, until relatively recently, the Delta had been a land of men and mules. Their personal relations were good. But mules were not of the highest efficiency, and there is little room in our highly competitive society for an inefficient man or work-animal. They were subject to various ills of the flesh. Sometimes anthrax killed them in droves. Large fractions of the cultivable land of a farm went into feed crops to sustain them; else, at high cost, you had to import oats, hay, corn from the Middle West. There were two schools of thought about this. One school held it was better to raise your own feed even if this meant less land devoted to cotton. The other school maintained it was better to put all your land in cotton and buy feed. The argument was never resolved and for long years the Delta bought trainloads of mule feed from other sections. Sometimes the one school seemed to be "right," then the other. Yet members of both schools often went broke, or lived for many seasons on short rations. It was only with the coming of the "guvment program" in the early nineteen-thirties, when farmers were subsidized to put cotton lands into feed crops, that the Delta began to grow most of its animal feeds at home.

There are long intervals on the farm when there is little for men to do and less for mules. It requires only about one-third of the year to make a cotton crop: Underemployed men sit on their porches. Underemployed mules stay in the stable lots and "eat their heads off." Farmers had always regarded Negroes, cotton, and mules as a "natural combination." But the combination, however "natural," awaited only the coming of the tractor to disarrange it.

When the tractor came to the Delta in 1915, the mule began to go. According to the 1940 census, 2939 farms in the ten Delta counties were using a total of 4964 tractors. Within those counties were 46.9 per cent of all tractors in the State, and if we include the nine additional part-Delta counties, 59.6 per cent of the State total. As a variation on the theme, the ratio of tractors to crop and cotton acres was higher on the smaller plantations than on the larger ones.

Reflecting increased mechanization on the farm, the Delta mule population dropped 18.67 per cent from 1930 to 1940, while its horse population in the same period decreased by 43.03 per cent.

But the tractor-using farm remained burdened with a heavy labor force. It has two periods of furious activity. The first runs from May until approximately the middle of July, when cultivation and hoeing are in progress. Then every available hand turns over the soil and fights grass and weeds. The plantation bell rings as early as three o'clock in the morning, and everybody works from "can to can't" — from the time in the morning when men can see until the time at night when they can't see. The second period runs from late August until the latter part of November when cotton is usually picked. The farmer races with the weather. He tries to gather his crop before rains stain it and reduce its value, or destroy it by beating it out of the boll. At hoeing and picking time he seldom has enough labor and must often hire more hands. But except for these periods, his tenants are idle much of the time.

The peculiar necessities of cotton cultivation were unfortunate for farmer and tenant. Since much labor is needed during peak periods of operation, the acreage per tenant family is usually limited to the amount that can be effectively handled during such periods. The result is that the tenant family works only a limited number of days annually, and its volume of production and earnings are low.

The farmer's dilemma was also painful. In order to have all of the labor he needed some of the time, he kept a force that was idle most of the time. But he nonetheless often had to hire more labor for hoeing and picking. These labor charges were held against his tenants and thereby reduced their earnings. But they also increased the farmer's risks and, in a bad crop year, might get him into serious financial difficulties.

The tractor offered farmers at least a partial way out of their difficulties, and they began to take it. Some gave up share-cropping altogether, and operated their farms on a day-wages basis through hands hired in near-by towns. Others adopted the median course of operating part of their farms on a wages basis, and the remainder on a share-cropping basis. Still others stuck to share-cropping as it had traditionally been employed.

Yet share-cropping, in the long run, is doomed to go. It is to go for the same reason that many planters, long before the Civil War, abandoned slavery. Humanitarianism apart, it did not pay. The old and the infirm had to be maintained until death. Property interest demanded that the sick be treated. There were children too young to work and the aged who were too old to work. At any given time illness, injuries, pregnancies, reduced the labor force. Bad years as well as good, slaves had to be fed, clothed, sheltered. Plantation records of the times show that the percentage of effective workers out of the whole number of slaves held, was extremely low. Slavery, many planters saw, did not pay and they began to abandon it.

Share-cropping, no heaven for the tenant, is no paradise for the farmer. He therefore began to give it up as the tractor came, or worked important modifications in it. This ought to be the definitive answer to those who have claimed that it was a vicious system deliberately designed to enslave the cropper. Ignoring the fact that it was born of the necessity of the times after the Civil War, they could not, or would not, see that it would go as soon as the need for it had disappeared. The Northern press long denounced cotton farmers who allegedly grew rich at the expense of their tenants. Well-meaning but equally mistaken Southerners joined in the cry. Share-cropping became a topic of heated discussion everywhere in the land. But now that farmers are throwing it over as rapidly as possible, those who once bewailed its existence are changing their lament. Now they talk of the inhumane way in which people are being put off plantation soil.

The tractor-farmer had to rely upon a mobile labor reserve to be found in near-by towns. But his success depended upon uncontrollable factors. The towns might lack labor. If it was in short supply, farmers competed for it with industry and with one another. Sometimes they went far afield for hands; often as far as Mexico. Town labor, moreover, was highly disadvantageous in one respect. Cotton picked by seasonal workers is often from one to three grades lower in quality than that picked by croppers and tenants who have a direct financial interest in the crop.

Nor is this all. The Delta's Negro population is decreasing. The probabilities are that it will continue to decrease. The fewer the available hands, the higher their wages. If the farmer's costs rise and cotton prices do not rise disproportionately, he goes broke; or is saved, temporarily at least, by government subsidy. If his costs rise and cotton prices rise with them, he may price himself out of the market. Low-cost foreign producers will take his foreign markets, and cotton substitutes will seriously invade his domestic market. He saw that his task was to produce cotton far more cheaply than in the past, but to do it without impoverishing his already none too prosperous cotton workers. Failing to do this, he might be forced off the land, or only a relatively few cotton farmers would remain to supply the small irreducible domestic demand for the staple. He knew what the combination of high cotton prices and the economic maneuverings of a disordered world had done to him in the period between the world wars.

Once the United States had enjoyed a virtual monopoly of the world's cotton markets. Exports formerly took from fifty to sixty per cent of the nation's raw cotton. But in the period between the wars, foreign cotton competed sharply with our staple. Foreign consumption of American cotton declined, for example, forty-six per cent in the years 1935-39. But at the same time, consumption of foreign cotton increased sixty-nine per cent.

These are cold statistics. What they mean in terms.of human misery and hardship I once saw with my own eyes, as our cotton, unwanted abroad, slumped to panic prices, and the federal government sold a large part of a community in bankruptcy proceedings. The story is perhaps worth retelling here for the light that it casts upon the cotton farmer's lot a short while ago; because it bears directly upon the mechanizing of plantations, with its incalculable consequences, which is now in progress.

"I'm mighty sorry about it, sir," said the clerk of the Wyndham Hotel in Dukeville, Mississippi. "We haven't got a room left in the house. Folks been piling in here since early yesterday morning to go to the auction that's going to be held today. I don't believe I can do anything for you till it's over."

"Auction?" I asked. "What auction?"

"Why, haven't you heard?" he replied. "Uncle Sam's men are down here from Washington to sell off the property of the Unger National Bank that failed. They busted and like to cleaned out everybody around here. They had mortgages on about everything in town and nearly every plantation in the county."

Shocked by the news, I checked my bag and walked out into the town. I had not visited Dukeville for years. What had happened to the Ungers? I wondered. Their forebears had come to the town from northern New York shortly after the Civil War, bringing with them large sums of money and a sound business equipment. They had been renowned throughout the state for their integrity and ability. Their bank had been a symbol of stability.

Now the Ungers were bankrupt and their proud bank and confident customers were ruined.

Dukeville is a cotton town. It lives for, through, and by cotton. Its rich surrounding acres have always produced good crops of silky long-staple cotton that commanded a special price premium in the markets of the world. (Thousands of bales used to be bought by the lace-makers of Calais.) Cotton is the one crop.

The people of the county cannot imagine themselves growing other things. . . .

There had been for years an apparently insatiable demand for cotton. Famous steamboats, the *Robert E. Lee,* the big *Jim White,* the *T. P. Leathers,* and others, had stopped at Dukeville and loaded huge cargoes of cotton for New Orleans. There they were transhipped to England, Germany, Italy, France, and other countries. And trains moved heavily out of the railroad station at Dukeville, bound for the cotton mills of New England.

Year after year, out of every ten bales grown in the United States, six were shipped overseas. Then came the dislocations of the period after the First World War: the rise of nationalism in the world; the coming of an era of high foreign tariffs and embargoes in whose creation the United States played a leading part; the dying away of demand for our cotton abroad; the piling up of surpluses at home and the falling of prices to disastrous levels, with the bankruptcy of farmers, the breaking of banks, and disaster to entire communities. I walked back to the Wyndham lost in wonder that the world had become so delicately interdependent that the policies of a Hitler in faraway Germany, or the actions of a Mussolini in Rome, or plows breaking the virgin soil of Uganda in distant South Africa, could paralyze the merchants of Dukeville whose little stores I was passing.

Opposite the hotel on the main street were three newly erected platforms upon each of which stood a man with a megaphone and another with a big ledger lying open upon his knees. A Negro band seated on a truck played jazz tunes, while the gathering crowd shuffled its feet in accompaniment to the music and stared pop-eyed at a huge sign over the center platform. It read: THIS SALE OF THE ASSETS OF THE UNGER NATIONAL BANK IN LIQUIDATION IS BEING HELD BY ORDER OF AND UNDER THE DIRECTION OF THE COMPTROLLER OF THE CURRENCY OF THE UNITED STATES.

The crowd slowly assembled. People came from the town, from the county, and from adjoining counties. It is not often that the majesty and dignity of central government personified in the person of the Comptroller of the Currency of the United

States descends upon an isolated town in Mississippi for the somber purpose of pronouncing a funeral oration upon the prosperity of half its population.

Negro women cooks temporarily deserted the white folks' kitchens and joined the crowds. Housewives on holiday came in their best dresses. Merchants who had left their empty stores. Children on their way to school who loitered to see this circus that was no circus. Prospective bidders sniffing bargains in the warm morning air. Farmers and friends of the banker, and those who were about to be forever dispossessed of their farms and homes.

Minute by minute the crowd grew. Automobile traffic through the main street soon became impossible. The mass of people stood close-packed and sweltering under the sun. The chief auctioneer raised his hand in signal to the jazz band. A sob died in the throat of a trombone. Silence fell upon the throng. The sale was about to begin.

"Ladies and gentlemen," said the auctioneer, "we are here today by order of the Comptroller of the Currency of the United States to sell the assets of the Unger National Bank of Dukeville which is now in liquidation. The various parcels of property that will be offered will be sold to the highest bidder. Most of you are probably familiar with the plantations, stores, houses, and other things that are comprised in this sale, because most of you live here and you have had ample opportunity to familiarise yourselves with everything. If there should be an questions that you want to ask at any time, don't hesitate to do so. I'll be glad to answer them to the best of my ability, and I'm sure I can say the same thing for the gentlemen on the other platforms who are assisting me today and who are known to all of you because they belong right here in Dukeville — Sam Goldrick and Fred Hays.

"Now the first thing on the list is Sun-Up Plantation, sometimes known as the old Ashley Place, located about six miles northeast of town on highway number twelve, consisting all told of six hundred and forty-two acres. What am I bid for Sun-Up Plantation with all its stock, feed, gear, houses, seed, and other equipment? A walk-out proposition. Lock, stock, and barrel."

Up and down the long street ran the refrain as the assistant auctioneers caught it up from their chief and bellowed it through megaphones: "What am I offered for Sun-Up Plantation, sometimes known as the old Ashley Place, situated about six miles northeast of town . . . ?"

Sun-Up was sold. Then Dunbar Plantation, 1150 acres, was knocked down to a bidder from a near-by county. Laughter ran through the crowd when Wade Rogers, a well-to-do man of the town, bought for a ridiculously low price, twenty-six acres of land on Rattlesnake Bayou.

"Shucks, dat patch ain't big enough for a vegetable garden," said a Negro in the crowd to his companion. "What you reckon Mr. Wade gwine do with hit?" he asked.

"Man, ain't you got no sense in yo' haid?" his friend replied. "When a big white man buy a cabbage-patch he doing it fer a nigger, sho's you bawn."

The speaker was right. This was the second time that Mr. Wade had restored George Jacob Washington to his little tract of land.

Then Sunnyside Plantation was sold. Wilbur Hammond had owned it for thirty-five years. He had brought his bride home to Sunnyside from New Orleans long ago. Their son, Wilbur, Junior, had died in France during the war. Helen, one of their daughters, was married and lived in St. Louis. Alice Bell, the other daughter, was the wife of a successful physician in Dallas. People in the crowd seemed to feel that the Hammonds were lucky. They could live with their children.

Proud Name, a plantation of 1200 acres, went next. It had been owned for a long time by the Johnson Jacksons. "Son," his father had told the young Jackson when he became manager of the property, "Jackson is a proud name. Hold it high."

Young Jackson through twenty years of hard work had added many acres to the original plantation, and had ruined himself financially in his effort to hold it against the tide. Now it was forever lost to him. There were rumors on the street that he would go to keeping books for the Dukeville Wholesale Grocery Company. Everybody in town knew that Johnson Jackson had a good head for figures.

In quick succession Tiger Trot Plantation was sold; then Willow Vale, Shiloh, Bridal Wreath, Big Water, Deep Snow, Morning Glory, Moonvine, and Ivanhoe.

One by one plantations big and little passed from the hands of their former owners into the hands of their new owners — banks, insurance companies, and anonymous persons acting for their unrevealed principals. The men on the platforms made notations in the ledgers balanced on their knees. At night they would use them to let the Comptroller of the Currency in Washington know how much Proud Name had brought on the auction block, the liquidating value of Bridal Wreath, the sum realized from the forced sale of Morning Glory.

Through the long hot morning the sale continued. Up and down the street ran the monotonous refrain: "What am I offered? What am I offered? Five thousand I hear. Five thousand once. Five thousand twice. Going! Going! Gone! Sold for five thousand dollars. What's the name, sir? Yes, sir, just step up here to the clerk and fix it up with him."

When the waterworks whistle blew the hour of noon but few people went home to dinner. The majority remained and bought sandwiches and Coca-Cola from Negro vendors. They ate, mopped their sweating faces, shifted from foot to foot, and stared in fascination at the rough platforms on the main street — sacrificial altars where the pride and hopes of so many local men lay dying.

The afternoon dragged on wearily. Several town buildings were sold, a number of lots, a few tracts of timber, a gin, two drugstores, and parcel after parcel of land. It seemed astonishing that a farming community had failed so miserably at the business of farming. Yet the voices of the auctioneers continue to cry out into the warm air, the ledger pages were turned, and the end was not yet come.

Late in the afternoon the chief auctioneer, wet with sweat, hoarsely croaked: "Item number one hundred and twenty-six is the Unger National Bank Building." A hush fell upon the crowd. They knew now that the end was come. They could no longer delude themselves into believing that at the end of the performance men in top hats and Prince Albert coats would circulate among them, offering for sale bottles of Indian Chief Blood Remedy. They were facing inescapable reality.

In less than five minutes an unknown man had bought the bank building for a small sum. The sale was over. The tired crowd slowly dissolved. The golden sun began its long, slow plunge into the river. Then the Negro jazz band, silent during the interminable day, burst rapturously into a blues song. Goldtooth Sam, its baritone, opened his mouth wide and ecstatically sang:

> I hate to see that evening sun go down,
> I hate to see that evening sun go down,
> O, I hate to see . . .

One of the potent reasons for the South's loss of its foreign cotton markets, was our own tariff policy. High tariffs had enraged the section before the Civil War. Northern idealists may honestly have thought that this war was fought to free the slave. But Northern business men were little concerned with Negroes. In the powerful industrial state of Pennsylvania, a herald of things to come spoke shortly before Lincoln was elected President. He was for white supremacy; the industrial supremacy of the Northern white man:

> . . . Curtin, the Republican candidate for governor (of Pennsylvania), said not a word about abolishing slavery in his ratification speech but spoke with feeling on "the vast heavings of the heart of Pennsylvania, whose sons are pining for protection of their labor and their dearest interests. This is a contest involving protection and the rights of labor. . . . If you desire to become vast and great, protect the manufactures of Philadelphia. . . . All hail, liberty! All hail, freedom! *Freedom to the white man!* All hail, freedom general as the air we breathe!" (Beard, *The Rise of American Civilization,* vol. II, p. 35.) (My italics.)

In January, 1867, a young Frenchman then in this country was acting as correspondent for *Le Temps* of Paris. As part of his *Lettres des États-Unis,* he sent the following dispatch:

> . . . The Assistant Secretary of the Treasury, Mr. Wells, has just proposed a revision of the tariff, leaving in operation most

of the semi-prohibitions of the old law. Protectionism is rampant in this country. When an industry is interrupted for a couple of weeks, importation of foreign goods is given as the reason, and men set to work to frame a new tariff. Owing to this custom, people have been made to pay ridiculous prices for articles of primary necessity, the Treasury has been defrauded of customs duties, which are no longer collected when they become exorbitant, and a few big men in the East have grown exceedingly rich.

The correspondent was Georges Clemenceau.

High tariffs were contributory to the Civil War. Later, they helped keep the South poor. The Deep South especially, partly through tariffs, freight rates rigged against the section, and northeastern banking control; and partly through its own shortcomings, assumed many of the aspects of an American India. It had nearly everything that India still has except the rope trick and snake charmers: poverty, malaria, dysentery, hookworm, illiteracy, and, along with these, a few local rajahs who lived in painted houses, and served ladyfingers with canned peaches at Sunday dinner.

Yet the South has done little to change the situation tariffwise. On the contrary, hamstrung by tariffs, it votes for tariffs. This in order to "protect" its extra-long staple cotton, vegetable oils, cotton textiles. For every phantom dollar the South obtains in this way, it spends a hundred hard dollars buying its needs from tariff-protected industries.

By 1933, when the Roosevelt administration came into power, the cotton farmer was on the ropes. If he had a dollar to spend at all, it had a purchasing power of about forty-two per cent of its prewar value. His lands were mortgaged up to the hilt. Thousands of cotton farmers faced dispossession. Yet cotton was the life of the South. In the ten great cotton-growing states, the percentages of the people on the land varied from eighty-three per cent in Mississippi to fifty-nine per cent in Texas. These states contain nearly one-fourth of the total land area of the United States and were home to twenty-two per cent of its population.

How sharply differentiated were the occupations, and therefore the economic interests, of the people of important industrial states from the people of the cotton states, is revealed by a comparison of percentages of rural populations with the foregoing. In 1933 they were:

	Per cent
Rhode Island	8
Massachusetts	10
New York	17
Illinois	27
New Jersey	18
Connecticut	30
Michigan	32
Pennsylvania	33

The cotton states were distinguished by their poverty, if by nothing else. It was, however, a poverty not without aspects of optimism. Thousands of Southern farm women wore drawers made of discarded cotton sacks. Some of these, despite repeated washings, still bore the stenciled legend of a famous brand: EVENTUALLY — WHY NOT NOW?

There was good cheer in Mississippi during the blackest days of the depression of the nineteen-thirties, when people read about the action taken by Mr. Alfred Sloan, president of General Motors. He voluntarily reduced his salary from $500,000 a year to $340,000 a year. The pleasure of Mississippi cotton farmers was almost unbounded when they realized that *his cut in salary was nearly $30,000 more than the federal individual income taxes paid in 1932 by two million citizens of the state.* Infected with the sharecropper mentality which causes a Negro tenant to boast to other Negroes that his white folks own the biggest car in the county, they were proud to be citizens of a country that had such rich people in it.

The American India remained the classical American area of poverty and disease. When, therefore, the Democratic party came into power in 1933, it would have seemed reasonable that it should seek a thoroughgoing redress of its grievances. It contented itself instead with a patch on its economic overalls. Far from pressing for a drastic revision of the tariff which might have restored part of its lost foreign markets for cotton, it gratefully accepted the mild revisions of the Reciprocal Trade Agreements. The people were content to go on drinking Free List coffee; eating foods from Free List tin cans; gaping at Free List Titians in traveling art shows; worshiping at Free List altars; and occasionally being hanged with Free List manila hemp. Their economic masters up North were graciously pleased to grant reductions in the tariff on French perfumes and champagne; preserved duck eggs, sausage casings, and dried blood. The great schedules affecting steel, cement, wool, cotton textiles, were left intact. It was not likely that the changes made would open wider foreign doors to American cotton.

The cotton South merely asked for measures that would immediately relieve its distress. It is perhaps unreasonable to expect men to take a long-run point of view when the meal in the barrel is running low and they are down to their last slice of sowbelly. Yet the effect of the measures taken would artificially increase the price of cotton, make it more difficult for domestic cotton to compete with the foreign-grown staple, and encourage foreigners to plant larger acreages to cotton. And while cotton was losing its foreign market, it was simultaneously losing its domestic market.

Its greatest competitor is rayon. This man-made fiber, first introduced to the United States in 1911, has been prodigiously successful everywhere. Nowhere was it received more warmly than by the Delta. The area, struggling for its economic life based upon cotton, wallowed in rayon. Its hotels had bedspreads, tablecloths, and curtains made of the stuff. The farmer's wife used it lavishly in her house, while she herself was a walking showcase of rayon's versatility. She wore a rayon dress, rayon or silk stockings and, for all one knows, rayon underwear. Her husband, wondering how he could make his next crop, sweated out his worries in shirt, suit, ties, and socks of rayon. He buried his grandmother in a rayon-lined casket which was taken to the cemetery in a rayon-lined hearse followed by carloads of his friends, rayon bedight. He clutched the synthetic asp to his bosom and, not understanding what caused his pain, took synthetic headache powders to stop it. Some primitive peoples, unable to relate cause and effect, see no relationship between the coming of a child and the coupling of its parents. So it was, in the Delta, with respect to the use of rayon.

World production of rayon jumped from 450,000,000 pounds in 1930 to 3,000,000,000 pounds in 1941. This is equivalent to 6,000,000 bales of cotton. It has recently taken away from cotton a large part of its former monopolistic market for automobile tire fabrics, a most important market which annually took 600,000 bales of cotton. No one can assign limits to its future expansion and while cotton has latterly been increasing in price, rayon prices have remained fairly stable.

Paper is a sharp competitor of cotton in the manufacture of towels, napkins, twine, bags, and other items. Between 1925 and 1942, for example, the use of cotton in cement bags dropped by two-thirds while the use of paper trebled.

Cotton has long been in a desperate estate. It was saved, temporarily, by federal subsidies, and the demands of the war period. Its future salvation, however, depends upon the ability of American farmers to produce it so cheaply that it can successfully compete abroad with foreign-grown cotton, and domestically with rayon, paper, and other substitutes. But costs must remain high so long as cotton production requires an enormous amount of hand labor.

At the same time, the Delta saw that even if it could reduce costs by the cruel expedient of doing so at the expense of labor, this would simply lower its already low standard of living. The fact is, of course, that labor would not be available any more at starvation wages. How, then, could the Delta produce cotton profitably and competitively without taking it out of the hide of labor?

The answer is mechanization of cotton culture with the object of sharply reducing the amount of labor required to make a crop. It would bring grave social problems in its train, but it was the only way out and nothing would stop it.

Until recently, cotton-growing in the Delta was much what it had been in times of slavery. Picking cotton is still as time-wasting, back-breaking, finger-splitting as it was in the Nile valley thousands of years ago. In the late eighteenth century the invention of a machine — the gin — furnished the impetus that led to the plantation way of life and America's cotton empire. But the machine, in cotton culture, went little farther. While machines in industry, mining, and many forms of agriculture, enormously multiplied man's productivity and took crushing burdens off his back, they were little used in cotton fields. There man continued to grow the staple at a high cost in money and human effort.

How costly in human effort cotton culture is appears by a comparison of man-hour labor requirements per acre for cotton with other principal Delta crops:

Cotton	133.0
Alfalfa	20.0
Corn	27.3
Soybeans	16.0
Oats	9.0
All hay	4.7

Among new machines, aside from the tractor, now being used by the farmer, is the flame cultivator. It is designed to lower the high costs of eliminating weeds and grass in the crop row. Cotton growing is often a race between weeds and the cotton plant. Weeds and grasses grow rapidly in the warm, moist Delta earth, and three hoeings, done by hand, usually follow each other closely during May, June, and first half of July. Other hoeings may be necessary if there are abnormally frequent rains. This means that tens of thousands of acres must be worked as though they were a flower or vegetable garden; and scarcely had the weeds been eliminated before they were growing again. A man could laboriously weed only about one-half acre a day, and it was a strange reflection upon man's ingenuity that as the hoe-hand slowly went his way, overhead he might see an airplane dropping planting seed.

There seemed little hope, however, of escaping the burdens of hand-hoeing until twelve years ago. Then Colonel Price McLemore, an Alabama cotton farmer, saw someone using a kerosene torch to kill weeds along a sidewalk. He observed that the torch killed small weeds and grass but did not harm the large weeds. It immediately occurred to him that small weeds and grass in cotton fields would succumb to flame, leaving the cotton plant, like the large weeds, unharmed. He fastened an ordinary plumber's blowtorch on a turnplow, and found that he could kill weeds with it. His experiments continued until he developed an attachment for a tractor which is the present flame cultivator.

It is described as follows, by Thomas L. Baggette, Engineer for project on mechanization of cotton and other crops, Delta Branch Station, Stoneville, Mississippi:

> The flame cultivator is a revolutionary new piece of farm equipment that eliminates young weeds and grass in the crop row by the process of flaming. Burners are mounted on a frame back of the tractor in a staggered pattern so that two burners flame one row, one from each side. The flame is directed toward the base of the plants and extends well into the opposite middle. . . . Flame cultivation of the crop row may be carried on simultaneously with the conventional cultivation of middles. The practice of flaming cultivation eliminates the throwing of dirt to the plant that is being cultivated, thereby permitting flat cultivation. The throwing of dirt covers weeds and grasses; but the theory of flame cultivation is to kill these growths rather than cover them. . . .

Flame cultivation effects significant savings. At a cost of fifteen to thirty-five cents an acre, depending upon the weed growth, the machine can clean up a field. Even under the miserable wage scale of fifty cents to a dollar a day, once paid hoe-hands, the cost would run one dollar to two dollars an acre.

Chopping, or thinning, cotton also consumed much hand labor. Its purpose is to remove surplus plants, when they first emerge from the soil, so that the others may be properly spaced for weeding and healthy growth. Each season, thousands of choppers, working thousands of hours, remove millions of plants. But hand chopping need no longer be employed. It is eliminated by hill-dropping devices that plant seed at required spacings, or by mechanical choppers.

Cotton, a crop which only yesterday emerged from its

pharaonic swathings, now engages not only many machines, but often man's most spectacular machine — the airplane. It finds employment in cotton dusting — spreading insecticides on growing plants. This was once done by hand machines, but the airplane does it less expensively. It is also a primary agent in defoliation. Stripping leaves from the mature cotton plant by the use of air-dropped chemicals, produces several beneficial results. It eliminates hibernating insects, and it is useful — if not indispensable — to mechanical harvesting. But primarily it is a method for saving "bottom cotton." Bolls at the top of the plant, exposed to sunlight, open earlier than those at the bottom which are shaded by its leaves. This permits retention of moisture and causes rot, resulting in losses sometimes amounting to one-fourth or one-half of the crop. Leaf removal permits free access of air and sunlight so that bottom bolls may ripen and open fully. Thus rot is eliminated, the crop can be picked quickly, reducing the risks of weather and, if cover crops are to follow cotton, they may be put in ahead of the autumn rains.

Flame cultivation, the tractor, the mechanical cotton chopper, the airplane — all these appreciably reduce the hand labor required for growing cotton. There remained, however, the hitherto insoluble problem of reducing the amount of hand labor needed to harvest it.

Cotton picking is a laborious and painfully slow operation. A picker, dragging a long cotton sack suspended from his shoulders, walks up and down the rows plucking the staple from the boll. The amount of cotton that a person can pick in a day is, like other rural accomplishments, a matter of boasting. It is also a matter of money, for pickers are paid for the number of pounds of cotton they bring to the weighing scales. Princella Williams, a big, strapping Negro woman, once boasted to me of her strength in these terms. "Lawd Gawd," she said, "I doesn't know what's the matter with these niggers 'round heah. I can pick two hunnerd pounds o' cotton ev'y day the Lawd lets me in the fiel', cook my husband's supper, an' pleasure him before goin' to sleep 'thout no trouble 'tall." But the cold statistical evidence, gathered from various cotton-producing areas of the United States, reveals that the average hand-picker gathers about fifteen pounds of cotton an hour throughout a normal season, or one hundred and twenty pounds in an eight-hour day. Since fifteen hundred pounds of seed cotton produce a five-hundred-pound bale of lint (marketable) cotton, it would take the average picker twelve and a half days to gather a bale.

The mechanical cotton harvester has for decades been the dream of inventors and farmers. As early as 1850, two Memphis inventors were issued a patent on such a machine. Since then, hundreds of patents covering many types of mechanical pickers have been issued. But a successful cotton harvester has recently been marketed by the International Harvester Company, and it is likely that competitive machines will soon become available to farmers. The cotton South at long last has the instrument it feared and wished for almost desperately.

The harvest is the pay-off. Since fifty to sixty per cent of the man-hour labor requirements for the production of an acre of cotton is for picking, the regular labor force cannot usually gather the crop before weather damage becomes serious. Here, at the crucial point of the farm's operations, the mechanical harvester performs spectacularly. This machine, operated by one man, in a field of open cotton averaging five-eighths bale per acre (the Delta average is much higher), will gather fifteen hundred pounds of seed cotton in approximately ninety minutes, including fifteen minutes for turning at the ends of the rows and dumping the cotton out of the machine's basket. It would take forty to fifty hand pickers to equal its work.

In 1945 it cost about $40 to hand-pick a bale of cotton. The mechanical picker did it for $7.50. The net saving to the farmer is, however, far less than indicated. The picker collects bits of leaves and trash along with the cotton, thereby lowering its grade and selling price. But it is reasonable to believe that this defect will be remedied, while it is clear that the machine, even as it presently functions, affords significant benefits to its users.

There is now available to farmers a group of machines which will remove them from a hand-labor agriculture to a machine agriculture. Before discussing the extraordinary changes that this transition will effect, it is well to observe that, at the same time, there is a flight from cotton in the Delta as elsewhere.

As I have observed before, cotton growing in the Delta has been more than a way to earn a living. It has also been a way of life; almost a religion tinged sometimes with an aberrant fanaticism. The soil and climate of the area are ideally suited for cotton. There was an abundant supply of cheap, docile labor. Land, too, was cheap; the use of commercial fertilizers unknown. Under these circumstances, a propitious combination of factors might lead to large profits. There might also be, when things went awry, large losses. The Delta is, in any event, a land of excess. The hot sun, the torrential rains, the savage caprices of the unpredictable river, the fecund earth, the startlingly rapid growth of vegetation, the illimitable flat plains and the vast dome of heaven arching over them: all these environmental influences seemed to breed in the people a tendency toward the excessive. Its agriculture became an economy with all risked upon cotton, the winners taking large gains and the losers suffering bankruptcy.

For many years past, however, the odds have been against the one-crop economy. It could not, in any event, be pursued under the federal subsidy system which dictated that large percentages of cropland must go into crops other than cotton. The time had come to reduce the risks. Cotton would remain the principal money crop. It would still offer chances of the greatest money rewards. But it would no longer be the one crop of the area.

The Delta has therefore recently turned to the extensive cultivation of small grains — principally oats — and cattle growing. It had never before seen a grain elevator. Now it has what might be termed three farm-cathedral towns marked by the towering structures, lording it over the flat plains, of grain elevators owned by Quaker Oats Company. Greenville, as evidence of the area's intense interest in cattle growing, has an active stockyards where large cattle sales are held at frequent intervals.

The decrease in Delta cotton acreage in the decade 1930–1940 has been drastic. It has declined from 1,416,849 acres in 1930 to 862,589 acres in 1940, or a 39.1 per cent decrease. Expressed in another way, there was a reduction in cotton acreage from 78 per cent of all cropland in 1930 to 46.1 per cent in 1940. There was, on the other hand, an increase in the percentage of cropland in corn, oats, hay, soybeans, and plowable pasturage land.

During the decade mentioned, cropland in corn increased from 10.4 per cent to 28.2 per cent; in oats from 0.2 to 4.7 per cent; in hay, exclusive of sorghum, from 3.1 to 11.8 per cent; in soybeans from 1.5 to 12.9 per cent; in plowable pasture from 1.2 to 3.1.

These changes in crop emphasis, however salutary for the economic health of the farm, nonetheless measurably increase the problems that will flow from the coming mechanization of the Delta's farms. For the growing of grains and cattle require little hand labor, and therefore fewer people on the land.

The social effects of farm mechanization will first reveal themselves in a radical displacement of farm population in the Delta. The population density within its plantation area is little, if any, higher than that of the non-plantation areas of the Southeast. But cotton plays a much more important life in the economy of the plantation area than it does in other areas, while the plantation itself is much better adapted to mechanization than the small farm, and the broad level expanse of Delta fields is ideally suited to the operation of farm power equipment. The Delta is, moreover, the important plantation area of Mississippi and the super-plantation area of the United States.

It is difficult to forecast the probable displacement numbers that relatively complete mechanization would cause, but they will undoubtedly be high. A conservative estimate of probable labor displacement runs from fifty-five to sixty-five per cent.

A few plantations are already operating on a ratio of about one family for each 100 acres of cropland by utilizing seasonal labor for chopping and picking. In 1940 there was one family for each 27 acres of Delta cropland. Assuming that widespread adoption of the mechanical picker would make possible an adjustment of the labor force to 100 acres of cropland per family instead of 27 acres per family, then 73 per cent of the families presently on the land would not be needed.

A potential displacement of people is indicated whose proportions are staggering. In 1940 there were 64,683 farm families, or a total farm population of 287,111 in the ten all-Delta counties. A 73 per cent reduction of these families would mean that these counties alone would lose 47,218 families or 209,591 persons.

This is a phenomenon fraught with extraordinary and unforeseeable consequences for the people of the Delta; as well for those who remain as for those who leave. It might be assumed, then, that they would oppose mechanization, however futile such a gesture, or would regard it as inevitable but immensely disquieting. Such is not the case. Opinion has radically changed in the Delta. Less than a decade ago leading newspapers of the region were advocating that all mechanical cotton pickers be dumped into the Mississippi as anti-social instruments economically detrimental to the people's welfare. At the same time, the Triple A followed a policy of restricting or attempting to restrict farm labor displacements. Now, however, in the face of the coming mechanical revolution, while it is regarded by a minority with dismay, it is regarded in other quarters, among whites and Negroes, with complacency, even relief.

The reasons for this radical change of point of view are many and complex. There are general factors affecting it which apply to all farmers as well as those of the Delta. Farmers, by the very nature of their occupation, tend to be conservative, stubborn in their ways, slow to change. During the past twenty-five years, however, technical change has sharply affected agriculture as, for example, in the wide use of contour and strip plowing, the planting of hybrid corn, the careful selection of seed, the breeding of animals and poultry for greater production, the employment of labor-saving machinery, the careful keeping of accounts. County agents and home economics demonstrators brought to farmers and farm homes the latest innovations of research laboratories. The farmer's sons, and many of his daughters, attended agricultural colleges and proved to the Old Man, by demonstration, that old ways are not necessarily the best ways. Through these influences, the farmer became almost as receptive to technological change as the industrialist.

Subconsciously, he was affected by the convulsive world in which he has lived since 1914 — the year when the nineteenth century finally ended. Neither in his thinking nor his way of life has he been able completely to escape the earth-shattering revolutions, political and economic, of his times. In these days of federal subsidies, it seems a remote world indeed when President Cleveland in the eighteen-eighties vetoed a House bill appropriating ten thousand dollars to buy seed for midwestern farmers whose crops had been destroyed by floods. It was not the business of the federal government, said the President in his veto message, to assist farmers in this way.

Changing times have almost dissipated the farmer's once stubborn resistance to change. And here enters a strange paradox. Far less than the industrialist is the farmer master of his destiny. Despite technology, he still operates in a largely uncontrollable environment. His cotton may rot in rains that keep him from picking it. His turkeys, bronze-gold and healthy two weeks before Thanksgiving, may suddenly die. His wheat may wither for lack of rain, or his peach trees be stripped by hail. The farmer is perforce, therefore, something of a fatalist, and he may look upon the death of an old order and the birth of a new with as much complacency as the industrialist.

The farmer is not the same man as the city feller, but he is more like him today than he was twenty-five years ago. The coming of good roads and the Model T broke down the isolation in which he had lived for generations. The telephone put him in instant touch with the city as well as his neighbors. The movies had their way with him and his family when they went to town, while the radio brought the uproarious, ever-changing world to his fireside. He became outwardly indistinguishable from the city feller, and inwardly approached him more and more.

These factors prepared the Delta farmer mentally for the monumental prospective changeover from a primitive hand agriculture to a highly advanced machine agriculture. But he was also moved by elements bearing directly upon his problems. He saw that if he was to survive at all, he could survive only through the increased use of machines. The old devices had been tried and either found wanting or would not be continued. The government would not go on forever lending money to foreigners with which to buy his cotton; an arrangement which meant in practice that the United States was giving away a portion of its real wealth, since the loans would most likely not be repaid. Federal subsidies had the effect of relieving the farmer's immediate distress and so were welcome, but their long-range consequences might be disastrous. It was questionable, moreover, how long the country would continue to hand out subsidies, and while the farmer naturally took them, he was not altogether pleased. Faced by a dreary prospect, invention came to his aid. Now the wheel is coming full circle. After many experiments, machinery puts him again upon his own and returns him to the fiercely individualist doctrine which farmers long ago summed up in their maxim — "Hoe your own row."

The Delta farmer sees mechanized agriculture not only as a source of survival, but also of large profits. Mechanization will enormously increase his outlay for capital equipment. But he will no longer share his profits as he does under sharecropping. His labor costs will be low. He will not have to build and maintain dozens of tenant cabins. Acreage hitherto devoted to feed crops for animals may be put into cash crops.

He is moved also by emotional factors. He is fatigued by the constantly increasing racial tensions of the Delta; by migrations of Negroes which threaten his labor supply; by the spirit of unrest that is abroad in the land. Weary of all this, he looks with welcome upon the coming day of more machines and fewer men.

Similarly, although machine farming will cause a huge displacement of Negro labor in the Delta, its Negro leaders seem to accept the prospect with relief. The remarks on this score of Dr. T. R. M. Howard, who directs the Taborian Hospital, a private Negro enterprise, in the all-Negro town of Mound Bayou, Mississippi, are typical of those of other Negro leaders. He is quoted as follows in the New York *Herald Tribune*: "Anything that replaces plantation economy is good for the Negro sharecropper. As long as he had Mr. John [the white farmer] to depend upon, he is going to depend on him. Urban life will make the Negro more resourceful. If he suffers for a while it won't be much more than he is suffering here."

The opinions of others are quoted by the same newspaper. "The Rev. James A. McDaniel, executive secretary of the Memphis Urban League, knows about the mechanical cotton picker and can still remark with feeling: 'It will raze the plantation social structure. The sooner they put it into mass production the better. Nothing has contributed as much to the ignorance and poverty of the Negro.'

"According to H. L. Mitchell, of Memphis, president of the National Farm Labor Union, "There seems to be a growing realization among them [Negroes] that there is no future in cotton.' This view was substantiated by a forum at the Negro branch of the Young Women's Christian Association at Jackson, Mississippi."

The Delta plantation system has always shown a marked preference for Negro labor. Consequently, 81.1 per cent of the Delta's farm population in 1940 was Negro, and it is this group which will be most seriously affected by mechanization. It is not generally realized, however, that many Negroes who will be forced off the land by mechanization, are themselves migrants to the Delta. Their coming migration will be for them at least a second migration. In his *The Plantation Land Tenure in Mississippi,* Frank J. Welch, Head of the Department of Agricultural Economics, Mississippi Experiment Station, states that less than half of the present regular labor force of the Delta were born there. The majority of the newcomers, including many whites seeking better opportunities on rich Delta lands, came from the hill counties of Mississippi. Others came from the adjacent states of Louisiana, Arkansas, Alabama, Tennessee.

Negro migrants from the Delta will present a difficult problem in urban assimilation. Generally unskilled, used only to the ways of a primitive agriculture, they will be able to find employment, unless trained, only as common laborers. The rate of illiteracy among them is high. In his study of the educational status of 220 heads of plantation labor families in the Delta in 1940, Welch shows that 52.3 per cent cannot read and write. Wives of the group were somewhat less illiterate, the rate of illiteracy among them being 34.0 per cent of the total number.

Whatever the consequences of farm mechanization in the Delta, its coming is accepted by whites and Negroes as a fact. The shock will be cushioned because it cannot come overnight. Sufficient machinery is not yet available. The present plantation structure, adapted to one-family farming, must be changed by a rearrangement of drainage ditches, roads, and so forth, to permit the cultivation of large plots of land. Personnel must be trained in the operation and repair of machinery. Garages must be built; gasoline tanks installed.

Under mechanization, the arrangement of farm dwellings will not be that of the old plantation, but of European village agriculture. Presently houses are scattered all over the plantation, their tenants working assigned plots of land adjacent to them. In the morning they fetch mules from a central place, go to the fields, and return the mules at night to the same place. On the mechanized plantation, dwellings and garages will be placed together on a highway. Men will live in small villages as in European agriculture. Workers will go to the fields on the self-propelled vehicles that are their tools, and will return in the same way.

As the mechanical revolution proceeds, the very shape and form of the plantation landscape will be changed. No more will blue woodsmoke curl from the cabin chimneys to hang suspended like evanescent plumes against the deeper blue of surrounding woods. The typical clearings amid wide fields made by the cabins will disappear. Little children, stark naked in hot summer, will not play with squirrel tails on the sunbaked ground of the cabin yard. Pigs will not grunt in the grateful shade underneath the cabin, nor hang, richly larded, at the back door in hawg-killin' time, giving sweet promise to the farm family of cracklin' bread, porkchops, chitlins, pigs-feet, and hawg-head cheese. On cold nights of winter, when logs crackle in the hearth, and chillun abed pull their flannelette nightgowns the closer about them as the wind whistles upward through the floor, while their elders spell out the gospels before smoky coal-oil lamps, there will be no one to make answer to the hoot owl as he complainingly asks from the limbs of a distant oak:

> *I c-o-o-k fer my wife,*
> *Er, who c-o-o-k-s fer you a-l-l?*

The glories of the good Lawd will continue to be praised by the godly, the mercies of Sweet Jesus sought, golden song made, and reverent prayer intoned, but no longer, as now, in scattered plantation churches deep-buried on the honeysuckle-entangled banks of creeks. The tractor will clatter where the church stands, and its yard, presently filled at prayer-meeting time with cars, wagons, and riding mules, will be the seedbed of cotton. This way, too, will go the scattered plantation school where, in spring, the music piercing sweet of Bob White quail comes through the open window; and the plantation bell, ancient herald of the rising sun, will no longer summon it with bronze throat.

An era comes to an approaching end. An era celebrated in play, pageant, verse, music, song, ballet, and novel. Long ago, although this is not to gift him with clairvoyant powers, Uncle Remus who was of the heyday of the era, told in parable why it had to end. Telling the little boy how, one day, Brer Fox was hot after Brer Rabbit and was just about to catch him, he said that Brer Rabbit escaped by climbing a tree. The little boy doubted the story. Rabbits, he said, could not climb trees. Sagely, Uncle Remus answered, "Brer Rabbit was 'bleeged to."

By necessity plantation owners are adopting measures that will all but destroy the plantation system as it has existed since shortly after the Civil War. Large operating units under a single management will continue, but in the coming farm-factory the old paternalistic relationship between management and labor will go. It was a relationship that, whatever its defects, was often marked by human tenderness, understanding, and enduring friendships. As such it was without parallel in our national life. Sharecropping will go, and all those things that were the essence of an economic and social system that had become a distinctive symbol of a traditional agrarian way of life in the Delta. The plantation will approach the conditions of a factory. Farmers will become mechanics. Management will become impersonal; operation mechanical; time measured not by the sun but the stopwatch; the task geared to the capacity of machines.

Of those now on plantations, only one-third will remain when mechanization is a fact. They will constitute a mechanic's élite. They will live, it is planned, in sound, fireproof, electrically lighted houses, with running water, bathtubs, and sanitary appliances. They will have ground for a garden, for the raising of the family's pigs and poultry, and the maintenance of a cow. House and grounds will be rent-free, and they will be paid monthly salaries, rain or shine, of not less than one hundred dollars a month. In terms of real wages, therefore, the Delta farm laborer of the future will have a standard of living higher than that of most of his fellows in the United States, and superior to that of many industrial workers and members of the white-collar class.

Whether this élite will be white or Negro is problematical. Some plantation owners are already choosing the brightest of their young Negro tenants and training them in mechanical tasks to become the nucleus of a mechanized order. There is no doubt of the Negro's aptitude for the tasks. But white men in the Delta, as elsewhere, have already taken over many jobs and occupations which were once exclusively the province of Negroes. It is likely, therefore, that they will try to push them off mechanized farms because of the rich perquisites of their jobs.

What will be the effect upon the urban Delta of the displacement of thousands of farm Negroes? Local industry cannot absorb them. They must emigrate to other places in the South, or, most likely, outside the South. The prospect is a matter of concern to merchants and others of the little Delta towns whose livelihood depends so largely upon Negro trade. If the movement from the area were sharply accelerated, it could work great hardship upon the towns, while it seems likely, in any case, that many of them must wither on the vine when the rural population sharply decreases. But others believe that the only white victims of Negro migration will be those catering to the lowest income groups. They hold that the economic level of the future farm mechanics will be so high that their expenditures will equal the expenditures of the present large group whose incomes are low. The event is not predictable.

More predictable perhaps is the social fortunes of the minority of Negroes who will remain in the Delta. Their conditions of living will improve in nearly all things. Once their numbers have dropped from a present sixty to seventy-five per cent of the population of Delta counties, to perhaps twenty-five per cent, there will undoubtedly be a marked rise in the Negro's educational opportunities. In Coahoma county, for example, there are five thousand Negro children and one thousand white children in school, while uncounted numbers of Negro children do not attend school at all. In order to consolidate the seventy-two small Negro schools of the county, one hundred buses would be required. The cost of these alone is prohibitive. If, however, the Negro population of the county should largely decrease, there is little doubt that Negroes would then be provided with schools equal to white schools in quality.

No matter what the Supreme Court of the United States may hold, the Delta's resistance to Negro suffrage will not be relaxed so long as its Negroes overwhelmingly outnumber its whites; when there are as many as five Negroes to one white person in a county. But here again, there is little doubt that a sharp drop in the Negro population would bring about a complete change of the white point of view on this bitterly contested issue.

The likelihood is, therefore, that Delta Negroes who survive farm mechanization, will find their lot improved. Once the enormous disparity in numbers of the groups has been removed, racial tensions will ease; many of the white man's fears will be dissipated; and the communities will live together in greater harmony than ever before.

The coming problem of agricultural displacement in the Delta and the whole South is of huge proportions and must concern the entire nation. The time to prepare for it is now, but since we as a nation rarely act until catastrophe is upon us, it is likely that we shall muddle along until it is too late. The country is upon the brink of a process of change as great as any that has occurred since the Industrial Revolution. In its brochure, *Reconversion of Cotton Farming*, the Department of Agriculture estimates that five million persons will be removed from the land within the next few years. They must go somewhere. But where? They must do something. But what? They must be housed. But where is the housing?

Most of this group are farm Negroes totally unprepared for urban, industrial life. How will they be industrially absorbed? What will be the effect of throwing them upon the labor market? What will be their reception at the hands of white and Negro workers whose jobs and wages they threaten?

There are other issues involved here of an even greater gravity. If tens of thousands of Southern Negroes descend upon communities totally unprepared for them psychologically and industrially, what will the effect be upon race relations in the United States? Will the Negro problem be transferred from the South to other parts of the nation who have hitherto been concerned with it only as carping critics of the South? Will the victims of farm mechanization become the victims of race conflict?

There is an enormous tragedy in the making unless the United States acts, and acts promptly, upon a problem that affects millions of people and the whole social structure of the nation.

CHAPTER 5

The Negro Moves North[1]

THE STORY is an old, unhappy one. The Civil War had been over but a few years when the Mississippi Valley Labor Convention met in the battle-scarred city of Vicksburg in 1879 to consider the emigration of Negroes from the Valley. There was much concern in many quarters because they were leaving in considerable numbers. Democratic politicians claimed that the movement was fostered by Republicans so that they could get more votes. But the convention, with General N. R. Miles as president, held otherwise. It said that Negro unrest arose from the low price of cotton; the credit and sharecropper system; the fear of Negroes that their civil rights, granted them under Reconstruction, would be removed; and opportunities for plenty which had been reported to them as existing elsewhere — especially in Kansas.

Ever since that day, the hope of emigrating from the South has stirred the minds of Negroes. Hundreds of thousands of Negroes have left the section since the beginning of this century, and the movement will continue, in my opinion, until there are more Negroes outside the South than in it. So, too, the overwhelming majority of Negroes in the Delta may be so reduced that they will become a numerical minority. It is necessary, however, first to consider the question in relation to the whole

[1] For many of the figures in this chapter pertaining to education and health, I am indebted to Rupert Vance's *All These People,* published by the University of North Carolina Press.

331

South, and then in its aspects that apply peculiarly to the Delta.

The logic of the situation is clear. The white South must decide whether or not it wants to retain its Negro population or risk losing a large part of it by emigration to other sections of the country. It can no longer retain its Negro population entirely upon white terms. If it wants to keep Negroes in the South, it must make many adjustments that will satisfy at least the more urgent demands of this claimant and highly race-conscious group. Otherwise it is reasonable to assume, both from the facts of the immediate past and from the present mood of Negroes, that they will leave the section in great numbers.

There are roughly ten million Negroes in the South and thirty million whites, so that Negroes constitute a quarter of its total population. In some of the Southern states, the proportion is as high as a third or half, while in certain counties of the deep South — as the Delta — there are three Negroes for every white.

Nowhere else in the nation do such ratios apply. Negroes make up only 9.8 per cent of the total United States population; only 1.2 per cent of the New England community; and only 4.8 per cent of a great Middle Western state such as Illinois.

Negroes are obviously a stupendous fact in the economic life of the South. They are not only labor but they are (or have been) cheap, ubiquitous labor that does the heavy work of the community and is, generally speaking, docile. They hoe the corn, pick the cotton, sweat in the sawmills and cottonseed oil mills, and tamp the ties of the Yellow Dog railroad in the blazing Mississippi sun. Negro women are the classical and almost the sole domestics of the region. They are the cooks, maids, children's nurses, and washerwomen, whose low wage-scale made it possible for even the small-income Southern home to have one or more servants.

The South is a section of low-cost labor. Its wages are generally below those of the rest of the country. It has long maintained that, for various reasons, it could not compete with richer, more experienced, more highly industrialized sections of the nation if it had to pay the same wage-scales; and, faced with uniform Federal wage legislation, it has sought wage differentials weighted in its favor.

At the risk of oversimplification and without taking into account various economic factors that have handicapped the South's growth (some imposed from without and some stemming from conditions within), one may say that it is largely the presence of Negroes which has made possible the low wage-scales of the South. The South's progress, economically and culturally, has been hindered because, unlike other sections, it received few fresh infusions of immigrant blood but has continued to live, since its beginnings, in a state of inbreeding. Immigrants would not go there in considerable numbers before the Civil War because there was little place for them inside the plantation system and they could not compete with slave labor. They did not go South after the war because they did not want to compete with low-wage free labor. The very abundance of Negroes made for a cheap labor market, while the fact that they could exist at an almost Oriental standard of living, and yet multiply, tended to perpetuate it.

There are other considerations. The South has long been bitterly opposed to labor unions; when it has not prevented them from starting, it has tried to hamstring them. Here the Negro unwittingly has played a valuable role for anti-unionists. Excluded largely from white unions, docile, accustomed to hard labor and a low standard of living, he has done much, by his mere presence, to prevent the growth of unionism — although by so doing he has injured both the white worker and himself. It is clear, therefore, that the emigration of large numbers of Negroes from the South would sharply change the system of non-unionism and low wages which many Southern industrialists have tried to perpetuate on the ground that their industries could not otherwise survive.

It is equally clear that a greater part of Southern industrial-agricultural productivity depends upon Negro labor. Their emigration might work serious economic harm to the region, retard its progress toward an industrialization balanced with agriculture, and place it perhaps at a marked disadvantage in competition with other sections of the nation. Negroes are both producers and consumers. Thousands of Southern merchants support themselves largely by Negro trade, and these merchants in turn affect their communities as property owners and taxpayers.

Yet Negroes have long been leaving the South in great numbers and, unless there is a change in their status, it is reasonable to believe that they will migrate in even greater numbers.

A minority suffering persecution, oppression, or a wide denial of its rights may, if all else fails, use the right or weapon of emigration. It was the method employed by immigrant hordes who came to the United States to escape oppression in their homelands or to improve their economic condition. It is the age-old method of the poor, the obscure, the politically weak. It is a form of active non-resistance against which nothing avails except a removal of the emigrant's grievances.

This method has been employed by Southern Negroes for the past fifty years. It has been intensified during the past quarter century. To illustrate, the Negro population of Detroit increased from around 40,000 in 1920 to 149,000 in 1940; of Cleveland, from 34,000 to 84,000; of New York, from 152,000 to 458,000; of St. Louis, from 69,000 to 108,000.

The great modern movement of Negroes from the South began during the First World War. Its effects were striking. By 1930, when Northern Negroes numbered some 2.4 millions, the loss to the South amounted to nearly 2 millions. This is more than 20 per cent of its Negro population and more than 5 per cent of its total population.

There were many reasons for the emigration, including a coincidence of three factors: the war had created a great demand for labor, the demand was increased by the shutting off of European immigration, and the boll weevil struck heavily in the old South cotton areas. Labor agents, disguised as insurance men and salesmen, worked incessantly among Negroes on behalf of Northern industry. They promised unheard-of high wages, attractive living conditions, less unemployment, a shorter working day than on the farm, a Jim Crowless land where every Negro man was "Mr." and every Negro woman "Mrs." to the white people, and better educational opportunities.

Southern Negroes already in the North, and those who had

recently gone, wrote glowing letters to friends and relatives in the South urging them to come to the promised land, while the Northern Negro press chimed in. The prospect was irresistible to thousands. Negro emigrants said they were leaving because of low wages, bad housing on plantations, unsatisfactory crop settlements, rough treatment by law officers, and unfairness in the courts. Some Negroes were even advised by their white friends to leave areas where the crop outlook seemed hopeless. But many were moved by nothing more than a desire to travel, while others were swept from their moorings by a movement that sometimes assumed hysterical proportions.

An observer of the unparalleled exodus described it as follows:

> The most interesting thing is how these people left. They were selling out everything they had or in a manner giving it away; selling their homes, mules, horses, cows, and everything about them but their trunks. All around in the country, people who were so old they could not very well get about were leaving. Some left with six to eight small children to feed and babies half clothed, no shoes on their feet, hungry, not anything to eat and not even a cent over their train fare. Some would go to the station and wait there three or four days for an agent who was carrying them on passes. Others of this city would go in clubs of fifty and a hundred at a time in order to get reduced rates. They usually left on Wednesday and Saturday nights. On Wednesday night I went to the station to see a friend of mine who was leaving. I could not get in the station, there were so many people turning like bees in a hive. Officers would go up and down the tracks trying to keep the people back. One old lady and man had gotten on the train. They were patting their feet and singing and a man standing nearby asked, "Uncle, where are you going?" The old man replied, "Well, son, I'm gwine to the promised land." (Emmett J. Scott, *Negro Migration during the War*, p. 41.)

Within a period of ninety days during the twenties, twelve thousand Negroes left the cotton fields of Mississippi, and an average of two hundred were leaving Memphis every night. Georgia was especially hard hit. It is estimated that, between 1920 and 1923, its available labor supply was reduced by two fifths. The *Macon Telegraph* expressed the consternation of the white community:

> Everybody seems to be asleep about what is going on right under our noses — that is, everybody but farmers who waked up on mornings recently to find every Negro over twenty-one on their places gone — to Cleveland, Pittsburgh, Chicago, Indianapolis. It was a week following that several Macon employers found good Negroes, men trained in their work . . . had suddenly left and gone to Cleveland.

There were three main streams of migration. The largest stream flowed from Georgia through the Atlantic coast states and terminated in New York and Pennsylvania. A second stream began in Mississippi and Alabama but split into three branches in Ohio — one going to Indiana and Illinois, another to Michigan, and a third remaining in Ohio. The third stream flowed from Louisiana through Arkansas and Missouri into Illinois.

The South did not willingly suffer the exodus, and attempted to stop it by methods ranging from repression and exhortation to raising wages. Strong measures were taken against labor agents. License fees were $1250 in Birmingham, and $25,000 in Macon, Georgia. Agents were beaten, jailed, run out of town. Negroes hanging around railroad stations were arrested on charges of vagrancy. Sometimes migrants were taken from trains and put in jail. Attempts were made to keep Northern Negro newspapers from reaching their Southern readers. The Southern press denounced the industrial North in terms reminiscent of the *ante-bellum* struggle between slaveowners and abolitionists. It described the opportunities for Negroes in the South and the kindly relationships long existing between thousands of individual whites and Negroes.

In the Delta, the whites gave a large picnic for Negroes. There were free pop and hamburgers. White and Negro speakers addressed the crowd on the advantages of the Delta as a home for Negroes. Privately, Negro leaders told the whites that their people would prefer to remain in the South if their principal grievances were removed.

None of these methods was successful. Negroes continued to leave the section until stopped by the stark facts of the economic depression of the thirties. Some day they would again be on the move. In the summer of 1944, this is how *Time* saw conditions in the Delta, and in Mississippi:

> Over all the black rich delta land of Mississippi, which produces 7 per cent of the nation's cotton crop, Southern whites last week were lifting their own loads, toting their own bales. In the hills, white women and small boys sweated behind the mules down the long hot rows of cotton and corn. . . . For Mississippi . . . was running short of Negroes.
>
> Since 1940, when Mississippi whites outnumbered the Negroes for the first time in a century, an estimated 50,000 Negroes have left the state, headed north in the hope of better pay and a better life. Mississippi, proud of its pleasant way of life which had depended for more than a century on Negro labor . . . fretted and fumed at doing the hard work.

This movement reaches back a long way.

> With the exception of the decade 1900–1910, the net movement of native-born Negroes out of the Southeast has grown greater with each decade since 1890. The loss of 129,000 in the decade 1890–1900 grew to a loss of 615,000 by 1920–30. *In the nineteen-twenties the region lost 8.2 per cent.* The states with the greatest losses were Georgia, South Carolina, and Mississippi. . . . (Rupert B. Vance, *All These People,* University of North Carolina Press, 1945.) (My italics.)

In the face of the reality, Southerners are likely to say, and with much truth, that the lot of the Negro in the North is not a happy one — that in the North the Negro is the last to be hired and the first to be fired; that many of the repressions which run against him in the South also run against him in the North and are often brutal in their application — untempered as they are by that complex mutuality of understanding and sympathy which so often prevails among Southern whites and Negroes. They say that New York's Harlem is a cesspool of disease, filth, and crime; that many avenues of economic opportunity are closed to Negroes so that, unless they are in the professions or private business, they are normally in demand only as domestics or doers of heavy, dirty work which whites reject. All these things may be true; yet they do not alter the situation. Southern Negroes, in my opinion, will continue to migrate so long as they *believe* they will be better off elsewhere. Apparently migrants believe they are better off, because only a tiny minority return to the South.

Negro migration from the Delta, present and prospective, is affected by elements general and particular. Negroes of the area are subject to the same disaffections which are common to all Southern Negroes, and to special disaffections which flow from their presence inside the plantation system. One cannot, however, understand the complexities of the case without taking into consideration the following:

(*a*) The fear of farm mechanization is not the root cause of Negro migration from the Delta. The movement began before mechanization was started.

(*b*) Mechanization is not being undertaken because of Negro migration. Its roots lie in the stark facts of cotton economics.

(*c*) Migration from the Delta in the recent past has flowed, and in the future will flow, from the Negro's general dissatisfaction with his lot. At the same time, it will be accelerated by mechanization.

(*d*) Neither the Delta nor the South is taking repressive measures to halt migration, as they did twenty-five years ago. It is taken for granted, at least in the Delta, that large percentages of its Negro population will leave the area for reasons of their own, or because farm mechanization will displace them.

Before examining the reasons why Negroes leave the Delta, it is well to note the population shifts in the area during the twenty-year period 1920–40.

It must first be remarked that, as Paul Foreman has shown in his population studies of Mississippi, there has been a comparatively small increase in its Negro population during the half century ending in 1930. He says:

> The native white population grew steadily decade by decade. Its increase in this half century amounted to a 110 per cent gain;

since 1900 a 56 per cent gain. Among the Negroes, however, the fifty-year trend shows only a 56 per cent gain; that since 1900, only slightly more than 10 per cent. (Paul Breck, Foreman, *Mississippi Population Trends* (Doctoral dissertation), Vanderbilt University, 1939.)

Foreman found that Negro women between the ages of twenty and forty-four in the Delta counties have comparatively fewer children under five years of age than do either white or colored women in the other counties of the State. It is clear, therefore, that in view of the comparatively low birth rate and the high migration from the Delta, the Negro population would not have been maintained at its present levels except for the importation of new people from the outside.

In the period 1920–40, the white population of the Delta increased by approximately 40 per cent. During the same period the Negro increase was 12 per cent. In 1920 Negroes constituted 81.2 per cent of the total population, but this had decreased to 73.6 per cent in 1940.

It is notable that while all of the Delta counties in the period mentioned have shown a decrease of Negroes in relation to whites, towns in the same area do not exhibit similar changes. The percentage of Negroes to whites in Washington county decreased from 81.5 per cent in 1920 to 72.3 in 1940. But during the same period, Negroes continued to make up 60 per cent of the population of the county's principal town — Greenville. This is also true of the neighboring towns of Greenwood and Vicksburg, while the percentage of Negroes to whites in the area's great metropolis — Memphis — rose from 37.7 per cent in 1920 to 41.5 per cent in 1940.

It would seem that Delta Negroes are moving into the towns as an escape from the farm; because they feel they have greater freedom in the towns than in the country; or because the towns are temporary havens for them on their way North.

As I have pointed out before, Negroes leaving one plantation for another, rarely give their true reasons to their employers. Negroes intending to migrate from the Delta tend to keep their migration secret. This attitude is evidently in part a hangover from slavery; a fear that white men will try to prevent their emigration. In one notable instance, however, a plantation owner went to considerable pains to find out precisely why his tenants were going North. He is W. K. Anderson, a member of the planting firm of King & Anderson, who operate a sixteen-thousand-acre plantation in the heart of the Delta. This is what he told me over the luncheon table one day in February, 1945:

"For several years we have been trying to improve farming conditions on King & Anderson. We have been losing labor to the North, the East, and the West; and some to neighboring farms and counties. We wanted to know just why Negroes were leaving us. So we sent a Negro shop worker who had been with us for some time to Chicago, to make contacts for two of our white managers to talk to the people about returning to the plantation. Mr. Harpole and Mr. Russell then went to Chicago. They talked with the Reverend Jackson, who has a congregation of some twelve thousand Negroes. They told him that King & Anderson had made some changes in personnel to get the best possible plantation managers. Also that they were getting out detailed tenant's accounts so that the tenant would not have to come into the office and ask to see his account. All charges are itemized; crop charges are broken down into detailed statements if the tenant desires.

"We did this because we realize that some tenants are either reluctant or afraid to come in and ask for these charges because they fear it might be offensive to the plantation manager or the office force. Mr. Harpole and Mr. Russell also told the Reverend Jackson that we now give our tenants a statement of their accounts around July first, and again at picking time. Also, prior to preparing the land for a new crop, the manager would make a detailed list of the crop charges that would most likely be made against the tenant during the year. In these ways, the tenant would know by detailed statements where he stood all the time.

"We plan to continue our practice of putting electricity into tenant houses where lines are close enough to serve them. We plan to continue our program of farming on a live-at-home basis. We propose to see that tenant houses shall be relocated on hard-surfaced roads wherever this is possible. In other words, we want to make farm life more attractive for our tenants."

When the plantation managers had told all this to the Reverend Jackson, he made his reply. This is what he said, as his remarks were reported by the managers to Mr. Anderson:

"I know all about the Delta. My grandfather lived around Jonestown. [This is the vicinity from which Mr. Russell, one of the managers, came.] At the present time Negroes are coming North much faster than they are going South. [Mr. Anderson interjected the remark that his Negro emissary reported that the three Negro coaches going North were so crowded he had to stand most of the way from Memphis to Chicago. But there was ample room in the coaches returning to Memphis.] Negroes will continue to come North because they can find jobs. They will continue to come North until they can get some of the things down South they are receiving up here. A Negro that applies for work in Chicago is first asked where he is from. If he says he is from a Southern state, he is given an opportunity right away. A Northern Negro, by contrast, is questioned pretty closely and his references checked on carefully. Southern Negroes are preferred because they are docile, know how to work, are obedient, and so are given preference. From what you have indicated, you are making a step in the right direction — making farm life attractive. However, there are other conditions that will keep the Southern Negro from his native home, which is the South. When those conditions are improved and objectionable features removed, these Negroes will want to move back South. The Negroes up here will know when that happens. At that time I would not hesitate to go into the pulpit and counsel my people to return when conditions are generally improved."

The meeting of the managers with the Reverend Jackson, whose words pontifical and patriarchal are reminiscent of a fifteenth-century serf-owning bishop, was held on an afternoon. A night conference had been arranged in the meanwhile by the managers' Negro emissary with members of what might be called the King & Anderson colony in Chicago. As European immigrants to this country grouped themselves, so far as possible, in physical relationship to their old neighbors in Vilna, Stavanger, Cortina d'Ampezzo, so Southern Negroes group themselves in the Northern cities to which they emigrate. On the evening after the meeting with Reverend Jackson, the managers attended a conference which is perhaps without parallel in the history of the Delta.

Escorted by their plantation guide, they went to the apartment of a Negro laundry worker who had been a tenant on the King & Anderson plantation. Here were present a number of ex-tenants of the plantation. The women brought with them hampers of edibles — fried chicken, hot dogs, biscuits. The men brought beer and a bottle of whiskey. There was a festive air of reunion about the gathering, as old friends and former neighbors met again — this time under novel circumstances. The Negroes were gravely polite and cordial to their guests; and, after such conversational detours as good manners dictated, members of the conference got down to business.

Mr. Russell, one of the managers, outlined to his audience what was happening on the plantation. He soon found that this was superfluous. As in India, all that the white sahib does, and much of what he thinks, is known to the Indians around him, so in the Delta, Negroes know nearly everything that occurs in the white community. They have a grapevine which functions with extraordinary rapidity, and it stretches everywhere that Southern Negroes go for those who leave are kept aware of happenings in their former home by friends and relatives. Thus ex-tenants of the plantation could tell Mr. Russell that they knew what had been done, and what was going on; even that "Mistuh Billy" (W. K. Anderson) was the father of a recently arrived son. The Negroes were cordial, good-tempered, and were willing to talk freely, saying, in passing, that they approved of the new type of settlement of accounts which had been worked out on the plantation since their departure.

Asked why they had left the plantation, they said they had been dissatisfied with their accounts. The Negro tenant is deeply suspicious of the honesty of the plantation owner. This suspicion, often well founded in the past, is far less well founded today.

There were always planters who dealt honestly with their tenants. There were some who ruthlessly gouged them. But the latter have reformed wholly or partially, not out of conscience, but out of fear of losing their labor. The tenant's suspicions are ineradicable. No matter how much money he may earn in a given year, no matter how honest his white boss, he still believes in his heart that he was swindled out of something. One might assume that this attitude has its roots in race consciousness, were it not for the fact that Negro tenants are equally suspicious of Negro landowners. A Negro witness (according to the New York *Herald Tribune*) testifies as follows on this score:

> Mayor Benjamin A. Green . . . of Mound Bayou, says that there is no generalization one can make about plantation owners. He explained that some owners have a reputation for . . . "fair settlement." It marks the time of the year when the landowner weighs the cotton yield, deducts his share, and then makes adjustments for food, clothing, and doctor bills advanced.
>
> Where the reputation obtains, sharecroppers . . . have made a fair living, said Mayor Green. . . . Where there is no such reputation "they catch hell." He said that in this respect there is no appreciable difference between Negro and white plantation owners.

Given the Negro tenant's lack of business experience; the suspicions common to all rustics; the legend or the fact of bad faith toward him on the part of landowners; and it is unlikely that he will completely believe in the planter's honesty, however scrupulously honest he may be, or whatever his reputation for fair dealing.

King & Anderson's ex-tenants complained bitterly about being "royally cussed" by plantation managers. Their principal grievances were against these men, and they named those who had allegedly mistreated them. Continuing, their spokesman said, "Up here we have a little more freedom. If we get off from work, buy us a bottle of whiskey and take a drink, nobody objects. If we get a little too much, as all of us do sometimes, the police take us to jail. Next morning they let us out without having beat us over the head or making us pay a fine. We think we get better protection from the law up here. Going into towns down home the Law would get us, beat us up, handle us rough. We don't get that treatment here." None of the group indicated an intention of returning to the plantation.

After the Chicago conference, similar meetings were held in St. Louis and East St. Louis, Illinois. Here the grievances of extenants were much the same as those stated in Chicago.

Armed with these facts, Mr. Anderson told his plantation managers that if they cussed or physically maltreated tenants, he would fire them. Then he went to the neighboring town of Clarksdale to discuss with its officials the acts of which his migrant ex-tenants had complained. This town, unlike other Delta towns, has long had a curfew under which Negroes must not be found in white residential sections after ten o'clock at night. "I talked with Clarksdale's City Commissioner," said Mr. Anderson. "The curfew was started to keep prowlers out of white people's homes. Clarksdale seems to think it has plenty of labor for us on the farm. But Clarksdale is just one stop on the way North and as fast as its Negroes leave the city, others from the farm move in. The town is a drain on farm labor, and its abuses are taking our labor."

A curious situation is presented. Delta towns are almost entirely dependent for their livelihood upon surrounding farms. The farms rely almost entirely upon Negro labor. Yet, migrant Negroes state as a principal reason for leaving the Delta, the rough treatment given them by town police officers. But planters have great influence in the towns by virtue of their economic strength and prestige. If, therefore, they do not remedy the conditions complained of, it is because of an apathy so great that it runs counter to their self-interest.

The next step was taken when white leaders of Clarksdale asked Negro leaders of the town for a statement of grievances which in their opinion were leading to migrations of Negroes. These were presented under five broad headings:

1. Better Economic Conditions.
    (a) Low wages in Clarksdale versus high wages elsewhere.

    (*b*) Unsatisfactory crop settlements and abuses by plantation managers.
    (*c*) Discrimination in employment and inequalities in wages for the same work.
2. Constant Intimidations.
    (*a*) Wanton killings of Negroes without recourse.
    (*b*) Intimidations on public conveyances.
    (*c*) Law officers forcing women to work who are not vagrants.
    (*d*) Unfavorable newspaper publicity and scurrilous references to Negro soldiers.
    (*e*) Maltreatment of Negro soldiers while home on furlough.
3. Lack of Educational Opportunities.
    (*a*) Poor school buildings.
    (*b*) Short school terms.
    (*c*) Low salaries paid Negro teachers.
    (*d*) Lack of high school facilities.
    (*e*) Lack of recreational facilities.
4. Activities of Loan Sharks.
    (*a*) Excessive rates of interest charged.
    (*b*) Refusal to give receipts.
    (*c*) Threatening borrowers with bodily harm.
5. Lack of Sanitary Facilities.
    (*a*) Failure to collect garbage in Negro areas.
    (*b*) Lack of sidewalks and drainage in most Negro residential sections.
    (*c*) Lack of hospitals for Negroes.

Most of these grievances, if well founded, are within the remedy of the white community. Failure to remedy them would be a grave indictment of that community. But those relating to lack of schools and hospitals — about which Negroes are understandably bitter — are not remediable without huge grants from the Federal government in the case of schools, and huge contributions from the outside in the case of hospitals.

Since these are matters about which a great deal of emotion is expended, it may not be amiss to look at the facts. First, those pertaining to Mississippi, and second, those pertaining to the Delta.

Mississippi is the poorest state in the union. Only fifteen years ago it was on the verge of bankruptcy when an incoming Governor found about $13,000 in the state treasury and immediately payable bills of about $200,000. The prompt passage of a sales tax saved the day, and put the State on a better financial basis than it had enjoyed for years. At that time the national average of wealth per school child (five to seventeen years of age) was $10,200. In Mississippi it was only $3600 — or one-third the national average. The national average of annual income per school child was at this period $2171. In Mississippi it was $512 — or less than one-fourth of the national average.

In terms of the nation's wealth, we are a badly educated people. Exactly half of the United States population aged twenty-five and over have had no more than 8.7 years of schooling. The best educated people of the nation live in the Far West where exactly half of the adults have spent over 9.7 years in school. If this is the educational condition of the whole United States, it is not surprising to find that in its poorest section — the Southeast — the people attain a median of 7.4 completed years of schooling.

It takes money to keep school doors open. In 1938 the average number of days attended.by pupils in the nation's schools was 149.3. But in Mississippi the average was only 109.7. Here, however, there enters not only the money factor but another. Mississippi is overwhelmingly rural, exceeding all other states in this respect. The people, rural and on the whole poor, need their children on the farm, and they spend fewer days in school than urban children.

What are the educational attainments of those who teach the nation's children? Only 25.3 per cent of the nation's teachers have had more than four years of college training. California leads with 63.2 per cent, but the next state, New Jersey, has only 30.5 per cent of teachers with graduate training. Mississippi ranks lowest with 8.7 per cent.

Such is the gulf between our pretensions and our actions, we speak of education as though it were as dear to us as God, or our wife, or even — our business. Our tongues running wind-mill fashion, we piously say we want our children to have more "advantages" than we had. Nothing is too good for our dear little ones; may they all enter into the heaven of plenty through the sweet uses of education. But we pay teachers less than janitors, elevator operators, or firemen. In 1938 the rich United States paid an average annual salary of $1374 to school teachers. Mississippi paid only $479 to its white teachers, and only 30.1 per cent of this miserably small sum to its Negro teachers.

What of school buildings and equipment? The average American pupil in 1938 had the use of property valued at $274. The average in the Northeast was $382. But in Mississippi the average per white pupil was $147; per Negro pupil $11.

This does not mean that Mississippi exerts little effort in the field of education. It spends over forty per cent of its total revenues for education, but it has little to spend per school child. The State's fortunes have improved during the past decade for business reasons that apply to all other areas, and because it derives considerable revenues from recently discovered oil and gas fields. It is making as much of an educational effort as possible within the limits of its funds. Calculating a model tax plan to support education, Rupert Vance says that "Mississippi, which is at the bottom of many lists, is found to spend currently on public education 138 per cent of the revenue that would be raised by the model tax plan." Yet it falls far below the nation's average in expenditures for education and in other measurements of educational standards. The hard fact is, as Vance shows, *that Mississippi's educational need is 4.24 times its financial ability.*

It seems impossible, therefore, that educational opportunities in Mississippi, for whites or Negroes, can be appreciably improved without Federal grants or in the absence of a large migration of Negroes from the state. Nearly half of the state's Negro population is in the Delta. It derives only 39.4 per cent of its school income from the State Treasury. The rest comes from local taxation. The area's meager funds are insufficient to provide a sound education for its minority of white children, and hopelessly inadequate for its majority of teeming thousands of Negro children. If the funds were evenly distributed, the Negro standard of education might be raised a little, and the white standard depressed sharply below its present level, but neither group would be adequately educated. The inescapable fact was stated by the Negro superintendent of schools in the Delta county of Coahoma:

Many white superintendents of schools in Mississippi say frankly that the solution of our educational problem is for many of the Negroes to get out. I think this is right. The white schools are bad enough in our state and we cannot expect improvement of schools for the multitude of Negro children under those circumstances. (Washington [D.C.] *Post*, May 7, 1945.)

Health conditions in the Delta are worse even than those of education, and for the same reasons. The Delta, with its great density of Negro population, is well aware of the desperate need for increased medical services for Negroes. Commenting upon a report of five years' public health service for Negroes of the Yazoo-Mississippi Delta, the Delta Council (March, 1944) said:

. . . The responsible citizenry of the Delta and Mississippi must not fail to recognize a great existing need for expanded health service and enlarged health facilities. . . . Every county of the Delta should have a colored hospital. The rapid-treatment venereal disease clinic at Greenwood should be expanded to six or eight similar clinics. There is desperate need for an isolation hospital for incurable colored tuberculosis patients. Every county should be able to afford hospitalization and treatment for cancer. Through further enlightenment and education the leading white population should make available to every Negro in the Delta the already existing health services as well as those which we hope will be part of the postwar reconstruction of the Delta.

These recommendations, sound and well meant, require for their realization sums of money which are beyond the capacity of the community; and this without considering its large numbers of poor whites whose economic (and health) condition is not above that of the generality of Negroes, and is often below it.

Here again we note the poverty-born backwardness of Mississippi. In 1940 there was one physician for every 751 persons in the nation; one for every 610 persons in the Northeast. But the number of possible patients for every doctor in Mississippi was 1459. Consider hospital beds. In 1939 the United States had 9.7 medical-care beds for every 1000 population. Massachusetts had 15.3 beds for every 1000 population. But Mississippi had only 4.4 beds for the same number of people. The State has many shortcomings but it is false to say of it, as is often said, that its lack of medical-care beds for Negroes is evidence of a deep-rooted anti-Negroism. Whites have only a few more available beds than Negroes, and there is an appalling lack of them for both groups.

One striking index of the economic ability to secure medical services is the percentage of births attended by physicians. In 1940 physicians attended 90.8 of all live births recorded in the United States. But only 50.2 per cent were attended by physicians in Mississippi; the remainder being attended by midwives.

Lacking physicians and hospitals, the Delta undertakes the task of dealing with its health problem on a county-wide basis — the plan best suited to rural areas. County public-health services deal overwhelmingly with Negroes. They make up the largest part of the community. They are the poorest of the poor. Excess illness and mortality among them derives from the same causes that cause excess illness and deaths among the poor everywhere. These are rough, heavy work, bad housing, inadequate nutrition, poor medical care, and ignorance which prevents them from improving their nutritional standards or seeking better medical care when it is available.

Diseases of Delta Negroes differ from those of the poor in any group in only two respects. They have a greater incidence of venereal diseases and respiratory tuberculosis than whites. The dimensions of the whole problem can be made clear by considering health work in some of the counties of the Yazoo-Mississippi Delta.

Holmes county has a population of 10,000 whites and 30,000 Negroes. Its Health Department consists of a Health Director, Sanitation Supervisor, Venereal Disease Investigator, four graduate nurses, clerk, and health aide. It operates nine free venereal disease clinics each week, located in different parts of the county. They are used almost entirely by Negroes. In 1943 these clinics made 2900 Wassermann tests and gave 28,800 venereal disease treatment to Negroes.

The two counties of Issaquena and Sharkey, located in the southern end of the Delta, maintain a joint health department.

The first of these counties has a population of 1229 whites and 5204 Negroes. The second has 4342 whites and 11,091 Negroes. The department conducts chest clinics twice a year to detect or deal with tuberculosis cases. But when physicians find tubercular patients, where shall they send them for adequate treatment? The only available hospital, the Mississippi State Sanatorium, is hopelessly overcrowded. It has therefore had to put the counties on a quota basis. Sharkey county's quota, with its population of over 11,000 Negroes, is two. Issaquena's quota, with its population of 6500 Negroes, is one. Several cottages, for the use of Negro tuberculosis patients, have been built by the Sharkey County Negro Teachers Association. But, generally, the Negro tubercular must go home to die slowly, to expose others to infection, or to recover eventually, by the grace of God.

The Tunica county health department takes a portable X-ray machine around the county for use in suspected tubercular cases. Humphreys county conducts a monthly tuberculosis clinic. Bolivar county, with a population of 67,000, three-fourths of which is Negro, is taxing itself to build a county tuberculosis hospital. But adequate work in this field is beyond the financial capacity of the counties.

County health services, offer free immunization against smallpox, diphtheria, typhoid, whooping cough. They conduct maternity conferences and train Negro midwives. As a result of these efforts, there was not, for example, a death from puerperal fever in Issaquena-Sharkey counties in the six-year period ending December, 1943. The health services do as much dental hygiene as possible; install sanitary privies and drinking fountains; visit Negro schools; teach the necessity of screening houses to prevent malaria. But in the beginning, they had to overcome some of the difficulties which are encountered by medical missionaries in primitive regions of the world. These arose from fears that white physicians would use Negroes for experimental purposes; the belief that if a white doctor ever got a Negro into a hospital he would never emerge alive. This difficulty is touched upon in the report of the Director of Quitman County Health Department:

When I began public health work twenty years ago, the colored people were, in a sense, wild and afraid to take any kind of a shot. It took lots of patience, diligence, and coaxing to educate these people to the necessity of these immunizations, but at present, they visit my office practically daily asking for a health shot. The young, or school children, are much different from what they were twenty years ago. I say without fear of contradiction, that one could visit any colored school in this county, and the children could tell you how malaria is transmitted and its prevention. . . . They are doing much better than I ever expected them to do.

In summary, educational and medical facilities for Negroes in the Delta are grossly inadequate. They cannot be improved by good will alone, and it is not good will, but money, that is lacking. If, then, Negroes leave the Delta because of educational and health conditions, there is little the area can do about it. The solution of its difficulties in these fields lies either in the emigration of large numbers of Negroes, thereby reducing the numerical dimensions of the problem, or in Federal aid for education and private (or Federal) aid for health.

It is pertinent in this respect, however melancholy the reflection upon American life, to note what the migrating Delta Negro may expect to find if he should go to the nation's capital. The District of Columbia is one of the richest communities in the United States. Its annual income per family ranks among the highest in the land. It is the seat of our national government. There Congress may see what is going on with its own eyes. Many Congressmen come from states where Negroes have much political power — New York, Pennsylvania, Ohio, and others. Every important hospital in Washington, with the exception of Freedman's, practices some form of segregation or discrimination against Negro patients and bars Negro doctors from practice. Even at Gallinger, where 70 per cent of the patients are Negro, Negro physicians are refused admission to the hospital. The life expectancy of Negroes in the District is ten to twelve years less than that of whites. The Negro death rate from tuberculosis, is 4½ times higher than among whites. The Negro-white maternal mortality rate is in the ratio of 4 to 1.

I have observed before that nowadays, by contrast with the past, the Delta is not taking futile and repressive steps to halt Negro migration. It regards the prospect calmly, whether out of weariness from wrestling with the question, because it has come to believe that a better balancing of the numbers of the two groups is essential to better race relations and the social welfare of the community, or that farm mechanization will remove its dependence upon Negro labor. Much of that dependence has already been removed by the use of the tractor and other machines, but in the transitional period before mechanization becomes a fact, planters are obviously deeply concerned about holding their tenants. Yet the community's attitude toward migration is remarkably unlike what it was ten years ago.

In 1937, a research associate of the Yale Institute of Human Relations, studying Negro-white relations in a small Delta town, wrote:

> . . . The alarm of the whites and the exultation of the Negroes at the mass migrations to the North are evidence of how effective this pressure can be; *it will continue to be so long as Negroes are needed for plantation labor, but of course no longer.* (John Dollard, *Caste and Class in a Southern Town,* p. 301.) (My italics.)

The alarm of the whites has been succeeded by calm. The exultation of Negroes at migrations, interpreted by Dollard as an expression of aggression, must nowadays proceed from another source because they no longer keep whites awake at night.

Ten years after Mr. Dollard's study was published a New York *Times* reporter took a look at Yale University and the city in which it is located. His findings were noted under these headlines:

NEGROES FIND YALE IS NEGATIVE IN AID
Leaders in New Haven Report the University
Does Little to Improve Race Relations
South Lures Graduates
Colored Pastor, an Alderman, Says Prejudice Crops
Up With Subtlety in City

Negroes have lived in New Haven for over two hundred years. It is the seat of Yale University. The city's Negro population of 7500 is a small minority of the whole population. One might conclude that the Negroes of New Haven live in an atmosphere of sweet reasonableness. This is what the reporter found:

> Negroes are not sure of the effect that Yale University exerts on city culture, but they agree that the school does little to improve relations. . . . "Race prejudice is very subtle up here, and it slaps you when it is least expected," they said. (New York *Times*, July 23, 1946.)

The Reverend R. A. G. Foster is pastor of the 126-year-old Varick African Methodist Church, and has been a Republican member of the New Haven Board of Aldermen since 1943. He said that "in the South, Jim Crow is so plain, one does no guessing, but up here, it crops up when least expected." Strangely, according to the Reverend Foster, the few Negroes who have been graduated from Yale "usually go down South." What of Southern Negroes who come North? The same witness said, "Most of our professional people have followed the Negro worker from the South since 1930. Conditions down South, oddly enough, seem to give our people more ambition to help themselves."

Asked about economic discriminations against the Negro in New Haven, the Reverend Foster said that the town had "three (Negro) policemen, no city firemen, no bus or trolley-car drivers and the Connecticut company which controls transportation still opposes hiring Negro drivers. . . ."

Questioned about all this by the reporter, the Mayor of New Haven indulged in a generalization slightly wider than a barn door. "The Mayor maintained that the Negro problems of New Haven could be solved when more leaders were willing to sacrifice their leisure and 'put their shoulders to the wheel. . . .'"

About three hundred miles to the South of the Delta is the city of New Orleans, with which it has had long cultural and economic relations. There, on December 1, 1946, Walter White, president of the National Association for the Advancement of

Colored People, addressed the Southern Conference on Human
Welfare. His remarks, as reported by the Associated Press, were
something less than statesmanlike. They belong in the realm of
the emotional rather than the factual, and so contribute to the
highly combustible elements always present in Delta race relations.

He saw "moral degradation" as the basic cause of the South's
backwardness. He said it had grown out of "the conviction
among Southerners that the most ruthless, cruel, and hate-creat-
ing individual is by these methods assured of being most successful." Then he added that racial segregation had to go. "It is
as utterly impossible," he said, "to segregate the physical persons
of Americans as it is to segregate their ideas. There are, perhaps
some of you in this audience who are frightened by such a
prospect. But the alternative to one world and one nation is no
world and no nation."

So far as the Delta is concerned, nothing could be better
calculated to destroy racial good will, or to lessen the area's
waning resistance to migration, than such remarks on the part
of a responsible Negro leader. For the speaker not only indicts
all Southern whites as "morally degraded," but adds that its most
sacred taboo — racial segregation — must go.

Essentially, race relations in the Delta have long been de-
teriorating, although few overt acts occur to mark it. Retrospectively, it seems wholly improbable that forty years ago Washington county had a Negro Justice of the Peace who, elected by
the white community, obviously served with its approbation;
or that, twenty years ago, a Negro had long conducted his sta-
tionery store on the main street of Greenville.

Since the First World War, however — the racial situation has
changed for the worse. Negro veterans of 1918, having seen
something of the world, were dissatisfied when they returned
to the Delta. Some left the section. Some who remained adjusted themselves to the old life; others never became reconciled
to it. Then there came the great migrations of the twenties.
Migrants from the Delta encouraged their friends and relatives
to join them. Delta Negroes avidly read the often incendiary

outpourings of the Northern Negro press. Younger Negroes, better educated than their elders, became keenly conscious of rights and opportunities for advancement which they felt were denied them in the Delta. The Second World War came, and eighty-three thousand Negro servicemen went out from Mississippi (and the Delta) to every part of the world. They went farther and stayed longer than their predecessors of 1918. Some of those who left the Delta have not even returned to say howdy to their families, but have settled outside the region. And with all this, there is now a firmly established pattern of migration. The normal restlessness of the American is accentuated in the Negro by factors peculiar to his status. And even if these factors were not present, many a Negro, like many a white, might leave the Delta in search of wider economic opportunities elsewhere.

On the white side, paternalism and *noblesse oblige,* as I have said before, are at an end. The older white stock of the Delta is now perhaps outnumbered by poor whites — themselves migrants from the poorer lands of Mississippi and adjacent states — who bitterly hate Negroes. Farm mechanization is gradually reducing the farmer's dependence upon Negro labor. The flight from all-cotton to cotton and other produce such as oats and cattle, further diminishes labor needs. And decade by decade, the percentage of Negroes to whites in the Delta decreases.

It has slowly become apparent to thinking members of both races that better race relations and better economic opportunities are impossible so long as Delta Negroes are in the proportion of seventy-five per cent to the white population, while the nationwide ratio of Negroes to whites is ten per cent. A marked improvement of relations is therefore contingent upon the migration of Negroes until their overwhelming majorities in the Delta shall be reduced, so to say, to workable numbers. As it is, both races are prisoners of their environment. The white man's society is conditioned by the presence of masses of Negroes. The Negro's life is dominated by the fact of the white man's presence. Each lies upon a Procrustean bed for all that it is honeysuckle-scented and luminous with yellow moonlight. Upon such a bed men toss uneasily at night and arise fatigued in the morning.

I believe that Negroes will continue to leave the Delta; that those who remain will be better off than before; that the whole social and economic system of the area will change. It is more than two hundred and fifty years since the ship *Hannibal* of London brought a cargo of Negro slaves to Barbadoes. When, and where, shall their descendants, and the descendants of all the others who came in other slave ships, find a permanent home on the American earth?

CHAPTER 6

Black Troubadour

In Newtown, where most of Greenville's Negroes live, there are many kinds of men and women. As individuals, their diversity is so great that it is fully comprehended, one is sure, only by God. It could perhaps be partially comprehended by the novelist of genius. God and the great novelist are concerned with the human heart. But God is wherever he is and novelists of genius do not come to Newtown. Sometimes anthropologists visit it; also sociologists and students of the race question. They measure and pry; ask questions; and later publish a book or report. This is all to the good. The book may add to man's knowledge if not to his understanding. So, too, men trap tigers for zoos; others shoot them for museums; and still others photograph them in their natural habitat. (It is notable, however, that no tiger, whether because of his dignity or his gentlemanly instincts, has written a book about man.) We study the live animals, the dead ones, and their photographs. And this, too, is salutary, for man is an endlessly curious animal, forever engaged in illuminating the darkness that surrounds him. Yet when the facts have been collated and the data weighed, we remain without answer to William Blake's question:

> Tiger! Tiger! burning bright,
> In the forests of the night;
> What immortal hand or eye
> Could frame thy fearful symmetry?

If, then, one cannot see with the all-seeing eye of God, nor

even with the profound penetration of a Tolstoy or a Stendhal;
if the facts, so called, merely glow with a transitory luminescence
like that given off by the silver sides of a herring gasping to
death in bright sunlight, there is nothing to do except to portray
the images that flicker upon the retina of one's eye and one's
spirit, and let it go at that. It is meet, therefore, simply to say
that out in Newtown where the majority of the Negroes of
Greenville live, there are many kinds of men and women. The
proud and the servile. The intelligent and the stupid. The gentle
and the brutalized. The greedy and the generous. The honest
and the dishonest. The hopeful and the hopeless. These are
qualities also of those who occupy the large houses on Blanton
Street, where, in the polite Negro phrase, white whoreladies
used to live in that ordained segregation born of our moral code
which dictates that the blunder of detection is greater than the
crime of commission; that, in a wider sense, to save the surface
is to save all. But since men cannot escape their common inheritance, it follows that the Negroes of Newtown are characterized
by most of the attributes, good and bad, appertaining to the
white folks living on the other side of Nelson Street that is the
boundary between the two worlds of Greenville.

Among other residents of Newtown was Alvin Jones. Through
him I came to know Joe Moss, the black troubadour. They are
illustrative of that myriad diversity which attaches both to snow-
flakes and men; even of that tiny group of human beings who,
living on a microscopic spot arbitrarily designated Newtown in
a state and a nation arbitrarily called Mississippi and the United
States of America, revolve with the planet denominated earth
around another planet denominated sun. Alvin was the child of
a broodingly proud father who killed himself years ago. Suicide
is rare among Negroes and his parent's act gave him a kind of
somber distinction in the community. He wore it lightly. He
did not play upon it but accepted it serenely as one might
a caul or wen which indicates that its possessor has been
marked by the fates as a diviner of things to come. He had
a superb ear for the people's talk; an eye for the unusual; an
extraordinary sense of detachment about his own people. His

was indeed the dangerous gift of the comic spirit. It enabled him to see clearly the patent absurdities to which Negroes (as whites) are subject. He would stigmatize them with a phrase; cauterize them with a laughing jest. The pomposities of preachers, the social pretensions of ignorant but wealthy undertakers, the grandiloquent language of the half-educated: these he artfully and accurately mimicked.

Negroes are not incapable of laughing at themselves; certainly not less incapable in this respect than whites. But, like whites, they fear and dislike the rare comic spirits who appear among them to blow away their pretensions with laughter, strip them of their protective pomposities with a word, reveal them shining plain — like a wall fly caught in a shaft of light — with a phrase. Humanity does not like such men against whom, whatever the garments worn, it is always naked. It neither sees nor cares that satirists are moralists, and how often has it crucified moralists who were not satirists. It has hanged them, jailed them, burned their books. In what we are pleased to call our more enlightened times, it condemns them to obscurity and loneliness. Alvin Jones was, therefore, a lonely man within his own community. Three years ago he killed himself as his father had before him.

It was Alvin who brought Joe Moss to me. On a night of autumn rain Joe came to Will Percy's house to play his harps for us, and Will, himself an excellent musician, listened with wonder and delight as the itinerant troubadour made his wild and sorrowful music. I talked with him at length on several occasions; heard of him as I went about the town; but when I again inquired for him, he had gone — as mysteriously as he had come.

Joe Moss is a harp-blowing black man. When he bears down hard on his two-bit harmonica he can make trouble leave your weary mind, set your tired feet to stomping, bring Sweet Jesus to your backsliding soul. Joe Moss is a one-harp, two-harp, three-harp-blowing man. Sometimes on hot nights in summer when folks are sitting out on the front porch catching air, talking, or sleeping on a mattress stuck in the front doorway to get the benefit of the draft blowing through the open back door and at the same time to keep the dog from leaving the house, Joe takes a stand on the corner of Redbud Street and Cately Avenue. He draws a harp out of the belt that holds up his red corduroy trousers and slowly eases up on the blues just like a lonesome man sidling up to talk to a lady who has a mean and jealous husband.

The first notes of the long, lonesome, mournful tune scarcely seem to disturb the stillness of the night. They merge with it. For a little while you are unaware that anything new has come into the night; that music must always have been there. It must always have been part of the dusty road in the moonlight; of the smoky coal-oil lamps in the shacks; the querulous whine of mosquitoes; the howling of dogs lost in the anguish of mating under the street light at the corner; the slow, reptilian crawling of crawfish in the muddy ditches; the pools of shadow between the close-packed shotgun houses; the broken picket fences and the fecund sunflowers heavy with dust and seed; the quiet voices talking, giggling; the sweaty hands seeking, searching; the black oily clouds scudding past the moon; and the far-off rumbling of the Cannon Ball train rounding the curve up above the oil mill. Joe bears down harder and harder. The notes of his harp tremble on the night like a weary sinner laying his head at last on the bosom of Sweet Jesus. Gawd, save us sinners on Judgment Day.

Joe Moss is a rambling, rolling, train-riding, harp-blowing man. They know him on Rampart Street in New Orleans; in the hotcat parlors and dice dens of Beale Street in Memphis; in Natchez, Vicksburg, Greenville, Helena; in all the river towns up to Cape Girardeau; as far west as Dallas, Texas. Winter and summer, fall and spring, Joe rambles the land, a sweat shirt and red corduroy trousers covering his nakedness, and a ragged hat on his nappy head. It ain't no need to work. A man with music in his body can win hisself a woman and a home whenever he lights. A nigger ain't gonna have nothin' nohow, so it ain't no need to try to have nothin'. And it sho ain't no sense to stay in one place, 'cause when yo' foots itches to travel they's trains goin' whichever way you wants, and somebody, white or black, to feed you when you's hongry.

Joe was born to be a harp-blowing man, but he didn't know it until he was past twenty-one and the Albino Preacher told him right out in church before all the folks that he had the gift of song and music. Up to that time he had worked on Deep Snow Plantation just like any common man, chopping cotton, hoeing grass, ditching, clearing land for the white people, never going farther from home than Greenville, fourteen miles away, and living with only three women from the time he was fifteen years old until he became twenty-one. Nowadays Joe laughs when he sees people chopping cotton in the hot sun; picking cotton on frosty mornings in the fall; felling trees in icy swamps. He rares back and laughs when they flash by him as he crouches on the blinders of that Pan-American train leaving out from New Awleens for Birmingham, Alabamer; when he rides that Manifest Freight from Memphis to Fulton, Kentucky.

As Joe plays the lonesome blues, up and down Redbud Street folks stop talking. Across the road in the jailhouse prisoners come to the windows of their cells and stick their heads close to the bars to drink in the music lingering on the air. Two high-yaller young couples driving down the street in a V-8 Ford automobile, on their way to the Chinaman's store to get something t'eat, pull up and stop. By this time everybody in the neighborhood knows that Joe Moss, the harp-blowingest man in Mississippi, is back in town. Suddenly Joe sticks the harp in his belt and begins to sing in a warm, rich baritone that can be heard two blocks away:

> I's a po' boy long way from home,
> I ain't got no money
> Ain't got nowhere to go,
> Just stand at de railroad crossin',
> Waitin' to hear de whistle blow.

Up and down the street women cock their ears to catch every word, every note, every tiny evocation of sound. Men listen, too, their souls wooed by the song, their hearts touched with jealousy and vague, uneasy stirrings. The song ends. The night is given over again to the whining of mosquitoes, the brittle crashing of heavy-bodied insects against the dazzling street lamp on the corner, the howling of dogs, and the rumbling of the Cannon Ball train as it moves slowly through Newtown on its way to the near-by station. The air is heavy with heat. There is a ring around the moon. Gwine rain tomorrow sho'. Lawd Jesus, he'p us. We's heavy laden.

Then Joe pulls two harps out of his belt. Once, long ago, when he was a fatherless chile and got religion, he promised the Lord that he would quit blowing the blues and play nothing but church songs. But Joe is a man who is messed up in his weary mind, and he can't always remember what he promised the Lawd and what he didn't promise. But shucks, if you blows the blues now and then and plays church songs now and then, the Lawd sho' ain't gwine be vexed with you.

He stands now under the street light, two harps gleaming silver in the great black gash of his mouth, and blows like Gabriel on Judgment Mawnin'. Tiny rivulets of sweat chase one another through his kinky hair and roll down his neck and throat to merge in little streams lost in the sea of his broad back and thick chest. His torso moves in slow circles on his hips; his feet tap time in the dust; his neck moves in convulsive jerks while his hands tremble on the harps, and the pupils of his eyes dilate until they become spots of black in pools of cream-white. Jesus, come take me home.

> Well, don't you mind me dyin',
> Lawd, don't you mind me dyin',
> Lawd, don't you mind me dyin',
> Jesus gwine make up my dyin' bed.
>
> Well, I'll be sleepin' easy,
> Well, I'll be sleepin' easy,
> Well, I'll be sleepin' easy,
> Jesus gwine make up my dyin' bed.

Across the street in the jailhouse, Bubber Armstrong stands with an ear hard against the iron bars of his cell, listening. He knows that Joe is singing the gospel truth. His mama told him it was the truth long ago when he was a little boy on Sunup Plantation. Reverem Green, the pastor of his church, told him it was so when he was baptized in Possom Slough. Even the white folks — and they ain't got much sense no matter if the Law is on they side — believe you're going to Jesus when you die. Now Bubber is on his way— on his way to know the truth beyond all dispute; on his way unscarred from his life on this earth except for a tiny dislocation of his vertebrae that will occur when he drops through the trapdoor of the newly erected gallows that stands in the back yard of the jailhouse. Bubber listens to Joe Moss blowing on his harps, laughs out loud, and shouts to the prisoner in the adjoining cell: "Nigger, ain't dat de beatin'est, harp-blowin'est man you ever has heerd?"

Once more silence falls on Redbud Street as Joe's song is ended. Then the Law walks up on him out of the darkness — the white-faced Law in a sweaty shirt, dust-stained shoes, gleaming badge beneath sagging suspenders, and black-and-silver pistol stuck in a sweat-stained holster.

Joe takes off his hat as the Law approaches and holds it respectfully in his hand. It wasn't no need to run, and besides Joe hadn't done nothin'.

"Good evenin', Cap'm," Joe said.

"Good evenin', Joe," the Law said.

"Boss Man, how come you knows my name?" Joe asked.

"'Cause every nigger in Newtown say they gonna kill you if you keep comin' around here blowin' them harps and monkeyin' 'round with their women."

Joe smiled complacently. "Cap'm," he said, looking at the ground, "I'm a man don't never kick in no other man's stall."

"Well, maybe you do and maybe you don't. That ain't no skin off my teeth, and if you get killed messin' around here that won't be nothin' new. Anyhow, it ain't gonna be tonight. You been givin' me the creeps with them songs you been singin'. Now let's hear something lively."

"Yassuh, Boss," replied Joe energetically, a note of vast relief in his voice. This was not the first time he had played for the

Law, but it was the first time as a free man. Once, down in Natchez, Joe had been arrested and had blown himself clean out of police court. Judge Patterson had asked him to play a tune to see if he was just a jackleg musician, and then had kept him playing all morning long while the other prisoners awaiting trial joined in the singing, and when it was all over the Judge told Joe to come back and see him whenever he was in town and gave him a dollar bill to boot. It ain't no way on earth to tell what white folks will do even if you's a two-headed man. And here Joe was facing the Law again under novel circumstances. "Cap'm," he said, "how 'bout a mess of dem St. Louis Blues?"

"Go 'head," said the Law, as it whittled a match into a toothpick and began to explore the cavities of its teeth.

Joe took three harps out his belt, put them in his mouth, and began passionately to celebrate the immortal fame of that St. Louis woman who tied men to her apron strings. Up and down the length of Redbud Street the music ran. Up and down the length of the street bare feet, shoed feet, stockinged feet, black feet, brown feet, chocolate feet, tan feet, *café-au-lait* feet, smooth feet, splay feet, flat feet, calloused feet, began to beat time. Up and down the length of the street bodies swayed. Fat bodies, thin bodies, fecund bodies, sterile bodies, old bodies, young bodies, flat-chested bodies, full-breasted bodies, swayed with the music. Bodies moved closer to bodies; lips to lips; chests to breasts; thighs to thighs — moved closer, swayed, beat time. Up and down the length of the street, children stirred in their sleep; stirred, awoke, and crept to the front door sensing rather than hearing something strange in the night. Up and down the street, women hissed to their children to git back in bed 'fo' I busts you wide open. Up and down Redbud Street, old men and old women dreamed of their hot lost youth when they could have talked under their clothes with the strongest in the land.

The harps stopped blowing. The Law walked away, moonlight on its badge, moonlight on its black-and-silver pistol, moonlight on its dusty-silver shoes, moonlight on its wet shirt sloping over rounded shoulders. The hot air pressed closer on Redbud

Street. The ring around the moon pressed closer on the moon. Frogs croaked in the stagnant ditches; an automobile coughed in the distance and was still. From the river came the mournful wail of the *Tennessee Belle* as she backed out into the stream bound down for way landings and New Awleens. Silence and heat and moonlight lay heavily on Redbud Street.

Then doors up and down the length of the street began to bang. Doors popped, screeched, slammed, and boomed as they were violently shut. Porch swings, suddenly deserted, swayed for a moment or two and then were still. Mattresses vanished inside the shacks. Soon the street was deserted except for old men and women who remained rocking in their chairs, catching little puffs of breeze that came up from the river, and slapping with weary hands at the mosquitoes that sang about their ears and legs.

Joe Moss stuck three harps into the belt that held up his red corduroy trousers, and walked slowly over to Mee Hop's café on Nelson Street to get him a can of sardine-fish and some crackers. Chinermens was funny. Funnier even than white folks. They wouldn't give you nothin' for no music if you blowed yo' lungs out. But it might be some niggers there and them sardine-fish could be turned into a mess of chitlins.

A few minutes later the chitlins were frying on Mee Hop's stove, and Joe sat smoking a Two Orphans cigar, voluptuously sniffing the rich, satisfying, mingled aromas of fat entrails and tobacco. Around him clustered a little group of his admirers. He took the cigar out of his mouth, spat on the floor, and laughed. "I swears to Gawd," he said, "de way dem niggers banged dey doors sounds like de time Wetherbee's Hardware Store caught on fire and fawty thousand shotgun shells went off at de same time. I doesn't keer where de niggers at or who dey is, when Joe Moss tears off a piece on his harps de mens shuts dey doors and tells dey wimmens to stay back to I done passed by."

"Hit's sho de truth," said Virgie Mae Willis, as she put twenty cents on the counter and Joe Moss lifted a forkful of steaming chitlins from the plate.

THE END

Index